BEHAVIOUR MODIFICATION FOR PEOPLE WITH MENTAL HANDICAPS

Second Edition

BEHAVIOUR MODIFICATION for people with mental handicaps

Second Edition

Edited by
William Yule and Janet Carr

CROOM HELM
London • New York • Sydney

© 1980 W. Yule and Janet Carr
Second Edition © 1987 William Yule and Janet Carr
Croom Helm Ltd, Provident House, Burrell Row,
Beckenham, Kent BR3 1AT
Croom Helm Australia, 44–50 Waterloo Road,
North Ryde, 2113, New South Wales

British Library Cataloguing in Publication Data

Behaviour modification for people with
    mental handicaps. — 2nd ed.
    1. Mentally handicapped children —
    Rehabilitation 2. Behaviour modification
    I. Yule, William II. Carr, Janet
    III. Behaviour modification for the
    mentally handicapped
    362.3′088054   RJ506.M4
    ISBN 0–7099–2918–8

Published in the USA by
Croom Helm
in association with Methuen, Inc.
29 West 35th Street
New York, NY 10001

Library of Congress Cataloging in Publication Data

ISBN 0–7099–2918–8

Filmsetting by Mayhew Typesetting, Bristol, England
Printed and bound in Great Britain by Mackays of Chatham Ltd, Kent

For Jack Tizard

Contents

ACKNOWLEDGEMENT

We are grateful to Professor Joan Bicknell, the Reverend John Foskett, Professor Peter Mittler and Dr Norma Raynes for their helpful comments on the first draft of Chapter 15.

Contributors

Maria Callias, MA, MSc, is Lecturer in Psychology, University of London Institute of Psychiatry

Janet Carr, BA, PhD is Regional Tutor in the Psychology of Mental and Multiple Handicaps, St George's Hospital, London

Hilary Davison, BA, BSc, MPhil, is a clinical psychologist with the Oxfordshire Health Authority

David Felce, PhD, is Director of the British Institute of Mental Handicap

Chris Gathercole, BSc, DCP, is Top Grade Psychologist with Blackburn, Hyndburn and Ribble Valley Health Authority

Rosemary Hemsley, BSc, MSc, is Lecturer in Psychology, University of London Institute of Psychiatry

Patricia Howlin, BA, MSc, PhD, is Senior Lecturer in Psychology, University of London Institute of Psychiatry

Judith Jenkins, PhD, is Senior Clinical Psychologist, Winchester Health District

Ursula de Kock, BA, is a trainee Clinical Psychologist, University of Exeter

Jim Mansell, MSc (Econ) is Director of Studies in Mental Handicap, University of Kent

Glynis Murphy, BA, MSc, PhD, is Senior Lecturer is Psychology, University of London Institute of Psychiatry

Chris Oliver, BSc, MPhil, is Research Psychologist, University of London Institute of Psychiatry

Sandy Toogood is a member of the Special Development Team, University of Kent

Mona Tsoi, BSocSci, MPhil, PhD, is Senior Lectuer in Psychology, University of Hong Kong

Barbara Wilson, BA, MPhil, PhD, is Senior Lecturer in Rehabilitation, University Department of Rehabilitation, Southampton General Hospital

William Yule, MA, Dip Psychol, PhD, is Professor of Applied Child Psychology, University of London Institute of Psychiatry

Ewa Zarkowska, BA, BSc, MPhil, is Lecturer in Psychology, University of London Institute of Psychiatry

1

Introduction and Overview of Behaviour Modification for People with Mental Handicaps

William Yule and Janet Carr

Figures for the prevalence of severe mental handicap vary according to geographical area, age group and date of the survey. Figures from five English surveys range from 2.9 to 3.4 with an average of 3.2 per thousand (DHSS, 1980). What this stark statistic conceals is the large number of individuals who are severely handicapped in many ways — so handicapped as to pose considerable problems to their families and the community. According to recent estimates, there are 148 000 people with severe mental handicaps in England and Wales (Johnson, 1985). There are a great many more people with milder degrees of mental handicap. In 1983 there were 40 000 hospital places in England for people with mental handicaps, of which 1300 were for children. Over the last decade overall prevalence has changed little, but hospital provision, especially for children, has been dramatically reduced.

In 1971 a major change, which has had far-reaching effects for all people with mental handicaps, occurred with the implementation of the 1970 Education (Handicapped Children) Act. Until 1971, children who were found to be 'severely retarded' were deemed to be ineducable, and they became the responsibility of the Health Departments. From April 1971 it was recognised that no child is ineducable, when education is interpreted in its broadest sense of preparation for living in the community. The momentum of change continued when the Education Act of 1981 followed the Warnock Report and encouraged the closer alignment with as much integration as possible of special with mainstream education. There resulted greater involvement of parents in the assessment of their child and the choice of school, and a change in terminology to 'children with special educational needs' and, in particular, 'children with [severe] learning difficulties'. The publication in 1971 of the White Paper,

1

Better Services for the Mentally Handicapped, represented the culmination of a quarter of a century's thinking on how to change and humanise the care of people with a mental handicap. In particular, the White Paper argued strongly for the need for care within the local community. As Bayley (1973) argued, care *in* the community is not synonymous with care *by* the community: all too often it means overburdened parents coping with a difficult situation without any real, practical help (Tizard and Grad, 1961). The White Paper recognised this danger and placed strong emphasis on domiciliary help and advice on management of problems.

Over the succeeding 15 years, the development of community care has been uneven, due in part to some uncertainty as to whether this was in the best interest of all people with mental handicaps. Community care has also been found to be very expensive, and ways are now being found to transfer finance from health to social services. Nevertheless, there has been a great expansion in educational and housing facilities and in the development of community mental handicap teams, with an emphasis on using ordinary services wherever possible (Sines and Bicknell, 1985).

The hospitals are becoming smaller because very few people with mental handicaps are being admitted for long-term care, and those people remaining are essentially multiply handicapped and may well have behaviour problems. There will also be many in the community who have behaviour disorders where the expectation is of community care with services in the locality. Both in hospitals and in the community, therefore, are to be found people with mental handicaps with challenging behaviours who require help and treatment.

But how are all these laudable goals to be achieved? More active care and education presuppose more appropriately trained personnel. Caring in the community implies an improvement in the domiciliary services, and in particular a shift from passive 'understanding' on the part of social services personnel to an active advice-giving role. What techniques are available that can be used by so many varied professionals which can be of value in training people with mental handicaps?

The Mental Health Act 1983 introduced a new legal concept, that of mental impairment and severe mental impairment. This definition combines a reduction of intelligence with behaviour problems which cause the person to be seriously irresponsible or abnormally aggressive. Only those who are mentally impaired can be compulsorily detained for treatment or placed on a Guardianship order. While no doubt the value of this concept is still to be ascertained, it is important that the Act be used to *enable* good management and treatment to be provided rather than to legitimise custodial detention.

THE GROWTH OF BEHAVIOUR MODIFICATION

Simultaneously with the change in social attitudes towards the mentally handicapped in Britain, there was a revolution in intervention techniques developing primarily in the United States of America. Although there is a long tradition of experimental psychologists applying themselves to the problems of people with mental handicaps, the bulk of the early work in this field was more related to diagnosis and the study of psychological process for their own sake, rather than to therapeutic endeavour. All this changed radically in the mid-1960s.

This is not the place to attempt a historical account of the growth of behaviour modification. Future psychology historians will probably point to the coming together of a number of different influences, ranging from the emergence of applied psychology as a separate profession from its mainly medical beginnings to the arrival of experimental analysis of behaviour as a respectable subdiscipline having its roots in the animal-experimental laboratory but its new applications in individual human single-case studies (Kazdin, 1978).

Clinical studies and controlled experimental studies of single cases began to appear in the literature in the mid- to late 1960s. Larsen and Bricker's *Manual for parents and teachers of severely and moderately retarded children* was published in Nashville, Tennessee, in 1968, the same year that Patterson and Gullion's more general, semi-programmed text, *Living with children: new methods for parents and teachers*, appeared from Oregon. After this, the floodgates opened. Many manuals appeared from America. Gardner's *Behavior modification in mental retardation* appeared in 1971, and was followed two years later in 1973 by Watson's *Child behavior modification: a manual for teachers, nurses and parents*.

The message from all of these sources was optimistic: children with mental handicaps can be taught a great deal more than most of us have hitherto accepted, provided we use appropriate techniques. The techniques of behaviour modification were presented in simple form, often in near-cookbook terms. The secondary message of these texts was that parents, nurses, teachers and other care-takers could be taught to carry out the 'therapy' with the child. There was

3

no need for all treatment to be carried out by expensively trained (and thin-on-the-ground) psychologists.

As the promise held out by behaviour modification techniques became recognised, so individuals in Britain began to try out the techniques. Some workers visited centres in America to witness at first hand what such methods of treatment could achieve. Visitors from America held more and more symposia and workshops. By the early 1970s, one or two centres were well established in the application of behavioural techniques to the problems of the mentally handicapped. By 1975, a major symposium could examine both theoretical and practical problems in this new area (Kiernan and Woodford, 1975b). Behaviour modification as a therapeutic tool in mental handicap was established.

SERVICE NEEDS

It soon became evident that there were valuable treatment skills which could be taught to nurses, parents, teachers and others. A major problem facing those with responsibility for providing services for the mentally handicapped was how to ensure that these skills could be provided where they were most needed.

At an 'Action Workshop' organised by the Institute for Research into Mental and Multiple Handicap (Kiernan and Woodford, 1975a) it was recognised that psychologists trained in applying behaviour modification techniques to the problems of the mentally handicapped were the key figures in expanding the services. There were, and still are, too few psychologists working in this area. None the less, a few psychologists could train many other personnel. This had already been recognised by the Joint Board of Clinical Nursing Studies (1974) and their Scottish equivalent when they formulated their syllabuses for specialist nurse training in behaviour modification with people with mental handicaps.

To accelerate these developments, it was recognised by many people that short, intensive courses in the techniques of behaviour modification could serve a very useful function. This sort of thinking lay behind the writing of this textbook.

THE PRESENT BOOK

This book saw its beginnings in two one-week workshops run for psychologists and other professionals working with the mentally handicapped and held at the Institute of Psychiatry in May 1975 and November 1977. These intensive skills training workshops were planned by staff of the psychology department with the participation of two other colleagues.

As described in more detail in Chapter 16, the format of the workshop was that after a lecture and discussion on a particular topic (usually a set of related techniques and their theoretical underpinnings), the course members divided into smaller groups of about eight participants and two group leaders. During workshop sessions, the techniques discussed earlier were actively rehearsed, one staff member simulating a child, the other acting as model, tutor and director. The main emphasis of the course was on skills training. This sort of format derives from the precision teaching methods of Keller (1968) used to such good effect by Vance Hall in training teachers (Hall, 1971a, b) and by Montrose Wolf and his colleagues in training teaching-parents (along the Achievement Place lines) to work with young delinquents (Phillip et al., 1971).

When preparing for these and related courses, it soon became evident that the material on which we wished to base the workshop was scattered throughout many related books and journal articles. We could find no suitable text which drew it all together in a manner relevant to this sort of skills training approach. One particular difficulty which all teachers face is that examples of good work in different social and cultural settings sometimes need elaborate explanations and interpretations before their value can be fully appreciated. The sorts of programme found suitable in a hospital setting may need considerable alteration before being suited to a community setting. In any case, it is always more meaningful to trainees if their tutors incorporate examples from their own hard-won experience, and this is what we have tried to do in this text.

In compiling the book, we have tried to keep in mind the needs of all the various professionals who work with people with mental handicaps. We believe it is relevant to clinical and educational psychologists, teachers, nurses, social workers and occupational therapists. It will be of interest to specialist health visitors, paediatricians, child psychiatrists and other members of district handicap teams. We have not written this text specifically for parents, although many may find it helpful. A separate book has been prepared with parents in mind (Carr, 1980). We have used the material in this text in workshops that we have organised for psychologists, nurses, teachers and other professionals in Britain, Denmark, Sweden and

Australia. Subsequently the demand for training has spread still further, and courses have been run for field social workers, for social services staff in day centres and in hostels and for nursery nurses and health visitors, besides teachers and nurses.

The book opens with a discussion on selecting appropriate goals and targets when faced with a person with problems. This is followed by five chapters on a variety of ways of increasing desirable behaviours and one chapter on decreasing undesirable behaviours. Having discussed some of the basic behavioural techniques and some of the theoretical background on which they are based, there are three chapters that deal with applications to areas of particular importance in meeting the needs of the mentally handicapped: self-help skills such as feeding and dressing, toileting and language development. Next comes one chapter discussing ways of disseminating these skills to all those who work closely with people with mental handicaps and one describing the use of the techniques in a community-based residential facility for adults. The penultimate chapter discusses some of the ethical issues raised by applying this powerful technology for the benefit of individuals with mental handicaps. Finally, the issue of how to run short courses to train caretakers in behavioural skills is addressed.

We recognise that no amount of book learning can substitute for good skills training. However, we hope that, having read this book, the reader will be better prepared to benefit from opportunities to participate in future workshops. We have included a chapter describing the workshops that we have run. We hope that this will prove useful in guiding others who may wish to mount similar ventures.

In revising this text for its second edition, we aimed to update the material on behaviour modification in general and to illustrate its application to adult clients. Behavioural techniques have developed considerably from the days of simple contingency management, and this is reflected in the increased space given to discussing stimulus control of behaviour (Chapter 6) and imitation (Chapter 7). The chapter on decreasing undesirable behaviours (Chapter 8) is completely rewritten to reflect both the greater realism and the exciting developments in working with clients showing self-injurious behaviour. Those chapters dealing with self-help skills and language development reflect the achievements of many colleagues over the past decade in bringing ingenuity, dedication and scholarship to bear on these important areas of every-day living.

Chapter 12 has been expanded to allow adequate discussion of the burgeoning literature on passing these skills on to 'front-line' caretakers. Chapter 14 describes the use of behavioural techniques with a well-thought-out community residential facility. Many beginners will marvel at the apparent ease with which well-trained staff analyse problems, gather detailed data and work on individually planned programmes. The emphasis must be on *well trained*. Good programmes can and do work, but they take a great deal of planning.

We feel it is important that all interventions should be monitored, and so have retained the chapter on evaluating treatment programmes. As we have continued to use the text in training courses, we have felt the need to add a chapter on ethical issues — not because we feel that there are any more ethical issues involved in behavioural treatments than drug treatments or other forms of intervention, but rather because it is important that all therapists think carefully about what they are doing. Moreover, we found when we ran courses for people from the newer caregiving professions that these issues were uppermost in their minds, and it became even more important that the issues should be discussed and clarified in detail.

All of this new and expanded material forced us to abandon the earlier Appendices which detailed how to set up the role-playing sessions. These are in the first edition of the book which, if all else fails, can be borrowed from the British Lending Library.

The first edition of this book was written by and for people working with children with mental handicaps. Since that time not only have many of the authors moved into work with adults with mental handicaps but there has also been considerable broadening of interest in this field, and a recognition that behavioural methods have much to offer to adults as well as to children. Consequently the second edition focuses on work with all age groups.

On a terminological note, throughout this edition we have tried to refer to people — adults and children — with mental handicaps, and to eschew such terms as 'the retarded' and 'the handicapped', which are still to be found in publications in the 1980s (van den Pol *et al.*, 1981; Konarski and Diorio, 1985).

In the first edition we said that we would welcome comments and constructive criticism from people who use this text. The necessarily delayed feedback came partly in private comments and partly in the form of book reviews. We were delighted by their overwhelmingly positive tone and have done our best to incorporate constructive suggestions in this second edition. It is heartening to know that the text has been welcomed by such a wide and diverse readership. Again, we seek comments from readers so that the text can continue to serve the needs of people with mental handicaps.

2

Identifying Problems:
Functional Analysis and Observation
and Recording Techniques

William Yule

Children and adults with mental handicaps present their caretakers with a constant stream of problems. At times, the net result is overwhelming so that, by the time outside help is sought, it is difficult to know where to begin to help. Which problem should be tackled first? What should be the goals of intervention? There can be no single, fixed set of answers to such questions. Rather, what is needed is a problem-solving approach — and that is what behaviour modification offers.

As we see it, there are four main stages in implementing a behaviour modification programme:

(1) defining the problem objectively;
(2) setting up hypotheses to account for observations;
(3) testing these hypotheses;
(4) evaluating the outcome.

In other words, a behaviour modification approach is a self-correcting approach. Problems are clearly defined, data are gathered before, during and after some treatment programme, and success or failure is made self-evident. Where progress is made, the therapist can continue the programme with increased confidence; where little or no progress occurs, this will be evident at an early stage and so steps can be taken to alter the treatment strategy.

A whole technology has grown up around the practicalities of gathering data — clearly the key to good behaviour modification. On the whole, these technical treatises are valuable for the researcher, but overwhelming for the clinician. What we intend to do in this chapter is to present a brief overview of a strategy which should enable any clinician to analyse any problem at an appropriate level:

that is, the analysis should be sufficiently complete to allow for efficient intervention, but neither so cumbersome nor so time consuming as to become an end in itself.

IDENTIFYING PROBLEMS

Problems are problems for someone. It is the parent, the nurse or the teacher who will complain about a child's or another adult's behaviour. It is one of the tasks of the therapist to help the caretaker to define the problem behaviour more exactly. Such complaints form the starting point of identifying problems which can be the subject of behaviour modification programmes.

Of course, the problems complained of may not be the most important behaviours from the client's point of view. Exasperated caretakers may seize on a florid difficulty such as temper tantrums which interferes with them rather than report that, for example, the client's lack of self-occupation and play skills results in temper tantrums when the staff cannot give him undivided attention. More careful questioning of what goes on around the time the problem manifests itself might prompt one to ask whether the client has skills of self-occupation and play. In other words, spontaneous complaints must be noted and fully investigated, but the pattern of the client's overall behaviour and adjustment must also be enquired into systematically.

In questioning the informant, one wants first of all to have a good, objective description of the client's behaviour.

DEFINING BEHAVIOUR

The behaviour in which the therapist is interested must be defined in observable, objective and measurable terms. In every-day life, we are used to discussing behaviour at a fairly global, trait level. When a parent complains that her eight-year-old boy gets jealous of his three-year-old sister, most of us would have a fair idea of what she meant — or would we? Does the boy hit his little sister? Does he sulk when his mother talks to his sister? Does he throw a tantrum when she snatches one of his toys? Some or all of these acts, together with countless others, could pinpoint what the mother means by 'jealous'. One of the tasks of the therapist is to help the complainant (parent, teacher, nurse or whoever is seeking help on behalf of the individual) to translate their concerns into detailed observable behaviours (Mischel, 1968).

To emphasise the point, consider the question of what constitutes a tantrum. For one parent, any occasion when their child refuses to comply with a request within a short time may be seen as a tantrum, whereas another parent may reserve the label for a full-blown outburst of screaming, hitting, pulling hair and throwing objects around. It is the job of the therapist to investigate how the parent views the problem. As is obvious from the examples, problems do not exist independent of some social context.

In addition to getting some idea of what the person does, how often it is done and how severe the problem is, an initial, systematic interview can also form the basis of a useful functional analysis of the problem. The therapist is interested in understanding the behaviour in relation to the effective environment in which it occurs. Are there any circumstances which 'set off' the problem? Are there any events which deliberately or inadvertently reinforce the maladaptive behaviour, thereby perpetuating a problem? Under what circumstances will the individual show appropriate behaviour, however fleetingly? What aspects of the environment are found reinforcing?

FUNCTIONAL ANALYSIS

Within the framework of behaviour modification, the therapist is interested in the relationship between a behaviour and its immediate social environment. The therapist is concerned not only with maladaptive behaviour, but also with positive behaviours on which further progress can be built. The therapist wants to identify those aspects that maintain a problem or those that prevent a more adaptive behaviour emerging. Crudely put, the ABC of a functional analysis consists of a systematic enquiry into the following:

(A) antecedents or setting events;
(B) behaviour, its frequency, duration, etc.
(C) consequences.

In subsequent chapters, you will see how, in planning and executing treatment programmes, one constantly returns to this form of analysis. At present, one must ask how detailed such an analysis must be.

As Kiernan (1973) points out, functional analysis has its origins in traditional operant conditioning theory. Through a thorough functional analysis, the therapist hopes to identify the 'sufficient and necessary conditions for a particular response to occur and persist' (Evans, 1971). This may involve gathering detailed observations on both the client's behaviour and selected aspects of the environment over lengthy periods, or it may involve systematically varying the environment and observing the effects on the patient's behaviour, the aim being to specify those environmental conditions that affect the behaviour to be modified. Recently, a sophisticated set of single-case experimental designs has been described which can assist in this process (see Chapter 13).

Careful functional analyses of disruptive, aggressive and self-injurious behaviour have recently resulted in the development of a new method for the assessment of severely disruptive behaviour. Carr et al. (1980) studied the disruptive behaviour of two children with severe mental handicaps and aggression. Very careful and detailed observations of the children under different conditions in which the difficulty of tasks was systematically varied led to the conclusion that children use disruptive behaviour to escape from a demanding situation. Various ways were found to reduce such 'escape-motivated aggression'. A later paper (Carr and Durand, 1985) confirmed with other children that disruptive behaviour was, in large part, a function of the difficulty of the task, but that there were individual differences. Some children were less affected by the task difficulty than by the availability of adult attention. In other words, disruptive behaviour is controlled in part by negative reinforcement (escaping from different tasks) and in part by positive reinforcement (adult attention, albeit intermittent, to the difficult behaviour), to different degrees in different children. As Murphy and Oliver discuss in greater detail in Chapter 8, these observations have been utilised by Iwata et al. (1982) to develop a useful way to analyse the functional significance of other, severe, self-injurious behaviours.

As noted earlier, a functional analysis of a presenting problem will be more broadly based, taking into account a great deal of information. Hypotheses concerning the relationship between the problem behaviour and the effective social environment will be developed both on the basis of careful interviews with parents or other responsible adults, and from a knowledge of similar problems treated in the past. Holland (1970) outlines 21 points to structure an interview with the parents, and Wahler and Cormier (1970) outline their 'ecological' interview. Both papers emphasise the need to get information on adaptive as well as maladaptive behaviour.

Kanfer and Saslow (1969) and Kanfer and Grimm (1977) suggest fairly comprehensive schemes for arriving at functional analyses of problems. They argue that most complaints can be categorised as belonging to one or more of five classes of behaviour: behaviour deficits; behaviour excesses; problems involving inappropriate stimulus control; inappropriate self-generated stimulus control; and problems in reinforcement contingencies. This way of categorising problems has heuristic value in that it points the way to appropriate techniques of intervention.

By far the most practical advice on analysing problem behaviour has come from Gelfand and Hartmann (1984). Following initial data-gathering through interview, they suggest that preliminary observations be made of the client in the situation where the problem manifests. At this stage, observations are recorded in a semi-structured format whereby the client's behaviour is described succinctly and notes are made about the antecedent and consequent social events. This allows one to check more precisely any hypothesis formulated on the basis of the interview, and also allows one to focus down on more circumscribed aspects of the total situation in subsequent, more formal observation sessions.

Thus, interview data and direct observational data can be merged in order to understand the presenting problem and thereby to help identify appropriate targets for behaviour modification programmes. Continuing observational data are also required to monitor the effectiveness of programmes. This can be complex and is discussed at length later. For the moment, let us consider the whole question of identifying appropriate therapeutic goals.

SELECTING TARGETS

Just as we want parents to be clear what it is that they are complaining of, we also want to make the goals of treatment explicit. This helps to let us see whether the goals are being reached. But how are these goals decided upon?

These questions are considered in detail in Chapters 9–11. For the present, we should note that goals are selected on the basis of what is in the best interests of both the child and his social setting. There is little disagreement that individuals with language handicaps should be encouraged to develop as much language as possible.

There might be some disagreement as to whether it is right to encourage a child to sit quietly if such a goal is more to meet the needs of staff than the child himself. In other words, goal-setting is value-laden, and this needs to be acknowledged.

Initially, many parents may set goals which are too far removed from the child's present level to be attainable within a relatively short time. For example, parents may wish their child to talk, and can be helped to achieve this aim by working initially on, say, simple motor imitation. In other words, one task of the therapist is to help break down complex behaviours into component skills. One way of helping people to select appropriate goals is to use developmental charts such as those published by Gunzburg (1965). By asking parents to report in detail on what their child *can* do, this often has the helpful effects of focusing their attention on hitherto unnoticed positive achievements. It also makes clear what, in terms of normal development, the next milestones are and, in the absence of evidence to the contrary, these become the next goals. Of course, some developmental charts are too gross, and the next goal may have to be analysed into many sub-goals, but the principle remains: mentally handicapped children should be regarded as very slow developers who achieve the same milestones as normal children in the same sequence.

The same principles apply in goal-setting with adult clients. Discussion with the adult, wherever possible, and the caretakers at home, the day centre or elsewhere will help to pinpoint areas where help is needed. Formal checklists of social and personal skills will help to systematise the planning, but specific goals may need to be analysed in considerable additional detail (Mash and Terdal, 1981; Hartmann, 1984).

Mager and Pipe (1970) present a scheme for analysing problems which is particularly relevant to devising programmes of treatment for those with mental handicaps. One of the basic questions which they pose is whether, when presented with a problem, the problem is one of skill deficiency or of motivation. If the patient's life depended on it, could he do it? Where the answer to that question is, 'Yes', then one is faced with a problem of motivating the patient to put his existing skills to better use. Techniques of positive reinforcement (see Chapter 3) are particularly relevant here. If, however, the answer is, 'No', then the therapist has to devise ways of training the patient in a new skill. The techniques discussed in Chapters 3 and 5 are particularly relevant here.

Thus the sequence of a behavioural analysis is as follows:

13

(1) Gather data from interviews on both problem and adaptive behaviour.
(2) Conduct preliminary observations to clarify hypotheses.
(3) If necessary, conduct more formalised observations as described below.
(4) Select target behaviours and begin treatment.
(5) Continue recording to monitor progress.

It is not possible to give hard and fast guidelines about which level of problem analysis is most appropriate in any given circumstances. At times, it will be clear from an informant's initial account what the problem is, and a solution will be suggested. It may be sufficient to accept the informants' assurance that the problem disappears.

At other times, expected solutions will not work. Then, one needs to be able to conduct a much fuller, more formal analysis of the problems, and this is where more detailed direct observational techniques will be necessary (Sackett, 1978).

MEASUREMENT TECHNIQUES

According to Hall (1971a), there are three major groups of recording techniques used in behaviour modifications. These are:

(1) automatic recording;
(2) measurement of permanent product;
(3) observational recording.

As will be seen, the third group is the most relevant to behaviour modification and so it will be considered in a separate section.

(1) Automatic recording

In laboratory studies of animal behaviour, a sophisticated array of automatic recording devices has been developed. Sensitive microswitches can record the areas of a cage entered by a rat. The relationship between a pigeon's pecking at a target and the delivery of grain are both recorded automatically and, as is well known, such sensitive recording procedures have yielded rich results in understanding the nature of reinforcement.

Similar automatic recording devices have been used in studying the behaviour of human subjects, but almost always in a laboratory setting. Hyperactivity in children with severe mental handicaps has been studied by recording their fidgety movements on a special seat (Sprague and Toppe, 1966). However, such devices are expensive and are not suitable for recording behaviour in the more natural environment. Although there may be occasions, particularly in institution settings, where such equipment will be installed to help deal with specific problems, in the main, automatic recording is not recommended.

(2) Measurement of permanent product

One method of gathering data which is often overlooked is the direct measurement of any permanent product produced by the child or adult in whom we are interested. In workshop situations, the number of completed units can be easily counted. In a school setting, the number of words written or copied can be counted. The beauty of this type of measurement is that it can be obtained simply and reliably, often at one's leisure.

Fewtrell (1973) used a permanent product ingeniously to monitor treatment of enuresis in an institutional setting. Since there is a high relationship between wetting and soiled linen sent to the laundry, they weighed the amount of linen sent for laundry one day each week. As their treatment programme proceeded, and as their patients improved, so the amount of soiled linen fell from 80 pounds at the beginning of treatment to 15 pounds after about 20 weeks.

OBSERVATIONAL RECORDING

In most cases when setting up a behaviour modification programme, the therapist will have to rely on observational recording. Someone will have to observe the patient and record relevant aspects of his behaviour. The type of observational recording selected will depend in large part on the type of behaviour being worked on. Practical constraints such as the availability of observers and the environment in which the problem occurs will also partially determine the recording procedure. In what follows, practical considerations will be emphasised.

(1) Continuous recording

It is impossible to record continuously everything that is happening in a given situation. Many beginners, or at least those who have never tried it, believe that they can write down all that someone else does. Although anecdotal records emerge, it can be quickly established that no two people will record the same events. This is a useful exercise to carry out in order to convince people of the need for some structured method of observing.

Even with the greater availability of videotape recording, continuous recording is not a practical venture, mainly because it is too time-consuming to extract data from the tape at a later time. For example, in studying the effects of training the parents of autistic children to use behaviour modification techniques, it was found that every one hour of audiotaped mother–child conversation took no fewer than three hours to transcribe later on (Howlin et al., 1973a). After that, it took untold hours to reduce the transcriptions to manageable data.

This is not to say that unstructured observation or videotape is not of value in behavioural treatments. Unstructured observations approximating to continuous recordings can be very useful at the beginning of a programme when trying to pin-point the problem. Likewise, one can study a videotape over and over again in an attempt to isolate particular difficulties. Where videorecorders are not available, eyes, hands, stopwatches and paper have to suffice.

(2) Event recording

Once the behaviour of concern (the 'target behaviour') has been defined, if it is a relatively discrete act such as hitting, waving, raising a cup to the mouth or whatever, then it may be decided to count each occasion that the behaviour occurs. When the number of events is divided by the time during which the patient was observed, the result is a measure of the *frequency of occurrence* of that behaviour.

Event recording is a relatively simple procedure. Tally marks can be made on a piece of paper, or a simple wrist counter (of the sort used by golfers) or a knitting-needle counter can even be used. Anything more elaborate can intrude too much into the situation.

Despite the ease of gathering data, it can be too time-consuming to record occurrences over a whole day. It is necessary to reduce the time spent observing to practical limits. As soon as one samples the whole day by choosing a portion of it, the question of validity, or rather representativeness, is raised. Unless one is reasonably certain that the target behaviour occurs (or does not occur, if one wants to increase it) more or less equally frequently throughout the day, then it is too easy to be careless and bias one's results. To take a glaring example, let us say that a man with severe learning disabilities is reported to be aggressive in the day centre. If the numbers of aggressive acts, however defined, were counted only during occupational activity sessions, one might miss the fact that he made most assaults while waiting to collect his midday meal. Worse still, if pre-treatment measures are taken at times when the target behaviour occurs most frequently, and post-treatment measures are taken at other times (either because of the availability of observers, or because the timetable is altered), then the apparent change in behaviour will not be a valid indicator of the change in the man's aggressive behaviour.

In summary, event recording is easily made when the class of behaviour of interest has been clearly defined. It is usual to observe for only short periods of the day. Unless there are times of greatest interest — e.g. mealtimes, bedtimes, free-play — then it is necessary to ensure that the selected time is truly representative of the longer period. Unless the patient is observed for the same length of time each day, the results are usually expressed as a frequency count per unit of time (i.e. a rate measure).

(3) Duration recording

With some behaviours, one is more interested in *how long* they last. For example, a frequent complaint is that individuals are slow in getting ready in the morning. Assuming that the person has all the necessary skills for getting ready without assistance, then it would be reasonable to target the length of time between being called to get out of bed and arriving washed and dressed at the breakfast table. The time taken is best recorded by stopwatch, although any clock or watch will serve.

It is worth noting that duration can be a more sensitive measure than merely noting occurrence. For example, during the early stages of a retraining programme, a child may still have the same number of temper tantrums in a day, but their intensity and duration might be less. Since it is always desirable to use the index which is most sensitive to change, duration recording is frequently employed.

17

(4) Interval recording

As with other forms of psychological measurement, ways have to be found to sample the behaviour of interest. One method is to divide the total length of observation into equal intervals, and then to note whether the target behaviour occurred at all during each interval. By recording in this manner, for the first time, the sequence of events is noted. This extra information can be made use of, particularly if more than one behaviour is monitored simultaneously.

Hall (1971a) comments that 'the chief advantage of the interval recording method is that it gives an indication of both the frequency and the duration of the behaviour observed . . . A disadvantage of interval recording method is that it usually requires the individual attention of the observer'.

Many workers have developed elaborate observation systems using variations on the interval recording technique. Patterson *et al.* (1969) used a 29-item coding system to record interactions between family members in their own homes. Hemsley *et al.* (1978) have developed a reliable method for studying mother–child interactions using 17 categories to classify the child's behaviour and 19 to describe the mother's behaviour. It should be noted that the more complex the coding system, the more training is needed by the observers, and the more difficult it is to obtain reliable measures.

Continuous monitoring is very tiring. In any case, no matter how skilled the observer becomes, he is likely to miss occasional target behaviours while recording. It is usual to allow some time for recording, for example, 10 seconds of observing, followed by 5 to 10 seconds for recording. The disadvantage of this is that sequences of behaviour cannot be so readily recorded.

The precise meaning of the recorded data should be understood. Although, as Hall (1971a) notes, the data *indicate* both frequency and duration, they reflect neither accurately. Take someone who is self-injuring by scratching his face. If he does it once, a check mark is placed in the appropriate interval. If, however, he has a sudden burst of many scratches, still only one check mark is placed in the one time interval. If he is indulging in a slow, deliberate scratch, it may stretch across two time intervals: will it be counted in both, or only in the interval in which it starts? Obviously, coding rules have to be worked out, and these will further distort the data collected.

It is in the nature of coding rules that they are hierarchical. To stick with the self-injury example, it would usually be the case that this behaviour would occur less than four times per minute. Even so, when it does occur, it is vital that it is noted. Thus, when the patient survives nine seconds of a recording interval without scratching, but commences scratching in the last second, scratching is recorded.

For other purposes, other hierarchical rules of coding may be more appropriate. If the target behaviour is 'co-operative play', then that might take precedence over 'fighting'. If, as is more likely, one is operating a multiple treatment programme to reduce fighting and increase co-operative play, then both behaviours would be recorded separately, but simultaneously.

Recently, the validity of interval sampling has been called into question. Powell *et al.* (1977) carried out a series of empirical investigations to test whether different forms of observing introduced different biases. They concluded that interval sampling contains so much error as to have little to recommend it. Instead, they find that momentary time sampling (see below) is both more accurate and more easily accomplished. This was confirmed in a study by Murphy and Goodall (1980).

In summary, interval sampling can be used to sample a stream of behaviour. It has the advantage that it records the sequence of occurrence of behaviour, but it loses out on precise measurement of frequency and duration. What is recorded is the number of intervals in which the target behaviour occurred, however momentarily. The coding rules adopted by the observer can distort the observations made. Moreover, recent evidence suggests that the method yields unreliable data.

(5) Time sampling

A different way of sampling is to observe the patient or client only at the end of a particular predetermined interval. The length of the interval will, as always, depend on the frequency of the target behaviour as well as the time at the disposal of the observer. This method has the advantage that it does not require continuous observation.

One disadvantage of the method is that it requires precise timing to avoid biasing the results. For example, take the case of a nurse on a busy ward who is observing a patient every five minutes to record whether the patient is rocking or participating in some other self-stimulatory activity or is sitting, usefully occupied. Unless the nurse does look at exactly the end of the five-minute interval, then she may find herself remembering to record only when she sees the patient engaging in the undesirable activity. Again, the recording can be interrupted if another patient demands immediate attention.

Despite the potential biasing factors, time sampling is often the most acceptable and least time-consuming method of observation that is practicable when the observer has other things to do. An ordinary wall clock can serve as a sufficient cue for timing, but a kitchen timer or automatic timer that emits a tone every few minutes is to be preferred. Patients usually habituate quickly to such tones, as can observers if they are not careful.

RELIABILITY AND VALIDITY

During the preceding description of the basic observational techniques, it has been repeatedly stressed that the observer must ensure that observations are truly representative of the broader class or classes of behaviour of interest. To readers familiar with the concepts of traditional psychometric measurement, this will appear self-evident. At all times, one must be concerned with the reliability and validity of the measures being made.

For reasons which are not altogether clear, but which appear to be related to a general movement to get away from psychometric *tests* as the sole measures in intervention studies, many behaviour modifiers have shown a great concern to establish the inter-rater reliability of observations almost to the exclusion of establishing the validity of the observations. As will be shown in the next section, even the calculation of inter-rater agreement is full of difficulties, many of which have been overlooked in early studies.

An interesting methodological study by Wahler and Leske (1973) underlines the point being made here. They made 15 videotapes of six-year-old children who were apparently engaged in silent reading. There was no sound on the tapes because what the children were actually reading was a 'script' of how to behave. Every 20 seconds each child had to act through one of five responses for the remainder of the interval. The responses included 'reading' and four distractible activities such as talking to a neighbour. One child was programmed by her script so that she was distractible for 75 per cent of the time in the first tape. With each successive 15 minute tape, her percentage of distractible behaviour was reduced by 5 per cent until in the fifteenth tape it was reduced to only 15 per cent. All the other children were scheduled to be distractible around 40 to 60 per cent of the time.

These tapes were then viewed by teachers, one at a time. The teachers thought they were helping to devise a scale of distractibility. One group of teachers viewed the tape and then related distractibility for each child on a seven-point scale. This was the 'subjective' group. The 'objective' group of teachers had first to count behaviours and then make summary ratings.

There were interesting differences in the ratings made by the different groups of teachers. The 'subjective' observers agreed very well among themselves: they agreed that the target child was extremely distractible, but they continued to agree that she was extremely distractible until the thirteenth tape, by which time she was significantly less distractible than her classmates. By contrast, the 'objective' observer did not have such good inter-rater agreement, but as a group their ratings of the target's distractibility dropped consistently. This study clearly demonstrates to behaviour modifiers what testers have known for a long time, namely that high reliability does not necessarily guarantee high validity. As Wahler and Leske (1973) conclude, 'while our untrained observers demonstrated good agreement on the target subject's behaviour, they were not responding to reality; their beliefs were consistent, but erroneous . . . One cannot glibly assume that a reliable observer is also an accurate observer'.

Put another way, observers are human, and human beings process their observerations before reporting them. Observers will behave differently during occasions when they are participating in reliability studies than when they are on their own. This has been well demonstrated in a series of studies by Reid and his colleagues in Oregon (Reid, 1970; Taplin and Reid, 1973). Reid has shown that inter-observer agreement is higher when observers are aware that they are being checked up on but that, afterwards, there is a gradual drift away from satisfactory levels of agreement. His solution is to employ professional observers who are retrained weekly — not a solution that can be translated into the every-day situation. Perhaps one should bear the problem in mind, and demand spot checks on the reliability of observations throughout a study rather than, as is typical, merely at the beginning. This is one remedy suggested by Johnson and Bolstad (1973) in their methodological critique.

Clearly, if simple observational measures of behaviour can become unreliable, and if they can be readily biased by factors both in the observer and in the situation, then it is unwise to rely on single measures as outcome criteria in any investigation. The results of treatment will be more convincing if a number of independent measures all point to change occurring. This is what investigators such as Patterson (1973) and Johnson and Bolstad (1973) call convergent validity.

COMPUTING RELIABILITY

While avoiding the term 'reliability' in preference to 'index of observed agreement', Johnson and Bolstad (1973) discuss a number of pitfalls to avoid when calculating observer agreement. First, it is important to be clear about which ratings are being compared. If there is a complex coding system in operation, such that an 'X' is scored if either A or B or C or not D is observed, then two observers could apparently agree by recording 'X' whereas one sees A and the other sees C.

Secondly, comparing overall percentage agreement even on a single-item scale is pretty meaningless. Let us say that in the course of an hour, employing a 15-second interval recording technique, two observers each agree that the subject engaged in co-operative play during 27 intervals. If on inspection of the record forms it is discovered that the first observer recorded all 27 play intervals within the first 10 minutes, and the second observer only noted play during the last 10 minutes, should one then conclude that the observers agree? Only a point-to-point or interval-to-interval check can indicate agreement, and this is a very stringent criterion.

Thirdly, it is no good reporting some composite measure of over-all-categories agreement and then using data from only one category to illustrate change in behaviour. It is necessary to quote separately the percentage agreement for each category that is used in any data presentation. Apart from being an obvious move once it is drawn to the attention, there is another good reason for insisting on this — and that has to do with the base-rate frequency of the behaviour of interest.

Consider a simple two-choice observational situation, where the patient's behaviour at mealtime is rated acceptable or unacceptable. Let us assume that acceptable behaviour generally occurs only 20 per cent of the time. In ten consecutive intervals, the following may be recorded by two observers.

I	U	A	U	U	U	A	A	U	U	U
II	U	A	U	U	U	A	U	U	U	U
Intervals	1	2	3	4	5	6	7	8	9	10

U = unacceptable   A = acceptable

Classically, for both time and interval sampling, reliability is calculated by the formula:

$$\frac{\text{Number of agreements}}{\text{Number of agreements} + \text{number of disagreements}} \times 100\%$$

In the above example, there are nine intervals in which the two observers, I and II, agree in what they recorded. Thus the percentage agreement is

$$\frac{9}{10} \times 100\% = 90\%$$

However, now consider the reliability of the less frequently noted category of acceptable mealtime behaviour. Here, observer I recorded three As, while observer II recorded two As, which agreed with two of observer I's recordings. Thus their percentage agreement for acceptable behaviour is

$$\frac{2}{3} \times 100\% = 67\%$$

Obviously, no reader of this volume would ever express percentages on such a low number of observations, but the moral is clear. The reliability of low-base-rate behaviours may be masked by the agreement obtained on high-base-rate behaviours. Where one is interested in low-rate behaviours — as one always will be when shaping up a new skill in a client with severe mental handicaps — then the agreement on the class of behaviour must be computed separately.

It is always problematical to decide what level of agreement should be obtained before using the observation schedule. Johnson and Bolstad (1973) suggest that it is possible, knowing the frequency of occurrence of the behaviours, to calculate the level of agreement

23

which should be obtained by chance. It is clearly desirable that the actual level of agreement should be substantially greater. In practice, levels in excess of 80 per cent can be considered usable.

Before leaving the issue of translating observations into numerical data, two other sets of issues should be raised. The first of these has already been touched upon, and that is the question of observer bias. The second issue concerns the mathematical properties of observational data.

A number of reviews have indicated some of the biasing factors that may affect the behaviour of both the observers and the observed (Johnson and Bolstad, 1973). Up until this point, observer error has been concentrated on. These reviews also note the effects of the observer on the behaviour of the people being observed.

Whilst few observers can become 'flies on the wall', it is generally agreed that it is desirable for non-participant observers to avoid interacting with their subjects. In particular, a good tip is to avoid eye contact. Then, it is generally found that the effects of the presence of the observer are minimised.

It should be borne in mind that the presence of the therapist to undertake observation may become a discriminant stimulus for any caretaker to alter their interaction with their charges. In a way, this relates to the point on the representativeness of the observation, and no easy solution to the problem is forthcoming. All one can say is that therapists should at all times remember that the presence of observers may have uncontrolled effects on the behaviour of the client.

This is not the occasion to go too deeply into the mathematical properties of observational data, except to draw attention to the writings of Jones (1973, 1974) on this subject. Basically, Jones presents the case for observational data being different (in mathematical terms) from the sort of psychological test data which are more familiar to most of us. As he says, 'The measurement characteristics of behavioural observation scores may differ from psychometric test scores for at least three reasons: (a) temporal dependencies among observation raw scores, (b) comparability of assessment conditions under which observations are collected for different individuals, and (c) ipsatising features of observation scoring procedures' (Jones, 1973).

In elegant examples, Jones demonstrates that the operations performed on raw observations to reduce the data to manageable proportions can unintentionally render the data unusable within conventional mathematical procedures. In essence, the problem is that, whilst frequency counts and rates of occurrence yield numbers which are cardinal in nature and have a fixed zero point, the proportion scores which are yielded by interval and time sampling procedures yield scores which are 'ipsatised' or interdependent within the boundaries of the coding system employed. The figures so derived cannot be added or correlated in the usual way without yielding meaningless results.

Thus, it can be concluded that, by following the earlier guidelines, behaviour can be sampled and recorded. However, even when all the practical difficulties involved in gathering the observations have been overcome, the resulting data must be handled with care. Data processing, data reduction and data analyses are all sophisticated procedures, each having its own internal logic and requirements. Applied behaviour analysis is not a task for the innumerate.

PRESENTING DATA

It has become customary to present data from behaviour modification studies in graph form. Although traditional operant work with animals was often displayed as cumulative records, few people are trained to read these. Since one of the functions of the visual display of data is to provide feedback to both the therapist and the client, the method of data presentation should be kept as simple as possible.

One of the simplest methods of presentation is to graph the data. The vertical axis is usually marked off in percentages — so that data are transformed into the percentage of intervals in which a target behaviour occurred, or the percentage of time samples at which the behaviour was recorded. Alternatively, the vertical axis is calibrated in terms of the absolute number of events recorded in a fixed time period (permanent product or event recording), rate of occurrence of behaviour (frequency per time unit) or duration.

The horizontal axis is marked off into units of intervention, be they treatment sessions or days of treatment. It is conventional to record the level of occurrence of behaviour prior to the start of intervention — i.e. to obtain a basal level or *baseline*. This is then separated from the treatment phase by a vertical line so that, at a glance, one can see whether any change occurred when treatment began (see Figure 2.1).

More will be said about appropriate single-case general designs in Chapter 13. At this point, it is as well to deal with the question of

Figure 2.1: Graph of treatment

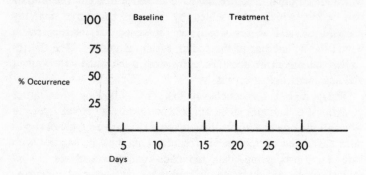

how long a baseline to obtain before starting treatment.

Often it is argued that one wants a stable baseline, and therefore that recording should be continued until a stable baseline is obtained. This is an oversimplification. The purpose of a baseline is to obtain a valid index of the patient's behaviour before treatment. The behaviour may already be improving, getting worse, remaining steady or even fluctuating in a regular or irregular manner. Ideally, then, the baseline observations should be continued until the patient's behaviour is reliably represented.

Reality is far removed from this ideal picture. The time which staff and patients will tolerate observations without treatment will vary a great deal and, in part, will depend on the presenting problem. Thus, it would be unethical to continue observing self-injurious behaviour merely to get a 'stable' baseline. Considerations such as these have to be accommodated in selecting the most appropriate research design which will both monitor change and allow the therapist to infer whether his intervention has been successful.

CONCLUSIONS

In the technology of behaviour modification, there are powerful techniques for improving the self-reliance and the general quality of life of individuals with mental handicaps. Broadly based methods of functional analysis can assist in pin-pointing problem areas. Once identified, problems can be objectively defined, observed and recorded. Although the observational techniques are, in concept,

26

quite simple, in practice observation is a skilled activity. The data yielded by observational techniques have certain properties which make them tricky to handle by conventional data reduction techniques. Even so, with adequate precautions, good data collection is the key to good behavioural intervention. The data should quickly reflect change, allowing for alterations in the treatment programme. The following chapters will describe the principles and practices of good behavioural treatment.

3

Ways of Increasing Behaviour: Reinforcement

Rosemary Hemsley and Janet Carr

It is a commonplace to point out that reinforcement, like others of the methods used, is not peculiar to behaviour modification but is widely used in every-day life. Few of us, apart from the affluent or altruistic, would go regularly to work if we were not paid to do so. Teachers and parents expect to help children learn by encouragement, praise and prizes. What distinguishes reinforcement in behaviour modification is the systematically careful way in which it is analysed and applied so as to make it maximally effective.

DEFINITION

Reinforcement may be defined as any event which, when it follows a behaviour, strengthens the probability or the frequency of that behaviour's occurrence. Or as Baumeister (1967) puts it, 'the frequency of a response is subject to the consequences of that response'. We can then bring the frequency of the response under control by identifying and arranging the consequences. If a certain consequence is found to strengthen a behaviour, that consequence is described as a reinforcer. This way of describing a reinforcer makes no assumptions as to its qualities: it does not describe a reinforcer as 'something nice' or 'pleasant'; it would come nearer the mark to describe it as 'something the individual likes very much' but that too may be mistaken. It is not uncommon for a programme to be embarked on using as a 'reinforcer' something the person is said to like very much, only to find that he didn't like it enough to work for it (Moore and Carr, 1976). Only if the consequence, when it follows the behaviour, results in an increase in the frequency of the behaviour can the consequence be described as a reinforcer. This is an important principle, and one sometimes overlooked by those drawing up behaviour modification programmes.

This definition of reinforcement is often found to be confusing to people new to the area. Some critics object that the definition is 'circular' — i.e. if a behaviour is *not* strengthened, then the stimulus which was applied contingently was not reinforcing. Within the logic of operant conditioning, this very 'circularity' is seen as a strength, not a weakness. It means that the therapist should never make any assumptions about what the person will find reinforcing. All assumptions have to be put to the harshest of all tests: they have to be shown to work by producing an effect in the desired direction on the behaviour.

Another source of confusion is that frequently the adjectives 'positive' and 'negative' are used as alternatives for 'pleasant' and 'unpleasant' when describing the stimuli which are applied contingently. This can lead one into the semantically strange situation of stating that applying a negative stimulus such as shouting at a child can act as a positive reinforcer when, as happens not infrequently, the child's naughty behaviour is strengthened. The point is that *reinforcement* is always defined retrospectively in terms of its actual effect on the behaviour. Having said that, then it must be noted that there are two types of reinforcement: positive reinforcement and negative reinforcement. Both have the effect of strengthening behaviour and can best be understood diagrammatically (Table 3.1). Punishment is discussed in detail in Chapter 8.

Table 3.1: The relationship between applying or removing stimuli and strengthening or weakening behaviour

Stimulus	Applied	Removed
Positive or pleasant	Positive reinforcement — behaviour strengthened	Punishment by removal — behaviour weakened
Negative or unpleasant	Punishment by application — behaviour weakened	Negative reinforcement — behaviour strengthened

TYPES OF REINFORCER

Reinforcers may be divided into four categories: primary, secondary, social and stimulating. Primary reinforcers are those that are essential for life — food, drink, warmth, sleep. In work with human subjects, our use of foods as primary reinforcers is not quite as simple as it sounds, in that these subjects are seldom so deprived as to be reinforced by *any* food or drink (although this may occur in animal studies). Instead we have to discover which are the preferred foods that are reinforcing. Secondary reinforcers are those events or things which, although not intrinsically of value, have acquired reinforcing properties through pairing with primary reinforcers. Money is highly reinforcing to most adults not because of the metal, paper and print of which it is made up, but because the money represents a vast range of back-up reinforcers for which it may be exchanged. Tokens, stars, points and so on may similarly acquire reinforcing properties. (These are discussed further in Chapter 4.) Social reinforcers — attention, praise, smiles, hugs and so on — have often been included among the secondary reinforcers, the assumption being that they only become reinforcing for the young child through being paired with primary reinforcers, especially food. This hypothesis may seem improbable, but for ethical reasons has never been tested with human infants, and it has continued in vogue (Jordan and Saunders, 1975). Other work with young infants, however, has shown that social stimuli may be responded to in the absence of any previous pairing with primary reinforcers (Schaffer and Emerson, 1964). It seems uncertain as to whether social reinforcers are a class of primary reinforcer, but equally they do not appear to be secondary, and should perhaps be in a class of their own. In the fourth category, stimulating reinforcers, are those objects or events whose reinforcing properties appear to lie in the stimulation that they provide. Without falling into any of the other three categories they are valued because of the engagement and interest that the person experiences through them. Music, and other sensory stimuli, are examples of this category, as also are toys, games, activities such as swimming, and many of the outings and leisure pursuits that may be used as back-up reinforcers in token programmes. A special example in this category is free time, which has been used successfully as a reinforcer in a number of studies (Couch and Clement, 1981; Salend and Kovalich, 1981).

Most reinforcers used in the natural environment are secondary or social. They have many advantages over primary reinforcers, especially to those delivering them: they are more convenient, less bulky and messy, easily available, acceptable to the general public, and probably less subject to satiation than are most primary reinforcers. Social reinforcers in particular may be favourably regarded in contrast to primary reinforcers (Kiernan, 1974) and may be thought of as preferable in being less like bribes. However, praise is not always an effective reinforcer, especially for people with more severe handicaps (Heitman *et al.*, 1980), nor for all types of task (Heitman and Justen, 1982). The crucial point, with social as with all other reinforcers, is: do they have the effect of increasing the frequency of the behaviour they follow? If they do not, then, regardless of how convenient and acceptable they are, they are not reinforcers in this case, and it may be profitable to return to using primary reinforcers. When a person does not respond to social reinforcers, we usually attempt to increase their influence by pairing them consistently with effective primary reinforcers. This may well be successful with those with no or only mild handicaps, but may be more difficult to achieve with people with severe handicaps. Lovaas *et al.* (1966b) found that autistic children were not reinforced by the comment, 'Good', after numerous pairings with food. When the children were required to attend to the social reinforcers, by approaching the therapist for the food when he said, 'Good', it then became a reinforcer for new behaviours.

SELECTING THE REINFORCER

It is obvious, from the preceding discussion, that what is a reinforcer can only be defined *post hoc*, when its effect on the behaviour is apparent. However, in order to arrive at that position we have to select a probable reinforcer for trial, using a variety of approaches to make an intelligent guess at what is likely to be effective.

(1) Ask the individual directly. This is the most straightforward way of determining preferences (Clements and McKee, 1968) but may not be possible with people with severe handicaps.
(2) Ask those people most familiar with the person — parents, sibs, nurses and so on. We stress that we are looking for things that the client likes *very much* as otherwise we may be given a catalogue of things he is mildly interested in or even of things that he barely tolerates.
(3) Use the indirect preference technique. If other methods have not elicited an effective reinforcer, a variety of possible reinforcers — foods, drinks, music, flashing lights, toys, etc. — may be offered on a number of occasions to see which one is selected most often. This method was used with severely handicapped children, and repeated testing over 10 days showed a high stability of choices (Kiernan, 1974). Wacker *et al.* (1975)

31

established the preferences of adolescents with mental ages below six months by the use of microswitches activating different stimuli such as taped music, marble games, coloured lights or an electric fan. The switches were triggered by the responses being trained, and individuals showed stable preferences for certain reinforcers. Other stimuli elicited responses little above baseline levels. For individuals with severe handicaps, who may be deaf and blind in addition to having profound mental handicap, it may be necessary to be highly inventive in the choice of reinforcers and in the evaluation of their efficacy to increase rates of responding. Pace *et al.* (1975) describe a two-stage procedure whereby 16 types of reinforcer were presented to people with profound handicaps and later assessed for their reinforcing value by their efficacy at increasing target behaviours. In this way it was possible to order the reinforcers for future use with each individual based on their proven effectiveness rather than on preferences alone. The type of reinforcers used included a plastic flower, a vibrator, a hug, coffee, and a taped song.

(4) Use the Premack principle. There are some children and adults who appear to have no particular preferences, are uninterested in toys, unaffected by cuddles, attention or scolding and are so uninterested in food that they may be difficult to feed. In this case it can be useful to observe the person to see what he does when left to himself. According to the Premack principle (Premack, 1959) this preferred, high-frequency activity, whatever it is, may be used to reinforce a less preferred, low-frequency one. For example, some children with severe mental handicaps spend much of their time in stereotyped behaviour, flapping their hands, rocking, twisting scraps of paper or string and so on. These stereotyped behaviours may then be used as reinforcers, by allowing the child access to them only after he has shown another more desirable behaviour. For example, one boy would usually sit twiddling a plastic cup on his thumb. When we wanted him to do a more constructive task — threading a wooden ring over a curved wire — he learned to do this when he was allowed his 'twiddler' only when he had performed the task. Wolery *et al.* (1986) describe a study where ritualistic behaviour (hand-flapping and licking or saliva play) were used as reinforcers for two autistic children. They monitored the rate of these behaviours in free settings after the training sessions to see if there was an increase in ritualistic

behaviours at other times. The authors found no such increase, but urge caution and careful monitoring of such possible side-effects when using reinforcers which are themselves potentially undesirable.

A dilemma is reached when the individual's preferred activity is in itself undesirable, such as overactive running about, masturbation or head banging. Whether or not we make use of these sorts of activities as reinforcers depends first of all on whether other reinforcers are available for that person, in which case it may be preferable to use them. If no other reinforcer is available, the decision will depend on whether the need to teach the new behaviour outweighs the undesirability of the preferred activity. For example, it might well be worth allowing a child to run about or rock repetitively if this helped him to learn some constructive play; it would be unlikely to be worth letting him bang his head. Other preferred activities such as masturbation or regurgitation can be highly embarrassing in public situations, especially in adults, so that they would reduce the outings or social events in which he would be included. It would be unwise to use these as reinforcers for other activities, especially for adults with mental handicaps.

VARIETIES OF REINFORCERS

Probably the most commonly used kinds of reinforcer are foods and social approaches such as attention, hugs and praise. Where these are either ineffective or undesirable, it may be necessary to be both imaginative and ingenious in seeking other reinforcers. Clapping may be an effective social reinforcer, as may gentle stroking and tickling. Music is reinforcing to some: an 18-year-old girl with severe mental handicaps was taught to obey simple commands using as a reinforcer snatches of her favourite record. Another child liked to look at a mirror for a few seconds while he was wearing sunglasses; another to sing nursery rhymes and carols at the top of his voice; another, with a passion for bizarre-tasting foods, liked to lick an ice-cube, bite raw potato or lick at a bar of soap. Sensory stimuli of various kinds — bright lights, music, doorbell chimes, synthesised sound, vibration — have been found to be as or more effective than edibles or praise (Goodall et al., 1981; Murphy, 1982). Microelectronic technology can be employed to bring such reinforcers under the control of people with even the most severe

handicaps (Lovett, 1985). Vibration has received particular attention, and was shown to be an effective reinforcer for 13 out of 16
children with profound mental and additional sensory handicaps
(Byrne and Stevens, 1980) and more effective than praise for
adolescents with mental ages below 5½ (Ottenbacher and Altman,
1984). Jones (1980) found similar effects but pointed out that 'vibration is not a universal reinforcer', that the intensity at which it is
reinforcing is an individual concern, and that in some cases vibration
can act as a punisher. Other sensory stimuli should be explored:
bright or flashing lights may be particularly reinforcing to partially
sighted children; one autistic boy would work for the reinforcement
of short periods of an electric toothbrush in his mouth. A systematic
study of a wide range of sensory stimuli and their effect on retarded
children has been made (Campbell, 1972) in an attempt to provide
novel reinforcers for children who are difficult to reinforce.

The methods described in considering the selection and varieties
of reinforcers have suggested ways to attempt to discover what the
person likes. The next essential step is to use the chosen reinforcer
in a treatment programme to find out whether it is powerful enough
to change that person's behaviour. Only if it is can it be described
as a reinforcer.

It is important to remember that, if a powerful reinforcer exists,
it may function to increase or maintain any type of behaviour,
desirable or undesirable. For example, someone who enjoys
attention may find that the quickest way to get people to attend to
him is to tip over furniture or pull the hair of the person next to him.
It is our job to ensure that, once reinforcers have been identified,
they are as far as possible made contingent on desirable behaviours
only.

NEGATIVE REINFORCEMENT

Negative reinforcement, like its positive cousin, *increases*
behaviour. Therefore the term is not synonymous with punishment,
which aims at *decreasing* behaviours (see Chapter 8). In negative
reinforcement the desired behaviour is followed immediately by the
removal of an unpleasant stimulus. The use of negative reinforcement is seen most simply in the example of a person's behaviour on
a freezing cold day. Experiencing the cold is aversive to most
people. As soon as he puts on a warm coat, the aversive circumstances are avoided. Thus, the act of putting on the coat is

(negatively) reinforced by the removal of the sensation of cold (Craighead *et al.*, 1976). Negative reinforcement is seldom used in work with children, but it can sometimes be seen having an effect on adults. For instance, a mother taking her child to the supermarket may be assailed from the minute she sets foot in it by a non-stop barrage of whining: 'Wanna sweetie! Wanna sweetie! Mum give us a sweetie.' When the mother can stand it no longer she seizes a packet of sweets and thrusts them into the child's hands. Instantly the whining stops, the *mother* is negatively reinforced by escaping from its unpleasantness, and she may be likely to buy the bag of sweets more promptly next time. Simultaneously, of course, the child is being positively reinforced for his undesirable behaviour, and the situation for the mother may actually get worse. The effect of negative reinforcement on the trainer may help to explain why some ineffective programmes are continued. Some mothers who smack their children for bad behaviour do so because the smack has the effect of stopping the behaviour at the time, so relieving the mother of the immediate unpleasantness, although they may realise it does not have any more permanent effect: 'It works, but it doesn't really alter his behaviour' (Carr, 1975).

HOW TO PRESENT REINFORCEMENT

There are four important rules as to how reinforcement should be presented if it is to be maximally effective. Mnemonically, we may say that reinforcement should be delivered with a CICC.

Contingency

Reinforcement should be given when the desired behaviour occurs, and not at other times in the session. When tangible rewards are being used for teaching, they should, if possible, be limited in their availability at other times of the day to ensure their continued motivating properties.

Immediacy

Reinforcement should be given as soon as the desired behaviour is shown, with the smallest possible time lag. This means that the teacher must be alert to what the client is doing, so that he will notice the appropriate response as soon as it occurs. He must also be ready with the reinforcer; if it is a tangible one, it should be already in his hand before the response occurs, so that he can deliver it at once and not have to search or fumble for it.

If reinforcement is not given immediately following the desired behaviour, there is the possibility that another, less desired, behaviour may take place in the intervening period and it may be this that is reinforced. For instance, a child who has just correctly imitated a sound may then resort to rocking or hand-flapping. If the reinforcement is delayed until this ritual has begun, it may be the ritual and not the imitation that is reinforced. Delay in reinforcement may also delay learning; Schoelkopf and Orlando (1965) found that delay of as little as five seconds between the behaviour and the reinforcement was sufficient to slow down learning.

Consistency

A new behaviour will be most rapidly established if it is reinforced every time it occurs. Therefore at the beginning of a training programme best results are achieved if responses are reinforced consistently. Once a behaviour has been firmly established, different reinforcement patterns are more effective for maintaining the behaviour (see the section on schedules of reinforcement).

Clarity

It is essential for the individual to be clearly aware that reinforcement has been given. This applies especially to social reinforcement. Praise should be enthusiastic, smiles broad and hugs and kisses given warmly. The restrained British mumble of 'Well done' may, to a person with a severe mental handicap, be indistinguishable from other verbal communication, whereas the more frenetic approach described above, besides being more pleasurable, gives him a clearer indication of his success. It is also important, especially for those with good understanding of speech, to state clearly which behaviour is being reinforced; to say, 'Good. I like the way you did up that button', rather than merely to say 'Good' mechanically.

SCHEDULES OF REINFORCEMENT

Reinforcement may be given on either a *continuous* schedule (following every appropriate response) or on an *intermittent* schedule (following certain responses only). We have already discussed briefly a continuous reinforcement schedule, or CRF (see the section on consistency, p. 36). The advantage of this type of schedule is that, beside being relatively easy to administer within a structured session, it is the most effective for establishing a new behaviour. In a recent study demonstrating the effect of various reinforcement schedules, three children with severe mental handicaps learnt to discriminate words, letters and numerals more quickly and with fewer errors when reinforcement was given for unprompted responses on a CRF (continuous reinforcement fixed) and prompted responses on an FR 3 schedule, rather than vice versa, or with CRF in both cases (Touchette and Howard, 1984). An intermittent reinforcement schedule has the advantage of being much nearer to the kind of reinforcement pattern likely to be met with in the natural environment; in the every-day world, people are likely to notice and enthuse about only a minority of our commendable actions. Busy parents or staff with other demands on them cannot reward each person for every correct response throughout the day. Secondly, and more importantly, behaviour that has been maintained by intermittent reinforcement is very much more resistant to extinction than is behaviour maintained by continuous reinforcement (Bandura, 1969; Baumeister, 1967). Some researchers have attempted to discover whether behaviours which have been maintained on an intermittent schedule will become more subject to extinction if they are transferred to a continuous schedule (Spradlin and Girardeau, 1966). This, if it were established, would be extremely important in cases where undesirable behaviours, maintained by intermittent reinforcement, are strongly resistant to extinction. Unfortunately, the studies have not shown that moving from an intermittent to a continuous schedule makes the behaviour more subject to extinction, though the authors point out that the experiments may have been too brief for such an effect to be shown. The disadvantages of an intermittent schedule are that it is, first, less effective for establishing a new behaviour and, secondly, rather more difficult to administer systematically (see below).

TYPES OF SCHEDULE

Reinforcement may be given on either a *ratio* or an *interval* schedule. On a ratio schedule, reinforcement depends on the frequency of appropriate responses; on an interval schedule, reinforcement depends on a reponse following a specified lapse of time. So a child on a ratio schedule might receive reinforcement for every second or third piece that he placed correctly in a puzzle; and on an interval schedule the child might be reinforced after every 15 or 30 seconds that he is working on the jigsaw.

Reinforcement schedules of either kind may be further categorised as *fixed* or *variable*. On a fixed schedule, reinforcement is given regularly, following a certain number of responses or after a certain length of time. So on fixed ratio schedules reinforcement may be given following, say, every third, tenth or twentieth response: these schedules are designated as FR 3, FR 10 and FR 20. Similarly, fixed interval schedules, where reinforcement is given following the response occurring after, say, 5 seconds, 15 seconds and 20 minutes, are described as FI 5 seconds, FI 15 seconds and FI 20 minutes. On a variable schedule, reinforcement follows after numbers of responses or periods of time that can vary considerably but which *average* out at certain specified numbers or times. For example, on a variable ratio schedule with reinforcement given for every third response on average (VR 3), the reinforcement pattern might be as follows (reinforced responses are indicated by an asterisk):

Responses	ꟾ ꟾ												
Reinforcements	*	* *	*	*	* *	*	* *	*	*		* *
Response No.	1	4 6	10	13	18 20	24	27 28	32	35		40 42
No. of responses intervening	1	3 2	4	3	5 2	4	3 1	4	3		5 2

With reinforcement given 14 times for a total of 42 responses, the average number of responses per reinforcement is 3, though the actual number varies considerably. A similar programme may be worked out for any variable ratio schedule (VR 5, 20, 45, etc.) or for variable interval schedules (VI 10 seconds, 60 seconds, 30 minutes), in which case it is the length of time rather than the number of responses that is varied.

Work with institutionalised children has shown that the use of different reinforcement schedules results in different patterns of responding (Orlando and Bijou, 1960). On a fixed ratio schedule there were high stable rates of responding with pauses following the delivery of the reinforcer. Variable ratio and variable interval schedules produced almost identical patterns of responding, high stable rates with short infrequent pauses not related to the time of reinforcement. Fixed interval schedules led to the greatest diversity in response patterns in these children. To those working with people with handicaps the most significant finding associated with reinforcement schedules is that variable schedules produce greater resistance to extinction (that is, the behaviour is maintained for longer after the discontinuation of reinforcement) than do fixed schedules (Spradlin and Girardeau, 1966). Since our goal must be to establish a behaviour which will function independently of extrinsic reinforcement in the natural environment, we should aim to 'thin out' reinforcement once the response pattern has been learned, the adoption of a ratio or interval schedule largely depending on the nature of the task being taught (see below).

It must be said that variable schedules are more difficult to deliver systematically and accurately than fixed schedules. The reinforcement programme must be planned in advance (similar to that on p. 38) whereas on a fixed schedule it is simple enough to determine that reinforcement will be given for every correct response, or every third or fourth correct response. If a variable schedule is to be applied strictly, then the programme must be strictly adhered to or the average rate decided upon will become distorted. It is of course quite possible to use a haphazard 'variable schedule', with reinforcement given at random, from time to time, and in real life — in the natural environment — this is what normally happens. The danger in moving from a fixed to a haphazard schedule is that reinforcement may rapidly become so infrequent that the behaviour is extinguished.

MAINTENANCE OF BEHAVIOURS

People with mental handicaps need not only to learn skills but also to use those skills on all appropriate occasions (generalisation) and to continue to use the skills after the teaching stops (maintenance). Generalisation has received much attention and is dealt with in Chapter 6. Maintenance, the continuation of a useful skill or behaviour, is also important if the teaching is to be of practical use to the learner. The part played by intermittent schedules of reinforcement in promoting maintenance through resistance to extinction has already been mentioned (p. 37) and there are some studies that have found the use of intermittent schedules to be crucial to the maintenance of the behaviour, both in children with mental handicaps (Koegel and Rincover, 1977); and in those without (Finley and Wakeford, 1984). In some cases continuing behaviour control may be necessary (Heidorn and Jensen, 1984) while in others behaviours may extinguish if the natural reinforcers for them are not forthcoming (Mayhew et al., 1978).

Many studies, however, describe maintenance over prolonged periods of time without giving details of procedures for the thinning of reinforcement or for moving from fixed to variable schedules (Faw et al., 1981, van den Pol et al., 1981). Since the behaviours were nevertheless maintained, it seems likely that they themselves produced reinforcing consequences. Examination of the studies suggests that one significant variable may be the task being taught; and that manipulation of reinforcement schedules may be necessary only where the task is relatively meaningless. Where the skills taught are directly relevant and valuable to the student, as for example sign language (Faw et al., 1981), eating out in a restaurant (van den Pol et al., 1981), dressing (Moore and Carr, 1976), appropriate menstrual care (Richman et al., 1984) or social skills (Gaylord-Ross et al., 1984), there seems to be a greater likelihood of maintenance occurring naturally.

SOME PROBLEMS ASSOCIATED WITH REINFORCERS

Satiation

Once a powerful reinforcer has been identified for a child, our troubles are not necessarily over. If it is repeatedly and invaryingly used, the child may get tired of it and cease to work for it. Satiation seems to take place most quickly with foods and least with social reinforcers, and sensory stimuli, which latter seem to be particularly resistant to satiation (Murphy, 1982). Two possible strategies to minimise the effects of satiation are, first, deprivation and, secondly, the use of multiple reinforcers. Most reinforcers are found to be more effective if access to them is allowed after a period of mild deprivation; this applies particularly to consumables: a child is more likely to work for these before rather than after a meal. An austistic boy who was said by his mother to be very fond of toast and honey was not making progress on the task she was teaching him. It transpired that she was working with him, using toast and honey as the reinforcer, after he came home from school and had had his tea — for which he had unlimited amounts of toast and honey. Satiation seems to occur particularly readily in the case of sweets, though these too may be subject to the effects of deprivation. Extended experiments have been carried out with institutionalised children using a lever-pressing task and candy reinforcement which was evidently so continuously effective that the authors concluded, 'Motivation is seldom a problem for the retarded' (Orlando and Bijou, 1960).

The use of multiple reinforcers avoids most of the problems of satiation. Either a variety of different reinforcers may be given in a session, so that at one time a food, at another a toy and at another a cuddle is given for each appropriate response, or a number of different reinforcers may be given in series for each response (Kiernan, 1974); for example, the behaviour could be followed immediately by praise, by a sweet 3 seconds later and by stroking 5 seconds after that. Once the client has learned not to grab handfuls of any reinforcer in sight he may be presented with several reinforcers at once from which to choose the particular one that appeals at the moment. This last approach has been found especially useful for the presentation of back-up reinforcers for people working on token programmes.

No research exists to show that any one method is particularly effective in avoiding satiation. The important thing is for the trainer to be alert to the possibility that satiation may result in reduced effectiveness of the reinforcer and to be prepared to do something about it.

Edible reinforcers and obesity and dental decay

Many of the early studies relied heavily on 'candy' as a reinforcer (indeed 'reinforcement' became almost synonymous with M and Ms, translated in Britain into Smarties), and sweet things are preferred by many children. This raises problems with people who are overweight or who have bad teeth. Our practice is always to explore first the effectiveness of non-edible reinforcers, and then that of other, less damaging, foods such as fruit, drinks, crisps, cheese, etc. Finally, if only sweets are effective reinforcers, we break them up into very small pieces (a Smartie is normally divided into four), thus also minimising satiation problems.

Reinforcers for particular behaviours

The behaviour to be changed may also to some extent affect the choice of reinforcers. If the person responds to a number of reinforcers, it may be possible to choose the most suitable one for the occasion. For example, when teaching a child to sit quietly it may be disruptive to use frolicking as a reinforcer. Similarly it may be thought inappropriate to use sweets as a reinforcer for eating meals; in fact in two cases known to the writers this has proved highly effective and has even, on one occasion, resulted in the child learning to eat foods that he previously would not tolerate. Edible reinforcers have been found to be inconvenient also in speech training programmes (Howlin, 1976) since the child spends several seconds in chewing and swallowing, which reduces the time available for training. In the writers' experience even quarter grapes took too long for one child to consume, since the child kept the grape skin almost indefinitely in his mouth: peeling the grapes got over that difficulty. Drinks are more quickly consumed than foods. The problems of spilling and of the amount of liquid taken can be overcome if the drink is given in a squeezy (well washed out) liquid detergent bottle.

Clearly where a choice of reinforcers is available it is sensible to choose the most appropriate one for the task in hand. If only one, less than ideal, reinforcer is available, then the decision has to be made whether to make use of it or to give up the idea of teaching the individual at all.

OBJECTIONS BY PARENTS AND OTHERS

Occasionally parents, nurses, teachers and others are found who object to the whole idea of using reinforcement. This is discussed more fully in Chapter 12. There is ample evidence that contingent reinforcement directly determines learning (e.g. Hekkema and Freedman, 1978), and on the whole it is found that *a priori* objections disappear when the individual can be shown to be making reliable progress.

OBJECTIONS BY PROFESSIONALS

It has been claimed that where extrinsic reward is given for a behaviour which is itself intrinsically rewarding, the strength of the latter, the 'natural reinforcers', is weakened. This is termed the over-justification effect (Lepper *et al.*, 1973) and its significance in behaviour modification has been reviewed by Ogilvie and Prior (1982). Since behavioural work with people with mental handicaps has as one of its final aims the increase of intrinsic motivation, this effect, if confirmed, could have serious consequences. However, numerous factors — subject expectations, type and salience of reinforcement, task and population characteristics — have been shown to have variable, sometimes conflicting, effects (Ogilvie and Prior, 1982) such that Karniol and Ross (1977) suggest: 'It appears entirely possible at this juncture that the detrimental effects of rewards on children's motivation may be limited to a narrow set of circumstances.' In particular the over-justification effect has been shown primarily in research with subjects whose initial interest in the task is high; whereas in work with people with mental handicaps level of interest is commonly very low or non-existent. One of the tasks of extrinsic reinforcement then is to persuade the client to participate in the activity, thereby providing him or her with the opportunity to discover the reinforcers intrinsic to it (Moore and Carr, 1976) so that the extrinsic reinforcers may then be withdrawn. Alternatively other ways must be sought, by thinning out and varying the reinforcement schedule, to ensure maintenance of the behaviour: a concern which Ogilvie and Prior point out has been generally disregarded in over-justification research.

IMPLEMENTING A REINFORCEMENT PROGRAMME

The following example, illustrating all the stages involved in setting up a behaviour programme, might help to clarify some of the principles of reinforcement and the sequence of events involved.

1. Specify the goal

Let us assume that we have been asked to devise a programme for a boy, John, who is hyperkinetic and has a mental handicap and that everyone concerned with his care and teaching — parents, nurses and teachers — have decided that getting him to sit for a few minutes and attend to some constructive activity would open the door to many possibilities for him. John is a very active child who is rarely

43

ill for even a few seconds. He will not sit still for meals, or to be taught any activities like puzzles or picture matching, nor will he stay on the toilet long enough for toilet training to begin. He has very little understanding of speech, responding only occasionally to his name. The initial goal is to have John sitting for 1 minute and attending to the therapist's instructions. We now have a clearly defined goal which we can reasonably expect John to achieve (asking him to sit still for 5 minutes would probably be too difficult at this stage).

2. Identify the reinforcer

The next stage is to identify the reinforcement for which John will be prepared to sit down for a second or two. Since John is such a hyperactive child, we expect that we will need quite a powerful reinforcer to teach sitting, since running about is itself so motivating for him. There are many possible reinforcers for John. He enjoys running and jumping, he loves orange juice, crisps and ice cream, and he also likes to be cuddled. All of these reinforcers could be used in teaching John to sit. The orange juice would be better in a squeezy bottle than in a cup, as this will save spilling if John knocks it over. The crisps should be put out on a plate, ready to hand, and broken up into smaller pieces. Ice cream is not an easy reinforcer to use as it is difficult to get it at the right consistency, neither rock hard nor melted; an insulated butter box helps to keep it from going liquid, and we should certainly keep the ice cream in mind in case John becomes bored with the other foods. Cuddles are easy to give, and a few moments of running about could appropriately be interspersed with the sitting. We plan then to use as reinforcement a cuddle plus a food or drink together with praise, followed by a few moments of running.

3. Teaching the behaviour

We begin to teach sitting using a plain bare room with as few distractions in it as possible. A chair for John is placed in the middle, preferably with arms to help prevent him squirming off it. John is called by his name to get his attention, told gently but firmly, 'Sit down', and then held and seated on the chair. Immediately we praise him — 'That's good, John' — and give him a crisp and a cuddle. With a very active and resistant or a large child it might be necessary to have a second trainer to hold the child while the reward is given, otherwise he may slip off the chair before receiving his crisp and inadvertently be rewarded for being off his seat. If this should happen (and accidents occur in the best-run treatment programmes even if they are not always written up in the journals), we withhold the reinforcer, repeat the command and the physical prompt and this time get the reinforcer in fast. Then John is released and allowed to get up and run around. (Here the Premack Principle comes into play: since running around is a high-frequency activity for John, it is likely to function as another reinforcer.) After a few seconds we carry out a further trial, calling John, leading him to the chair and seating him, then praising and rewarding him for sitting on the chair.

How many trials should be given per session and how long each session should last will depend on the individual child. On the whole, we prefer short sessions of 5–10 minutes with 10–20 trials per session, and several short sessions a day seem preferable to one long one. As the programme progresses, we may give more trials, but usually 10 minutes' intensive training is enough for both therapist and child. When we train staff or parents to do the sessions themselves, it is often difficult, especially at the beginning of a programme, to convince them of the need to keep the sessions short. Sometimes a parent will go on with a language session for 45 minutes and then wonder why the child is reluctant to co-operate the next time.

4. Fade out reinforcement schedule

Let us say that John has now had a week of training in sitting. He has rather lost interest in crisps and orange juice, so ice cream is now being used as reinforcement. He will now come to the chair when told to sit, and will wait there to receive his spoonful of ice cream and then get up and run around the room until the request is repeated. John probably does not yet understand the actual meaning of the command, 'Sit down', but has learnt that, each time he is given an instruction in this situation and he sits down, he receives ice cream; he is reacting to the cues of the environment. At this stage, when he is sitting each time he is told to do so and is anticipating the reinforcement, we can begin to fade out the rein- forcement, moving on to an intermittent schedule. Now John receives edible reinforcement every second time he sits to command, then every third time, after which we may, if we are sufficiently well

45

organised, move on to a variable ratio schedule (VR 3 perhaps). At the same time we may move on to training John in a slightly different task, that of remaining seated. For this we may begin with a fixed interval schedule — FI 5 seconds for example, so that John is now reinforced every 5 seconds that he is sitting down. Gradually we extend this to FI 10 seconds, 30 seconds, 1 minute and so on, eventually going on to a VI schedule when John is reasonably good at sitting still in order that this behaviour may be the better maintained. In addition, once John will sit for 30 seconds to a minute, we may insist that meals are only eaten when he is seated, or introduce constructional material such as simple form boards, colour matching and so on. Providing that we ensure that the constructional material is interesting and at a level appropriate for the child, we may be able to use these activities as reinforcement: the child is allowed to put the pieces of puzzle in the board if he is seated. Now we may be able to dispense with edibles as interest in the task and praise begin to function as reinforcers. If, however, under these conditions the child's learning slows down, we should always be prepared to go back to edible or other tangible reinforcers.

CONCLUSIONS

Reinforcement is not, as is sometimes implied by the critics, the whole of behaviour modification, but, some recent concerns notwithstanding (Balsam and Bondy, 1983, 1985; Epstein, 1985), it is an important aspect of it. Some people with mental handicaps receive little reinforcement in their every-day lives, and many have little expectations of success. They may on the contrary have well-founded expectations of failure or of the probability of aversive consequences. If we can identify, arrange and deliver reinforcers so that appropriate behaviours are strengthened, we shall increase that person's learning, his social acceptability and his own enjoyment of his life.

4

The Use of Tokens with Individuals and Groups

Janet Carr and Chris Gathercole

At times it is not convenient, practicable or possible to deliver tangible reinforcers immediately after a behaviour has been performed. For example, if you are teaching the components of good road sense, it may not be possible to reinforce stopping at the kerb by giving a sweet if, in turn, that means you have to wait for the sweet to be eaten and thereby miss the gap in the traffic. Equally, many parents despair of reducing temper tantrums during shopping trips. Threats of what will happen when the child returns home are ineffective; immediate corporal punishment brings the wrath of passers-by to bear on the harassed mother. How can behaviour be influenced in these settings?

As was discussed earlier, we aim to bring behaviour under the influence of social attention from parents and others. Where social attention is not yet a powerful reinforcer, some other way must be found of bridging the gap between the appearance of the behaviour and the later awarding of reinforcers. One way of bridging this gap and of delivering a form of reinforcement which need not unduly interfere with the ongoing behaviour is to use token reinforcement.

Tokens are one form of generalised reinforcer; others include points, stars, plastic money or indeed real money, which latter serves as an effective generalised reinforcer for most people. In each case the token, star, point or coin has no intrinsic value for the individual, but it has come to be valued because it represents the possibility of obtaining that which is of value. The tokens themselves then become of value; since the exchange of tokens leads consistently to reinforcement, the tokens acquire reinforcing properties. When we use tokens our aims are the same as when we use other reinforcers — to teach skills, to maintain established skills and to reduce undesirable behaviours.

47

The following examples illustrate the use of tokens with individuals:

(1) Roderick is receiving individual training in speech and language development. Whenever he gives an appropriate, well articulated verbal response to pictures shown him in a scrap book, the trainer gives him one penny in plastic money, which he puts into a plastic jar beside him on the table. At the end of the 10-minute training session, he takes his jar, with a screw-on lid, back to the ward, where he exchanges his plastic tokens for real money, which he can then spend in a real shop. This is a very simple token system, which is only used in his speech and language training sessions.

(2) A more complex programme has been worked out for Stephen who works in an Adult Training Centre, where he is extremely difficult to control. Each member of the training staff carries a number of coins, with impressions of footballers. These coins were used in a sales campaign by one of the petrol companies some time ago. Whenever Stephen follows an instruction and does what he is told he is given a token by the trainer. He is also given a token if he enters the dining area for a midday meal or a drink during the tea break, as well as for participating in the work of the Centre. Stephen may therefore be given tokens by any member of staff at any time of the working day. He can exchange his tokens for drinks during the tea break, and coloured stars, which he sticks on to a chart kept in the Manager's office. The token system is in operation at all times when Stephen is at the Centre.

ADVANTAGES OF USING TOKENS

Tokens have a number of advantages over conventional reinforcers. First, they allow for the use as reinforcers of a wide variety of events and items that could not be used in the conventional way: that is, delivered immediately and contingently on the desired behaviour. For example, if a person is very fond of swimming, it may be desirable to use swimming to reinforce, say, bed-making. However, it may not be possible for him to go swimming immediately after he has made his bed. If, then, he is given a token when he has made his bed, and if he has to give a token to be allowed to swim, then he is more likely to make his bed. Here the token bridges the time gap between the required behaviour and the back-up reinforcer. Furthermore, the use of tokens enables a large reinforcer to be used by requiring a number of tokens to be exchanged for it. Since each token is given for relatively minor behaviours, the reinforcer follows a series of desirable behaviours. So it might be that the person would be given the chance of going swimming only once a week and would have to earn seven tokens — make his bed every day — for the privilege. This aspect of tokens is particularly valuable with the more able person who has little interest in foods or drinks but is keen to have, and is willing to work for, a particular outing, record, article of clothing, and so on.

Tokens also have the advantage that they allow sequences of responses to be reinforced without interruption of the teaching. Sweets and crisps, for example, take time to be consumed, which can hold up teaching and cause particular problems in, say, speech training. If consumption of the back-up reinforcer can wait until the end of the training, then time is not wasted. Again, tokens maintain their reinforcing properties because they are independent of deprivation states, whereas other reinforcers are more likely to be affected by satiation (Gewirtz and Baer, 1958; Winkler, 1971). For example, after a meal, the effectiveness of food as a reinforcer is greatly diminished. Nevertheless, a trainee may still be willing to earn tokens, which he may be able to spend on food or sweets later. Tokens allow workers to exercise some choice in their selection of back-up reinforcers. They will use their tokens for the reinforcers they want most. This allows those with different preferences to select what is most rewarding for them at that particular time. The teacher then does not have to worry too much about possible loss of interest in one particular reinforcer, so long as a range of reinforcers is made available.

Tokens also have a number of advantages for staff. When she dispenses reinforcers, a teacher also gives praise and attention. This allows her to increase her personal social reinforcement value to the person she is working with, since she becomes a discriminative stimulus for the occasion of reinforcement. Since tokens are reinforcers, and since many tokens may have to be earned before exchange can take place, there are many opportunities for the teacher to increase her reinforcement value. Tokens may also be useful in situations where real money cannot be used or where the use of real money might require an elaborate accounting procedure. Tokens can, of course, provide a valuable preparation for the use of real money. A token system may involve counting, saving, checking of change, looking after tokens and possibly even a banking system. Again the use of tokens may help to shape staff training skills, and staff are often found to be particularly enthusiastic and positive when they are working with tokens (Fernandez, 1978; Kazdin, 1977). Lastly tokens may be used flexibly, for programmes for groups as well as for individuals. A start may be made with a simple small-scale system for one person and this may be gradually extended to include more people as required.

FORMS OF TOKENS AND STORAGE

There are many different kinds of token which can be used. Tiddly-winks are suitable, as they are robust and come in several different colours; plastic money as used in schools can lead on to the use of real money; coloured stars can be stuck on to a wall chart or on to cards which the person carries with him; ticks or crosses in a book or on a card, or points written as numerical values, can be used for those able to recognise numbers; tickets can be used which can be punched like a bus ticket.

Which form of token is to be used depends partly on the ability of those earning the tokens to keep and store them. If a points card gets torn up, it may have to be covered with plastic or stuck on to more rigid material to prevent its being destroyed. Tiddly-winks may be kept in a purse, and if the purse is attached to a belt they will be even more secure. A token in the form of a washer or plastic disc with a hole in the middle can be threaded on to string, or stored in a jar for safe keeping. For a group it can be useful to make a token bank out of transparent perspex, so that each trainee has a section with a hole at the top into which he can drop his tokens. If the bank is screwed to a wall, he can then see his tokens mounting up.

TEACHING TOKEN USE

Although token systems were originally developed for use with groups of people, as in ward management and subsequently class-room management, tokens can be very helpful in individual cases, whether in hospital, classroom, hostel or the home.

Even quite severely handicapped people can learn to use tokens if they are given individual tuition. The first step is to assess the person's ability to use tokens, by freely giving him a token and requiring him to present it in exchange for a back-up reinforcer, such as a drink of milk. It quickly becomes apparent whether he can look after the token and hand it over in exchange at the appropriate time. If he is not able to do this, then he is taught to do so. A task analysis of all the skills required in token use indicates that the person should be able first of all to hold out his hand to receive the token. Then he should be able to look after it safely in his hand or his pocket, in a purse, or in some form of piggy bank. Then he must be able to present the token when he wishes to exchange it for a back-up reinforcer. Reinforcement, shaping, prompting, modelling and fading are all used in teaching these skills.

So if the person does not understand the purpose of the tokens, he should first be given one and then, almost immediately, prompted to hand it back in exchange for his back-up reinforcer. When he has learnt, by repeated trials and fading of the prompts, to do this readily, he should be given a token and prompted to retain it for a short time, 10–15 seconds, before exchanging it. Later he must learn to retain two tokens, and later still he can be taught to keep the tokens for a longer period and to store them, for instance in a purse. Once these skills have been established and he is exchanging them appropriately for the back-up reinforcer, the tokens can begin to be given contingently on the performance of some skilled or required behaviour.

Teaching of this kind may not always be necessary, even for people with very severe handicaps. In one day-care facility a token system was set up for the five most able people in the group, with tokens earned according to individually devised programmes and exchanged at a 'token shop' for a variety of small items — pencils, postcards, sweets, etc. The remaining 20 people were thought to be incapable of learning to use tokens. One middle-aged man, autistic, with no speech and very few skills, picked up a token from a windowsill and took it, as he had seen others do, to the token shop where a kind-hearted worker exchanged it for him. After this, in view of his keen interest in the tokens, a programme was drawn up for him (with the result that many of his stereotypies disappeared). Gradually the other clients were similarly included in the token system until eventually all were participating in it apart from four who were very severely physically disabled as well as mentally handicapped.

With less severely handicapped people, it is often possible to explain the contingencies of reinforcement and even write down a list of the behaviours being reinforced, together with token payments, and a price list of back-up reinforcers for which tokens can be exchanged. The written statement is a useful reminder to the teacher of what the prices and wages are at any particular time. It can also be considered as a form of contract when the list has been agreed by both parties, and may even be signed by both parties to give it a more official status. Having a written contract helps to avoid disputes about what has or has not been agreed in the past. A contract is not essential, however, and for more severely handicapped people it is only necessary that they be exposed to the contingencies of reinforcement. It is essential, however, that once a token system has been worked out it should be adhered to consistently. If arbitrary changes are made or the teacher forgets to make token payments or omits to provide the back-up reinforcers, then the system will break down and become ineffective.

SCHEDULING REINFORCEMENT

When the tokens can be used appropriately and the person is not losing them, throwing them away, chewing them, allowing them to be stolen or giving them away, but is looking after them carefully, then we can begin to use them in actual training of other skills. To begin with, they would be used as reinforcers after every successful performance. As the behaviour becomes established, intermittent reinforcement can be introduced. Every other correct performance is reinforced, then every third, every fourth and so on, gradually increasing the number of correct performances before token reinforcement is presented. If the number of correct performances before token reinforcement is now varied, the behaviour will become even more strongly established, and it will be easier for other reinforcements in the natural environment to take over the reinforcing functions of the tokens so that eventually the tokens can be eliminated altogether. The benefits of intermittent reinforcement are discussed more fully in Chapter 3. The important point is that behaviour is more resistant to extinction when reinforced intermittently than when reinforced every time it occurs.

In the early stages of training, the person should be allowed to exchange her tokens for back-up reinforcers fairly frequently. Eventually it will be possible for her to work for 10 minutes, or 20 minutes, or longer, during which time she may accumulate 50 or 100 tokens before she makes her token exchange. At an even higher level of functioning, it will be possible for the token exchange to be delayed for half a day, or a day, or even longer.

SOME RULES FOR TOKEN ECONOMIES

Ayllon and Azrin (1968) describe a number of rules, very carefully worked out on the basis of both theory and practice, which provide essential ingredients for the success of a token system.

We need to describe the current behaviour which we wish to change in specific terms that require a minimum of interpretation. For example, it is more helpful to record that

Paula bit Brenda on the arm

than to say that

Paula was aggressive to Brenda

The first description is specific, whereas the second includes interpretation. On reading the second we would still have to ask, 'What exactly did Paula do to Brenda?'

We should also describe the objectives of training in behavioural terms. A good behavioural objective (Mager and Pipe, 1970) will state WHO — WILL DO WHAT — UNDER WHAT CONDITIONS — TO WHAT CRITERION; e.g. 'Paula will clap hands unassisted when you say, "Paula, clap your hands", and demonstrate, four out of five times'. Such an explicit statement of the required behaviour will enable the trainer to know when the desired behaviour has been achieved.

We should aim to select as behavioural objectives or targets for training as far as possible only those behaviours which will continue to be reinforced after training, so that time and effort are not wasted in teaching skills which are unlikely to be maintained after the training period. This means that we need to look at the reinforcers available in the person's natural environment and to judge how effective these will be and for which behaviours they are likely to be delivered; and thus which behaviours stand a good chance of being maintained. This is especially important with token programmes as the teacher will wish to wean the person from the arbitrary token reinforcement used during the training period.

SELECTION AND USE OF REINFORCERS

The basic principles governing the selection and delivery of reinforcers generally (contingency, immediacy, consistency, etc.) also apply to tokens. In addition, however, a token programme offers the opportunity to make use of a wide range of potential back-up reinforcers for which the tokens can be exchanged. Moreover, there is less danger of the person becoming satiated and losing interest in particular reinforcers, and the tokens are more likely to retain their reinforcing value when there is a wide variety of back-up reinforcers to choose from. Since multiple reinforcers are valuable in token programmes, it is also important that the different reinforcers are equally available, and that choosing one does not automatically exclude another. For example, if swimming and riding were scheduled to occur at the same time, the person could not choose to exchange his tokens for both, even if he had sufficient tokens for both. If these events were scheduled at different times, he could exchange his tokens for both activities and enjoy a wider range of back-up reinforcers.

Before using events as reinforcers we may have to provide opportunities for the person to try them without having to pay tokens for them, to see whether or not he likes them. To take a, perhaps extreme, example: one young man was so unwilling to participate in the light industrial work on offer at his day centre that he was taught to do so with the aid of edible reinforcers. Once he had experienced this activity, however, he became so interested in it that it was then possible to use these industrial tasks as back-up reinforcers for learning other skills. Similarly other potentially enjoyable experiences may be made available, so that the person can decide whether he or she will want to earn tokens in order to gain access to them. In effect, we are helping the person to make use of many potential reinforcers and to enjoy a wide range of activities. The more he wants to exchange his tokens, the more effective they will be in training, so we have to do all that we can to interest him in the reinforcers that are available. If possible he should be able to see, touch, smell or hear the reinforcer: supermarkets and salesmen have long recognised the importance of exposure to reinforcers. It may help to have him watch someone else actively enjoying it (Doty et al., 1974; McInnis et al., 1974).

RECORD KEEPING

It is important that a record be kept of the number of tokens earned, and of their exchange. Some systems, such as stars or points on a chart or tokens accumulating in a locked 'bank', provide their own record, but if tokens are stored by the person earning them, for example in a purse, then it is useful to have an independent record to check both that the person is not losing them and that he is not illicitly acquiring extra tokens.

In some cases this record will also serve as a record of behaviour change: if, for example, it shows the frequency of a desirable behaviour which may be compared with a baseline. In other cases it may be necessary to keep separate records of the target behaviours, in order to determine whether or not the programme is having the intended effect.

FIXING WAGES AND PRICES

Fixing the level of token payment is a fairly arbitrary matter. There are no rules to say exactly how many tokens should be paid. Token payment will partly depend on its value to the person, that is, what it will buy for him. A bag of crisps may cost 1000 tokens, which could be earned by his making his bed each day. It would be just as effective to arrange the payment for making his bed to be 1 token if the price of the crisps is 1 token. Wages and prices therefore have to be considered together. Payment should not be too low in relation to prices, otherwise the tokens will be ineffective. If the level at which they are set is such that the reinforcer is effectively unavailable to him, the person will simply not work for them. If they are too high, the teacher may have difficulty in providing enough back-up reinforcers and the person will be able to get all the reinforcers he wants too easily.

The number of tokens required for the purchase of a back-up reinforcer has to be specified. For example, 20 tokens may be required in exchange for one toffee, three for 30 minutes of television viewing time. One telephone call home, lasting not more than five minutes, might cost ten tokens. Price fixing will be determined by the availability of reinforcers, how many tokens can be earned, how keen the person is to purchase the particular reinforcer, and prices of other available reinforcers. It is possible to increase or decrease the prices to be paid for the reinforcers or the token payments made to the person. Inflation and deflation occur in a token system, just as they do in a wider monetary economy.

It may become apparent, after the scheme has started, that wages and prices are not sufficiently in balance and that one or other is too high or too low. Some change will be needed to achieve a better balance. The teacher may fix the prices, or he may negotiate them in discussion with the person. Obviously in changing prices and wages, care has to taken that changes are introduced in such a way as to maintain the desired behaviour. If wages are lowered too quickly or prices increased too much, the person may go on strike. To avoid resentment, then, changes should be introduced slowly. The ratio of reinforcement to performance can be altered as was described in the section on scheduling reinforcement in such a way as to maintain the behaviour. The effect of this is that during a training session the number of tokens earned may stay the same but the person is gradually working faster or longer or harder.

Another way of avoiding difficulty is for the person to select tasks each day or each week. The wage for each task is set for the period but at the end of the period the wage may be reset. The person could opt for the same task he had the previous week or for another. In this way he would get used to changes in wage levels and, should he object to the wage for a particular task, he can vote with his feet by choosing to do something else.

In group work, a decision has to be made on whether to introduce a standard scheme in which everybody is paid at the same rates for the required levels of behaviour and the prices of back-up reinforcers are all standardised, or whether each person will have an individually tailored programme. It is probably easier for staff to run a standard scheme, because if wages and prices vary for each individual then the whole system can become very complicated. However, a standard scheme may not cater for individual needs in sufficient detail and therefore may be less effective than individualised programmes. It may be possible to combine the two approaches so that a standard scheme forms the basic system but individual variations are used for particular people.

WEANING FROM TOKENS

The aim of training with tokens is to help the person improve her skills to the point where they become so useful to her that she does not require tokens to maintain them. The token system therefore should have built-in procedures for weaning off tokens at the earliest opportunity.

As a first step, reinforcement may be changed from a continuous to an intermittent schedule. This has been discussed already in the section on scheduling reinforcement (p. 52). Then opportunities should be sought for moving from tangible to social reinforcers. Praise should always be given when tokens are being given, so that, in time, praise should acquire reinforcement value and, as the token reinforcement is reduced, the behaviour can be maintained by social reinforcement. The significant people in the person's natural environment should be taught to maintain the desired behaviour using reinforcers other than tokens, especially praise and attention where these can be shown to have reinforcing value. This means that other members of the family, teachers or nurses, should be able to recognise and reinforce the behaviour acquired during the training when tokens were used.

If the desired behaviour is firmly established and is being maintained by tokens exchangeable for the back-up reinforcers, it may be possible to tell the person that, so long as the behaviour remains at or about the present level, she will no longer be asked to earn tokens but the reinforcer(s) will be freely available to her: but that if the behaviour falls below an acceptable level, she will need to return to earning and paying tokens.

PUNISHMENT

For the punitively minded, one of the attractions of a token system is that tokens can be not only given but also taken away. Token-fining can be used as punishment, but in our view should be used only with great caution, and never excessively, or the person may get to a stage where he is never able to exchang tokens for back-up reinforcers. Indeed, he may be constantly in debt. When fined for some undesirable behaviour, he could be given a chance immediately to earn back, say, half his fine by practising the desired behaviour. This provides an opportunity for positive teaching rather than merely suppressing unwanted behaviour. However, the teacher has to be creative in thinking up a task on the spur of the moment, and in fixing appropriate payment for it; this might be set at roughly half or a quarter of the fine previously imposed.

A major problem involved in using fining is that workers usually dislike giving up their tokens, and resentment, or even physical struggle, can occur. An ingenious way round this problem is provided by the approach described by Salend and Kovalich (1981). Working with a class of eleven adolescents (mean IQ 66) they first determined the baseline level of disruptive behaviour: talking out of turn. With an average of 16 occurrences per half-hour session the group was given eleven 'tokens', strips of paper taped to the blackboard. The group was told that any occurrence of the behaviour would result in the loss of one token, but that if *any* token remained at the end of the session the group would receive the reinforcer, of 20 minutes' free time, in full. This programme resulted in an immediate reduction of the target behaviour, and, by gradually lowering the number of allocated tokens, the behaviour was brought, over a period of six weeks, to an acceptable level of one to two incidents per session. The authors comment that they 'noted no negative effects', and attributed this to the fact that individual occurrences of the behaviour did not mean the withdrawal or partial withdrawal reinforcement.

GROUP-ORIENTATED CONTINGENCIES

Token reinforcement may be arranged for members of a group in several ways. In a workshop, where several people contribute to the output of the team, payment can be made contingent on the productivity of the group. Another form of group-orientated contingency is demonstrated when an isolated child's peers are given tokens to give to him when he approaches them, and they too receive tokens at the same time. (The more usual procedure would be for a teacher to reinforce the child's approach.) In getting the other children to present the reinforcement, not only are they taught to shape his behaviour but also their social reinforcement value is enhanced. This approach can also be useful when the behaviour of the target subject is reinforced by attention from the group: members of the group as well as the subject receive reinforcement consequent upon appropriate behaviour of the subject, so decreasing the incentive for group members to egg on the subject in his or her inappropriate behaviour. The focus of interest in this situation is on the behaviour of one particular member of the group.

Yet another form of group-orientated contingency operates when all group members have to achieve a criterion before tokens are dispensed to everybody. An example might be the requirement for all children in a family to have tidied their rooms before pocket money is given.

The aim of using group-orientated contingencies is to make use of the peer group. The members of a group can arrange contingencies which may be more powerful and more effective than those arranged by the teacher. It may be necessary to ensure that peers do not arrange unacceptable punishing consequences for group members who hold the group back.

THE EFFECTIVENESS OF TOKEN ECONOMIES

Reviews of the extensive research on token economies (Fernandez, 1978; Gripp and Magaro, 1974; Kazdin, 1977; Kazdin and Bootzin, 1972) show that token schemes can effectively change behaviour. Many client groups have been helped in many kinds of situation, including not only children and adults who have mental handicap or autism but also delinquents in foster homes and institutions, psychiatric in-patients, especially chronic schizophrenics in long-stay wards, and children in classrooms and at home.

A wide variety of token programmes have been used with people with mental handicaps, and many different behaviour deficits have been targeted. Several programmes run in hospitals have been concerned with general behaviour and skills on the wards, including self-help and social behaviours and the decrease of inappropriate behaviours (Bath and Smith, 1974; Brierton et al., 1969; Girardeau and Spradlin, 1964; Musick and Luckey, 1970; Sewell et al., 1973; Spradlin and Girardeau, 1966). Lent et al. (1970) reported improvement in the behaviours of adolescent girls in hospitals; at follow-up a year later, significant improvements were being maintained in self-care, personal appearance and deportment but not in social and verbal skills. Two programmes (Horner and Keilitz, 1975; Wehman, 1974) have concentrated on tooth-brushing and oral hygiene; in the former, tokens were exchangeable for sugarless gum and, using a multiple baseline, the effectiveness of the use of tokens in teaching correct tooth-brushing was demonstrated.

Hunt et al. (1968) used tokens to improve the personal appearance of 12 men with mild mental handicaps who were being prepared for discharge from the institution. Tokens were awarded for such things as being clean, shaved and laundered, having keys in pocket, not dangling from the belt, and wearing not more than one pair of trousers. Tokens delivered on either a continuous or an intermittent schedule produced high levels — 80–90 per cent — of appropriate appearance in the group as a whole, which declined to 62 per cent at the end of a 10-day period in which no reinforcement was given. However, there were considerable differences in response to the programme; three men appeared unaffected by the tokens, showing relatively high levels of appearance through all three phases of the study.

The effect of tokens has been more extensively studied in classrooms than in any other setting, and are reviewed by Kazdin (1977). Birnbrauer *et al.* (1965), in one of the earlier studies, looked at a group of 15 children with mild mental handicaps working in class in a token system. When the tokens were withdrawn for 21 days, the achievement and behaviour of ten of the children deteriorated, and returned to normal when the tokens were reinstated. For five children no changes were observed, suggesting that their behaviour was not controlled by the tokens; while another child's behaviour may have been more influenced by the reinforcement from other children for his disruptive behaviours, which was discontinued when the tokens were in force ('Leave me alone, I've got work to do'). A group of young deaf behaviourally disturbed children received tokens for attentive behaviour in class (van Houten and Nau, 1980). Results showed that although both fixed and variable schedules of token reinforcement produced improvement in behaviour, variable schedules were more effective, with VR 8 rather more effective than VR 12, and were preferred by the teacher.

A novel use of tokens is described by Fabry *et al.* (1984). Six adolescents with mild to severe mental handicap, who were already in a token system for academic work, were taught to identify unknown words, written on the tokens, when these were being handed in in exchange for back-up reinforcers. This minimal teaching procedure resulted in four out of the six students learning to identify previously unknown words with a high degree of reliability. Although the author points out that they had no evidence that this approach was more effective than 'programmatic instruction', they saw the token exchange occasion as a potentially valuable time which could be used to enhance, and aid generalisation of, a variety of skills.

Recent studies have examined the effect of token reinforcement on intelligence-test performance. Young *et al.* (1982) and Johnson *et al.* (1984) showed that, in groups of children aged 7–12 with mild levels of intellectual impairment, scores on the Verbal and Full Scales of the WISC-R (Wechsler Intelligence Scale for Children — revised edition), were significantly improved when tokens were used for reinforcing correct responding. They recommended the use of tokens as motivational agents for assessing such individuals in the future. However, Johnson *et al.* failed to replicate this effect for older subjects (13–15 years). They pointed out that children whose

IQ scores are raised through the use of token reinforcement may need similar motivational enhancement in the classroom, and suggest that this may be less available to students whose higher IQs have put them beyond the special educational services. Nevertheless where tests are given without the use of extrinsic reinforcers the opposite effect may also be seen, with some children being inappropriately kept in the special educational services because they were not able to demonstrate their abilities to the full.

In another study, tokens were used indirectly to bring about change in children with mental handicaps. Muir and Milan (1982) used tokens (lottery tickets) as reinforcers to mothers for progress shown by their developmentally handicapped children to whom the mothers taught elementary language skills. The children's progress, monitored by an independent observer, was markedly more rapid when the token system for the mothers was in operation than under baseline conditions, eliciting the rueful comment from the authors that 'improvement in their children's behaviour [was not] a powerful reinforcer for parents' instructional efforts'.

Zimmerman et al. (1969) and Hunt and Zimmerman (1969) used tokens in a sheltered workshop and found that productivity increased, although the latter study found productivity also increased in periods of the day when tokens were not in operation. Goldberg et al. (1973) used an ABAB design to study the effect of tokens on the productivity of seven young people with mild mental handicaps. Group mean production rates rose when tokens were in operation and fell when they were discontinued, but again there was considerable individual variation, with two subjects showing no extinction effect in Phase 2 and one actually increasing production in Phase 1 when tokens were discontinued.

The programmes discussed above have looked at the effects of token programmes in changing behaviours. Some studies have compared the effectiveness of tokens with other forms of treatment (Baker et al., 1974; Stoffelmayr et al., 1973) and a few have compared the effects of tokens with that of various drugs on the behaviour of people with mental handicaps. Christensen (1975) and McConahey (1972) found tokens to be more effective than the drugs in increasing attention, working, self-care, etc., and in decreasing undesirable behaviours such as aggressiveness, and this was supported in a subsequent study (McConahey et al., 1977). Sandford and Nettelbeck (1982) compared the efficacy of a token system and drugs on both the desirable and undesirable behaviours of four people with mild mental handicaps. Desirable behaviours increased immediately following the introduction of the token system and did not alter when drugs were added in; in only one case was the undesirable behaviour significantly affected by the drugs. The authors conclude that the usefulness of the phenothiazines in the management of people with mild mental handicaps is doubtful.

Apart from the comparison with drugs, comparisons with other forms of treatment reviewed by Kazdin (1977) do not in any case refer to mentally handicapped populations. Perhaps this should not be seen as surprising since, apart from behavioural methods and drugs, treatments in mental handicap are thin on the ground. One approach which has become important in recent years has been that of normalisation, and the attempt to provide optimal living conditions for people with mental handicaps (Gunzburg, 1976; Nirje, 1970). In view of the findings of Baker et al. (1974) that changes of ward and of routine had effects on the behaviour of chronic schizophrenic patients that were not subsequently surpassed by the addition of tokens to the regime, a comparative study of the effect of a normalised environment with that of a token economy for mentally handicapped people is surely overdue.

SOME PROBLEMS INVOLVED IN TOKEN PROGRAMMES

1. Non-responsiveness

Many studies have found that, although the use of tokens has a favourable effect on the behaviour of the majority of clients, a minority do not alter their behaviour as a consequence of the use of tokens (Birnbrauer et al., 1965; Goldberg et al., 1973; Hunt et al., 1968). In some cases clients working under conditions of tokens delivered contingently are not adversely affected by the withdrawal of tokens (Birnbrauer et al., 1965), and in others clients do not respond positively when a token system is instituted (Goldberg et al., 1973). Explanations for the latter (failure to respond positively to tokens) have received the most attention. Kazdin (1977) suggests that the explanation may lie in the ineffectiveness for individuals of the back-up reinforcers; or in the possibility that the required responses are not in the clients' repertoire; or that the clients may not understand the relationship between performance and reinforcement. Kazdin suggests strategies to deal with these problems, and says that the variability of response patterns in different subjects 'should come as no surprise' (p. 154).

The second kind of non-responsiveness is shown by the client whose performance does not extinguish when tokens or other extrinsic reinforcement is discontinued. This event seems to dismay many behaviour modifiers, who appear to regard it as undermining the proven effectiveness of their intervention. However, in some cases at least, such an event may point to a highly successful intervention in that the client, having been persuaded by the use of extrinsic reinforcers to undertake an activity, later finds reinforcement within the activity itself. Far from being ineffective, the intervention allows the client to sample, and to discover reinforcement in, an activity he would not otherwise have attempted (cf. Carr, 1980). Other explanations for the failure of a behaviour to extinguish include the possibility that those administering the programme (teachers, parents, etc.) have changed in their behaviour towards the client and may continue to provide more effective reinforcement than they had done previously, even in the absence of a systematic programme (Kazdin, 1977, p. 176). Such an effect has certainly been observed where parents are taught to use behaviour modification methods, and constitutes one of the most hopeful aspects of such teaching (Carr, 1980).

2. Adverse effects of token programmes

More serious than the possibility that some clients may not respond to token programmes is the finding that some are made worse by the programme (Hemsley, 1978). In some cases this may have been due to distress caused by disturbance of routine. In others, Hemsley suggests that cognitive factors in the clients may be important and that these should be taken into account when selecting patients for this type of treatment. The clients considered here were chronic schizophrenics; how far similar effects may be found in the mentally handicapped is unknown, but their possibility should obviously be borne in mind.

3. Difficulties in the maintenance of benign effects

Token programmes, like others undertaken to change behaviour, are intended to produce changes which are permanent, and which will eventually be maintained by reinforcers, especially social reinforcers, that are readily available in the natural environment (Kiernan

1974). Thus the tokens should gradually be faded out, and generalis-ation to normal — ideally, community-based — living conditions should be the goal from the start. Fernandez (1978), visiting ten institutions in the United States where token programmes were in operation, found that all attempted to programme generalisation, though this tended to be unstructured and to rely on gradually substituting social for token and other reinforcers. Kazdin (1977, p. 175) states that 'behaviours *usually* extinguish when a programme is withdrawn', and goes on to suggest ways of counteracting this, including the selection of behaviours likely to be maintained by the natural consequences of the environment, the use of intermittent token reinforcement contingencies and the gradual fading of these, and also the gradual expansion of stimulus control.

Although it is generally agreed that tokens should not last for ever but should eventually give place to other, less artificial, forms of reinforcement, it may not always be possible to achieve this. Lindsley (1964) has distinguished between a therapeutic environ-ment, designed to teach new skills, and a prosthetic environment, designed to maintain behaviours already established. A token economy is usually established with therapeutic aims in mind, but it may in some cases be impossible to wean all clients off it, if only because the 'natural' reinforcers, especially the social reinforcers, may continue to be ineffective for these clients. In this case the token economy may have value as a prosthesis, if this allows for higher-level behaviour to continue in these clients; but opportunities to supersede it should be constantly sought.

ETHICAL ISSUES

The use of tokens and of token programmes has come under attack for their potential in violating human rights, freedom and dignity. Concern has centred round the external control and manipulation of human behaviour; the possibility that this control may be exerted for undesirable ends, or ends not related to the client's welfare; that methods of control may be used which interfere with the client's basic human rights; and that treatment methods may be employed which have not been agreed to by the client or his relatives.

Clearly these concerns do not relate only to behaviour modifica-tion programmes. Human beings have made determined and vari-ably successful attempts to control and to influence the behaviour of other human beings, whether as parents, teachers, police, judiciary or government, since the beginnings of social organisation. Similarly, society has always made use of rewards and punishments, and especially of the latter, in order to control or eliminate what is seen as socially undesirable behaviour. Nevertheless, perhaps because behavioural methods are seen as constituting a powerful technology whereby one group may be able to control the actions of others, particular ethical issues have been raised.

These issues are well discussed by Kazdin (1977, pp. 255–77), and it is not possible to cover them all here. However, two that particularly affect the operation of token, and other, programmes with people with mental handicaps are, first, the question of human rights and the restrictions thereby placed on the availability of back-up reinforcers; and, secondly, the question of consent to treatment. Early token economies made use of a variety of 'privileges' which were not freely available to the clients but had to be earned and paid for in tokens (Ayllon and Azrin, 1968). These 'privileges' included such things as a comfortable bed, recreational activities, particular items of food, etc., which may now be regarded as due to the client as of right, and not to be withheld (Wyatt v. Stickney, 1972). Consequently these 'privileges' may not be used as back-up reinforcers. The solution may be to provide additional privileges over and above the conditions available to all clients but, as the requirement for these conditions becomes higher, it will become increasingly difficult to surpass them in the 'privileges'. A particular problem posed by some people with severe or profound handicaps is the paucity of reinforcers that are effective for them. For example, a boy for whom other reinforcers were not effective learnt to dress himself only when his breakfast was used as the reinforcer (Moore and Carr, 1976) — a practice that might now be thought inadmissible even though there was no question of his missing or being deprived of any of his breakfast. In some cases the effective reinforcers are so limited that unless one which may constitute a basic right is used it may become impossible to devise treatment for some clients. It may be that for these clients permission may have to be sought for certain events, which in the normal way would be regarded as theirs by right, to be restricted and used as reinforcers, following full discussion with the client's parents or guardian. This permission would be sought only if it could be shown that without the use of these events adequate and beneficial treatment of the client would not be feasible.

There is a potentially damaging side-effect to the current climate of concern with the rights and protection of clients in token and other programmes; that is, that the strictures on those attempting to provide this treatment may become so severe that few will be willing to undertake it, with the result that clients who might have benefited from this treatment will not have the opportunity to do so. This position has not yet been reached in this country; it is to be hoped that therapists will be sufficiently alert to the needs of their clients and for adequate ethical safeguards in their treatment that such a position will never be reached.

The restrictions now placed on treatment programmes pose considerable problems for psychologists. Nevertheless, the fact that psychological, as well as other, treatments are now explicitly required to be humane and to inflict as little discomfort as possible, especially where these treatments are directed to relatively vulnerable groups of people such as those with mental illness or mental handicap, must be taken as a welcome sign of the greater sensitivity of society to its less fortunate members.

CONCLUSIONS

Token programmes have an important part to play in the teaching of people with mental handicaps. This applies particularly to those with moderate and mild handicaps, for whom tokens provide the opportunity to make use of effective reinforcers in a way which is closely similar, and may lead on, to the earning and purchasing conditions that operate for normal people. Among the many advantages of token programmes is their flexibility, which makes it possible to devise programmes for individuals or for groups, or indeed to allow for particular contingencies for individuals within groups. Hitherto, the published reports have been predominantly concerned with the results obtained from programmes on whole groups but, in view of some reports of variable response by individuals and even, in some cases, of adverse effects, it seems important that future reports should pay particular attention to these and to the attempts made to overcome the problems.

It has not yet been made clear what is the effective ingredient in token programmes. One that may well play a part in programmes run in institutional settings is staff enthusiasm; this is generally found to be high (Fernandez, 1978; Kazdin, 1977, p. 151), although this has been questioned by Tizard (1975), who sees the token economy as operating primarily for the convenience of staff and offering little of positive benefit to the clients. There may be particular dangers in large-scale, long-term programmes running in institutions that the behavioural principles on which the programmes were based will be forgotten and the token system will become an end in itself. Clearly, it is essential that all concerned with token programmes, and especially the managers and those responsible for the inception and development of the programmes, should keep ever before them the aims on which they must be based: of teaching skills and developing behaviours that will allow the person with a mental handicap to realise his maximum potential, and allow him and his family to enjoy their lives to the full.

5

Building up New Behaviours:
Shaping, Prompting and Fading

Mona Tsoi and William Yule

Many parents, teachers and nurses would claim that they already know about the importance of positive reinforcement. As Chapter 3 showed, 'knowing about' and 'knowing how to' are not synonymous. Even so, if one accepts that the adult knows how to reinforce a child, one is immediately faced with a problem: how do you get the child into a situation where reinforcement can be delivered appropriately? This chapter will focus on three groups of techniques which are used in building up new behaviours — a frequent problem when considering children who have severe handicaps.

SHAPING

Shaping is an art. It is the art of the therapist, using all the skills and ingenuity at his or her disposal, in getting the handicapped person to produce a novel response. Fortunately, it is an art form which has some ground rules.

Having carefully analysed the problem the child presents with, and having decided that there is really a skill deficiency (Mager and Pipe, 1970), one then has a clear picture of the difference between what the child can do now and what we want him to do. We could wait around until he does want we want by chance, and immediately reinforce that chance occurrence, but that is obviously an inefficient strategy. (That is not to say that one should not constantly be on the look-out for improvements in behaviour and reinforce them when they occur. It is just that skills teaching is too important to be left to chance.)

A more active way of intervening is to analyse the components of the skills behaviour you want to teach. Having done so, then

68

decide roughly on the steps needed between where the client is now and where you want him to be at the end of the programme. This means that you have to work on one aspect of the skill *which is already in the client's repertoire.* The handicapped person has to develop this skill in the desired direction under the therapist's guidance.

The therapist begins by reinforcing the existing behaviour. Once it is firmly established and can be reliably elicited, then the therapist begins to use differential reinforcement: concentrating reinforcement on those responses that approximate more closely to the desired goal, and ignoring (and hence extinguishing) those responses that are less like the required behaviour. Thus, the therapist reinforces successive *approximations* to a desired behaviour. An example will help to clarify this.

Let us say that the task is to teach a child to have good eye-to-eye contact. The child will sit on a chair, but will not look at the therapist's face. Having identified a powerful and convenient stimulus which is reinforcing, the therapist could sit opposite the child and wait. He would wait until the child happened to move his upper body towards the therapist. Immediately, the reinforcer would be delivered. Movement of the upper body would continue to be reinforced in this manner until it was reasonably established. Next, the therapist might wait until not only was the upper body oriented towards the therapist, but the child's head was also in the same direction. Then, he might withhold reinforcement until the child's face was showing opposite the therapist's. Finally, he would deliver reinforcement contingent upon their eyes meeting, however fleetingly. Having established that behaviour, it would be a simple matter then to withhold reinforcement until eye-to-eye gaze had been maintained for longer and longer periods.

Notice what is happening in this training sequence. The therapist selects a response which is already in the child's repertoire, which he can see is related topographically to the desired response. Reinforcement is made contingent upon successive alterations in the topography of that initial behaviour until the end point is reached. But how does the therapist know what speed to go at? What pitfalls lie in this approach?

Gelfand and Hartmann (1984) have some excellent advice on these issues, although they admit that their advice owes more to intuition and clinical experience than to experimental findings. They recommend that, when the desired approximation occurs, a powerful reinforcer should be delivered immediately. Otherwise, there is a danger that, with rapidly changing behaviour, the therapist might reinforce an incorrect response. Such reinforcement should be delivered at almost 100 per cent frequency.

There are no hard and fast rules for deciding when to move on to the next step. It makes sense to ensure that one step is reasonably mastered before moving on, but one can only know that one's judgement is right or wrong if the child duly masters the next step. If, when the requirements of correct performance are made more stringent, the child's performance breaks down, then one of two major errors may have been made. (1) The previous step was not sufficiently well established. This means that you should repeat the steps so that the child overlearns the previous one. (2) The therapist has demanded too big a jump. In this case, can the skill be further analysed into component steps? As Gelfand and Hartmann (1984) put it, the art of shaping is to *think small*!

A further practical tip to facilitate such shaping sessions concerns the way of ending a session. By their very nature, such sessions are proceeding from easy items to making successively greater demands on the child. But the training sessions should not become aversive for the child. Therefore, always ensure that the session finishes on a high note. If the child is beginning to fret and to fail; back down to a lower level of performance and ask the child to do something that is well within his capabilities. As soon as he responds correctly, give an extra big reinforcer and finish the session.

Risley and Baer (1973) argue that shaping or response differentiation 'is so consistently successful that it suggests that some sequence of shaping can *always* be found which will produce the behaviour change planned, if effective reinforcement is available'. This is a very strong claim and, as will be seen below, the availability of an effective reinforcer is probably necessary but not sufficient.

Even so, the technique has been put to good effect. A classical example adopting shaping techniques was reported by Wolf *et al.* (1964) who successfully taught a 3½-year-old autistic boy to wear glasses which were essential to preserve his vision following an operation for the removal of both lenses. The child had refused normal entreaties to put on the spectacles, and threw tantrums, banged his head, slapped his face and pulled his hair when asked to wear them. The therapist decided on new tactics. Just before lunchtime, the boy was offered empty spectacle frames. He was reinforced with food for holding the frames for longer and longer periods. Then, reinforcement was only delivered if he held them close to his face, and in the correct orientation. Once he was reliably placing them on his face and tolerating them for lengthy periods, the lenses were inserted. Then, reinforcers other than food were used so that the new behaviour would be maintained by a variety of reinforcers in a variety of settings.

Shaping can be used in combination with other procedures to attain treatment goals. For example, Tarnowski and Drabman (1985) reinforced successive approximations to independent walking in a 5-year-old boy by shaping him to stand upright and then gradually initiating appropriate leg movements to start ambulation. Shaping can be a very lengthy business. It depends on the child emitting the responses and the therapist sensitively perceiving minute changes and reinforcing them. Somehow, life would be a great deal easier and progress a great deal faster if the approximations to the desired response could be 'forced' out of the child. The next sections deal with techniques whereby this can be facilitated. Basically, there are two approaches: the therapist can manipulate the child so that he produces the desired response, or he can alter the environment in such a way that the restructuring facilitates the appearance of the new behaviour.

PROMPTING, CUEING AND FADING

Let us return to the example of shaping up eye contact. Although the technique as described should eventually be successful, the therapist would probably be ready to close his own eyes with exhaustion! To speed the process up considerably, the therapist could do the following: Sitting opposite but close to the child, he says, 'Johnny, look at me!' Then, he reaches over and physically turns Johnny's head until it is facing him. Again, fleeting eye contact is reinforced. If an edible reinforcer is being used, the process can be further accelerated by holding this at eye level. As the child looks at the reinforcer, he automatically looks at the therapist. Thus, a judicious use of physical prompting and placement of the reinforcer will maximise the likelihood of eye contact being made.

Prompting has been used to great effect in training in self-help skills such as feeding (Berkowitz *et al.*, 1971), as well as areas such as instruction following (Whitman *et al.*, 1971) and learning generalised imitation skills (Baer *et al.*, 1967). Again, an example will help to give a flavour of the versatility of this technique.

Zeiler and Jervey (1968) report on the case of a girl who was taught to feed herself. Initially, the therapist prompted (i.e.

71

manually guided) her through the whole sequence from picking up the spoon, scooping up the food, raising it to her mouth, to placing it in her mouth. After a few trials, the therapist gradually released the child's hand when it was near her lips, and the girl completed the sequence of feeding on her own. In subsequent trials, the therapist gradually reduced the amount of guidance (or faded out the prompts) so that the girl took the food to her mouth from a progressively greater distance, until eventually she could bring it the whole way from the plate. Notice that, in this instance, the prompts were first faded from those aspects of the sequence of behaviours closest to the final link in the chain of responses.

Mosk and Bucher (1984), using a pegboard task and a self-care skill task in which children with mental handicaps were taught to hang a washcloth or a toothbrush on a hook, employed a graded sequence of prompting. First, only a verbal instruction was given. If no correct response occurred, the trainer gave the instruction and pointed to the response board. If this did not work, the instruction was given together with a demonstration by the trainer, followed by the instruction and touching the back of the child's hand and finally the instruction plus a hand-over-hand prompt, in sequence, until a correct response was given. This contrasts with the example just given in that the prompts were introduced from the least intense level to the more intense one, thus allowing errors to occur. More will be said about such use of 'forward and backward chaining' of responses later in this chapter.

Crosson (1969) contends that, in the training of more complicated skills, the component tasks vary in difficulty and the more demanding ones may benefit from more intensive instruction. As Cuvo *et al.* (1978) have shown in teaching janitorial skills to young adults with mental handicaps, tasks that are difficult to communicate by verbal instructions have to be taught by more intensive or physical prompting. Clearly, using prompts can speed up the acquisition of new behaviours. But again, this process is slightly problematical in that it demands that the therapist must be very close physically to the child throughout the training session. There is a danger that the child may only go through the sequence when the therapist is seated next to him. In any case, where the therapist is a busy mother, teacher or nurse, they will want more 'remote control' methods which will allow them to get on with other things simultaneously. This is where other cues or discriminant stimuli become important.

For example, when the therapist is prompting a child through a potato-printing activity, instead of merely making encouraging noises he could clearly label each action — 'Pick up the potato', 'Dip it in the paint', 'Press it on the paper', and so on. Then, later, if the child gets in a muddle during printing, the therapist can get him back on track by calling the appropriate cue. This depends on the child's ability to follow the verbal instructions.

When children have learned to imitate the therapist, then gestural and other visual cues may be used. In fact, children can be taught to imitate by the judicious use of gestural cues and physical prompts (see Chapter 7).

The different quality of prompts and cues can best be seen in language training. Nelson and Evans (1968) paired arbitrary signs — e.g. tapping the teeth or touching the lips — with particular sounds. They hoped that these visual cues would serve as extra discriminative stimuli, thereby facilitating the learning of the different sounds. Notice, however, that the arbitary cues in no way force out the correct sounds, and therefore they cannot be considered prompts in the restricted sense that the term is used here.

Sometimes such extra cues can be more confusing than helpful. This seems to be particularly true of autistic children. Schreibman (1975) found that, if cues were added which bore no intrinsic relationship to the critical dimension in a discriminative learning task, autistic children were not helped. However, when the cue was an exaggeration of the relevant component of the training stimulus, then the children were greatly helped. In other words, just because extra cues serve as useful mnemonics for normal adults, this does not mean that children will be able to utilise them in the same way. Wolfe and Cuvo (1978) also supported this and cautioned the use of so-called extra-stimulus cues. They found that, in teaching children with mental handicaps to read, the prompts that emphasised a feature of the reading stimulus were more effective than the use of a pointing finger, which is a prompt unrelated to the reading material. Rincover (1978) underscored this issue by suggesting that the cue to be emphasised should be a distinctive feature of the stimulus.

Risley et al. (1971) describe an ingenious use of cues and fading to teach expressive language. Briefly, once the child is reliably imitating what the therapist says, they shift the stimulus control of the child's expressive language from imitating the total utterance to answering questions. Thus, the therapist holds up a ball and says, 'What is this?' Then, before the child has time to imitate the question, the therapist continues with the answer, 'It's a ball.' If the therapist gets his timing and emphasis correct, the child will answer (i.e. echo), 'It's a ball.' In subsequent trials, the therapist will gradually *reduce* or *fade* the verbal cues he provides, until the child's answer is reliably produced when the question is asked.

The use of prompting, cues and fading is very much an art form. The therapist must judge how quickly to remove the extra supports dependent on the child's performance. If the performance begins to fall off, extra cues are needed. This is an active process and, as Risley and Baer (1973) point out, by these methods the therapist actually produces behaviour change rather than merely waiting to reinforce it if and when it occurs spontaneously.

ALTERING THE ENVIRONMENT — THE USE OF GRADED CHANGE

Another way of forcing a response out of a child is to alter the environment in which the child finds itself. Physical aspects of the environment may assist the appearance of the required behaviour. Let us look at a few examples.

Wickings *et al.* (1974) were faced with a 10-year-old child with mental handicap who would not drink from a spoon — a slow and inefficient method. The problem here was not to teach him how to drink, but rather to shift the stimulus control of drinking from the spoon to the cup.

If Mahomet won't come to the mountain, then . . . in this case, if the boy won't approach the cup, the cup must approach the boy. Over a period of several weeks, the spoon the boy used for drinking was deepened (see Figure 5.1). Later, the handle was shortened, and finally bent over to become the cup handle.

The whole process took eight months, partly because of the need to make the spoon-cups. Care was taken to ensure that the boy's new skill was generalised to other settings, and six months after returning to his own school, his progress had been maintained. Follow-up four years later showed that he continued to drink from a cup.

A similar technique was used by Marchant *et al.* (1974) in the treatment of attachment to unusual objects in young autistic children. In one case, a 4-year-old boy was carrying a blanket to such an extent that it grossly interfered with his learning normal hand–eye co-ordinative skills. His mother was asked to cut bits off the blanket in gradual stages. After one week it was down to 2 × 8 inches without provoking any reactions from the child. Some three weeks later he had given up carrying the small bundle of threads and began to make strides in learning new tasks. The critical aspect of this approach

Figure 5.1

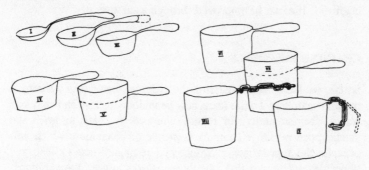

Source: Wickings *et al.* (1974), p. 6. Reprinted with the permission of the authors and editor.

appears to be the gradualness of the change, thus having a certain similarity with desensitisation approaches. The tasks used by Mosk and Bucher (1984) are essentially discrimination learning tasks, and systematically changing the stimuli has helped learning. For example, in teaching the children to hang their towel or toothbrush on a peg, the S^+ peg was present at all times, while the S^- pegs were introduced in steps into other positions and these S^- pegs ranged from short, medium to long in length. When this stimulus shaping procedure was used in combination with prompting, it proved to be a more cost-effective technique than simply teaching by prompting to criterion level. However, the way in which stimulus shaping was utilised in this instance may not be optimal. As Schreibman and Charlop (1981) have demonstrated with autistic children, discrimination was acquired faster and fewer errors were committed when S^+ was faded in first with S^- held constant than vice versa. It could be that, during the fading, the changing S^+ appeared novel and was salient for learning.

There are other ways of restructuring the environment to assist learning. Probably the most effective restructuring of recent years has been the introduction of feeder cups. Many toddlers can skilfully drink unassisted from training beakers — thereby upsetting many development checklists! Spoons can have their handles enlarged to make them easier for spastic hands to grip; plates can be placed on non-slip surfaces, thereby greatly facilitating feeding. Walking frames can aid walking. In many ways, these are prosthetic devices: without them, the skill disappears. The aim of therapy will be to fade

75

out these aids, but if that proves impossible then at least the patient's quality of life can be improved through their use.

CHAINING RESPONSES

So far, we have been discussing the different techniques whereby a therapist can help a child learn new behaviours as if each behaviour was a discrete entity. In reality, the task is often to teach the handicapped person a complex *sequence* of behaviours which will occur in the appropriate environmental setting. When a client fails to perform a complex task, the therapist asks himself the questions, 'Can this task be broken down into smaller sub-steps? If so, does the client have the skill to perform any or even all of these sub-steps?' Posed in this way, it can be appreciated that on some occasions handicapped people may fail to perform a complex piece of behaviour because they do not have one or more crucial skills in their repertoire. At other times, they may have all the skills, but they do not produce them in the correct sequence.

For example, the mobile child who responds to bladder pressure by pulling down his pants and urinating on the carpet does not necessarily need to be taught bladder control *per se*. He needs to have both the appropriate setting in which to urinate and the correct sequence of movements which will take him from wherever he is to the toilet. The task of the therapist in such an instance is to train the child to go to the toilet (initially on command), perform all the necessary undressing actions, urinate, dress, pull the chain, wash his hands and return to the class. Mahoney *et al.* (1971) describe such a programme in some detail.

What one is aiming for in these circumstances is a complex form of stimulus control whereby the completion of one act in a sequence is both reinforced by the commencement of the next act and also acts as a cue to begin the next act. Arriving at the toilet is the signal for pulling down the pants, which is the signal for urinating in the pot, which, in turn, is the signal for flushing the toilet and so on. Each behaviour forms part of an orderly chain which leads smoothly from the initiating step to the final action.

In training the handicapped to master a chain of behaviours, there are logically two ways of going about it. Either you start with the first step, master it, go on to the second step, and so on: this is *forward chaining*. Or, alternatiely, you can start with the final step, then move to the penultimate step, and so on in reverse order: this is *backward chaining*.

By and large, there is a consensus among therapists (although there are not many hard data) that backward chaining is the more efficient method for teaching skills, particularly skills such as feeding, dressing and other motor skills (Martin and Pear, 1984). The argument given is as follows. By teaching the client to complete the chain, he can be given a large reinforcer for this. By association, the last step takes on the characteristics of a secondary reinforcer. Therefore, whatever is done immediately prior to the last action is itself reinforced. A judicious use (at early points of the chain) of extrinsic reinforcers, which can thus be quickly faded, can establish the earlier actions in the chain.

Put in the jargon, the technique may sound formidable. In practice, what it means is that a careful analysis of the sequence coupled with good, sensitive data collection should quickly identify difficult stages. The therapist then decides whether the child is sticking because the step was too large, because a component skill was missing, because motivation (i.e. reinforcement) was not strong enough or because of some other problem. It is a matter of clinical judgement to decide how long to persevere in a training scheme before altering it.

Both forward and backward chaining have been used in programmes to teach dressing. For example, backward chaining was used by Moore and Carr (1976) in teaching a 15-year-old boy to put on his vest, pants and socks. A similar procedure was used by Minge and Ball (1967), and Martin *et al.* (1971a) successfully applied forward chaining to teaching dressing skills. Richman *et al.* (1984) pointed out the problem associated with forward chaining when they taught menstrual care to women with severe mental handicaps. Whenever the clients were asked to revise the last sequence of behaviour in a chain, they only performed the last practised behaviour. Consequently, it was necessary to ask them to start from the beginning of the chain each time.

As noted earlier, there is an absence of comparative data which would allow one to select between the two methods of chaining. In our current state of knowledge, therapists would be well advised to try backward chaining first.

It is as well to remember that where the problem is one of having to put old skills in a new order, then modelling (which is discussed in more detail in Chapter 7) is an extremely powerful therapeutic tool.

CONCLUSIONS

Although they have been presented separately for ease of exposition, the techniques described in this chapter are usually used in combination to establish new behaviours. For example, prompting and fading are often used together with backward or forward chaining. The decision to use particular techniques depends on the nature of the problem and the level at which the learner is performing. Thus, at the initial stages of teaching a child to use speech sounds, greater reliance may be placed on simple shaping techniques, whereas later, when the child has learned to imitate, more emphasis will be placed on his imitating in the presence of the correct cue.

What all these techniques have in common is a rigorous behavioural and task analysis. Shaping, prompting, fading and chaining all require that the large responses be broken down into small steps. Continuous evaluation of progress is important for isolating unexpected difficulties. Further task analysis then points the way to remedial action.

As is by now obvious, the application of these techniques in behaviour modification is an art, but it is an art form which is increasingly susceptible to rigorous scientific analysis. As this chapter has attempted to show, many principles underlying the techniques are derived from experimental studies and are at the same time applied and tested on skills that are relevant to the daily functioning of people with mental handicaps. The therapist must always be sensitive to the client's progress and needs. He or she must respond to the behaviour changes in the handicapped person, and alter the training techniques in a flexible manner to ensure the most effective progress. Undoubtedly, many of the spectacular successes in helping handicapped people stem from the sensitive and imaginative application of the techniques which have been described here.

6

Discrimination and Generalisation

Ewa Zarkowska

STIMULUS CONTROL

The skills that people perform in their every-day life rarely occur on a random basis but tend to be appropriate in a given context. A car driver will put his foot on the brake at the sight of a red traffic light but will keep his foot on the accelerator when the light is green. A traveller on the London Underground will find his way to the correct platform even though he has never been to that station and there are several platforms. A person will remove his shoes and put his feet up when watching television in his own front room but will sit up straight with feet firmly on the floor during a church service. People 'know' when it is appropriate to make a particular response. They know because the various stimuli present in the environment provide them with the necessary information (the red light, the formal church setting, the coloured symbols to direct travellers at the station).

Behaviours never occur in a vacuum but always within a context. The context might be a place, a time, an event, an object or a person. The context contains a variety of cues which, if consistently present when the response is reinforced during learning, gain control over the behaviour. When this happens, behaviour is said to be under *stimulus control*. Stimulus control is evident when a change in a particular property of a stimulus results in a change of behaviour (e.g. traffic light turning to red → foot on brake). Stimulus control enables the individual to be more efficient and effective in his or her interactions with the environment. Discrimination and generalisation are opposite ends of a single continuum of stimulus control. Discrimination is evident when an individual responds differently to different stimuli (red light → stop; green light → go). Generalisation is evident when the individual responds consistently to similar stimuli across a number of situations (red light → stop — all road junctions and pedestrian crossings).

DISCRIMINATION

Discrimination is the basic component of many skills, and it is evident in most behaviours which a person performs. In order for discrimination to occur, individuals must be able to detect differences in the events/environment around them. At the simplest level they need to discriminate between the things they touch, the things they see and the things they hear. Thus, in order to match a pair of socks an individual needs to be able to make colour discriminations. To operate a television or tape recorder, he or she needs to discriminate positions of the buttons on the control panel. To respond appropriately to the verbal instructions 'Give me the ball' and 'Give me the bell' a person must make a subtle auditory discrimination between two vowel sounds. Many situations necessitate discrimination of multiple cues. For example, responding to conversational language requires making auditory discriminations of sounds, pitch and volume and also visual discriminations of facial expressions, gestures and situational cues.

Learning discriminations

Discriminations are established through differential reinforcement of responses. When a particular response is consistently reinforced in the presence of a certain stimulus, that stimulus becomes a signal, for reinforcement. It is known as the discriminative stimulus (S^D). A stimulus in whose presence responses are ignored or punished is known as S-delta (S^Δ). S^Δ is a signal for non-reinforcement or punishment. Thus a child will learn to respond with the word 'dada' to a specific person in his environment because a special fuss is likely to be made of him whenever he uses the word appropriately and because whenever he calls the word 'dada' the same individual consistently responds with attention. When he applies the word to other persons he is more likely to be ignored or corrected. To give another example, for many children the bedroom doubles as a playroom and sleeping room. The bed itself can be associated with sleeping and playing. However, most children 'know' when it is time to sleep because of a history of associating the various cues in the environment with differential reinforcement. Wearing pyjamas, a darkened room, the curtains drawn, feeling tired, mother saying 'Time to go to sleep' are all cues which are likely to have been associated with parents showing their pleasure at their child lying quietly with eyes closed and displeasure at their child running around the room playing and shouting. Through differential reinforcement these stimuli become an S^D for sleeping and an S^Δ for playing. To give one final example, parents sometimes complain that their children display unacceptable behaviours such as tantrums when out in public, particularly in crowded supermarkets. This is likely because in this setting behaviours such as crying, shouting and stamping of feet have been reinforced with crisps or sweets (in order to keep the child quiet), whereas co-operative behaviours have been ignored because the parents are too busy getting their shopping. The supermarket, therefore, comes to act as an S^D for 'naughty' behaviour and an S^Δ for 'good' behaviour.

There is ample evidence that people with learning impairments can make discriminations and that these are related to the reinforcement history of the individual. Redd and Birnbrauer (1969), for example, showed that children who had been reinforced for their play behaviour by certain adults performed these behaviours more readily in the presence of these adults. In the presence of adults who had not reinforced their play behaviour, they displayed very little play until these adults also began to reinforce their play. Kiernan and Saunders (1972) showed similar results in a study which looked at the imitative behaviours of children. However, it is a consistent finding that people with serious learning disabilities can experience problems with learning even simple discriminations through the use of differential reinforcement alone. Failure to learn discriminations can seriously impede the learning of new skills. It can also result in 'problem' behaviours because a person is unable to discriminate when a particular behaviour is appropriate and when that same behaviour is inappropriate. Wing (1975) believes that the bizarre behaviours of many autistic children are due to their inability to discriminate the appropriate cues for various situations.

Overcoming problems with discrimination learning

Failure to learn discriminations can occur for a number of reasons. It can occur because the individual does not attend to the task itself, because the individual does not attend to the relevant dimension of the stimulus, because the stimulus to be discriminated is very complex or because the individual has difficulty attending to more than one stimulus dimension. It is important to assess the nature of the difficulty so that an appropriate strategy can be adopted to help the individual learn important discriminations.

Enhancing attention to the task

Many people with profound learning disabilities will not attend to a task long enough to learn discriminations. For such individuals it may be important to use stimuli which can enhance attention to the task long enough for learning to occur. Bell and Richmond (1984) taught a position discrimination to adults with profound learning disabilities by hiding different objects under cups in different positions. They found that, when sweets were used as stimuli, learning occurred faster than when toys were used, even though the sweets were not used as reinforcers in the learning situation. Another way of enhancing attention to a task is through the use of multidimensional cues. A cue that employs size and shape, for example, may be attended to more readily than one employing shape alone (Gardner, 1971). Care should be taken, however, when using multiple cues, as some individuals have difficulty focusing attention on more than one or two stimulus dimensions (e.g. Anderson and Rincover, 1982) and for these the use of multiple cues may impede rather than facilitate discrimination learning.

Focusing attention on relevant stimulus dimensions

Failure to learn discriminations may be due to the fact that the individual is not attending to the relevant dimension of the discrimination. For example, a child learning a colour discrimination may focus on the shape of the objects presented or their position rather than their colour. An adult learning to recognise bus stops may focus on the shelter next to the bus stop and not recognise the bus stops which have no shelters. The relevant dimensions of the discrimination must therefore be brought to the attention of the individual. One way of helping a person focus on the relevant stimulus dimension is to accentuate a distinctive feature of the discrimination. For example, Rincover (1978) found that, when teaching adults to discriminate between the letters J and S, altering the letter J by thickening its cross bar (a distinctive feature) was better than thickening the curve of the J (a non-distinctive feature). Similarly Meador (1984) taught graphic communication symbols by using colour cues to direct attention to the distinctive elements of the shape of the lexigrams. This resulted in faster learning than simply using coloured backgrounds or training with lexigrams that were completely coloured (non-distinctive features).

For individuals who fail to learn discriminations even after prolonged teaching, an errorless discrimination training procedure known as fading may prove useful. This procedure entails first establishing a response to just one stimulus (S^D) through reinforcement and then gradually fading in the other non-reinforced stimulus (S^Δ). Thus, a discrimination between the colours red and blue might be taught by presenting a red card and several blank (white) cards and asking the child for the red card. Once the child is responding correctly to the colour card, colour is gradually introduced to the blank cards so that they become progressively brighter and more clearly blue. Hedbring and Newsom (1985) used a similar procedure to teach children to match objects, such as a spoon or cup, with line drawings of the objects. The task was analysed into perceptually manageable steps: object-to-object matching, object-to-photograph matching, photograph-to-photograph matching, photograph-to-line-drawing matching, and object-to-line-drawing matching. The task was then taught using a graded approach, thereby minimising the large differences between stimulus cues by the use of gradual shifts in stimulus topographies.

Simplifying complex discriminations

Many naturally occurring stimuli consist of complex and subtle cues which need to be simplified if correct discriminations are to be made. Recognising which bus stop to get off at to get to one's work place, for example, requires discriminating very complex visual cues. Many bus travellers seek out a salient, arbitrary stimulus such as a single large department store, a park or a bus garage which can act as a signal that the stop is approaching. People with learning impairment may need to be helped to focus on such arbitrary stimuli in their natural environment to help them with complex discriminations.

Problem behaviours can also be related to complex, subtle stimuli. They are frequently defined in a contextual rather than an absolute manner. Thus, undressing is an acceptable skill when it occurs in the bedroom or bathroom, but is unacceptable when it occurs in the street. Hitting another child may be acceptable when it is a response to an aggressive attack. However, hitting the same child to obtain a desired toy may be considered unacceptable. Such complex cues may be difficult for people with learning impairments to discriminate. Woods (1983) in an interesting study decided that the stereotypic behaviour of an autistic girl which consisted of repetitive 'flipping' of books and magazines was only inappropriate when valuable or important books were 'flipped' since she tended to destroy the books. Flipping provided an important source of self-occupation for her and therefore could not be seen as wholly unacceptable. It would have been impossible for her to discriminate valuable books so a large red triangle (S^D) was attached to books which she would be permitted to 'flip'. She was reinforced with praise whenever she played with these appropriate books and punished using a brief restraint procedure whenever she flipped inappropriate (S^Δ) books.

Focusing attention on multiple cues

Most stimuli in the natural environment consist of a large number of components, yet people with learning impairments may sometimes fail to respond to cues that occur together. Instead, they respond to just one or two stimulus components (for example, one letter of a word, sign only when words and signs are presented simultaneously). This phenomenon is called *overselective responding*. Overselective responding can seriously interfere with learning. For example, when teaching discriminations, teachers often make use of prompts such as pointing to the correct choice, providing verbal cues or using materials that provide multiple cues to make the correct choice distinctive by virtue of its location, size or colour. Prompts are artificial stimuli which are not related to the task but which nevertheless come to control behaviour. Successful learning with the aid of prompts requires responding simultaneously to the prompt and the natural stimulus. Individuals who have difficulty focusing on multiple cues often have problems transferring control of their responding to the natural stimuli in the environment once the prompt has been removed or faded out (Rincover, 1978). Overselective responding has also been thought to contribute to a number of behavioural deficits in people with severe learning disabilities and autistic individuals, including impaired observational learning and impaired social development (Lovaas *et al.*, 1979).

When teaching discriminations to people who have difficulty responding to multiple cues, it may be important to consider teaching methods that avoid the introduction of artificial prompts. Enhancing the distinctive features of the stimulus (see earlier discussion) makes use of prompts which belong to the same dimension as the stimulus, and thus avoids the problem associated with transfer of control from artificial to natural stimuli. Delaying verbal or physical prompts by a few seconds rather than fading them may be another way of facilitating transfer. Halle *et al.* (1979), for example, used a prompt delay of 15 seconds to provoke spontaneous verbalisation in children waiting to be served at a lunch counter, and Touchette and Howard (1984) found that an 8-second delay in prompting accelerated stimulus transfer.

When multiple stimuli need to be attended to (including prompts and natural stimuli), a simple overtraining procedure may be useful. Schover and Newsom (1976), for example, continued to train a complex visual discrimination for fifty trials, using a continuous reinforcement schedule, after the criterion for learning had been reached and showed that students responded to a larger number of stimulus elements after overtraining than after initial learning. A second way to encourage the individual to respond to multiple cues is through the use of intermittent schedules of reinforcement. This requires reinforcing perhaps every third or fourth correct response rather than each correct response (e.g. Koegel *et al.*, 1979). By using intermittent schedules of reinforcement with breadth of attention may increase because the student is encouraged to look around more and compare responses. Specific training on multiple cues may be another way of helping people who are overselective in their responding. For example, Schreibman *et al.* (1982) showed that training children to respond to arbitrary compound stimuli (large circles, blue squares), facilitated responding to two simultaneously presented cues in the natural environment (prompt and natural stimulus).

Complex discriminations such as word recognition may occasionally require the use of more elaborate procedures if errors continue to occur at a high rate during training. A procedure that aims to avoid errors during learning is stimulus shaping. This procedure involves starting with an easy-to-discriminate meaningful object and gradually shaping it to approximate the correct stimulus. In an experimental study, Smeets *et al.* (1984) successfully taught a group of children a set of three words which consisted of scrambled combinations of Roman letters or modified Hebrew letters. A picture of the word (e.g. chair, ear) which was easily recognisable was superimposed on to the letters. Once responding was occurring consistently, the shape of the picture was gradually reduced and transformed into one of the letters of the word. This was done in such a fashion that, on the final step, the shape of one letter of the word was identical to that of the residual prompt.

85

GENERALISATION

When new skills are learned, they need to transfer out of the training situation to a number of new situations if they are to be useful to the individual. For example, having learned to initiate social interactions in the work setting, a person should be able to use this skill with people he meets at home and at social events. Having learned how to operate a washing machine at the training centre, an individual should be able to operate a washing machine in the local launderette. There are a number of situations to which newly learned skills may need to generalise: new places, a variety of people, different times of the day, novel materials and even to other related behaviours (Stainback *et al.*, 1983). In some cases new skills may need to generalise to just a few specific stimuli (bottle feeding → baby sister). In other cases they may need to generalise to a whole class of stimuli in order to be useful (crossing all roads, travelling on all kinds of buses). Responses themselves may need to generalise (initiating social interactions). In many cases a particular class of stimuli may require a particular class of related response (familiar people → being sociable) so that generalisation needs to occur both to other stimuli and to other responses.

Generalisation is thus a complex process. It will not occur unless behaviour is under the control of relevant stimulus dimensions within the stimulus array which are present in both training and non-training environments. It is also unlikely to occur if a response is under the control of just a subset of the relevant stimuli. Generalisation is thus intimately related to discrimination. Like discrimination, it involves responding in the presence of relevant cues and not responding in the presence of irrelevant cues. For example, a person who has learned how to greet his workmates needs to generalise his skill to his friends and fellow residents but not to strangers in the street or on buses. A child who has learned to tug at an adult's sleeve for attention needs to generalise this skill to suitable and appropriate times, appropriate adults and appropriate situations.

For some individuals generalisation does not occur spontaneously. It is a consistent finding that people with learning impairments fail to use their skills in novel situations unless generalisation training has been specifically programmed (Stainback *et al.*, 1983; Stokes and Baer, 1977). This may, in part, be due to difficulties in learning discriminations but may be due also to teaching methods which are commonly employed in this group. New skills are often taught under highly contrived conditions. Settings are tightly controlled to avoid unnecessary distraction and to maximise consistency between teaching sessions; artificial cues in the form of prompts are used to elicit new skills; and artificial reinforcement may be employed in order to provide maximum information to the student about his performance and to increase his motivation to learn. Teaching is often carried out by a single trainer on a sessional basis using discrete teaching trials, at arbitrary times of the day. Such techniques, designed to create optimal conditions for learning by minimising the opportunity for errors during teaching and increasing the individual's motivation to learn, may paradoxically make it difficult for the student to apply skills subsequently to appropriate new situations, since he or she will not 'know' when to use them (Donnellan and Mirenda, 1983). In order to facilitate generalisation it is important when planning teaching to look towards the long-term applicability of the skills being taught, to the conditions in which they will ultimately be performed, and to incorporate conditions into the teaching situation that will increase the probability that the skill will generalise to appropriate novel situations.

Selecting appropriate skills

If skills are to generalise to new situations, they need to be reinforced by naturally occurring events in the new environment. Skills that are functional (i.e. required or valued within the natural environment) are more likely to be reinforced by people within that environment and, hence, are more likely to be used. Thus, Gable *et al.* (1978) obtained generalisation of social behaviours taught to two children with severe learning disabilities by selecting behaviours which prior to intervention were observed to be most likely to elicit positive responses from others in the environment where they were to be used. These included shaking hands and mutual toy play. Carr (1979), in a discussion of the selection of a signing vocabulary for autistic students, reported that signs related to obtaining functional and reinforcing items (e.g. food, toys) are more likely to generalise than non-functional signs. Although the evidence on curriculum selection is still rather sketchy, there is, nevertheless, a strong logical appeal in the argument that functional skills — ones that are likely to receive positive reciprocal feedback from others in natural settings — are likely to generalise more readily than non-functional skills.

Training under 'naturalistic' conditions

When features of the natural environment (the environment in which skills need ultimately to occur) are incorporated into the training situation, generalisation is more likely to occur than when wholly artificial conditions are used in teaching.

Settings. There is some evidence that teaching skills in the environment in which they are to be produced facilitates generalisation. For example, Coon *et al.* (1981) showed that individuals taught bus-riding skills in the natural environment generalised their skills better than did students trained in simulated conditions. Similarly Hill *et al.* (1982) showed that generalisation of leisure skills (use of pinball machines) did not occur until training had been conducted in natural settings. Richman *et al.* (1984) generalised menstrual care skills in a group of learning disabled women by teaching them in the environment in which the skills would most often be used: the bathroom adjacent to their bedroom, where the ladies' personalised cabinets were available for easy and immediate access during menstruation.

Training in the 'natural' or real environment is not always feasible, nor is it always desirable, particularly if the natural environment is highly distracting. When training needs to be conducted in artificial environments, key stimuli from the natural environment can be introduced to the artificial teaching situation to act as discriminative stimuli for the target skill and thus facilitate generalisation. Koegel and Rincover (1977) found that autistic children who were trained on task-readiness skills in a laboratory setting only generalised their skills to the classroom when classroom stimuli (e.g. furniture and people) were brought into the artificial training setting. Petersen *et al.* (1979) taught socially reciprocal behaviours, such as playing ball, to adolescents with severe or profound learning disabilities. The same stimuli (i.e. the same games and materials) were brought into the novel setting to facilitate generalisation.

Materials. When selecting materials for use as teaching aids, faster generalisation is likely if natural (real, three-dimensional) materials are used rather than artificial ones. For example, Welch and Pear (1980) showed that children with severe learning disabilities taught to identify object labels generalised these skills more readily when real objects were used in training rather than photographs or line drawings.

Prompts. The use of prompts in teaching may result in students attending to irrelevant stimulus dimensions (prompts rather than natural stimuli) during teaching. Since these artificial stimuli are not present in the new environment to which the skills should generalise, the student who is attending to an inappropriate stimulus may, as a result, fail to generalise his or her skills. For example, during language training programmes artificial verbal cues, such as 'What's this?' or 'What do you want?', which are used to elicit language behaviour, may inhibit spontaneous use of speech. Thus Woods (1984) showed that whilst acquisition of verbal labelling skills was more rapid for two autistic boys when verbal prompts were used, generalisation was better when natural rather than contrived cues were used. Teaching was carried out during predetermined walks and while looking through children's story books. Natural cues consisted of pausing in front of objects or pictures, looking at them, then turning to the child and looking 'expectantly' at him for approximately 7 seconds. Contrived cues consisted of trainer requests such as 'What do you see there?' or 'What's happening here?'. In the study by Richman *et al.* (1984) referred to earlier, menstrual care was taught using 'simulated' cues (an artificial stain on the clients' underwear and sanitary napkin) in order to increase the number of practice trials which could be carried out. However, to facilitate generalisation, naturally occurring menses were incorporated into training.

Reinforcers. During teaching, artificial reinforcers are often used to increase the strength of the reinforcement received by the student. In addition, reinforcement is usually given each time a correct response occurs in order to provide clear feedback to the student about his or her performance. Such continuous reinforcement is artificial since, in the natural environment, reinforcement tends to occur intermittently and at variable intervals. Although artificial reinforcement can dramatically increase the rate at which learning occurs, it can, nevertheless, decrease the likelihood of generalisation occurring. It is, therefore, important to incorporate natural reinforcers into training, either in place of or in addition to artificial reinforcers, so that artificial reinforcers can be gradually phased out leaving the natural reinforcer. In addition continuous reinforcement should be gradually reduced in frequency until it occurs on a variable and intermittent basis. Cone *et al.* (1978) failed to obtain generalisation of social behaviours after continuous reinforcement had been provided in the training environment. Generalisation occurred once continuous reinforcement had been gradually reduced to an intermittent schedule. Ivy and Dubin (1979) taught subjects to respond to the commands 'come here', 'sit' and 'stay'. Reinforcement was initially provided for each compliant response. Then it was provided after every second response, then after every third, finally on a variable schedule averaging one reinforcer for every six compliant responses. Responding then generalised easily to the 'natural' environment. Lancioni (1982) taught a variety of social behaviours to a group of students using edible reinforcement delivered on a continuous schedule. Generalisation was facilitated by a weaning procedure which moved gradually from continuous to intermittent reinforcement and from edible to social reinforcement (the natural reinforcer for social behaviour).

Baer and Stokes (1977) suggested that intermittent reinforcement leads to durable generalised effects because it is very difficult for students to discriminate or predict reinforcement occasions from non-reinforcement occasions. Some authors have used delayed reinforcement strategies (e.g. reinforcing at the end of a session rather than immediately following the correct response) as a way of making it difficult for students to discriminate which aspect of a behaviour is being reinforced or the time and setting in which reinforcement for a particular skill is likely to occur, thus encouraging generalisation across settings and across behaviours (e.g. Baer *et al.*, 1984). It is important, however, not to use delayed reinforcement procedures in the early stages of the acquisition of skills but to use them as a way of facilitating generalisation once skills are being reliably performed in training situations.

Training sufficient exemplars

When skills need to generalise to a whole class of settings, people, times or materials, or when a stimulus requires a whole class of similar responses, then a number of examples of the stimulus or response class may need to be trained before generalisation will occur to new stimuli/responses within that same class. For example, Lancioni (1982) obtained generalisation of social behaviours (co-operative play, positive social verbalisations) across a number of settings, peers and responses by using several peer trainers and by reinforcing a variety of social responses during training. Lowther (1980) trained a greeting response ('Hi') with the aim of generalising it to people and settings outside the training environment. He showed that generalisation could be obtained either by using several trainers in the teaching setting, or by using a single trainer in a number of different settings. When generalisation across time and activities is desired, training should be programmed across a variety of time slots and activities.

It has been suggested more recently (Colvin and Horner, 1983) that, when selecting exemplars for training, trainers should be careful to select examples which, between them, contain the range of critical attributes present in the whole 'class' of stimuli and ones which sample the range of responses necessary for that stimulus set. Sprague and Horner (cited in Colvin and Horner, 1983) trained adolescents with severe learning disabilities to use vending machines. They found that training students to use one easily accessible machine (single-instance training) or three similar machines (multiple-instance training) resulted in only limited generalisation. However, when training was conducted using three machines that sampled the range of stimulus and response variations necessary for this generalised skill (general case training), there was a significant increase in correct performance on non-trained machines. Gaylord-Ross *et al.* (1984) conducted a study to increase the initiations and duration of social interactions between autistic and non-handicapped youths. Training was carried out using a variety of trainers who were carefully selected so that, between them, they had a range of critical attributes (age, sex, familiarity) which would be present in the natural environment to which the skills were expected to generalise. Using the same principle of general case training, Haring (1985) trained young children with severe learning impairments to generalise play responses by training a specific play response to a set of toys. Several sets were used, including animals, people, aeroplanes, boats and motor-bikes. Each set contained five examples of each toy, varying in size, colour and abstractness. Toys in each set possessed the defining properties of that toy with progressively more and different details. The most abstract toy in each set consisted of cut-out wood forms with no details other than the defining configurational elements. Responses were specific to each set of toys. For example, with spaceships, students were taught to move the toy through the air in a circular motion and land it at right angles on the table. Once learning had occurred with one or two sets of toys, generalisation to other sets was facilitated.

Training loosely

Baer and Stokes (1977) suggested that one way to promote generalisation is to conduct teaching in a way which holds relatively little control over the stimuli presented and the correct response allowed.

91

An example of such 'loose' training is the incidental teaching approach to language training (Hart and Risley, 1980) in which classes of responses rather than specific responses are taught. In this approach, the natural environment is arranged so as to provide a rich variety of attractive and desired materials. The teacher is available to provide attention, praise and instruction whenever a child initiates an interaction. If necessary the teacher requests an elaboration or improvement in the child's verbal request. The teacher thus has little control over the particular stimulus a child will select to communicate about at any given moment, nor over the particular responses which may be required. Using this approach, Hart and Risley (1980) increased spontaneous language usage in a group of children by arranging the environment so that attractive materials which could function as natural reinforcers for spontaneous initiations ('Can I have X?') were available. Children were asked to elaborate their requests whenever initiations were made ('. . . so that I can Y'). Reinforcement was delivered regardless of whether or not they responded correctly.

Incidental teaching of language has been shown to be a powerful means of increasing children's spontaneous language usage. In addition to being a 'loose' training format, it incorporates a large number of the stimulus conditions described in the foregoing discussion which contribute to generalisation. Teaching is carried out within natural settings, in various places, with different people, materials and activities. It is conducted at various times throughout the day in various contexts, in relation to whatever aspect of the rich stimulus environment a child selects as a momentary reinforcer. Contingencies of reinforcement are likely to be hard to discriminate since teaching is carried out only when the teacher has time and an appropriate reinforcer-related prompt for elaboration. Thus, sometimes reinforcement is delivered without asking for language elaboration; sometimes prompting occurs once, sometimes more than once.

Training self-control

A potentially powerful medium for promoting generalisation of skills is the use of self-control techniques. Self-control procedures include self-monitoring, self-evaluation, self-reinforcement and antecedent cue regulation. It has been suggested that self-control procedures have generalisation capability because the individual can effectively control his or her own behaviour by delivering reinforcement immediately, any time and anywhere (Clement, 1973). The individual can also provide cues for himself which can serve as discriminative stimuli or mediators for behaviours across a number of settings.

People with learning disabilities have been shown to be capable of learning each of the components of self-control (Shapiro, 1981), and generalisation of the effects of these procedures to new situations has been reported. Thus, Ackerman and Shapiro (1984) trained a group of adults in a sheltered workshop to monitor their productivity by pressing a counter each time they completed a piece of work. They were praised for accurate monitoring and required to record their productivity at the end of each session. Work productivity increased as a result of self-monitoring training. When self-monitoring counters were made available during another period of the day, there was an immediate increase in work behaviour, despite no requirement to record productivity at the end of these sessions. Robertson *et al.* (1979) established appropriate classroom behaviours in a group of highly disruptive children with severe learning disabilities using a complex procedure that included self-evaluation. Training was carried out in several phases. First, the children were individually provided with feedback every 10 minutes about their behaviour (good, OK, not good). A token programme was then begun with students being rewarded 2, 1 or 0 points corresponding to the teacher's ratings. Points were exchanged for edibles or specific activities. During the next phase, students rated themselves and their ratings were expected to match with the teacher's ratings. Matching to teacher's ratings was then faded till students were managing their own behaviour. Finally points were also faded leaving only the self-evaluation component of the programme. A decrease in disruptive behaviour occurred and this generalised to other sessions during the day.

A few studies have demonstrated that people with severe learning disabilities can be trained to control their own behaviour through antecedent cue regulation, that is, by providing cues for themselves which serve as discriminative stimuli for appropriate behaviour. Sowers *et al.* (1985) trained a group of students to work independently by teaching them to use picture cues to regulate their own behaviour. Picture cues were a photo album sheet with pictures representing a day's tasks in their assigned order (e.g. wash soup pots, bring in garbage cans, clean refrigerator). Students were trained to go to the tasks corresponding to each picture, do the task, tick off the picture corresponding to that task, touch the picture of the next task and then begin the task. Once they had learned to use the picture cues without instructions or reminders, new pictures were introduced. The corresponding tasks were independently initiated by the students without the need for further training, suggesting that training had resulted in generalised use of the picture-cue system.

Whitman *et al.* (1982) showed that children trained through correspondence training to verbalise (say–do) or, if they had no language, to demonstrate (show–do) what they were going to do in class (sitting correctly or paying attention) and how they would do it (e.g. feet flat on the floor, back against the back of the chair, seat in the chair, both hands on the desk) not only learned these skills quickly but generalised them to new teachers and to unreinforced periods of the day.

CONCLUSION

The ability to discriminate between the stimuli present in the environment is an essential aspect of learning. Knowing which stimuli are relevant in any situation is also important if appropriate responding is to occur. A number of difficulties arise for people with learning impairments both in making discriminations and in attending to appropriate stimulus cues in the environment, either because the stimulus is a complex, multidimensional one or because the individual has difficulties attending to more than one or two cues simultaneously. Once skills have been learned, they need to generalise to new situations not encountered during training in order to be useful to the individual. It has been consistently shown that generalisation of skills to new situations rarely occurs without specific programming. This is not surprising since, for generalisation to occur, the individual must discriminate relevant cues which are shared by the training and non-training environment. Discrimination and generalisation are both evidence that behaviour is under stimulus control. A number of techniques have been described in this chapter which can help bring the behaviour of people with serious learning disabilities under the control of relevant stimuli. When planning teaching, a careful assessment should be carried out of the difficulties a person may be experiencing in discrimination learning and of the situations to which new skills are expected to generalise once learning has occurred. In this way appropriate strategies can be incorporated into the teaching programme that will simplify learning and make teaching more efficient.

7

Imitation

Janet Carr

This chapter follows on directly from the last in considering how behaviours may be acquired and developed in people with mental handicaps. In Chapter 5, we saw that new skills can be taught by shaping — that is, by successively reinforcing aspects of his behaviour that approximate gradually more and more closely to the specified behaviour. We saw too that the shaping method, though effective, is a slow and laborious way to acquire skills. In some cases other teaching methods may be more appropriate. 'No parent would take his (*sic*) teenage son into the car for the first time and then shape up his car-driving repertoire in a step-wise fashion, praising the skilled aspects and ignoring the bumps. Rather, the father will instruct his son, and in particular he will *show him what to do*' (our italics) (Yule, 1977). In other words, the son will learn what to do by imitating what he first sees his father do. In this case, as in many others, imitation is an effective and economical way to learn a skill.

Imitation is a basic means by which new behaviours may be learnt, and occurs readily in young normal children. Infants normally begin to imitate a variety of simple movements at around 9 to 10 months, and the two-year-old toddler may spend much of her time following her mother around and imitating her activities. 'She wants to do everything I do' is a frequent comment, mixing exasperation with acknowledgement of the child's need to learn in this way. Imitation in these normal children may appear unprompted or require very little prompting, and may be continued without overt reinforcement such as reward or praise (although other factors to be discussed later may be instrumental in initiating or maintaining the behaviour). Through imitation a child may acquire many behaviours, such as speech or social behaviours, which because of their complexity or inaccessibility to prompting might be slow or difficult to teach by other methods.

The capacity to imitate is, then, a valuable aid to learning, and one which children (and, less commonly, adults) with mental handicaps may lack — a deficit that may be related to another, that of spontaneous learning (Clarke and Cookson, 1962). Especially for these children it may be helpful, in the interests of speeding up their learning generally, to teach them imitation skills, using the methods described in Chapters 3 and 5: *modelling* the required response, *prompting* the response from the child (subsequently *fading* the prompts) and *reinforcing* the resulting response. Initially it seems best to train only one response. The trainer should give the command, 'Do this', and make the response herself: if the child does not respond and needs to be prompted, it is helpful to have an assistant to do this, so that the trainer can continue to model the response while the child is being prompted. The assistant should prompt the response and then gradually withdraw his own hands so that the child receives the reinforcement when he is holding the position without help (Bricker and Bricker, 1970). Two points may be noted here. First, it seems preferable that the trainer, and not the prompter, should deliver the reinforcement, so that the child's full attention shall remain on the trainer-model. Secondly, since the child is being trained not in specific actions but in imitation, the trainer should always use the command, 'Do this', for whatever action he models, and not, 'Stretch out your arms', or 'Touch your nose' (or whatever the action is to be). What actions the trainer chooses are, then, unimportant in themselves: what is important is that the child shall develop an imitative set to reproduce the actions whatever they may be. That this set to imitate can be developed in children with mental handicaps has been shown by Baer *et al.* (1967). At the start of their training the children never imitated an action at its first presentation, but they did so increasingly later in the programme. While imitation is being trained, reinforcement is given only if the child produces an action in response to a demonstration by the trainer: if the child produces the action spontaneously he does not receive reinforcement.

Large simple movements are often trained before finer ones, as they are easy to prompt, though whether there is any major advantage in this training sequence is open to question. Garcia *et al.* (1971) and Bricker (1972) found that imitation of responses trained in one topographical class — either of large movements or of hand movements — did not easily generalise to responses in the other topographical class. This finding, however, was not replicated by

Kiernan and Saunders (1972), who found no evidence that particular types of training resulted in a greater tendency to imitate a similar rather than a dissimilar probe task. In view of this conflict of evidence, and of the small number of subjects involved in these studies, the question of the best sequence of motor imitation training has not yet been satisfactorily resolved.

Another important factor to be taken into account in selecting early items for training should be the relative ease or difficulty for the children themselves. Garcia and his colleagues report that object-oriented actions (ring bell) are more easily imitated than are body-oriented actions (clap hands), and this is supported by Bricker and Bricker (1970), who found that, of 20 actions imitatively learnt by severely handicapped children, the first (easiest) six items were object-oriented and the last 14 body-oriented. Kiernan and Saunders (1972), however, found considerable variation in this difficulty among individual children; their data suggest that, if a child is having great difficulty with imitation of one type of action, it may be helpful to switch to another.

Where large movements are selected for initial training, for example of the arms, it is simpler to train movements of both arms rather than one-arm movements as this avoids the question of laterality or mirroring as the basis of the imitation. This question may have to be faced when finer, single-handed movements are trained, but the difficulties it involves will be more easily overcome when the child has developed some degree of imitativeness.

Training should continue on the one action until the child can produce it in response to only the verbal command and the modelled gesture, physical prompts having been gradually faded until they disappear. How often the child shall be required to respond appropriately before a second gesture is introduced is a decision for the trainer: the criterion set by Paloutzian *et al.* (1971) was 90 per cent accuracy over two sessions of 25 trials each. This seems heroic, and children can become bored with lack of variety. Kiernan and Saunders (1972) were unable to reach a 90 per cent criterion with any but one of their subjects, and finally accepted 65–70 per cent accuracy.

Once the child has reached criterion on the first movement, a second may be introduced and trained to the same criterion level. After this, the two movements may be mixed and given in random order, after which a third movement may be introduced, and so on. When several (8 to 10) large movements have been trained, smaller hand movements may be introduced, leading on to finger movements and then to movements of the hand, face and mouth. It is likely that as the child's repertoire of imitated responses increases he will need less physical prompting, while at the same time the proportion of responses given at the first demonstration of the action is likely to increase. For these reasons it should be easier to teach verbal imitation once motor imitation is firmly established; but there is as yet no research to show whether this approach is either quicker or more effective in training verbal imitation than an approach which focuses on verbal imitation from the start (Yule *et al.*, 1974). Imitation research, reviewed by Glidden and Warner (1982), has thrown up a number of conflicting viewpoints on, for example, the effect of developmental level on imitativeness. Five of the reviewed studies found that more advanced clients imitated better than did the less advanced, three studies found the reverse. As it appears that there were considerable discrepancies between the studies as to the age and overall level of the clients, and as to the imitation task, no firm conclusions on the place of developmental level on imitativeness can be drawn.

REINFORCEMENT IN IMITATION TRAINING

It has been suggested that the *model* should be reinforced for producing the appropriate response, both so as to facilitate the learning of complete chains of behaviour (Bandura, 1969, p. 145) and to indicate to the subject that reinforcement occurs. In this case it may be necessary to have a third person (besides the trainer and subject) as the model, and for the reinforcement to be something highly valued by the subject. Another technique used by Paloutzian *et al.* (1971) to demonstrate the availability of reinforcement was to give non-contingent reinforcement in the first session. It seems likely, however, that reinforcing the subject in the actions he is prompted (and not allowed to fail) to do, would be equally effective.

During the imitation training, the use of contingent reinforcement appears essential, with failure to acquire imitative responses shown under conditions of non-contingent reinforcement (Hekkema and Freedman, 1978). Once the child has learnt some imitative responses, reinforcement is not necessary for all subsequent responses. Baer *et al.* (1967) found that so long as some responses were reinforced, others, which were never reinforced, would be reliably produced. Obviously the subject would have to reach this level of responsiveness before he would imitate a new action on its first presentation. It seems likely that in some subjects some factor other than the presented reinforcer may become effective in maintaining the imitative behaviour; one of the subjects in the study by Baer *et al.* continued to respond when the reinforcer was delayed for up to 60 seconds after the subject's response, and only extinguished when the response was prevented. One might hypothesise that the subject 'enjoyed' the imitation activity, and indeed subjectively this often seems the case.

CHARACTERISTICS OF THE MODEL

A subject may be more willing to imitate the actions of one model than another. Gardner (1971) points out that behaviours modelled by a 'neutral or aversive' teacher may be less closely attended to and imitated than those modelled by a high-prestige peer. Subjects may be influenced by the competence of the model (Strichart, 1974; Strichart and Gottlieb, 1975) and by his age, sex and social and ethnic status (Bandura, 1969). Since these studies on model characteristics were done on mildly handicapped and normal people, it is uncertain how far the findings may be applied to those with severe handicaps; nevertheless the commonplace observation of the ease with which some severely handicapped children 'pick up' the behaviours of other children suggests that the use of peer models might be worth trying also with them. Indeed, Gardner (1971) suggests that modelling of new behaviours and their reinforcement may have particular importance for people with mental handicaps since new situations and new behaviours have often resulted in unpleasant consequences for them. They may need evidence that the behaviours will result in reinforcement before they are willing to attempt them at all.

EFFECTS ON BEHAVIOUR OF ITS IMITATION BY AN OBSERVER

Another aspect of the use of imitation as a teaching method concerns the effect on a person's behaviour of its imitation by an outside observer. In some cases imitation by the adult of a child's response results in a subsequent increase in the child's imitativeness of the adult's actions (Hallahan *et al.*, 1977). Here it appears that the child experiences the adult's imitation as reinforcing (Miller and Morris,

1974), while Hallahan also refers to 'the social norm of reciprocity [which] demands that the person imitate after having been imitated'. In other cases, however, imitation of the child's response by an adult results in a *decrease* in the child's imitated actions (see Case 1 in Kaufmann *et al.*, 1975; Kaufmann *et al.*, 1977), suggesting a possible mechanism whereby imitation could, besides its more conventional use in facilitating behaviours, be used to reduce undesirable behaviours. Owusu-Bempah (1983) describes imitation of severe self-mutilating behaviours which declined during the period of treatment; however, the effect shown was short lived, the behaviour returning in an exacerbated form shortly after termination of the treatment (J. Carr, unpublished). It remains unclear as to what are the different factors involved which result in imitation having diametrically opposed effects on the imitated behaviour. Kaufmann *et al.* (1975) suggest age and IQ as well as other characteristics of both imitator and subject, as possible differentiating factors; others might be the type of action imitated, the previous consequences of the action and other concomitants of the imitative process. Here is an area in which it is impossible to avoid the hackneyed conclusion that further research is needed.

Imitation, then, is a valuable means by which children and adults may learn desirable behaviours and, perhaps, unlearn some undesirable ones. Where a person lacks all imitative skills, these have usually been trained through motor imitation (as described on pp. 96 and 98). Once motor imitation has been established, imitation may be used to teach other useful skills such as self-grooming (Bry, 1969), social interaction (Paloutzian *et al.*, 1971), speech (Baer *et al.*, 1967) and social behaviours (Gadberry *et al.*, 1981), and many others are obviously possible.

CONCLUSIONS

The capacity to imitate provides a short cut to learning, especially of complex skills and those which, like speech, are difficult to prompt. Those who do not spontaneously imitate may well benefit from being specifically taught to do so: one perhaps unexpected bonus is that some people with mental handicaps appear to get pleasure out of the imitative skill itself, quite apart from any other benefits that may accrue to them from it. The first steps in teaching a person to imitate are usually slow and laborious but, as he acquires a number of actions that he is able to copy, so his ability to imitate increases and new actions are learnt more quickly. The aversive aspects of imitation, known we suspect for decades by persecuted children in school playgrounds, offer a novel and potentially useful alternative to more punitive methods of tackling problem behaviours that deserves systematic exploration in future research.

8

Decreasing Undesirable Behaviours

Glynis Murphy and Chris Oliver

Undesirable behaviour appears to occur more frequently among children with CNS damage and mental handicap than among children without handicaps (Rutter *et al.*, 1970; Stainback and Stainback, 1980). It is particularly common in severely and profoundly handicapped children and adults, with a number of studies showing an increasing prevalence of undesirable behaviour with increasing degrees of handicap (Eyman and Call, 1977; Maisto *et al.*, 1978; Schroeder *et al.*, 1978).

The use of behavioural techniques to reduce undesirable behaviour in people with mental handicap implies that there may be learnt components to their behaviour. To some parents and professionals this may appear a simplistic idea, and before proceeding to discuss the techniques themselves we shall consider the development of undesirable behaviour in more detail, not least because an understanding of the causes of such behaviour informs our attempts to reduce them.

CAUSES OF BEHAVIOUR PROBLEMS

A number of factors are thought to be important contributors to the increased likelihood of undesirable behaviour developing in mentally handicapped people. Many of these factors can be seen as background characteristics, which interact with the child's environment to produce conditions in which particular undesirable behaviours will be shaped up.

It is, for example, well established that increased rates of behaviour problems occur in children who have difficulties with language (Gould, 1977; Richman *et al.*, 1982). People with mental

102

handicaps, particularly those with more extreme impairments, are especially likely to have little or no linguistic ability. On occasions, undesirable behaviours can come to have linguistic functions in such non-speaking children, because of the way in which people in the environment react to such behaviour (Kiernan, 1986). Thus if a child hits or pinches his classmate, it is likely to bring the teacher over to him. This can become a useful though not necessarily a planned way of gaining teacher attention if the child has no other way of attracting it. Similarly, when presented with an unwanted task, a major tantrum may result in the removal of the task, or at least its temporary removal while the tantrum persists. Again, if a person has no other way of protesting about the level of task difficulty, tantrums may become a useful tool. Indeed, given any undesirable state of affairs (such as a dinner disliked, being sat on the toilet at the wrong time, being put in a jumper when it is too hot), one of the few ways of indicating disapproval, if a peson has no useful language, is by protest. However, many forms of protest, including screaming, shouting, hitting, kicking and struggling, are, of course, considered undesirable by all those others who have language by which to express themselves.

Secondly, many people with mental handicaps have additional sensory handicaps, and among those with severe and profound handicaps sensory impairments are both particularly common and frequently severe (Hogg and Sebba, 1986). For those individuals with impaired hearing and/or sight, every-day sensory stimuli of interest to normal children and adults may not be perceived. In these conditions, the handicapped person may begin to produce his or her own stimuli by what are normally termed stereotyped behaviours (Baumeister, 1978). The reinforcers for these behaviours, which include eye-poking, head and body twirling, hand-flapping and rocking, are now thought to be usually the sensory consequences, since a number of studies have demonstrated dramatic reductions in stereotypies with the provision of alternative sensory input (Murphy et al., 1986; Rincover et al., 1979). It is also possible that some people with mental handicaps and no apparent peripheral sensory impairment have central sensory processing problems which may result in similar behaviour.

Thirdly, it is known that people with mental handicap and impairments in social behaviour are particularly likely to show undesirable behaviours (Wing, 1987). It is probable that for these people the social rules that operate within a culture are difficult to comprehend so that they continually 'break' the social rules without

103

necessarily realising that they do so, and such behaviours are then seen as 'problems' by others. Such a lack of understanding of social rules is very common among people with severe and profound handicaps, but is also very prevalent, Wing feels, among mildly handicapped autistic people.

Fourthly, the social behaviour of people in whose care the person with a mental handicap finds him- or herself may unwittingly contribute to the appearance of behaviour problems. Many parents of handicapped children, because of their concern for their child, may alter their usual methods of child rearing, particularly in the early years. Such alterations may result in the shaping up of undesirable behaviours in the child. Thus, if a child has had an epileptic fit in the night, something not uncommon among handicapped children, parents will be more likely to keep him or her sleeping with them, or go in to him or her every time they hear a faint cry (if in a separate room), and so on. In the process, the child is unlikely to learn that night-time should be slept through rather than woken in, and night waking problems are likely to result (Clements et al., 1986; Douglas and Richman, 1984). Similarly, if a child is small for his or her age, especially if there were early feeding problems, both of which are common events in the handicapped child's life, parents will be understandably concerned to ensure an adequate food intake. Then misbehaviour at mealtimes, whether it be refusing to feed oneself, throwing the dish or being fussy over which foods are offered, is less likely to be followed by normal parental methods of management, such as deciding the child is not really hungry, can leave the meal and will make up for it tomorrow. Instead, the child will often be fed, cajoled or provided with alternative meals, because of the concern about his or her nutritional intake. As an unfortunate consequence, though, the contingencies that normally operate to reduce mealtime misbehaviour no longer hold, and problem behaviours at mealtimes will be likely to continue. Similarly, because a child with a mental handicap is likely to be interested in rather different activities from same-age peers, parents may be reluctant to let him or her visit, and be left with, local friends. They may worry that he or she will not 'fit in' or will be an extra problem to the adult in charge. As a consequence, the child may become clingy and over-dependent on his or her parents, and in the long term may be lonely.

The situations described are necessarily oversimplifications. However, it can frequently be seen in clinical work that the seeds of misbehaviour were actually sown some years previously. Usually these originated in a very real and appropriate concern for the person's well-being and, of course, it is not uncommon for professionals (such as care staff, nurses, teachers) to be similarly concerned and to shape up undesirable behaviour, quite unwittingly, for just the same reasons as parents may. The difficulty with such concern is that, although it generates desirable short-term consequences, it frequently leads to adverse long-term consequences, as Oliver (1986) has demonstrated for the particular behaviour problem of self-injury.

Fifthly, some of the residential facilities in which people with severe and profound handicaps find themselves leave much to be desired. In these settings, undesirable behaviour may arise partly as a function of environmental deficits. Poor resources, staffing levels or inadequate staff training, for example, may indirectly lead to low levels of appropriate occupation in facilities, such that undesirable behaviours are more likely to appear (Gardner and Cole, 1984).

Sixthly, the fact that the handicapped person is progressing developmentally less fast than those without handicaps has implications for the appearance of behaviour problems. Certain kinds of misbehaviour, such as tantrums, are tolerated in very young children (among whom they are common), perhaps partly because tantrums are usually part of a transient phase in childhood. In people with mental handicaps, though, such developmental stages may last far longer, and behaviour which may be in part a function of a person's developmental level may, therefore, continue for longer, exposing the person, in the process, to some of the social effects described above which may act to maintain the undesirable behaviour.

Finally, there is the possibility that extreme degrees of brain dysfunction lead directly to behaviour problems. This last hypothesis, often favoured by those with a medical training, may be true, but few specific links between brain damage and undesirable behaviour are known. (For example, it is well documented that people suffering from Prader Willi syndrome commonly have problems with eating control, and those with Lesch–Nyhan syndrome usually self-injure.) It is perfectly possible, though, that brain dysfunction is indirectly related to the appearance of behaviour problems, perhaps through one of the mechanisms discussed above (sensory handicaps, linguistic or social disability, deficient environments, developmental lags). Organic factors are thus probably best thought of as 'risk' factors, so that an extreme degree of handicap and the presumably extreme degree of brain dysfunction that accompanies it can be seen as altering a person's propensity for developing behaviour problems.

This consideration of why behaviour problems arise so commonly among people with mental handicap is not simply academic. For in deciding to design a behavioural programme to reduce a client's undesirable behaviour, on the assumption that the behaviour can be 'unlearnt', it is important to ask why the behaviour arose in the first place. Ten years ago it was uncommon for this to be thought an important issue but now, after some years of experience with behavioural methods, it has become clear that long-term effective change is more likely given some understanding of why the undesirable behaviour had reached problematic levels. Indeed, some early programmes, particularly where certain forms of punishment were applied without a real understanding of the function of the undesirable behaviour for the individual, now seem to have been treating the handicapped person as less than human.

Behavioural techniques for reducing undesirable behaviour involve either the alteration of antecedents preceding the undesirable behaviour or the rescheduling of consequences, following the undesirable behaviour, or other behaviours. The various techniques are described in detail, with examples, on pp. 115–41. First, however, methods for discovering which of the various events (which surround the client's undesirable behaviour) are acting as setting events and reinforcers, will be discussed. This stage of analysis is crucial to the design of effective treatment programmes because incorrect assumptions about setting events and reinforcers can lead to treatment programmes that worsen rather than improve behaviour (see, for example, the case described in the section headed 'Time-Out').

FUNCTIONAL ANALYSIS

One of the most useful tools in understanding the basis of a particular individual's undesirable behaviour is that of functional analysis. According to Kiernan (1974), this kind of assessment involves an analysis of the function of both antecedent and consequent stimuli in relation to the behaviour problem. In other words, functional analysis is essentially a search for the answer to questions like: What sets this behaviour off? When and where does it occur? What happens afterwards? What is maintaining the behaviour?

Such an analysis has always been considered an important part of the behavioural treatment of problem behaviours. In its simplest form, a functional analysis can be conducted by asking the person and/or others in his or her environment when and where the behaviour occurs, what sets it off and what follows. Alternatively, those caring for the person can be asked to complete a simple 'ABC' chart over a few days or weeks (see Figure 8.1).

These simple techniques may be adequate for some problem behaviours, though they are probably best supplemented by informal direct observation of the problem, since some informers may not be observant or may be so busy as to miss seeing and/or recording many instances of the undesirable behaviour. In complicated cases, however, it may be difficult to discern particular antecedent stimuli (for example, if the behaviour has generalised to many settings and times of day) and the consequences acting as reinforcers may be quite unclear. In these situations a more formal functional analysis may be necessary before a programme can be designed.

One way of conducting a formal functional analysis is to observe directly what the client does in a number of different settings and over extended periods of time (precisely how many observations need to be made will depend partly on the rate of the problem behaviour and partly on its variability, as discussed in Murphy, 1986). Edelson *et al.* (1983) adopted this kind of naturalistic observational technique in analysing the antecedents for a group of self-injurers. The observers simply sat in the residential setting (a hospital ward) and recorded antecedent stimuli, such as staff demands, denials and scoldings, and the levels of self-injury. The high levels of self-injurious behaviour (SIB) which followed these staff behaviours meant that it was possible to draw conclusions about what set off the SIB. They did not analyse the consequences of the behaviour, although this would be possible using a continuous observation technique (Murphy, 1986; see also Chapter 2).

Naturalistic observations of the kind that Edelson undertook are very time consuming. An alternative method of functional analysis is to set up particular situations and examine the effects of such settings on the problem behaviour. Carr *et al.* (1980), for example, discovered that their client's aggressive behaviour appeared only in sessions in which he was required to perform a task. When given free time, aggression did not occur. Carr and his colleagues concluded that the antecedents for aggression were task demands, and that the reinforcer, in the client's usual environment, had been escaping from an aversive situation (i.e. negative reinforcement, see Chapter 3).

Since Carr's early work, Iwata has developed a method of testing

Figure 8.1: An 'ABC' chart for recording antecedents (A), behaviour (B), and consequences (C), for an initial baseline and functional analysis

Date	Time	What happened before target behaviour	Describe target behaviour	What happened afterwards

out a series of possible antecedents and consequences by presenting an individual with a number of contrived situations (Iwata *et al.*, 1982). In Iwata's study, the clients showed self-injurious behaviour, and, because of the extensive literature documenting the importance of a number of different reinforcers for SIB, it was particularly important to understand the function of each individual's behaviour before proceeding to design treatment programmes lest the SIB was worsened by incorrect assumptions. Each individual was therefore observed in a number of different conditions in which either task demands were made of him, or he was verbally reprimanded for each self-injurious response, or he was alone (without toys) or toys were available and free play was allowed. When an individual's SIB was highest in the demands condition, Iwata *et al.* concluded (as did Carr above) that the probable past reinforcer was escaping from demands. When SIB was highest in the reprimand condition, Iwata and co-workers concluded that it had been positively reinforced in the past by adult attention (including scolding). If the SIB was highest in the 'alone' condition, but low in free play, the conclusion drawn was that the behaviour had sensory reinforcement properties for the individual. For several clients, however, the SIB was high in all situations, and for these people it was difficult to see what the antecedents and consequences were. Thus it is possible that their behaviour had generalised to a large number of situations, and/or had multiple functions, or that the particular antecedents which set off their SIB had not been tested (Iwata *et al.*, 1982, discuss these and a number of other possibilities).

The technique that Iwata and colleagues employed in their functional analysis may be appropriate for a variety of other high-rate behaviours (such as frequent tantrums, aggression, stereotyped behaviour, self-induced vomiting). In the three examples that follow, a rather similar technique was employed to provide information on antecedents and consequences for two self-injurious clients and one aggressive client (who also had other problems).

(a) Michael

Michael was a non-ambulant young man and had been self-injuring for many years. He had lived mostly in a large hospital setting but had now transferred to a hostel in a local community. Normally Michael wore a protective helmet because of his hand-to-head punching. Hostel staff were uncertain of what maintained Michael's

Figure 8.2: Duration and frequency of Michael's various behaviours when staff ignored and attended to him. During the full-attention condition, only minutes in which staff held Michael's hand for less than half the minute are used. All figures are prorated to take account of time hands held by staff

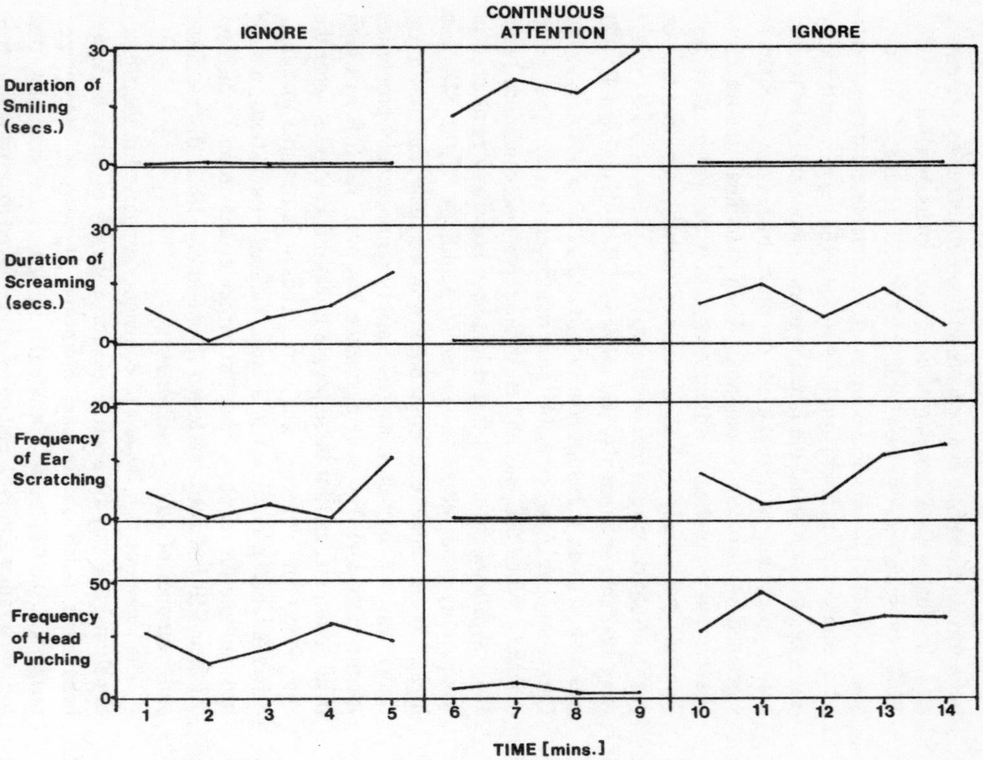

SIB, and said that they tried to manage the problem by putting the helmet on him and by ignoring the behaviour. One of the hostel staff was asked to spend several minutes next to Michael completely ignoring him and talking to another child. She was then asked to attend entirely to Michael and ignore the other children in the room. Michael's helmet had been removed before these observation sessions, as it was important to see his 'free' behaviour, so the sessions were very short lest Michael damage his head further. Figure 8.2 shows that, when ignored, Michael hit himself at a high rate and screamed a great deal. When the member of staff gave him her full attention, Michael rarely hit himself and smiled more. The effects on his behaviour were reversed when the member of staff turned away from Michael again, suggesting that we had identified reliable antecedents to Michael's SIB. It seemed likely that Michael was using his self-injurious behaviour to attract staff attention. He had no useful language and this may have been one of the reasons why Michael's self-injurious behaviour had taken on this function (particularly since he had lived in a poorly staffed hospital ward for many years). The problem was therefore construed as: how do we teach Michael a better method of gaining attention (and reduce his self-injury)?, rather than simply: how do we reduce Michael's self-injury?

(b) Nora

Nora was a non-ambulant three-year-old girl who was hitting herself on the mouth and cheeks with the back of her hands, and breaking down the skin on both hands. She had been wearing straight arm splints to prevent her self-injury. Her parents and the staff at the hostel where she lived were keen to stop using the splints but did not want Nora to injure herself. She had, incidentally, no language and was functioning in general at about a 6-month level.

Nora was admitted to a special behavioural treatment centre for several months (there were at the time no psychologists local to her hostel able to take on her assessment and treatment). During her time at the centre, Nora was observed in a number of contrived settings or analogue conditions (similar to Iwata's session), including sessions in which she was without nearby adults or toys ('alone'), with toys but no adults ('toys'), with adults who paid her full attention ('full attention'), and with adults who made her engage in a task ('demands'): see Figure 8.3.

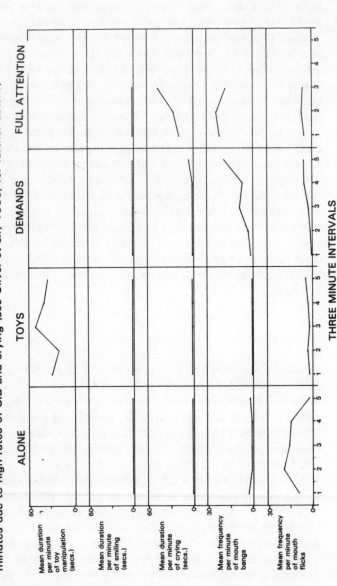

Figure 8.3: Duration and frequency of Nora's behaviours during 'alone', 'toys', 'demands' and 'full attention' conditions. Only one example of each session is shown, and toy manipulation is plotted only in the 'toys' condition. In the full attention condition on this occasion the session was abandoned at 9 minutes due to high rates of SIB and crying (see Oliver *et al.*, 1985, for further details)

As can be seen from the figure, Nora's behaviour, which was recorded on a continuous real-time basis, could be divided into flicks to the mouth, bangs to the mouth and cheek, toy manipulation, crying and smiling. Flicks to the mouth were highest in the 'alone' condition and lowest when Nora was occupied in the 'toys' condition (see Figure 8.3). It was concluded that this form of behaviour had a self-stimulatory function. On the other hand, bangs to her mouth/cheek area were highest in the full attention and demand conditions, and were accompanied by a great deal of crying. They also varied with the amount of physical contact made by the members of staff, being highest when they made most contact, and it was concluded that the bangs were a form of protest about physical prompting and physical contact, which had been reinforced in the past by escape from the aversive situation (Oliver *et al.*, 1987). Interestingly, Nora probably had Rett's syndrome, a neurodegenerative condition, and her self-injury, which was closely linked in topography to her more stereotyped hand flicks, was thought to have arisen when she began on a Portage teaching programme. The problem was thus construed: how do we teach Nora to like people again and how do we promote her development without her using self-injury to avoid tasks? It was not simply a question of how to stop her self-injury. (For Nora's treatment, see below under complex treatment examples.)

(c) Ella

Ella was a profoundly mentally handicapped, ambulant young lady, who lived in a small hospital unit and attended a community Social Education Centre (SEC). She was frequently aggressive, and showed high rates of stereotypy and also some self-injury. Her aggression took the form of pinching and scratching staff (sometimes at a very high rate). Ella was seen in a small bare room at the SEC in a number of conditions, like those we employed for Nora ('alone', 'toys', 'demands' and 'full attention'). She was also seen in a further condition, 'no attention' (like Michael above). Figure 8.4 shows that Ella's aggression occurred at a high rate during the full-attention condition but at a low rate during demands (the 'alone' and 'toys' conditions are not shown because in these sessions Ella was without staff in the room and thus could not be aggressive). Ella also cried more during 'full attention', and spent some of her time trying to push the trainer off her chair. It had been

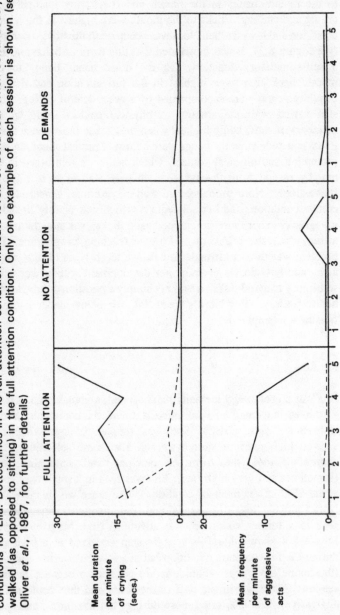

Figure 8.4: Frequency of aggression and duration of crying in 'full attention', 'no attention', and 'demands' conditions for Ella. Dotted lines in the full attention condition indicate levels of behaviour when continuously walked (as opposed to sitting) in the full attention condition. Only one example of each session is shown (see Oliver et al., 1987, for further details)

noted that Ella liked being walked around the centre (she needed some assistance in walking) and it seemed as if she was trying to persuade the trainer (in 'full attention') not to sit there talking to her but to get up and walk. Consequently in some 'full attention' conditions, the trainer walked Ella around the room, still paying Ella all her attention (dotted lines in Figure 8.4). Under these conditions, Ella's aggressive behaviour decreased markedly. It seemed as though Ella's aggression was a form of 'protest' about undesirable staff behaviour (from Ella's point of view) and it is probable that staff had come to interpret Ella's aggression as if it were a request. Certainly when staff did what Ella liked, tasks (see the demands condition in Figure 8.4) and walking (see full-attention-condition dotted line in Figure 8.4), Ella was no longer aggressive. (Her stereotypies and self-injury were more complicated, and are discussed in detail in Oliver *et al.*, 1987.) The plans for Ella's treatment are described under complex treatment examples below.

BEHAVIOURAL TREATMENT

There are a number of different techniques that have been found to be useful in the behavioural treatment of undesirable behaviour. Normally the techniques are employed in combination, and some programmes may involve a complex set of concurrent or parallel methods. Here the types of treatment will be described first with simple examples. Then more complex examples will be given, linking up with the functional analysis cases described in the preceding section. Other examples can be found in Jones (1983), Carr (1980) and elsewhere in the published behavioural literature.

(a) Positive reinforcement techniques

It follows from what has been said about the causes of behaviour problems and the analysis of the function of behaviour for particular individuals that at times it may be possible to eliminate undesirable behaviour by positive reinforcement methods. Such techniques may involve shaping, prompting, fading of prompts, imitation and chaining, as well as delivery of positive reinforcement, as has already been described in previous chapters in this book. Deciding precisely which behaviours should be reinforced is often quite difficult: usually the behaviours chosen will be physically or functionally incompatible with the undesirable behaviour (Luiselli *et al.*, 1985). Otherwise, the individual may learn the new behaviour but continue with the old one as well.

Often it may be helpful to employ a constructional approach (Cullen and Partridge, 1981), i.e. to ask what the client would be doing if he or she did not have this problem. A preceding functional analysis should provide the starting point for this approach. In the case of Michael, for example (described above), it appeared that self-hitting was gaining him attention, and it was clear that Michael needed to learn a more appropriate way of doing this. Most people gain social attention by verbal request (such as 'Come and see what I'm doing'), but Michael did not have this facility. He could, however, be taught to gain attention by other means (for example, by ringing a buzzer). It is also possible that, having asked what else he should be doing instead of head-banging, we might have discovered that Michael needed more self-occupational skills and/or a more structured curriculum, two other areas of development which may have required positive reinforcement techniques (see previous chapters in this book).

For those with less severe handicaps, positive reinforcement techniques can be combined with self-monitoring (Mace *et al.*, 1986a; Rudrud *et al.*, 1984), and the handicapped person can learn to run his or her own programme. Self-instructional techniques may also be appropriate, particularly where the problem behaviour is one of self-control. Thus for six adult clients with mild mental handicap and workplace problems, such as disruptive verbal and physical behaviours, Cole *et al.* (1985) employed a 'self-management' treatment package. Clients learnt by modelling, role-playing and rehearsal to self-monitor (recognise if they were yelling/hitting/ working well), self-evaluate (display a card which depended on current behaviour), self-consequate (provide themselves with monetary positive reinforcement for good work behaviour) and self-instruct (tell themselves not to yell or hit).

The two examples which follow concern individuals with more severe handicaps. For these clients self-monitoring and self-instruction were not possible. Instead desirable behaviour functionally incompatible with the undesirable behaviour was reinforced. David was 14-years-old, ambulant and had a profound handicap. He suffered from rubella embryopathy and had partial sight and hearing deficits. He lived in a mental handicap hospital and attended a special school in the hospital grounds. In school, when not given one-to-one attention David would sit and rock violently backwards, usually tapping a toy rhythmically on his nose at the same time (this tapping did not produce tissue damage). In baseline observation sessions David spent 90 per cent of his time engaged in stereotypies (Murphy *et al.*, 1986).

David was enrolled into a research project testing out the effects of special toys with handicapped children who showed no interest in ordinary toys. Two sets of toys were employed: in one set, interaction with the toy produced one of several intense stimuli (a sit-and-ride car produced vibration when the seat was pressed down, a pull-along train had a light which flashed when the wheels rotated, and a giant soft panda played loud electronic music when its stomach was pressed). These were the experimental toys. The other set of toys, the control toys, were identical except that they produced no special stimuli when played with. In a series of 30 sessions David was observed with the experimental and control toys (15 sessions of each). Figure 8.5 shows that during control toy session time David spent less than 6 per cent of the time in toy contact and manipulation, and 85 per cent of the time in stereotypies. In contrast, during the experimental toy sessions, David spent on average far less time in stereotypies and far more time in toy play (see Figure 8.5). This was particularly the case with the experimental car which David was in contact with or actively manipulating 94 per cent of the session time, on average, and his stereotypies reduced to less than 15 per cent of the time, except in one session (when he rocked while keeping his hand on the car).

These observations were designed as part of a research project rather than as a treatment programme (Murphy *et al.*, 1986), but they indicate the power of positive reinforcement of other behaviour (in this case toy play) in the reduction of even high-rate undesirable behaviour (stereotypies) in people with profound handicaps. Interestingly a parallel project, training constructive play using edible and social reinforcers, was much less effective in increasing toy play and reducing stereotypies (Murphy *et al.*, 1985). It seems likely that this was partly because the sensory reinforcers employed in the specially designed toys were replacing the sensory reinforcement normally gained from stereotypies.

It would, of course, be difficult to alter the whole of David's environment to produce stimuli of the kind he found reinforcing. It would, though, be possible to provide, at times in the day when he was not otherwise occupied, periods when David could be learning a variety of skills with vibration or other stimuli as the reinforcer, particularly if the stimuli could be computer-presented and linked with

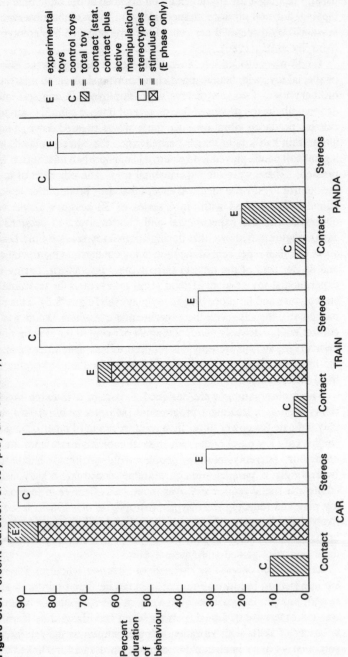

Figure 8.5: Percent duration of toy play and stereotypies for David, with experimental and control toys

E = experimental toys
C = control toys
▨ = total toy contact (stat. contact plus active manipulation)
☐ = stereotypies
⊠ = stimulus on (E phase only)

computer-run learning programmes. Ideally, of course, social reinforcers should be developed for David, by pairing them with sensory
reinforcers. However, this method of establishing social events as reinforcers is relatively unsuccessful (see Chapter 3), and particularly
given David's age it might not be possible. Other examples of the
use of positive reinforcement for multiply handicapped students can
be seen in Luiselli *et al.* (1985) and Slifer *et al.* (1986).

The second example of the use of positive reinforcement comes
from a recent report on the treatment of undesirable behaviour
(aggression, tantrums, self-injury, opposition, being out of seat) in
four autistic and brain-damaged children in a classroom setting (Carr
and Durand, 1985). Following functional analysis of the effects of
attention and task difficulty on the undesirable behaviour in question
(using a technique similar to that in examples on pp. 109–15), Carr
and Durand found that the four children involved responded with
disruptive behaviour to either low levels of teacher attention (one
child) or high levels of task difficulty (two children) or both (one
child). They proceeded to teach the children, who all had some
expressive language, one of two verbal requests: either to ask if they
were doing good work or to say they did not understand when asked
by the teacher if they had any questions. Subsequent observations
showed that when the verbal response taught was relevant to the
child's problem, the disruptive behaviour was drastically reduced
(for those whose disruptive behaviour was a function of task
difficulty, the relevant response was 'I don't understand', whereas
for undesirable behaviour produced by low attention the relevant
response was 'Am I doing good work?'). Where the response taught
was irrelevant to that particular child's problem, the disruptive
behaviour remained at a high rate. Carr and Durand concluded that
they had taught the children acceptable responses. In other words,
the children had been taught desirable methods of obtaining the same
ends (gaining attention or reducing task difficulty) as their previous
undesirable behaviour had achieved.

In these two examples of the use of positive reinforcement to
reduce problem behaviour, often termed differential reinforcement
of other behaviour (DRO), the alternative appropriate behaviour had
the same function as the maladaptive behaviour had had. It was
therefore not necessary to alter the consequences of the undesirable
behaviour. This may be why the relatively recent treatment of
antecedent exercise is effective in reducing some problem
behaviours (Bachman and Fuqua, 1983; Baumeister and Maclean,
1984). Sometimes, though, it may be difficult to eradicate the

problem behaviour without combining a DRO schedule with other techniques, such as extinction, for the problem behaviour itself.

In practice, although differential reinforcement methods are the most attractive techniques for reducing undesirable behaviour, they do have some disadvantages (Balsam and Bondy, 1983, 1985; Epstein, 1985). In particular, they may be difficult to operate, particularly in poorly staffed environments. It is, unfortunately, much quicker to react briefly to each undesirable response than to teach a person new behaviours. Punishment programmes (see below) frequently require less behaviour change on the part of the staff in the environment than do positive reinforcement techniques. In addition, the appearance of the undesirable behaviour probably acts as a reminder, or discriminative stimulus, to the adult to operate the agreed programme in the case of punishment. It is therefore very important to build into the DRO programme discriminative stimuli (such as the ringing of the kitchen timer) which will act to remind staff or parents to provide positive reinforcement, particularly when all-day programmes (such as token programmes) are in operation.

An alternative method of decreasing undesirable behaviours, also involving positive reinforcement procedures, is that of reinforcement of low rates of undesirable behaviour, DRL schedules (see Deitz, 1977). The use of the DRL schedule has mostly been limited to the reduction of classroom misbehaviours in educational settings (Deitz 1977; Deitz and Repp, 1973, 1974). These studies have demonstrated that it is possible to reduce the levels of undesirable behaviour by differentially reinforcing low rates of the undesirable behaviour, but it is not yet clear whether the use of DRL schedules is in any way preferable to the other techniques which have also proved to be effective in the reduction of such behaviours. It is possible, however, that such a procedure would be useful in reducing very high rate misbehaviours (which are extremely difficult to deal with) to a level where other techniques could then take over.

(b) Extinction techniques

An essential feature in any technique for teaching a new skill is contingent reinforcement of the target behaviour. Conversely, it is possible to reduce the frequency of a behaviour by not presenting contingent reinforcement. This process is termed extinction, and may be used in the reduction of undesirable behaviours.

Evidence from the animal literature (see, for example, Ferster and Skinner, 1957; Morse, 1966) gives two important characteristics of extinction: first, once extinction is begun, a temporary rise in the frequency of the target behaviour occurs before it drops off, and, secondly, the rate at which the behaviour reduces in frequency is, in fact, a function of the previous reinforcement schedule (intermittent schedules providing some 'protection' from extinction). It seems likely that these two characteristics also hold true for extinction in humans, at least on some occasions (head banging in Figure 1b, and self-biting in Figures 1a and 2a, Duker, 1975; jabbing in Jones *et al.*, 1974; self-injurious behaviour in Figure 6, Romanczyk and Goren, 1975). These two characteristics may explain the rare use of extinction by untrained staff and parents: for instance, if a child's misbehaviours are reinforced by the attention he receives, then although staff or parents may try ignoring the behaviour they will be discouraged first by the rise in the rate of the behaviour when they start ignoring it, and secondly (if they continue and if the previous schedule of reinforcement was intermittent) by its slow rate of fall afterwards.

Extinction was used in the following two examples for two severely retarded boys, one aged 4 and one aged 8, the latter presenting a problem because of persistent tantrums (consisting largely of loud screaming) and the former showing 'naughtiness' of various kinds. The older boy's tantrums usually occurred when he was being asked to do something he disliked (for example, to do a jigsaw puzzle or look at a book) and generally resulted in his teacher abandoning the task with him. The tentative functional analysis suggested that the boy's tantrums were being reinforced by being allowed to escape from tasks he disliked, contingent on screaming. The extinction programme entailed non-presentation of the reinforcement contingent on screaming, i.e. continuation of the task despite the tantrum. The reduction in the number of tantrums that followed was evidence of a correct functional analysis, and a favourable outcome ensued.

The 4-year-old boy's 'naughtiness' was mainly displayed when his mother's attention was directed towards others, particularly when visitors came to the house. At such times he would turn on the television or radio to full volume, swing on the curtains, hit the dog, go into the kitchen and pull things off the table. His mother's response was, of course, to interrupt her conversation at very frequent intervals to tell her son to turn the volume down or not to swing on the curtains. His undesirable behaviour seemed to be reinforced by contingent attention. During the extinction programme his mother ignored the 'naughty' behaviour and, although the undesirable behaviour increased at first, it soon reduced to mere verbal interruptions, which were felt to be acceptable for a 4-year-old.

Extinction may not always be an appropriate way of reducing undesirable behaviour, for the following reasons:

(1) It may be impossible to prevent the contingent presentation of the reinforcer. For example, when a child's aggressive behaviour to his peers is reinforced by their cries and screams, or where a child's continual masturbation is reinforced by the contingent sensory stimulation, non-presentation of reinforcers is difficult. Such cases usually involve peer reinforcement that cannot be controlled, or sensory reinforcement. An extinction programme then cannot be set up, and other methods (restructuring the environment, reinforcement of other behaviour, punishment) will need to be used.

(2) It may be undesirable to withhold the contingent reinforcer for practical reasons. This generally becomes a problem only when the reinforcer in question is adult attention and the target behaviour is part of a chain of behaviour normally interrupted by the adult. For instance, if the undesirable behaviour is stuffing towels and toilet rolls down the toilet until the toilet becomes blocked and/or overflows and the reinforcer is the adult attention involved in intervening before disaster ensues, then an extinction schedule requiring non-intervention would be rather impractical, as the damage done would be temporarily irreversible. Again restructuring the environment, reinforcement of other behaviour and/or punishment will be necessary.

(3) The expected increase in the rate of the undesirable behaviour at the beginning of extinction may make an extinction programme inappropriate or dangerous. For example, if the undesirable behaviour in question is self-injury or injury to others, the introduction of an extinction programme may result in added physical harm to individual(s). It is true that many extinction programmes have not resulted in a temporary increase in responding at the beginning of extinction (e.g. crying in Figure 2b in Duker, 1975; speech initiation of teachers and peers in Figure 2 of Sajwaj *et al.*, 1972; finger-feeding in Figure 1 of O'Brien *et al.*, 1972) and this phenomenon may be a result of the particular reinforcement schedule preceding extinction, as the schedule is known to affect response rates during extinction in animals (see Blackman, 1974). An absence of response rate increase cannot be relied on, however, unless the previous reinforcement schedule is certain; in clinical situations this is almost never possible, so that extinction is better not used for severely injurious behaviour.

(4) Extinction may be considered inappropriate where a quick

result is required, particularly if there is evidence that the behaviour has been only intermittently reinforced. This situation may occur if an undesirable behaviour is particularly upsetting to parents, teachers or care agents, or if only a limited time is available for a treatment programme. Although it is 'hazardous to compare general procedures with each other', Holz and Azrin found that with lower animals punishment was a quicker method for reducing response rate than was extinction, after a continuous schedule for reinforcement (Azrin and Holz, 1966; Holz *et al.*, 1963). Similar studies do not seem to be available in the literature dealing with the treatment of undesirable behaviours in people with mental handicap, but the same may be true. If, however, it is fairly certain that the target behaviour has been reinforced in the past on an intermittent schedule and extinction still seems to be the method of choice for reducing the behaviour, it may be possible to speed up the extinction process by altering the reinforcement schedule to a continuous one before beginning extinction. It would presumably be difficult to convince untrained staff of the logic of this kind of strategy, but there is one report in the literature (unfortunately not a controlled trial) of the use of this procedure (Galvin and Moyer, 1975). The crying of the young child (of one of the authors) was reduced by first moving to a continous reinforcement schedule for crying and then to an extinction schedule.

(5) In some situations, although it may seem to be appropriate at first sight to use extinction to reduce undesirable behaviours, practical problems may arise which would make the use of this technique unwise. Gilbert (1975) has discussed the difficulty of employing extinction procedures effectively in institutions when the reinforcer in question is some facet of adult attention. He points out that unless the programme planners can control the behaviour of all staff (including domestics, porters, voluntary workers, visitors and others not normally included in treatment action) in responses to the undesirable behaviour to be reduced, then this target behaviour may be reinforced unwittingly, on a sparser schedule than in the past, may not be extinguished, and may indeed be strengthened. Frankel (1976) has commented that, although this is a danger, the effects of intermittent reinforcement need not necessarily be disastrous as either the schedule could be stretched so much (if the majority of adults respond correctly), that the target behaviour does extinguish, or the child may learn to discriminate between 'reinforcing adults' and 'extinguishing adults' (the undesirable behaviour coming under the stimulus control of particular adults, appearing for some and not

for others, as a result of the reinforcement history).

Unfortunately, it would be impossible to guarantee in advance that either of these two conditions would hold, whereas it would be almost inevitable that someone not involved in the treatment programme would reinforce the target behaviour at some time. As Frankel (1976) says, it is probably unnecessary to recommend the abandonment of extinction procedures for attention-maintained behaviours in institutions: it is, however, important to be aware of the dangers and hence to maximise the chance of a successful programme.

A second, rather similar, problem that may arise is that of escalation of the intensity of the target behaviour. Again the difficulties apply mainly to attention maintained behaviours on extinction programmes, but the possible consequences are probably more dangerous than those discussed by Gilbert. Within a particular class of undesirable behaviours, such as biting others, there is a variation in the intensity of the behaviour (even within subjects), i.e. a child who bites others does not bite with exactly the same intensity every time. It is possible when an extinction programme is operating that adults will correctly ignore the majority of bites but will react in some way (a grimace, a cry, an orienting response even) to particularly hard bites. If their reaction is reinforcing to the child, the result will be that the average intensity of the undesirable behaviour will increase, as a result of differential reinforcement of 'high-intensity' responses. Similarly, if the child happens to bite by chance in a particularly painful place on one occasion and the recipient reacts instead of ignoring, then differential reinforcement of biting in painful places will result in the child's learning only to bite there (where he gets a reaction) and not to bite elsewhere (as he gets no reaction). An identical argument holds for many other undesirable behaviours which may be attention-maintained, such as hair-pulling, kicking, spitting, head butting, pinching, self-injury and so on, all of which can vary in intensity. Again, it follows not that extinction should be abandoned for attention-maintained behaviours, but that a wary eye should be kept on the possible dangers and alternative plans made in case the undesirable behaviours escalate in intensity to an unmanageable degree.

Despite the practical problems which have been discussed above, extinction is often the method of choice for reducing undesirable behaviours. If the technique of restructuring the environment (see below) cannot be used, and this is often the case, then extinction, if it seems likely to be successful, is probably preferable to punishment because of the ethical and practical difficulties involved in the use of punishment. It is normal to combine the positive reinforcement of appropriate behaviours with the non-presentation of reinforcement of undesirable behaviours (extinction) in clinical programmes, and certainly if the target behaviour is still being reinforced in some way, then a programme merely involving the reinforcement of other behaviours is unlikely to be effective. There appear to be few experimental tests of the importance of this combined approach in the literature. The principle can, however, be seen particularly clearly in a study designed to reduce finger-feeding in a child unable to spoon-feed (O'Brien *et al.*, 1972), where it was found that, in order to reduce the child's finger-feeding, it was necessary to employ not only extinction (involving prevention of edible reinforcement after finger-feeding) but also positive reinforcement of self-feeding skills.

(c) Punishment techniques

The *Oxford English Dictionary* defines punishment as follows: 'the infliction of penalty, the subjection (of offender) to retributive or disciplinary suffering, to handle severely'. Thus the ordinary English use of the word seems to refer to the procedure whereby the recipient is made to suffer.

The use of the word 'punishment' in operant theory was, for many years, parallel to the English usage, but more recently it has been redefined as follows: 'a consequence of behaviour that reduces the future probability of that behaviour' (Azrin and Holz, 1966), and this new definition seems to be being accepted (Johnston, 1972; Kazdin, 1975). The present meaning in operant theory and in the clinical field of behaviour modification is thus in terms of an effect on behaviour, and not a procedure. The definition is indeed precisely opposite to the definition of reinforcement.

The colloquial use of the word 'punishment', with all its connotations, has resulted in a reluctance to use the term, with its new meaning, in the clinical field and thus some will refer instead to 'negative reinforcement'. This is, of course, an incorrect use of the term. Here the word 'punishment' will be used throughout to mean a consequence of behaviour that reduces the future probability of that behaviour.

A thorough analysis is invariably required to define a punishing stimulus for a particular child in a particular situation, and the only genuine evidence of its effectiveness will come from the results obtained from its use. Nevertheless, there are several common types of stimuli which are often effective:

(1) time-out;
(2) response cost;
(3) other contingent aversive stimuli.

(1) Time-out

'Time-out' is short for 'time-out from positive reinforcement'. The procedure is as follows: in a setting in which positive reinforcement is continuously available, the reinforcement ceases for a short period of time contingent on undesirable behaviour. In the animal literature the procedure has been used in teaching matching-to-sample, time-out (unavailability of the edible reinforcer and switching off of the house lights) being contingent on errors. In clinical work, time-out is used in various ways, most commonly when the reinforcer concerned is praise or social attention and time-out involves a short period of isolation either in a separate room (e.g. Burchard and Barrera, 1972; Clark *et al.*, 1973; Wolf *et al.*, 1964) or in a semi-separated area, such as a chair facing the wall (e.g. Mace *et al.*, 1986a). It has also been used to correct inappropriate mealtime behaviour. Time-out involved either removal of the meal from the child for a short time or removal of the child from the meal (e.g. Barton *et al.*, 1970; Whitney and Barnard, 1966), and it could be used, in principle, in any situation involving presentation of positive reinforcement, where undesirable behaviours are occurring (see, for example, Lucero *et al.*, 1976; Myers and Deibert, 1971).

A number of controlled studies in the clinical literature have been concerned with the characteristics of time-out. (Alevizos and Alevizos, 1975; Clark *et al.*, 1973; Hobbs and Forehand, 1975; White *et al.*, 1972; Willoughby, 1969; Zimmerman and Baydan, 1963), and some of thse studies are reviewed in MacDonough and Forehand (1973) and Hobbs and Forehand (1977). Varying the duration of time-out has shown that time-out from social events becomes more effective as the period is increased towards several minutes (Hobbs and Forehand, 1977; Zimmerman and Baydan, 1963). Time-out periods over 15 minutes were found not to produce an increased effectiveness, however (White *et al.*, 1972), and evidence from the animal literature suggests that excessively long periods of time-out result in a suppression of appropriate behaviours (Zimmerman and Ferster, 1963). It has also been shown in one study (White *et al.*, 1972) that if the duration of time-out is altered for particular individuals, order effects occur: specifically, if short (1-minute) time-out is used first and is then increased to 15 and 30 minutes, the rate of undesirable behaviour drops progressively. If, on the other hand, the long durations are given first and then changed to shorter durations, there is an increase in the rate of undesirable behaviour. Thus, if unsure what period of time-out to employ, it seems advisable to begin with short periods and then, if necessary, to increase the duration, rather than the reverse. Similar findings have been obtained by Burchard and Barrera (1972) and Kendall *et al.* (1975).

Much as target behaviours increase most quickly when started on a continuous positive reinforcement schedule, it has been shown that undesirable behaviours decrease most quickly on a continuous schedule of time-out (Clark *et al.*, 1973). However, low-ratio schedules of time-out such as VR 2, VR 3, and FR 2 seem to be almost as effective as continuous schedules (Clark *et al.*, 1973; Calhoun and Matherne, 1975). High-ratio schedules (such as VR 8) are almost useless when used for high-frequency behaviours which have not been subjected to previous low-ratio schedules of time-out. It appears, though, that if a behaviour is first reduced on a low-ratio schedule of time-out, the high-ratio schedules can then be quite effective (Hobbs and Forehand, 1977).

Release from time-out could be considered to be a negative reinforcer of behaviour preceding the release, and consequently it is usual in the clinical situation to make the ending of time-out contingent on at least a very short period of good behaviour and to delay the ending of time-out until this is achieved. There is evidence with normal pre-school children that this contingency results in lower rates of disruptive behaviour during the time-out period, as would be expected, and that it produces an increased efficacy of the time-out in reducing undesirable behaviours outside the time-out period (Hobbs and Forehand, 1975). However, a more recent study with three young children (two of whom were mentally handicapped) suggested that time-out without contingent delay did not increase the rate of undesirable behaviour, either in time-out or at other times, when compared with time-out with contingent delay (Mace *et al.*, 1986a). If, then, the use of a contingent delay would cause a client to be in time-out for longer than about 30 minutes, it would seem unwise and unethical to employ a contingent delay rule.

127

Finally, just as positive reinforcement of alternative behaviours is used in extinction programmes, so the use of time-out to reduce undesirable behaviours is combined with reinforcement of other behaviours. There is some clinical evidence to support this. Willoughby (1969) showed that a partially effective time-out programme became fully effective only when combined with positive reinforcement of other behaviours. He concluded that 'if the punished response provides the only available means of reinforcement, it is unlikely that time-out will have lasting suppressive effects on the occurrence of the undesirable behaviour'. Equally, if positive reinforcement of some kind is obtainable during the time-out, it cannot be expected to be effective.

Three examples of the clinical use of time-out follow. In one case, a 10-year-old boy with mental handicap was screaming in the classrom at a baseline rate of about 29 times a day. The intensity of the screams had brought complaints from the residential area across the street and from other class teachers in the school, and of course the noise was disrupting the child's own class. A brief functional analysis suggested that the boy's screaming occurred when the teachers were not attending to him, and that it was reinforced by their consequent efforts to quieten him down (including allowing him to play on his favourite rocking horse). During the treatment programme a 5-minute period of isolation in an adjacent small room (time-out) was made contingent on even the smallest scream, while quiet working alone was reinforced approximately every 10 minutes with a teacher's praise and attention, and a short ride on the rocking horse. The results are shown in Figure 8.6. At 15-month follow-up the boy's behaviour remained excellent, with no screaming at all on most days and no more than one scream on the remaining days.

Before leaving time-out, it is important to note that when time-out involves exclusion from a situation, as it commonly does, care must be taken to ascertain that the child is already receiving positive reinforcement of some kind in the situation from which he is to be excluded. This is of course clear from the name for this technique (time-out from positive reinforcement) but seems to be frequently forgotten. Time-out from an aversive situation would in fact be negatively reinforcing and result in an increase in the undesirable behaviour. Two examples follow of clinical situations where this occurred. Further examples are provided by Vukelich and Hake (1971) and Solnick et al. (1977).

A 10-year-old deaf boy with a normal non-verbal IQ but total absence of language began to throw his food and hit his peers during

Figure 8.6: The effect of time-out on a boy's screaming in the classroom

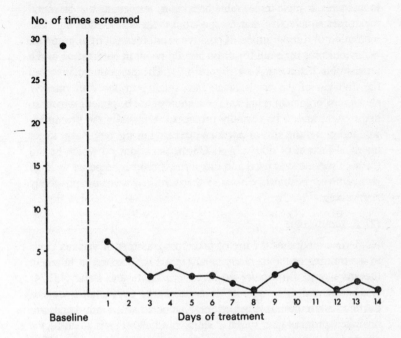

No. of times screamed

Baseline   Days of treatment

mealtimes. A brief time-out from the meal (exclusion from the dining room) contingent on such behaviour resulted in a reduction in this behaviour within a short period. However, the use of an identical procedure in a large-group situation resulted in an increase in his aggression. For this boy the large-group situation itself was aversive, and escape from it (brief isolation) was reinforcing. He did, however, love his food, so that brief exclusion from a mealtime was indeed punishing. This illustrates the dangers of a 'cook-book' approach: the use of a specific procedure (isolation) was effective in reducing one behaviour but ineffective in reducing another, for reasons that are clear on close examination of the situations in which the behaviours took place.

A 7-year-old boy, on the borderline ESN(S)–ESN(M) range in IQ, with language at about a 3-year level, frequently threw his full plate at the beginning of lunch, and sometimes this was preceded by throwing other objects on the table (salt and pepper, vases of flowers). His behaviour at other mealtimes was somewhat better,

129

but still occasionally resulted in throwing. Exclusion of the child from the meal contingent on throwing, i.e. brief 'time-out', resulted in an increase in the undesirable behaviour, suggesting that he found mealtimes so aversive that escape from them was reinforcing. The institution of a programme of positive reinforcement of appropriate behaviour plus time-out for throwing did result in elimination of the undesirable behaviour (see Figure 8.7). The programme involved the division of the boy's lunch into small portions with massive social reinforcement (plus stars) for appropriate behaviour which, to begin with, had to be partially prompted. Gradually the prompting was faded and the size of portions increased as the boy learnt to eat his meal instead of throwing it. On the occasions on which he did throw, time-out was used and did seem, from his response to it, to be aversive, presumably because the mealtime was now positively reinforcing.

(2) Response cost

Numerous reports of the use of token programmes of various kinds in the training of the mentally handicapped have appeared in recent literature (e.g. Birnbrauer *et al.*, 1965; Iwata and Bailey, 1974; Kaufmann and O'Leary, 1972; Lent *et al.*, 1970). One way of dealing with undesirable behaviours that occur when individuals are on token programmes (points, stars, plastic discs) is to deduct a number of tokens contingent on the undesirable behaviour. This procedure has been used as a punishment contingency for swearing, property damage, aggression (Burchard and Barrera, 1972); or being late for class or off-task (Iwata and Bailey, 1974; Kaufmann and O'Leary, 1972).

Many studies of response cost have not been concerned with individuals with a mental handicap, and it is not known whether the characteristics of response cost differ in this population. Burchard and Barrera (1972) investigated the effects of amount costed in adolescents with mental handicaps who were already on a token system. They concluded that response cost was effective only if the individual had few tokens and/or little opportunity to earn more.

One of the problems with response cost, as those who try it will discover, is that the procedure often evokes protests, struggles and temper tantrums from the individuals involved. Indeed, it can be seen as 'unfair' to remove tokens earned by good behaviour contingent on later behaviour, and it is usually preferable to arrange the programme so that undesirable behaviour results in 'not earning' rather than 'being fined'. Alternatively, 'free' points can be given

Figure 8.7: The increase in mealtime misbehaviour produced by supposed 'time-out', and the effect of introducing positive reinforcement procedures during the mealtime

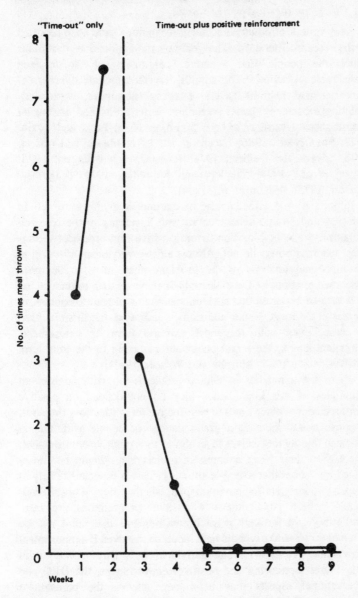

at the beginning, which are then deducted after undesirable behaviour (Salend and Kovalich, 1981).

(3) Other contingent aversive stimuli

A great variety of other punishment techniques have been reported in the research literature. They employ the application of stimuli, which the people find aversive, contingent on the targeted undesirable behaviour. The stimuli described include overcorrection, personal restraint, aversive-tasting substances, unpleasant-smelling substances, facial screening, water spray and contingent electic shock (Azrin et al., 1975; Foxx, 1976; Foxx and Azrin, 1972; Foxx et al., 1986; Lucero et al., 1976; Measel and Alfieri, 1978; Myers and Deibert, 1971; Romanczyk and Goren, 1975; Sajwaj et al., 1974; Salzberg and Napolitan, 1974; Singh and Winton, 1985; Winton et al., 1984).

Reports of the effectiveness of contingent aversive stimuli in reducing undesirable behaviour are still appearing in the research literature. Some employ concurrent positive reinforcement techniques, whereas others do not. Almost all pay very scant attention to the functional analysis of the problem: they seem to be more concerned to suppress the undesirable behaviour than to understand it. It is to be expected that such an approach will lead to short-term success at the most. Some studies have indicated that this is indeed the case, even with the most extreme form of punishment, contingent shock, the target behaviour recurring in the long term (Griffin et al., 1984; Murphy and Wilson, 1981).

There are a number of ethical problems too with punishment techniques of this kind. Since they do not depend on positive reinforcement at other times to be effective (cf. extinction, time-out, response cost), there is a grave danger of people with mental handicap finding themselves in an almost total punitive environment, where even their weak attempts at protest may simply be consequated by yet another aversive stimulus. This is especially likely to happen in poorly staffed environments, whether they be hospitals or hostels, where labour-intensive positive programmes are rare. Furthermore, it is likely in such environments that there will be minimal (or absent) psychological input, so that even if a punishment programme begins with one individual in a careful way, with behavioural monitoring and positive reinforcement, the DRO and observational aspects may peter out, leaving the punishment programme which sometimes may be transferred to other individuals in an unplanned way. This is particularly likely to happen if staff are under stress and feeling angry with individuals who are repeatedly provoking them with challenging behaviour. Even Itard, in a moment of frustration, once tried to teach his pupil, the wild boy from Aveyron, by employing an aversive consequence. The experience produced no positive effects, however, and Itard later greatly regretted the incident (Shattuck, 1981, p. 126–8).

In America, there has been a concerted attempt to eradicate the use of punishment procedures, largely as a result of privately brought court cases (e.g. Wyatt *v.* Stickney 1972). Many States have now had behaviour modification guidelines for some years (e.g. May *et al.*, 1974; Peek and McAllister 1974), and it is now almost impossible to conduct programmes involving aversive procedures in some States (for example, in Michigan), even when undesirable behaviours are liable to harm the individuals in question. Thus Nolley *et al.* (1982) had to devise positive reinforcement programmes for 16 severely self-injurious clients in Michigan without using anything more aversive than time-out. It is interesting to note that they reported 12 out of 16 were nevertheless successful programmes (at least in the short term).

In Britain there are no similar legal restrictions on the use of punishment procedures, although occasionally inquiries are held into mental handicap hospitals because of reported misuse of such methods. However, most districts now have their own local ethical guidelines or ethics committees which all consider such programmes, among other matters. (See Chapter 15 for a full discussion of ethical issues.)

(d) Stimulus control technique

The operant view of behaviour is that not only is the future probability of a behaviour a function of its present and previous consequences, but also its occurrence is in part a function of its present and past antecedents. This is the concept of stimulus control (see Terrace, 1966) and it can provide a powerful treatment tool in the decreasing of undesirable behaviours. Thus if, during the preliminary functional analysis, it becomes clear that the undesirable (target) behaviour occurs only in one situation and not in others, then one possible method for reducing the frequency of the target behaviour is to prevent the presentation of the discriminative stimuli that precede the inappropriate behaviour. For instance, suppose a child is exceptionally distractible in a classroom situation, in that he frequently turns around and interacts with adults or peers, spending little time 'on task'. Suppose also that he turns around far less if his view of the classroom is blocked and then spends more time 'on task'. One way of reducing his 'off-task' behaviour might be to place a screen around him, to block off his view of the room. Clearly as a long-term solution here this technique would be inadequate, and so in practice other methods may need to be combined with the restructuring of a situation. In other cases (e.g. Sajwaj and Hedges, 1973) it may be sufficient merely to omit the discriminative stimuli altogether.

An example of the use of this technique follows. A 9-year-old child, verbal mental age approximately 4 years, presented a distinct behaviour problem at mealtimes when not at home. In the hospital situation he would throw his plate on to the floor (and eat off the floor if allowed to do so), steal food from other children, throw food, spit food and so on. If prompted to eat appropriately (by physical prompts), he would struggle, stiffen his arms, sweep food on to the table with his spoon, spit food out, and turn his head away. When eating meals at home he ate like a normal boy. The possibility was, therefore, that appropriate eating behaviour had come under the stimulus control of his parents sitting down at the table in his home dining room, whereas inappropriate eating behaviour had come under the control of the hospital unit stimuli and procedures. Experimentation revealed that the essential aspects of the stimuli controlled appropriate eating behaviour were not his parents *per se*, nor his home dining room *per se*, but the presence of adults sitting down at the table with him. Once this procedure was used in the unit, the boy ate as well as at home, this effect being immediate and not a function of further training in the unit.

Typically, stimulus control is exerted as a function of differential reinforcement of behaviour in the presence of different stimuli. If stimulus control is not complete (i.e. if generalisation occurs to other stimuli), then, even after the removal of a particular discriminative stimulus for an undesirable behaviour, it is likely that the behaviour will at some time occur in the new situation. If the deceleration target behaviour elicits reinforcement in this new situation, then, effectively, the subject is being taught to generalise, and the undesirable behaviour can become an equal problem in the new situation. Consequently it is essential to combine a programme involving the removal of discriminative stimuli for undesirable behaviour with one or both of the following:

(a) non-presentation of reinforcement if the undesirable behaviour appears in the new situation;

(b) reinforcement of appropriate behaviours in the new situation.

In the example given above, neither of these two procedures was included on the programme and, predictably, the child gradually learnt to behave in the previously undesirable ways even when adults also sat down at the table with him in the unit. Unfortunately, this inappropriate mealtime behaviour did generalise to some extent to the home situation, as might be expected.

The method of restructuring the situation can be an extremely effective and rapid way of eradicating or reducing an undesirable behaviour, or at the very least, with extremely frequent target behaviours, it can reduce the undesirable behaviour sufficiently to allow the occurrence of some appropriate behaviours which may then be reinforced in preference to the inappropriate ones. It will not always be possible to discover a situation in which the undesirable behaviour does not occur, and in such cases it will be necessary to turn to alternative methods (see above). Occasionally, however, it may be felt that the new situation, while preventing the undesirable target behaviour from occurring, is not in itself desirable. For instance, to use an earlier example, if a child is sat behind a screen to reduce off-task classroom behaviour, it will at some stage be necessary to remove the screen and integrate him back into his peer group. The success of the reintegration will depend in part on the adequate reinforcement of the 'new' appropriate behaviour when it occurs again. The preferable method to use for such a return to the original situation is probably a gradual fading from the new situation back to the old one, with the aim of gradually establishing stimuli from the old situation as S^Ds for appropriate behaviours, by contingent reinforcement.

Sometimes it may be useful, especially when beginning treatment sessions in a complex treatment programme, to deliberately include a special stimulus to indicate that the treatment session is in operation. The reason for doing this is that, in the long term, the stimulus may well come to exert control over the client's appropriate behaviour, i.e. it may become a discriminative stimulus for such behaviour. Very often such treatment sessions take place in a particular room, and this may become an S^D for good behaviour, but this is clearly not a very useful kind of S^D. Sometimes the trainer becomes an S^D for good behaviour but, again, this is not particularly useful. Probably the best deliberately constructed S^D

135

(when such a programme is being generalised) will be one which can accompany the client whenever and wherever he or she goes, to act as a signal both to the client (for good behaviour) and to the care staff, teachers and/or parents (to operate the agreed programme).

(e) Combined and complex programmes

For those people with mental handicaps who are showing very high rates of behaviour problems or very extreme kinds of behaviour, the programmes designed may need to be quite far reaching and complex in order to achieve lasting change. Very often the most difficult part of such programmes is not thinking them up, but persuading staff or parents to operate them consistently. It is probably most important for all the people involved to understand the reasoning behind particular programmes. This does not mean that they need to have particular kinds of professional training, but it does mean that spending time at the beginning of the programme explaining the functional analysis and the logic behind a treatment plan will be time well spent. In addition, if the programme designer is acting as a visiting advisor, as opposed to being one of the people currently caring for the child in question, then it is essential for him or her to be sensitive to programme suggestions from parents or care staff who usually know the client extremely well (see also Chapter 12). Even the best programmes will need reviewing at regular intervals, and most will require alterations from time to time. Three examples follow of complex treatment programmes that illustrate some of the techniques and problems involved.

Nora

Nora has already been described in the section on functional analysis (page 111). The aims with Nora's programme were to provide some appropriate form of self-stimulation (to reduce hand flicks) and to teach Nora that social interaction with adults could be pleasant and would not be avoided by bangs to the mouth. Since, at the beginning of the programme, Nora found social contact unpleasant, it was impossible to employ a natural event like cuddles as a reinforcer. Instead an edible reinforcer was employed and paired with a very gentle form of social interaction (the kind Nora least disliked, such as whispering 'Good girl, Nora'). The programme involved two main parts:

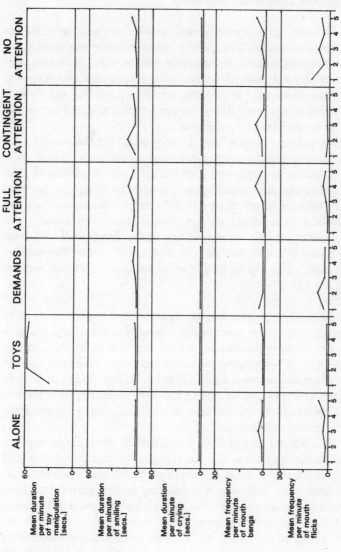

Figure 8.8: Duration and frequency of Nora's behaviours at follow-up, during 'alone', 'toys', 'demands' and 'full attention' conditions. Only one example of each session is shown, and toy manipulation is plotted only in the 'toys' condition

(i) Nora was given a circular rattle to wear on a necklace. This was chosen because Nora showed high rates of toy manipulation and mouthing when it was available and low rates of flicking. Her mental age (around 6 months) suggested that mouthing was developmentally appropriate for Nora, so it was not discouraged at this stage. The rattle was attached to a necklace so that it would always be available.

(ii) In order for Nora to learn to enjoy social interactions, a graded training programme began on a sessional basis. During these sessions, to begin with a trainer sat some distance away from Nora (because contact was aversive for her), and provided edible reinforcers for every 30 seconds Nora did not bang her cheek. The edible reinforcer was paired with gentle social interaction. If Nora banged herself, her hands were held down away from her face and the trainer said loudly 'No banging, Nora'. This was the kind of social interaction we knew Nora did not like.

As the sessions progressed, the trainer moved closer and closer to Nora provided she successfully managed not to bang. After a number of these sessions the trainer was able to sit very close to Nora without her banging and had dropped the edible reinforcers to one every few minutes. Up to this point, no tasks had been given to Nora and no physical prompting had been necessary. Over the next few weeks, tasks and prompts are gradually reintroduced, again using edible reinforcers.

After several months Nora was tolerating life in the special unit well, including her teaching and occupational therapy sessions, and the programme had been generalised to all staff. A number of meetings were held with her referring hostel, parents and local school to explain the functional analysis and treatment programme, and Nora was then discharged home. About four months later she was visited at the hostel, and the functional analysis assessments were repeated (one session for each condition). The results are shown in Figure 8.8).

Nora's banging no longer occurred in response to full attention and demand conditions. However, it appeared to be occurring in the contingent attention condition (a condition involving social disapproval contingent on SIB), where it was accompanied by some laughing and smiling. This suggested that Nora was now using the bangs to obtain adult attention (which previously was unpleasant to her). It was therefore necessary to instigate a programme of ignoring bangs and providing the attention that she liked when she behaved appropriately.

This programme illustrates the need for a continued close follow-up of treatment programmes where staff have not been trained in behavioural analaysis techniques. In such circumstances, it is possible for parts of the programme to be dropped, while other parts are maintained, and for the undesirable behaviour to be unwittingly 'trained up' in new situations to have new functions which an unadjusted programme would not deal with.

Ella

Ella appeared to have learnt to use aggressive behaviour to 'ask' people to give her walks or do tasks with her (see functional analysis, page 113). Her treatment programme involved a number of aspects:

(i) Ella seemed to enjoy doing structured tasks with assistance from an adult, including physical prompting. Regular sessions involving a listed set of activities were begun, the activities ranging from table-top tasks to self-help tasks. During these sessions Ella was not allowed to have her favourite toy (to reduce the related stereotypies during the sessions) but she was allowed to have the toy back at the end of each session (this would presumably act as a reinforcer). In addition, during these sessions, there was a programme operating to reduce her aggression (see (ii) below).

(ii) It was very important in Ella's long-term interests that she learn not to hurt other people. As a start, sessions were begun in which Ella wore palm splints (Spain *et al.*, 1985) in which she found it difficult to pinch people. During these sessions, Ella was reinforced for gradually lengthening periods without aggressive responses (DRO), and any attempts at aggression were ignored. At first, the time in the sessions was taken up doing tasks (see (i) above) or going for walks, both activities which Ella enjoyed. In the long run, it was planned that the palm splints would be somewhat faded (i.e. made very small) and the DRO generalised to other times of the day. It was intended that the palm splints, or their faded equivalent, should act as an S^D for appropriate behaviours and an S^Δ for aggression (see above, under stimulus control).

Tom

An accident at the age of eleven months, damaging the spinal cord at C4, had left Tom paralysed from the neck down and dependent on positive pressure ventilation. He lived on a busy children's ward in a large children's hospital and was referred at about 2 years to the psychologist when he became difficult to feed. On investigation, it appeared that Tom spent all his time on his back or in his Matrix chair in the ward, and was apathetic and unable to occupy himself in any way except by making requests of the nurses. His main request was for them to pat a ball or balloon up repeatedly in front of him and to bounce it off his forehead. When it came to mealtimes, Tom was refusing to eat, had to be force-fed on occasions and eventually had a naso-gastric tube.

After informal observations of Tom and his life on the ward, the psychologist concluded that his refusal to eat was probably his only way of protesting about his life and constituted one of his few possible methods for exerting any environmental control. A treatment programme was planned to provide Tom with a generally more rewarding existence, including the opportunity for controlling his environment, for learning new skills and for self-occupation (Douglas and Ryan, 1987; Douglas *et al.*, personal communication).

The feeding problem was targeted directly only in so far as the demands to eat were reduced and mealtimes were introduced gradually as enjoyable activities, with modelling of appropriate behaviour by adults. Thus adults, particularly his speech therapist, would eat lunch in his room and chat and offer him bites of their sandwiches. Once Tom was enjoying these small amounts and sampling a variety of tastes, the amounts were gradually increased until Tom was eating normal meals. This procedure (shaping) took some time: Tom's naso-gastric tube was finally removed several months later and his eating and weight gain have not since been cause for concern.

In parallel with these change in Tom's eating, there were major developments in other parts of his life. Before the programme began, Tom had been able to leave the ward only with two nursing staff and an unwieldy apparatus (a Matrix buggy with two cylinders of compressed air and oxygen connected in close proximity). During the programme, after a number of false starts, a chair was found which suited Tom's degree of handicap (Everard turbo chair with a Matrix seat) to which his oxygen cylinders could be attached (in a concealed position). A mouth joystick control was designed, which Tom rapidly learnt to operate, and, after 5 months of intermittent sessions with his chair, he was able to manoeuvre in crowded rooms, through small doorways, in and out of lifts, could move around the hospital independently and could go outside along pavements too (Douglas and Ryan, 1987).

In addition, he was provided with a personal microcomputer, and after trials with a variety of different interfaces two main ones were selected: a head-switch control and a tongue-switch control. At the time, very few appropriate programs were available in commercial software, so a number of games and tests were designed and, eventually, some training programs for developing new skills (Douglas *et al.*, 1987).

By the time Tom was 4-years he was eating well, driving around in his chair independently and occupying himself for considerable periods of time. He was no longer apathetic but enjoyed much of his life, including being naughty (for example, refusing to solve a problem on his computer until no-one was watching when he would rapidly complete the task). His language had developed very rapidly and he was using a number of active verbs about himself ('I'm driving', 'I'm coming', 'I'm getting', etc.). Indeed, from appearing to be a severely mentally *and* physically handicapped child, he had emerged as a physically handicapped child with at least some near normal abilities.

Tom's programme exemplifies the need, in providing help with behaviour problems, to examine the maladaptive behaviour within the context of the child's whole life. Had the psychologist (J.D.) simply tackled the child's eating problems, the programme would have been doomed to fail. The success probably lay in building up the positive side of Tom's life and giving him some control of his world.

CONCLUSION

Over the last ten years there have been major changes both in the philosophy and in the techniques employed in reducing undesirable behaviours in people with mental handicap. Whilst it is recognised that people with mental handicap are more likely to develop behaviour problems than many other groups of people, there is a growing understanding of the reasons why this may be. There has been a parallel alteration in the kinds of techniques included in treatment programmes aiming to reduce difficult behaviours, with a move towards positive programming and away from aversive control. The emphasis in this chapter has been first to understand the reasons for difficult behaviour, secondly to design as positive a programme as possible, and thirdly to consider the problem behaviour in the context of the person's whole life.

9

Self-help Skills:
Washing, Dressing and Feeding

Janet Carr and Barbara Wilson

Normal children become increasingly independent as they grow older, acquiring the self-help skills we are discussing here through a combination of imitativeness and iron-willed determination to be independent. The only one of these skills likely to cause the parents of a normal child any concern is toileting (discussed in Chapter 10). Washing, dressing and feeding she learns effortlessly and almost before her elders have realised what is happening. For the handicapped child, however, the acquisition of these skills may not be so easy; without special teaching she may remain dependent on help from others at almost every moment of an ordinary day, and, in the case of those with the most severe handicaps, may remain so into adult life. With special teaching most people, even if profoundly handicapped, can learn at least some of the self-help skills. With every skill that the person acquires she becomes more nearly 'normal', and this can result in a change for the better in people's attitudes towards her; she herself may gain great satisfaction from her own prowess, which she can demonstrate repeatedly throughout the day; the work-load of those caring for her, whether parents, nurses, teachers, or hostel or day centre staff, is lightened; not least important, her ability in these areas may determine to some extent whether or not she can continue to live in the community.

For all these reasons, the self-help skills are ones that we want to teach to handicapped people. Behaviour modification methods can improve the effectiveness of our teaching.

WASHING

We need to wash or be washed not only at the beginning and end

143

of each day but also before meals, after using the toilet and at other times when we are particularly dirty, for instance after working in the garden. Washing, then, can occupy a considerable amount of time in the day, and inability to wash herself may be an added burden to those caring for a handicapped person. However, among the self-help skills washing is the one that has been the least discussed in the literature. Only one experimental paper on washing (apart from those on tooth-brushing) has been reported in sufficient detail to allow for replication. Treffry *et al.* (1970) trained 11 girls with severe or profound mental handicap whose average age was 14 and average IQ about 20 (none was above 30). A 12-stage scale for washing and drying hands was used and the girls were trained by a forward-chaining method, using sessions of 5 to 15 minutes after meals for a 9-week period. One girl made no progress, four showed varying increase in skill, and six were able to wash independently at the end of the programme.

Other papers have mentioned washing amongst various self-help programmes but have not discussed it (Mackowiak *et al.*, 1978) or have referred to scales devised and used (McDonald *et al.*, 1976) and results achieved (Song *et al.*, 1976) but without giving any detail of the programmes.

Manuals written for parents of mentally handicapped children are, like the Treffry *et al.* paper, more helpful, giving detailed instructions for teaching washing including backward-chaining scales for hand and face washing, bathing, hair washing, etc. (Baker *et al.*, 1976; Baldwin *et al.*, 1973; Carr, 1980). The number of steps in a scale, for example for hand washing, varies from 8 (Baker *et al.*) to 12 (Treffry *et al.*) to 16 (Carr) to 26 (Baldwin *et al.*), the latter including separate steps for washing each separate finger. Treffry *et al.*, whose 12-stage scale includes drying, pointed out that the majority of the steps they give had to be broken down into smaller ones for effective teaching; although not all of these smaller steps are described, it is clear that in practice the scale was considerably longer than that given. Baldwin *et al.* (1973) present programmes for washing hands, cleaning teeth and combing hair only, and say that these may be extended to washing face and bathing; Baker *et al.* (1976) give separate programmes for these. Other programmes for drying hands and for hair washing are set out in Carr (1980) and in Baker *et al.*, who also give one for hair brushing, while Carr includes one for teaching the child to be aware of the need for a wash.

Many of the chaining scales may seem not entirely appropriate for a particular person, either because they are overdetailed or because the steps are not small enough, or because some other approach to the task is preferred. No one scale can be expected to suit everybody, and readers of all three parent manuals are encouraged to regard the scales given not as a sacred text but as a guide, and to be prepared to adapt them to suit themselves. The following is an example of one scale, for hand washing (Carr, 1980):

(1) Go to basin.
(2) Put in plug.
(3) Turn on cold tap.
(4) Turn on hot tap.
(5) When sufficient water in basin turn off hot tap.
(6) Turn off cold tap.
(7) Take soap.
(8) Put hands and soap in water.
(9) Take soap and hands out of water, rub soap between hands.
(10) Put soap down.
(11) Rub palms and fingers together.
(12) Rub hands together, interlacing fingers.
(13) Rub palm and fingers of right hand over back and fingers of left hand.
(14) Rub palm and fingers of left hand over back and fingers of right hand.
(15) Rinse hands in water.
(16) Pull out plug.

At first the person is physically prompted, the teacher's hands moving his hands, through the whole sequence, and reinforcement is given as soon as the plug has been pulled out. After some repetitions the teacher may sense that the person is beginning to participate in the task; she may then begin to fade the prompts, starting with those for pulling out the plug. When the person can pull out the plug by himself, it will be time to begin fading the prompts for rinsing hands. And so on.

There is a special problem with teaching washing, which is that it involves quantities of water. Children often love playing with water, and this may be an advantage in teaching washing, in that the child enjoys it. However, what he enjoys doing with the water may be quite unconnected with washing — overfilling the basin, drinking from the tap, smacking the water in the basin or pressing a hand under the tap to make the water fly everywhere. The teacher may have to continue with a certain amount of prompting or at least of shadowing of the child's hands, even when he has become quite skilful at some of the steps in the chain, to ensure that he does not make an almighty mess. (It may also of course be an excellent idea to allow him to indulge in this messy water play at other times when he and his surroundings are suitably prepared.)

Because hand washing is relatively enjoyable, it may be better to regard it as one complete task, while the less enjoyable hand drying may be regarded as another, to be taught separately. Baker *et al.* insist that drying should be taught before washing, presumably because they see the two as a single chain of events. However, there seems no need for this, and indeed there may be some advantage in teaching, and reinforcing, the two tasks separately; if chaining scales are better constructed in really small steps, it may also be helpful if the scales themselves are not too extended.

TOOTH BRUSHING

Cleaning teeth has received more attention in the literature, perhaps because it seems technically more demanding than washing. Abramson and Wunderlich (1972) trained nine boys (mean CA 12.4, mean PPVT MA 2.8). Out of a maximum possible score of 19 the mean pre-training score for the eight boys who completed the programme was 11, and the post-training mean was 16. The boys were trained first to select their own brush and paste, then to apply paste to brush, finally to brush the left, middle and right sides five times each. The major change was found in the last stage: pre-training they brushed only 10 per cent of the time, whereas in post-training checks they were observed to brush 81 per cent of the time. Wehman (1974) used a token system to improve tooth brushing by 15 institutionalised women. Stars, exchangeable for a variety of treats, were given for proper tooth brushing, which was checked by an independent observer. Over a 60-day period the success rate was 92 per cent (831 stars earned out of a possible 900), and at the end of the period other women on the ward had asked and been allowed to join the scheme. Smeets *et al.* (1976), in a replication of the study of Horner and Keilitz (1975), used a 14-stage tooth-brushing programme with four young adults with severe mental handicaps, all of whom had some speech. Observations of normal ward procedure showed that attendants would turn on a tap, put toothpaste on the brush and then leave the residents to get on with it. Some residents, however, 'would just dispose of the toothbrush, swallow the excess water and toothpaste and wait for the attendants to wipe their mouths'. The programme, using verbal instructions, demonstration and physical guidance which was gradually faded, resulted in considerable improvement in the performance of all four subjects. A subsequent study (Bouter and Smeets, 1979) explored ways of teaching another group of similar young adults to brush the inside surfaces of their teeth (which had been mastered by none of those in the previous study), and of facilitating maintenance through the systematic fading of feedback during training. Seven of the eight young people learned and maintained the skill, but the authors point out that generalisation may not have been achieved and suggest ways in which this could be tackled in future studies.

Other tooth-brushing programmes are given in the parent manuals, with the number of steps ranging from 5 (Baker *et al.*) to 22 (Carr) to 29 (Baldwin *et al.*), the differences being accounted for by differences in the size of the steps and in the extent of the programmes; Baldwin *et al.* and Carr include putting the toothpaste on the brush while Baker *et al.* suggest this be done by the mother. Carr points out that the most difficult part to teach will usually be the brushing of inner surfaces, and this was found to be the case in the study by Smeets *et al.*.

Electric toothbrushes are commended (Baldwin *et al.*), and an earlier study (Aronwitz and Conroy, 1969) found that an electric toothbrush was more effective than a conventional one in reducing gingival inflammation and in cleaning the teeth, but was slightly less effective in reducing plaque (the substance responsible for the destruction of tooth enamel). A plaque-identifying material may be bought at chemists which, used as a mouth-wash, shows up plaque as a cherry-red substance on the teeth, and this may then be removed by scraping or brushing with a conventional toothbrush; probably both kinds of brush have a place in the dental care of people with mental handicaps.

DRESSING

While dressing is not the most important of the self-help skills, a child or adult who can manage her clothes by herself has taken another step towards independence and one that she may find very gratifying. Although the major dressing occasions are limited to morning and evening, the skills may also be practised at toileting times and when changing for games, swimming, going out and so on.

As with other self-help skills, teaching dressing relies on observation and functional analysis, prompting, fading, breaking down the task into small steps, chaining and reinforcement. The first step is to observe what the person is able to do for herself and where her difficulties occur. In making these preliminary observations it may be helpful to use a chaining scale for each garment, either one of the published scales (Baker *et al.*, 1976; Baldwin *et al.*, 1973; Carr, 1980; Martin *et al.*, 1971a; Minge and Ball, 1967; Moore and Carr, 1976) or one devised for the occasion, and to note at which stage the person fails to complete the task. Supposing it were decided to look at a child's ability to put on her vest and to use the scale given by Moore and Carr (1976). The teacher will start at the beginning of the task, at Stage 6; he will lay the vest on the bed and say to the child, 'Put your vest on'. If the child does not carry out the instruction, the teacher moves to Stage 5, and then if necessary through the whole scale, as follows:

Stage 5. Vest handed to child.
Stage 4. Vest handed to child rolled up ready to go over her head.
Stage 3. Vest put over child's head.
Stage 2. Vest put over child's head, one arm pulled through armhole.
Stage 1. Vest put over child's head, both arms pulled through armholes and vest pulled down to rib level.

If the child succeeds at any stage, then the following stage is the starting point for teaching. Let us say that the child can manage Stage 1 — that is, that she can pull the vest down from rib level — and that the teacher has decided to use backward chaining. The teacher then begins by putting the vest over the child's head and putting one arm through an armhole. He then tells the child, 'Put your vest on' and prompts the child to put the second arm through its armhole; after this, the child pulls down the vest and is given her reinforcement. Subsequently, the teacher fades the prompts on Stage 2, and, when the child has mastered this stage, moves on to training Stage 3. And so on through the stages until eventually the child is able to put on her vest with no help from start to finish.

Other garments, pants, socks, shirt, trousers, dress, jumper, cardigan, etc., may be taught similarly, using available scales or, if preferred, drawing up new ones. The teacher who wants to draw up a new scale should herself go through the process of putting on or taking off the garment, working slowly step by step, and noting where in the process difficulties are likely to occur. (It is a salutory experience; normally we dress and undress so mechanically that we have little idea of how we go about it.) Undressing may be taught in the same stepwise fashion, and as a rule is rather easier to teach. If at any point difficulties arise in teaching either dressing or undressing, the teacher should check, first, whether the reinforcer is really an effective one; and second, whether the step he is teaching is too big. For example, supposing that the child learning to put on his vest made little progress at Stage 2 (putting the second arm through the armhole). The teacher would break this step down into a series of smaller ones: 2a, teacher puts second arm halfway through armhole; 2b, puts wrist of second arm through armhole; 2c, puts hand up to but not through armhole, 2d, doubles arm up against ribs under vest. When the steps are smaller the chances of the child's success are greater.

Many people prefer to teach dressing and undressing at the normal times for these activities — morning and evening — and to give only one trial of each garment on each occasion; so the child learns in a way similar to that for normal children. This will probably save the child from becoming bored with the task, but may mean that, because of limited practice, the teaching is spread over a long period. If the teaching cannot be carried out at normal times, it is worth-while using training sessions at other times (Martin *et al.*, 1971a, Minge and Ball, 1967), and teaching may still be successful even if not carried out every day of the week (Moore and Carr, 1976).

When a child or adult is being taught to dress himself, the teacher has to decide how far the teaching should go. Is it enough to ask that the person should simply get the garments on to his body or should he also be expected to do up fastenings — buttons, poppers, zips, buckles, laces? Should he start with his clothes laid out for him or be expected to get them out of the cupboard? Should he be told what to wear or choose his clothes himself? All of this will depend partly on the person's ability and partly on how his progress goes. Fastenings often seem impossibly daunting to teach, but even people with severe handicaps can master buttons and zips. Even shoe laces, which at first sight seem to demand a near-genius level of combined manipulative and spatial skills, can be taught providing the steps in the task are small enough, and the use of broad football-boot laces, each of a different colour, also helps in the early stages.

Programmes for tying shoe laces in a knot and bow are given in all three parent manuals and in Martin *et al.*; all four use different approaches, so there is ample choice. On the printed page, even with illustrations (Martin *et al.*, 1971a; Baldwin *et al.*, 1973) these programmes are difficult to follow, but they become clearer when the instructions are tried out in practice.

Besides programmes for basic garments and fastenings, others are described which are less usual but potentially useful: threading and buckling a belt, and hanging up clothes on a hanger (Baker *et al.*, 1976), knowing inside from outside (Martin *et al.*, 1971a; Carr, 1980), putting on a bra (Martin *et al.*, 1971a), and knowing which shoe to put on which foot (Carr, 1980).

All the studies and manuals draw attention to the fact that a particular part of a particular dressing programme may cause difficulties and that this may be different with different people. Minge and Ball (1967) found that some girls had great difficulty in learning to remove a dress when given only a spoken direction, and some to take and put on a dress — the difficulty here being apparently in grasping the garment. Martin *et al.* found that over two-thirds of the total average time (10 hours 54 minutes) spent in teaching girls to put on a sweater went in teaching them to discriminate inside from outside. For the boy in Moore and Carr's study the major difficulty was in pulling up a sock placed half-way over his heel. Responses that occur later in the chain in a backward chaining programme have been found more difficult to teach than those that occur earlier (Kazdin, 1977), perhaps because they are further removed from reinforcement. This explanation could apply to the results of Minge and Ball, who used backward chaining, but not to those of Martin *et al.*, who used forward chaining and found the greatest difficulty with the first step; nor to that of Moore and Carr, where the major problem occurred in the second step of the (backward) chaining scale. It may be that although some parts of a process are generally found especially difficult — getting a pullover over the head (Baker *et al.*) or the second arm in a jacket (Carr, 1980) — other difficulties may arise idiosyncratically, and teachers should be prepared for and ready to tackle these.

Although dressing skills can be taught, it is not always easy to do so, and the group programmes reported (Martin *et al.*, 1971a; Song *et al.*, 1976; Minge and Ball, 1967; Monaco *et al.*, 1968) describe limited success in the limited time for which the programmes ran, although it is possible that within the groups there were individuals who became independent in dressing, as has been described elsewhere (Moore and Carr, 1976). Minge and Ball's programme, with six girls chosen because they were 'amongst those with the fewest self-help abilities in the hospital', ran for six months, each girl receiving two 15-minute training sessions a day. Mean scores, on a situational test, improved significantly from 7.88 to 19.75, the comparable figures for a control group being 13.4 and 15.6. However, the greatest improvement was found on attentional items ('Look at me', etc.), with virtually no change in the girls' ability to put the garments on. Martin *et al.* used 15- to 30-minute training sessions each day; the average number of sessions per garment varied from 36 (lacing and tying shoe on foot) to 3 (putting on undershirt). Not every girl was trained on each item, and the percentage of the number undergoing training (ranging from 8 to 2 girls) who reached competence varied from 100 (e.g. putting on undershirt) to 50 (putting on sweater). Much greater success was achieved by Azrin *et al.* (1976). In a characteristically rapid programme seven 'profoundly retarded' adults were taught to dress and undress themselves. The average time taken in training to reach criterion was 12 hours over three or four training days (compared with a maximum estimate of 65 hours over 6 months in the study by Minge and Ball). The students in the study by Azrin *et al.* had an average CA of 31 and an average MA under 1½ years on the Stanford Binet. Each student had two training sessions a day, each session lasting two to three hours; undressing was taught before dressing; a 'forward sequence' was used, with the student participating fully in the early as well as in the later stages of each dressing process; each trial involved all garments, instead of concentrating on one at a time; and emphasis was laid on the use of physical prompting and on the use of near-continuous praise and stroking as reinforcers. A dressing–undressing test showed that, before training, students averaged less than 10 per cent success, whereas the average score after training was 90 per cent. This study demonstrates remarkably effective teaching of people with very severe handicaps. It will be interesting to see whether other workers using these methods are able to replicate these results.

Azrin *et al.* excluded from their study twelve students with physical disabilities, and it seems probable that whereas some people with mental handicaps will be able to attain high levels of competence others will have particular difficulties. For them it may be unrealistic to aim for the most advanced skills, and we may instead try to give them as much independence as possible, while not making too many demands on them. This may mean using clothing adapted

151

to their needs (Waters, 1970) — loose garments and simplified fastenings, jumpers with wide necks, trousers with elasticated waists, slip-on shoes. Even for potentially capable people these may be valuable in the early stages of teaching (Azrin *et al.*, 1976); for more limited people they may make the difference between incompetence and independence. More able people on the other hand may need to learn more advanced skills, such as selection of appropriate clothing (Nutter and Reid, 1978) and grooming skills (Doleys *et al.*, 1981).

FEEDING

Self-feeding is one of the most enjoyable of the self-help skills to teach, partly because it is a relatively simple skill and partly because most people like their food, so that the food itself may be a powerful reinforcer, although Richman *et al.* (1980) suggest that the effectiveness of food as a reinforcer may vary significantly from one person to another. Before starting a feeding programme it is necessary to find out just what the person can and cannot do for herself during mealtimes. Indeed the problem may be not that she cannot feed herself but that she engages in some inappropriate behaviour during the meal such as spitting out food, stealing food from others or hurling her plate across the dining room. The checklist in Table 9.1 shows one way of making a preliminary assessment of assets and deficits (others are also available — e.g. Gunzburg, 1965).

It is not possible to cover all these problems in detail, but some examples will be given from each of the three areas: self-feeding skills, social training and behaviour problems.

Before beginning to teach the person to feed herself, it is important to see that she is comfortably seated, with her feet resting on the floor, or if she is not tall enough for that, on a box or other support; the table top should be at her waist level so that she can see and reach over the table easily. For those who have difficulty in manipulation, a number of aids are available, such as rubber handles to slip on to cutlery for easier gripping, suction mats to prevent crockery from slipping, and plateguards to help scooping (for a selective list of aids and stockists, see Carr, 1980). During assessment food preferences should emerge, and it is of course best to start training using foods that the person is fond of. Some foods may be selected as being specially appropriate to some stages in training; for instance in teaching finger-feeding, pieces of toast, apple, biscuit or banana are

Table 9.1: Self-care at meals

A. Eating skills	Cannot	Can with help	Can by self but messy	Can by self neatly
Chews adequately				
Tries to feed self with fingers				
Eats with spoon				
Eats with spoon and fork				
Eats with fork alone				
Uses fork and knife				
Uses knife as pusher				
Cuts with knife				
Spreads with knife				
Drinks from cup				
B. Social Training				
Finds own place and sits				
Sits still during meals				
Waits for others to finish				
Lays table				
Pours from jug				
Serves with spoon				
Carries plate				
Passes plates				

C. Behaviour problems	Often	Sometimes	Rarely	Never
Uses fingers unnecessarily				
Tips drink over				
Throws or tips food				
Grabs other people's food				
Regurgitates food				
Faddiness about food				
Bolts food				
Excessively slow				
Eats from plate with mouth				

good, and in teaching spoon-feeding soft rather glutinous foods which are easy to scoop and keep on the spoon, like mashed potato, mince and apple sauce, are best.

Teaching self-feeding

Spoon-feeding

This task may be seen as a series of small steps. The teacher first loads the spoon, scooping some food into it: this is the most difficult step in self-feeding and is best taught last. The steps are:

(1) holding the spoon;
(2) taking the loaded spoon from the plate to the mouth without spilling;
(3) taking the food from the spoon into the mouth;
(4) returning the spoon to the plate.

The teacher should position herself behind the person rather than to the side of or facing him, so that the teacher's hand can move the person's hand in a natural hand-to-mouth movement. The teacher closes her hand over the person's hand (not over the spoon) and prompts the person to take the spoon to his mouth, tip the food into his mouth and return the spoon to his plate. Having prompted the person in this way for several mouthfuls, the teacher can begin gradually to fade the prompts as she feels the person begin to participate in the action. This procedure is known as graduated guidance (Westling and Murden, 1978). Since for many people the food itself is the reinforcer for taking the spoon to his mouth, it is often preferable to regard replacing the spoon on the plate as a separate task. In this case the prompts will be faded first on step (3), the teacher releasing her grip on the person's hand just as the spoon is going into his mouth, so that the person completes this last step himself. When this stage is done successfully, the teacher now slackens her grip when the spoon is very slightly further from the mouth. There are in fact a number of sub-steps between steps (3) and (2), and it is important not to try to go too fast or failure may ensue. As already mentioned, the most difficult part to teach in the spoon-feeding chain seems to be loading the spoon and this should be taught after the chain of steps involved in taking the spoon to the mouth and replacing it on the plate has been mastered. Since the scooping does not lead immediately to the reinforcement (the food), it may be worth giving extra reinforcement (a word of praise, perhaps, or a stroke of the cheek) immediately the scooping has been accomplished. Where the difficulty has an unusual cause, an unconventional remedy may be called for. One boy who persistently failed to learn to scoop his food was found to be failing because he would use his fingers to push the food on to his spoon (Song and Gandhi, 1974). This was dealt with by tying one hand to his side and putting a sock over the other, the spoon being then tied to the sock-covered hand in a convenient position for scooping. The boy then successfully learnt to scoop the food, and when two weeks later the sock was no longer put over his hand he continued to use the spoon appropriately.

In the following example we describe how a 13-year-old with an estimated mental age of 6 months was taught to feed himself within 5 days. Tony had been fed all his life. At 13 he was admitted to a special unit on a short-term basis, and it was decided to try to teach him to feed himself. As Tony was particularly fond of ice cream he was given this as a dessert and, after having been fed his first course as usual, he was prompted to feed himself the first four spoonsful of ice cream, the rest being fed to him as before. Initially the nurse teaching him had thought to use praise as an additional reward but each time she said, 'Good boy, Tony!' he turned round to look at her for several seconds. She stopped using praise, and the teaching progressed faster. Over the next two days Tony progressed from feeding himself four spoonsful of ice cream to feeding himself the whole course, and by the third day he needed help only in loading the spoon. The nurse gradually faded her prompts on this part of the action, letting Tony take over more and more of the scooping. At first Tony often used his unoccupied hand to play with the food so the nurse held this hand on the edge of the plate, which also helped to steady the plate. By the end of the fifth day Tony was eating independently and without a great deal of mess.

Using the same methods of prompting, fading and backward chaining, other self-feeding skills, such as drinking from a cup, using a fork and cutting and spreading with a knife, may be taught; programmes for these are found in the parent manuals (Baker *et al.*, 1976; Baldwin *et al.*, 1973; Carr, 1980). An additional technique, also aimed at fading prompts but in a rather different way, is that of 'tactile cue fading' (Westling and Murden, 1978), in which prompts given first to the child's hand are gradually shifted to the wrist, then if necessary up the arm to the elbow and shoulder (Larsen Bricker, 1968, quoted in Song and Gandhi, 1974). Alternatively, modelling may be considered as a teaching method, and was used by Nelson *et al.* (1975) and by O'Brien and Azrin (1972), although both studies found prompting to be superior. Modelling may also be useful for those people averse to prompting, though some of these may be helped by desensitisation.

Most programmes to teach self-feeding have assumed that this is best done in normal mealtimes. Richman *et al.* (1980) compared two groups of children with severe to profound mental handicaps who were taught to use a fork. One group was taught in normal mealtimes, the other received prior teaching in the classroom using bite-size pieces of make-believe 'food' (which was removed from the fork when it was three inches from the child's mouth) and social reinforcers. Despite the apparently artificial nature of this training, the three children taught by this method learnt and maintained their skills better than did the three taught by the more conventional method, suggesting that it is not essential for all teaching of feeding skills to take place at mealtimes.

Teaching chewing

For people who will only eat very smooth, liquidised food it may be possible to introduce first very small and then larger lumps into their food, or to make the food gradually thicker. Four-year-old autistic Lisa only ate liquidised food or else sucked food such as biscuits until it dissolved in her mouth. For a few days her food was made very slightly thicker each day, then, when the consistency had become fairly solid, it was thoroughly mashed with a fork rather than being liquidised. At this time only foods that could be easily mashed were used, such as potatoes, and peas mixed with gravy. Then a few small pieces of minced beef or carrots were added. In this way Lisa progressed to being able to accept a more normal meal although her food was always cut up into small pieces. Concurrently, Lisa was given long pieces of food to hold in her fingers such as carrot sticks and hard rusks that she could not dissolve by sucking, and she was encouraged to bite off a piece: one end was placed in her mouth and the teacher prompted Lisa to pull gently at the other end. When a piece was bitten off Lisa's jaws were gently moved up and down to encourage her to chew the piece of food. Someone who imitates well may watch and imitate the teacher's chewing: sometimes letting the person watch himself in a mirror helps.

When appropriate eating skills have been learnt, care must be taken to ensure that they are maintained; without post-training, both staff and learners may revert to pre-training levels (Albin, 1977; O'Brien *et al.*, 1972).

Teaching appropriate social behaviour at mealtimes

Although some people with mental handicaps will not be able to learn all the skills listed in the assessment chart, most should be able to learn to sit still between courses or wait to be served, perhaps to lay the table, help serve the food, stack the plates and clear away after the meal. Indeed these tasks may even be used as reinforcers for appropriate mealtime behaviours; 12-year-old Joey, who enjoyed clearing away, was allowed to do this if he did not throw food during the meal. Other people with more severe handicaps may need to learn to sit at table or wait their turn to be served. Timmy would not sit at table and so was fed by an adult who followed him around the room popping in a spoonful whenever he was stationary enough to receive one. Staff tried prompting Timmy to sit at the table, but he reacted with tantrums and aggression, so it was decided to use a shaping procedure. Instead of being fed wherever he happened to be, Timmy was only fed when he wandered within three feet of the dining table. When he was spending most of his time within three feet he was fed only when he was within two feet, then one foot of the table. Following this the teacher sat at the table and Timmy had to come to her when he was ready for his next mouthful; then he was required to touch his own chair before being fed, then have his arm over the chair, then his arm and one leg. Within two months Timmy was sitting at the table for all meals, and was then ready to begin learning to feed himself.

A different problem was presented by Sam, a large 14-year-old who would sit down at the table as soon as he was taken to the dining room but, if his dinner was not given to him immediately, would scream, kick the table over and flail about. Similarly if his second course did not appear as soon as his first was finished, he would go through the same procedure, and as soon as he had finished eating he would leave the table. These problems were tackled by very gradually increasing the length of time that Sam had to wait. At first his dinner was always ready for him when he sat down, but when he had finished that a helper held him still for three seconds, praising him for sitting before giving him his pudding. Over two days the three seconds were extended to five, then to seven, and so on until Sam would cheerfully wait three or four minutes for his second course. Later on, waiting at the beginning and end of meals was dealt with in the same way.

An important feature of the programmes for both Timmy and Sam was the fine grading of the steps by which they progressed. Each new requirement of the child was only marginally more difficult than the last, thus maximising the chances of the child's co-operation and success.

Good table manners and special skills in ordering, paying, etc. are required when meals are being taken in public. Van den Pol *et al.* (1981), working with three young adults, used ten hours of classroom training to teach appropriate behaviours, then checked the students' performance in two different fast-food restaurants and found this to compare favourably with a normative sample. The authors comment on the economy of classroom training but speculate that this may have been successful partly because the students had all had considerable prior experience of restaurant eating, and suggest that if this is not so then students might need more *in vivo* training.

Other mealtime problems

The most frequently encountered undesirable behaviours are inappropriate use of fingers: troughing, or pigging (putting the face down to the plate or eating food spilled on to the table); eating too fast or too slowly; stealing; throwing or tipping plates; and excessive faddiness. A number of studies have described procedures to deal with these (Barton *et al.*, 1970; Henriksen and Doughty, 1976; Martin *et al.*, 1971b), the most often used technique being time-out (Westling and Murden, 1978). Time-out (from access to food) is effective in reducing undesirable mealtime behaviours if the food itself is a reinforcer (although it will not be useful for those people who do not like or are indifferent to food). If on the other hand it is attention from adults or peers that is maintaining the undesirable behaviour, then time-out from this type of reinforcement may solve the problem. Overcorrection and brief restraint may also be considered, but which techniques are used in any one case will depend on the person, and the programme should always be evaluated in the light of his response to it. More rapid learning of appropriate behaviour may be achieved by using the 'mini-meal' method (Azrin and Armstrong, 1973). Each meal is divided into three portions and the child is given hourly training in feeding throughout the day. Not only does this enable the child to have more teaching sessions each day, but satiation problems are reduced. The 'mini-meal' method may be used to teach self-feeding skills as well as to reduce unpleasant eating behaviour.

Helen, a seven-year-old with Down's syndrome, exhibited a variety of unacceptable eating habits but all were eliminated over a period of seven weeks. The main problem was food stealing; as soon as Helen finished her own meal she helped herself from other children's plates, and when the meal was being served she would grab food from the serving dishes. In addition she would push food on to her spoon with her fingers, and she gobbled, shovelling in one mouthful after another. The result was unsightly and unpleasant mealtimes for everybody around and particularly for her mother, who felt that Helen should eat with the rest of the family. Stealing was tackled first. As soon as Helen attempted to steal food, any that she had managed to get was removed and her hands were held to her sides for a count of 20. Food stealing rapidly decreased. A fork in her other hand solved the problem of Helen's using her fingers to push food on to her spoon. When gobbling was the target behaviour, time-out was considered (removing her plate for 20 seconds), but as brief restraint had been so successful in eliminating stealing this was used again. Each time Helen attempted to put food in her mouth before she had swallowed the previous mouthful, she was told, 'Hands down', and her hands were held as before. Helen gradually learnt to put her hands down when she was told to without the need for restraint. Eight weeks after the start of the programme Helen's mother reported that mealtimes were no longer a nightmare, and that the family could sit down at table knowing that Helen would eat without making much mess and only from her own plate.

An interesting programme to deal with disruptive mealtime behaviours in an adult woman with severe mental handicap is described by de Kock *et al.* (1984). Using the 'least aversive' approach, they focused on differential reinforcement of appropriate behaviours, resulting in a significant increase in these and a decrease in disruptive behaviours at mealtimes.

CONCLUSIONS

Teaching self-help skills to people with mental handicaps takes time and effort. It is not surprising that some parents and other caregivers are slow to embark on it, the more so because people with mental handicaps themselves tend to accept help and do not, as normal young children will, insist on trying to do things for themselves. Specialist teaching using behaviour modification methods can enable even those with severe handicaps to attain some of the skills, though many questions remain as to the most effective ways in which these methods may be applied. No research exists to show, for example, whether forward or backward chaining is the more effective. Until such research is done we prefer backward chaining, since this teaching leads directly to completion of the task and hence to reinforcement; others, however, have specifically preferred forward chaining (Azrin *et al.*, 1976).

The skills discussed in this chapter and the next are the essential ones for daily living, but others may also be seen as potentially valuable and worth attempting. Among the programmes described in the literature are those to teach people with mental handicaps to use public transport (Gunzburg, 1968; Hughson and Brown, 1975; Neef *et al.*, 1978); to differentiate between coins (McDonagh *et al.*, 1984; Wunderlich, 1972), and to go shopping (Matson, 1981); to swim (Bundschuh *et al.*, 1972), to use a telephone (Karen *et al.*, 1985; Leff, 1984; Smith and Meyers, 1979), to do their own laundry (Thompson *et al.*, 1982) and mending (Cronin and Cuvo, 1979); to respond to a fire alarm (Bertsch *et al.*, 1984; Cohen, 1984; Luiselli, 1984); to live independently (Crnic and Pym, 1979; Perske and Marquis, 1973); and to make appropriate use of leisure time (Schleien *et al.*, 1981). These studies show that skills that might have been thought too advanced for the people concerned have been successfully acquired through systematic teaching.

The area of self-help skills is one in which parents are often keen to be involved with the teaching, and one in which they have been seen as particularly appropriate teachers (Baker *et al.*, 1976; Baldwin *et al.*, 1973). It is not always easy for parents (or others) to see how they should set about teaching these skills, and the published accounts and scales should be helpful. In future studies it is to be hoped that not only group results but also individual programmes will be reported, and that not only successes but also failures and the reasons for them, and difficulties and how these were tackled, will be described. Such details are often more informative than the more usual bland descriptions of plain sailing, and are a good deal more encouraging to others who have to contend with setbacks in their teaching.

10

Toilet Training

Barbara Wilson and Hilary Davison

Appropriate toileting is arguably the most important single self-help skill for people with mental handicap to learn. The incontinent child runs the risk of skin infections, causes a great deal of unpleasant work for carers, and is likely to remain socially unacceptable. Incontinence has in the past been a major factor in determining whether a child is admitted to long-term care (McCoull, 1969–71; Wing, 1971). A survey of three hospitals (Torpy, 1981) indicated that incontinence was a major handicap preventing certain members of the adult population with mental handicap from being resettled from institutions into the community. For such reasons continence is seen as an important skill which we must attempt to teach to virtually all people with mental handicap.

Toilet training involves several different skills. Besides learning bladder and bowel control and appropriate voiding, the person needs to learn to ask to go to the toilet, and eventually make his own way there. He may also need to learn skills such as pulling his pants up and down, wiping his bottom, pulling the chain and washing his hands.

TO TRAIN OR NOT TO TRAIN?

Usually, children without mental handicap are dry during the day by about two years of age, and by the age of three years normal urinary control should be established (Campbell, 1970; Muellner, 1960). Although in general, when devising behavioural programmes, developmental level should be taken into account, it should be recognised that people with severe mental handicaps may be capable of being toilet trained even though they may not have reached a

161

mental age of two years. Subjects with IQs below 20 were excluded from Sloop and Kennedy's study (1973), but Azrin and Foxx (1971) succeeded in toilet training nine adults with a mean IQ of 14 and a range of 7 to 45. An adaptation of Azrin's procedure has been used with handicapped children with a mental age of less than two years at Hilda Lewis House, Bethlem Royal Hospial, a unit for multiply handicapped children. One programme involved working with a 13-year-old boy functioning at a 5 to 6-month level on the Bayley Scales of Infant Development. Baseline data over six days showed that he used the toilet only once and was wet 14 times. At the end of two weeks' intensive toileting he was using the toilet between 5 and 13 times a day, and was wet less than once a day. He was discharged before completion of the programme, but his mother toileted him at home every half-hour during the day, and for two weeks he averaged one accident daily. The number of accidents then increased somewhat, but not to the baseline level. The findings suggest that children with a mental age below one year can be toilet trained, although greater success is likely with those of a higher developmental level. Smith and Smith (1977) found it quicker to train people below the age of 20 than those over 25, and with a Vineland social age of two years or more rather than below two years. Nevertheless, with longer training the older, less sociable group reached comparable levels of success, achieving an 89 per cent reduction in accident rate in an average of eight to nine weeks compared with five to six weeks for the younger, more sociable group.

GENERAL PRINCIPLES

1. Observation and recording

As with other skills, baseline data are needed prior to any training programme, on such questions as the timing and frequency of toileting accidents, presence or absence of constipation and so forth. A typical observation and recording sheet used at Hilda Lewis House is shown in Table 10.1. For some purposes simpler record charts may be adequate, recording, for example, for one week whether or not the child remained clean and dry over the morning period and again over the afternoon period.

Table 10.1: Toilet chart

NAME.....................   Week Beginning..............

CODES

Urine: Bowels:

Dry = dry pants   BOP = bowels open in pants
Wet = urinated in pants   BOT = bowels open in toilet
UT   = urinated in toilet
NU   = not used toilet

Time	Sunday	Monday	Tuesday	Wednesday	Thursday	Friday	Saturday
7.00–7.30							
7.30–8.00							
8.00–8.30							
8.30–9.00							
9.00–9.30							

and so on through the day

2. The principles of reinforcement

All appropriate behaviour should be reinforced. Depending on the level or stage the child has reached, reinforcement may be given for approaching the toilet, pulling down pants and sitting on the toilet, as well as for elimination in the toilet. Effective reinforcers should be sought (see Chapter 3). Some children, for example, find pulling the chain highly enjoyable and, for this reason, should only be allowed to do this following appropriate behaviour. A musical potty may also be an effective reinforcer and, in addition, will inform the trainer as soon as the child has urinated. It may also serve to draw the child's attention to what he is doing.

3. Providing the most suitable conditions for learning

This includes making sure the person is comfortably seated, so that his feet reach the floor or a platform, and seeing that he has something to hold on to if necessary. It may also mean choosing the best times, those at which the person is most likely to wet or soil, for toilet training — record charts are often useful here. It may also mean providing extra opportunities for urination to occur, by giving extra fluids in order to increase the frequency of urination.

4. Making use of the basic techniques

Shaping, fading, prompting and backward chaining may be necessary for teaching the additional skills needed for independent
toileting behaviour, for example pulling down pants and wiping
bottoms. Training pre-toileting skills may also be necessary. This
may include teaching the person to sit on the toilet for several
minutes at a time, and if a pants alarm (a device to signal inappropriate elimination) is being used, it may be necessary to shape the
person's behaviour so that he does not destroy, dismantle or switch
off the alarm.

DAYTIME ENURESIS

Habit-training

One of the most commonly used methods for eliminating daytime
wetting involves taking the person to the lavatory every half an hour
or 45 minutes and sitting on the toilet for several minutes. If he
urinates, he is rewarded and this procedure alone may result in the
person becoming toilet trained. This is not unlike the method used
by many a mother, who puts her baby on the potty after every feed
and thus manages to avoid several wet nappies. In both situations the
opportunity is provided to urinate in the appropriate place. With
some people this method is successful: they often urinate in the right
place and gradually become able to wait for longer periods before
needing to urinate. Alan was a seven-year-old with Down's
syndrome who had never been toilet trained. A five-day baseline
period during which he was toileted every 30 minutes showed that
he was dry 87 per cent of the time. It was decided, therefore, that
an intensive programme was not necessary and that it was sufficient
to continue toileting Alan every half an hour. Following two
accident-free weeks the intervals were gradually increased, first by
five and then by ten minutes, with continued success.

Other clients may use the lavatory each time they are taken but
are also frequently wet in-between times. In this case it may be
better to change to a shorter interval, say 15 minutes, and then
gradually extend the time. Others may never 'perform' on the potty
or lavatory and can, therefore, never be reinforced for elimination
in the appropriate place.

As this 'habit-training' method is so simple, it may be worth trying before beginning a more intensive type of programme. The trainer must decide how often to toilet the client and how long to leave him there each time. Information on this point may be derived from baseline records. If he is wetting roughly every 20 minutes, then the trainer should begin by taking him just before the next 20-minute interval is over. How long to wait each time is a more difficult question. If he urinates into the lavatory straight away, there is no problem, but if he does not, then three to five minutes seems a reasonable period for him to remain seated — if indeed he will stay seated for that long. Martin, the 13-year-old mentioned earlier, had to be taught to sit on the lavatory for five minutes at a time before toilet training proper could begin. Initially he stood up every 30 seconds or so but, with prompting and reinforcing, learned within four days to remain on the lavatory for five minutes.

There have been several studies in which parents successfully acted as co-therapists in such habit-training treatments for both enuresis and encopresis (Brown and Doolan, 1983; Herbert and Iwaniec, 1981; Slukin, 1975). Habit training has also been instituted successfully in school environments. Richmond (1983) trained four pre-school children at a development unit by getting the teachers to toilet them every 15 minutes in week one, 30 minutes in week two, 1 hour in week three, and so on. They praised the children if they voided appropriately, and reprimanded them and made them help clean and wash their knickers if there was an accident. Wigley *et al.* (1982) report a single case study where a young boy was treated successfully for encopresis using simple habit-training prompted by his teachers in a nurture group at school.

Parker (1984) surveyed 372 families with children suffering from mental and physical disabilities who had been in contact with the Family Fund and who had been recorded as incontinent (although this was not the problem they were seeking help for at that time). Over 200 of these families had received some training, usually in teaching simple habit training — albeit with some degree of rein-forcement. Although many of these training programmes had been co-ordinated between home and school, she found a significant number that had not. Twenty-eight per cent of the children had received training at school but not at home; and a further 13 per cent had received training at home but not at school.

Intensive programmes

The 'habit training' method does not work with all people with mental handicaps and other methods may be needed. The procedure used by Azrin and Foxx (1971) with institutionalised adults can be very effective. Two pieces of apparatus are required for this programme: a pants alarm which sounds whenever the trainee wets his pants, and a toilet alarm which sounds whenever he urinates into the toilet. The main features of this programme are greater opportunities for correct toileting through the use of extra fluids, immediate and consistent correction of reinforcement (made possible by the pants and toilet alarms), reprimands and time-out from positive reinforcement following any 'accidents' and a post-training maintenance procedure to ensure continued success.

Azrin and Foxx's method has been adapted slightly at Hilda Lewis House for use with the severely handicapped children seen there (and might need adapting further for use with adults). The adapted procedure is as follows.

Pre-programme arrangements

(1) Baseline observations and recordings are taken for five days.
(2) The child's day, from 9.00 a.m. to 3.30 p.m., is broken up into half-hour periods and a rota of volunteers is drawn up, each volunteer taking on one or more half-hour periods at a time. The volunteers are drawn from nursing staff, occupational therapists, teachers and psychologists. The child is taken off the programme for lunch (i.e. from 11.30 a.m. to 12.30 p.m.) with the other children.
(3) The toilet area is prepared. If a musical potty or potty chair is to be used, this is taken to the area along with the child's favourite drinks, toys, sweets and other reinforcements, spare pants, pencils, a seat for the trainers and materials for cleaning the child and cleaning the floor. Record sheets and instructions for the trainers are prepared and pinned up in the toilet area. An example of a record sheet is given in Table 10.2.

Table 10.2: Example of record sheet

INTENSIVE TOILET TRAINING

TIME	9.00 9.30	9.30 10.00	10.00 10.30	10.30 11.00	11.00 11.30	11.30 12.00	12.00 12.30
Amount of fluids drunk (number of cups)							
If used toilet (√ or X)							
Time from sitting on toilet to using it							
Reinforcer given for using toilet (√)							

IF DOESN'T USE TOILET, GET CHILD OFF AFTER 20 MINUTES (NO REINFORCEMENT)

If wet pants once off toilet (√ or X)							
Time from getting off toilet to wetting pants							
No. of dry pants checks (with reinforcement for this)							

Signature. . . . .

Comments:

Instructions for trainer

(1) Give the child as much to drink as he will accept. Record the amount on the chart.
(2) After one minute, seat the child on the musical potty/toilet chair.
(3) If he urinates the music will start. We hope this will reinforce the child as well as inform the trainer. In addition give lavish praise (or whatever social reinforcement the child likes) plus edible or other reinforcer if necessary. Remove child from potty/toilet chair.
(4) If he does not urinate, remove him after 20 minutes with no reinforcement.
(5) During the time the child is not on the potty he can play with toys, with the trainer or do whatever he likes. This period may last 10 minutes or may be almost 30 minutes, if the child used the potty immediately.
(6) At five-minute intervals during the time that he is not on the potty the child should feel his pants. If they are dry make a big

167

fuss of him and say, 'Dry pants, good boy'. If they are wet say, sternly, 'Wet pants, bad boy' and change the pants. (This procedure is sometimes changed. If, for example, the child is one who finds a scolding very reinforcing, then, 'Bad boy' is not used. Instead his pants are changed without the trainer saying anything.)

(7) At the end of half an hour the next volunteer will take over and repeat the procedure. Each volunteer should fill in the chart as appropriate throughout the session.

(8) At the end of the day, the chart is taken down, the observations are graphed and the chart for the following day is pinned up.

Ending the programme

If, after two weeks, there is little or no improvement, the teaching is discontinued at least for some weeks. If, after two weeks, the findings are ambiguous, the intensive toileting will be continued. If there is substantial improvement, the intensive training will gradually be faded out and replaced by a more normal toileting procedure. How this is done will depend on the child but it is almost always necessary to ensure that generalisation takes place. To hope that this will occur of its own accord is to invite trouble. The following examples illustrate how intensive toilet-training programmes were faded out for two children.

Following a successful intensive programme for Benjamin, it was decided that he should spend the mornings, i.e. until lunch time, in the toilet area and continue the intensive programme but he should spend the remainder of the day with the other children. During this time Benjamin was taken to the toilet area every half an hour, given his drinks and seated on the toilet. Following elimination, which always occurred within a few minutes, he was taken back to the group. Later Benjamin spent all day with the other children. He was toileted every half an hour, but had no extra fluids. For the succeeding three months Benjamin averaged one 'accident' each week and took himself to the toilet when he needed to go. Benjamin learned very quickly, but with many children it is necessary to proceed more cautiously. Alex, for example, after two weeks' training was taken just outside the toilet area when he was not seated on the potty. The trainer played with him there until the next toileting was due. Over the next few weeks the distance from the toileting area was increased by a few feet each day. Meanwhile the dry-pants check occurred every ten minutes, instead of every five minutes, then every 15 minutes and so on. The extra liquids were gradually reduced over the two weeks following the intensive programme and the schedule of edible reinforcement changed from continuous to partial, although Alex was always praised. Finally the interval between one toileting and the next was slowly increased from 30 to 35 to 40 and more minutes. When he did wet his pants, which was not often, he was scolded and made to wash his pants. The fading procedure took about three weeks, and after this Alex was toileted in the ordinary way with the other children, although occasionally his pants were checked too.

Besides teaching the person to generalised his toileting skills so that he is able to recognise and respond appropriately to the signals from his bladder when he is outside the immediate toilet area, it may, in some cases, be necessary to teach him to use different toilets. In this case it may be necessary to repeat the teaching process in other toilet areas and with other toilets, although it is usual to find that the teaching time becomes progressively shorter as he finds more toilets acceptable and becomes increasingly able to use them.

It may seem rather appalling that a child or adult should spend long periods each day sitting on a potty or lavatory but, in practice, many children at least seem to blossom during intensive programmes. They have the undivided attention of an adult and may well enjoy the finger games, singing games, musical toys and so on. Some trainers only use these games as reinforcement of appropriate urination whereas others play with the child while they are waiting for him to eliminate, using the games to reinforce the child for remaining seated on the toilet for fairly lengthy periods of time.

Smith *et al.* (1975) describe a toilet-training procedure which is also based on Azrin's work. Like Azrin and Foxx, Smith *et al.* used a pants alarm as well as a toilet alarm. The pants alarm is further described in Dixon and Smith (1976). A study by Smith (1979) compared three different toilet-training programmes. The first was 'intensive individual regular potting', i.e. each child was toileted every half an hour or some other regular interval. The second method was 'intensive individual timing' in which the trainer predicted when elimination was likely to occur and toileted the child around that time. The third method also used regular potting but taught several children at once. Both the individual methods resulted in greater reduction of incontinence and greater independence in toileting than the group method. Of the two individual methods regular potting was preferred to timing because it was easier to administer and all staff concerned preferred this method, but little difference was found in the results of the two individual programmes.

NOCTURNAL ENURESIS

Like daytime wetting, nocturnal enuresis is a widespread problem among people with mental handicaps. It has been reported that 79 per cent of four-year-old Down's syndrome children wet the bed at least once a week compared with 27 per cent of non-handicapped four-year-olds (Carr, 1975). Among institutionalised people with mental handicaps, it is estimated that 70 per cent are enuretic (Sugaya, 1967). Some of the main methods for dealing with this problem will be described.

1. Bell-and-pad

Meadow (1977) describes this method whereby the child sleeps on a mesh or foil mat connected to an alarm buzzer which is activated when the child urinates. Meadow also describes some of the common problems that arise in using the method with normal children and that many also occur with people with mental handicaps, though the biggest problem is probably the tendency of their users to disconnect, damage or otherwise interfere with the equipment. It may be worth-while shaping the person's behaviour so that he will accept the apparatus, but the method itself needs reasonable co-operation.

In recent years pants alarms have become more widely available, and as this equipment is more discreet and does not require the mesh or foil mat, it may be more acceptable to some people. However, Fleming (1982) observed that some older boys with whom she used the pants alarm disliked the equipment because they recognised the pad as a sanitary towel. In such cases it may be worth-while shaping the person's behaviour so that he will accept the apparatus. Usually, though, this method like the bell-and-pad requires a degree of reasonable co-operation from the start.

There are several studies of the use of the bell-and-pad method with normal children that have been summarised by Doleys (1977, 1984), Sorotzkin (1984) and Shaffer (1985). Both Sorotzkin and Shaffer, after summarising all the main treatments available for normal children suffering night-time enuresis, conclude that the bell-and-pad method offers the most effective treatment. Its major disadvantage is a high relapse rate: Doleys (1977) found a relapse rate of 41 per cent in his study, a rate also reported by Dische *et al.* (1983). However, the authors of the latter study found that 40 per cent of those who relapsed after initial treatment were successfully trained on retreatment. Others have explored the effects of over-learning (Johnson, 1980; Young and Morgan, 1972); and of inter-mittent schedules (Abelew, 1972; Finley *et al.*, 1973, 1982; Taylor and Turner, 1975). Both of these approaches appear to produce lower relapse rates.

Sloop and Kennedy (1973) found that a group of children with mental handicap treated with the bell-and-pad showed superior results to those treated by being potted several times a night. In an earlier study (Kennedy and Sloop, 1968), four out of eight children reached the criterion of 14 successive dry nights after a seven-week training period. In both these studies all subjects had an IQ above 26, and the age range was from 8 to 18 years. Smith (1981) success-fully trained five adults with mental handicap (IQ range from 18 to 30) using a bell-and-pad. All five subjects reached a criterion of two dry months. She found the amount of time each individual needed for training varied enormously, ranging from 18 to 92 weeks.

Parents of children with mental handicap are often reluctant to use the bell-and-pad method, partly, it seems, because they are afraid of the procedure owing to a lack of understanding of the principles and mechanics of the system. It is understandable that some parents are unwilling to have their child woken and possibly remain awake for some time; they may also have another child sleeping whom they do not wish to be disturbed. However, the latter problem can be overcome by having a buzzer ring in the parents' room. It is also possible to obtain a device that vibrates instead of buzzing when the child urinates, thus avoiding noise altogether. As Sloop and Kennedy have demonstrated, the bell-and-pad can be an effective treatment for some subjects, if parents and others working with children with mental handicap are willing to use it.

2. Retention control

Retention control aims to increase the amount of urine the child will retain before voiding. This method has been used to treat diurnal enuresis in a normal child (Doleys and Wells, 1975). The child is reinforced for not urinating at once when he has reported the need to go to the toilet. The intervals between wanting to go and urinating are gradually increased so that functional bladder capacity is increased. Doleys (1977) summarises eight studies of the effect of retention control training on night wetting. He found that six studies reported success, one had no success, and one achieved partial success. It may be worth trying this method with some people with a mental handicap, particularly those for whom a bell-and-pad seems unsuitable.

Fielding (1980) carried out a careful study of 75 normal children aged 5–14, 45 of whom were night wetters and 30 both day and night wetters. She compared treatments consisting of alarm only with treatments using both alarms and retention control training. She also measured the functional bladder capacity of all her subjects, both before and after treatment. Fielding found that retention control training made no appreciable impact on either daytime or night-time wetters. Furthermore, she found that success in treatment was not accompanied by changes in bladder size. Shaffer *et al.* (1984) found similar results, and both Shaffer (1985) and Sorotzkin (1984) conclude that the evidence for the effectiveness of retention control training is now seriously in doubt. However, Doleys (1984) still thinks that it may be useful for certain daytime wetters, and in some cases of night wetting when used in conjunction with other methods.

Progressive lifting, another method of treating nocturnal enuresis, may be similar to retention control. Progressive lifting (Carr, 1987) involves lifting the sleeping child earlier and earlier in the evening until a time is found at which he is usually still dry. After the child has been lifted at this time for several nights, the time at which he is lifted is very gradually increased, with the aim that he shall become accustomed to being awakened when his bladder is increasingly full (but before voiding). This method was used with Nicky, a nine-year-old Down's syndrome boy, after a star chart had been unsuccessful and his mother had adamantly refused to venture on a trial of the bell-and-pad. Nicky was first lifted at 9.30 p.m. and this was gradually increased over four months, with variable evening success, to 10 p.m. when Nicky, for the first time in his life, began to be occasionally dry in the morning. Nine months later, Nicky was dry through the night approximately 70 per cent of the time, and six months later again this increased to 100 per cent. Progressive lifting is known to have been used in only one other case (Robson, 1988) where dryness was achieved over a two-year period by gradually extending the lifting time to 7am. This method may offer another avenue to explore if other methods fail or are seen as impracticable.

Phibbs and Wells (1982) used a similar method of training with seven adult women with mental handicap who were living in hospital. They collected baseline data over a period of 29 days, each resident being checked every half-hour through the night to find out her usual accident time. The training consisted of each resident being wakened at her usual accident time and being asked if she wished to go to the toilet. If she did she was guided to the toilet. Subjects were also wakened at some point in the early hours of the morning and asked the same question. After seven dry nights the waking time at night was brought forward 15 minutes and the morning call was held back for 15 minutes, thus gradually extending the dry night-time period. During the first four weeks of training, independent visits to the lavatory increased while the number of accidents was reduced. Treatment lasted 14 weeks and all the women remained accident free at one- and four-year follow-ups. It is not clear whether this training increased the functional bladder size or helped the women become more conscious of the need to relieve themselves at night.

3. Dry-bed training

This procedure, described by Azrin *et al.* (1973, 1974), is similar in many respects to the intensive daytime toilet training described by Azrin and Foxx (1971). It requires considerable effort from the trainer over a short period of time but may solve the problem very rapidly. The main features of the programme are:

> positive reinforcement for having a dry bed and for using the lavatory at night;
> practice in getting up during the night to urinate;
> extra fluids to provide more opportunities for urination to occur;
> alarm systems to enable immediate detection of correct toileting;
> and punishment for accidents in the form of reprimands and cleanliness training.

Initially, the trainee is given extra fluids before going to bed, is woken every hour and is led to (or asked to go to) the toilet. If he uses the toilet within five minutes, he is rewarded, taken back to bed, praised for having dry sheets and allowed to go back to sleep for the remainder of the hour. If he does not use the toilet, he is taken back to bed and reinforced for having a dry bed. Reinforcement in both situations includes extra fluids. If the trainee wets his bed, he is woken, scolded, taken to the toilet and then made to change his sheets. After this he is given positive practice in using the toilet: he returns to bed for three minutes, is then taken to the toilet, returns to bed for another three minutes and so on for a 45-minute period. When there is one accident or less a night and the trainee uses the toilet on at least 50 per cent of occasions, he moves on to the second stage of monitored post-training. During this stage, wet beds result in reprimands, cleanliness training and positive practice, but there are no extra fluids and hourly awakenings. Stage two continues until there are seven consecutive accident-free nights when treatment is discontinued although the trainee's bed is inspected each morning and, if wet, he is required to change the sheets and remake the bed. Stage two is reintroduced if two accidents occur within a week.

Azrin and his colleagues used this method with twelve adults with profound mental handicap (mean IQ 12) all of whom wet the bed at least four nights out of twelve but were accident-free during the day. Eight of the patients reached criterion after one night of training, three after two nights and one after three nights. Following this brief period of training, bedwetting for this group occurred at an average rate of 9 per cent during the first week compared with a 50 per cent baseline. This was a reduction in incontinence of 85 per cent during the first week which rose to 95 per cent by the fifth week. There were no relapses during a three-month follow-up period. The method seemed promising in that it worked quickly and with individuals who were functioning at a very low level.

In later studies Azrin modified this package substantially. Most of the modifications had the effect of reducing the intensity of therapist input in administering the training programme, and making it more acceptable to parents. The enuresis alarm was eliminated and the first day of training was shifted to the earlier time frame of 4.00 p.m. to 12.00 midnight (Azrin and Thienes, 1978). Later, the parents conducted the first night of intensive training instead of a therapist (Azrin et al., 1979). Finally, the parents administered the training without any professional involvement, using only a manual (Azrin and Besalel, 1979; Besalel et al., 1980). With all these modifications Azrin and his co-workers found the package to be only marginally less effective than the original full programme.

Not all researchers have found Azrin's modified programme so successful. Bollard and Nettlebeck (1981) found the dry-bed training without the use of an alarm to be only slightly more effective than no training at all. Bollard *et al.* (1982) found that all the children in their study had to use the alarm before treatment was successful. Although studies have replicated Azrin's finding that it is possible to get equally effective results by training the parents to do the work of therapists (Bollard *et al.*, 1982; Griffiths *et al.*, 1982), it seems likely that there will be severe disadvantages in reducing clinicians' input to no more than handing out a manual. Griffiths *et al.* (1982) noted that parents who acted as therapists without either coming into hospital for a first night's training or having a therapist in their own home needed considerable support in the form of regular visits to the clinic and telephone support. Fincham and Spettell (1984) reported that parents who were only given the manual to implement the programme found the dry-bed training considerably less acceptable than those who were trained face to face. Bollard *et al.* (1982) also found that the training programme was more effective if parents were trained in small groups. Obviously, this method has the added advantage of being cost-effective.

To summarise the results of research using Azrin's programme with normal children, it seems that the alarm and the waking schedule are the most important items in the programme. Many of the studies have questioned the ethics of the positive practice and cleanliness training routines, and pointed out that both parents and children found these routines very tedious. In addition, it seems that parents with professional input can be as effective as a professional therapist in administering the programme. There has, however, been very little research looking at the efficacy of the various components of the programme with children with mental handicap.

ENCOPRESIS

Several reviews attempt to classify the various types of encopresis: for example, continuous or discontinuous encopresis; overflow incontinence due to constipation or retention due to anxiety; or the deliberate placing of faeces in inappropriate places (see Doleys, 1984; Hersov, 1985; Levine, 1982). It is likely that most faecal incontinence seen in people who are handicapped mentally is continuous (or primary) encopresis due to skills deficit. However, trainers should be alert to possible emotional or physical factors.

Hersov (1985) emphasises the complexity of the various muscle systems involved in enabling bowel control, and points out that breakdown of control can occur at various stages, the most common being failure to register a sense of urgency when the rectum is full. According to Levine (1982) a common reason for failure of this natural feedback system is stretching of the rectum, caused by retaining large quantities of faeces. This in turn may be caused by a period of constipation or deliberate retention. The faeces become hard as the water is absorbed by the intestine, and the rectal muscles stretch so that they become inefficient both at giving feedback and at pushing material out. Additionally, new softer material can simply seep out and around the old, impacted faeces, thus leading to overflow incontinence. Levine asserts that 'virtually all children with encopresis retain stools, at least intermittently'. There seems to have been no work done looking at the degree of retention among children and adults with mental handicap.

Levine goes on to outline a treatment programme for faecal incontinence, based on his model (above). Many other programmes incorporate the use of mild laxatives in order to promote the number of occasions a child can practise the skill of defaecating. By contrast Levine advocates that after careful assessment, a cathartic dose of laxatives should be given in order to clear the passage fully of old impacted material. Then a regular habit-training toileting programme should begin, accompanied by the use of a mild laxative such as mineral oil. He notes that treatment should continue for a minimum period of six months. Wakefield et al. (1984), like Levine, emphasise the importance of regular toileting and a high-fibre diet. They, however, give great importance to family support and therapy. They teach parents how to do abdominal massage in order to help restore mobility to the colon and rectum.

Another recent development aimed at increasing a child's anal responsiveness has been reported by Olness et al. (1980). Fifty children were given biofeedback training for the purpose of achieving anal-sphincter control. Feedback was in the form of oscilloscope tracings which the children learned to produce by contracting small air-filled balloons positioned at the internal and external anal sphincters. However, such complicated equipment is going to be way beyond the scope of the average clinician or parent, and may be of doubtless use for the person with mental handicap.

Although enuresis and encopresis are physiologically and behaviourally different (Neale, 1963), sometimes teaching bladder control will indirectly result in bowel control (Epstein and McCoy, 1977). Furthermore, behavioural treatments of the two conditions have much in common. Positive reinforcement, for example, is an important part of treatment for both the enuretic and encopretic person and maintains inappropriate bowel habits as well as establishing correct ones (Lal and Lindsley, 1968). It may be more difficult to 'catch' bowel movements than it is to 'catch' urination, as the former occur less frequently. However, just as we can give extra fluids to provide increased opportunities for bladder training, so also it is possible to provide extra opportunities for bowel training, for example with the use of a suppository (Lal and Lindsley, 1968). Ashkenazi (1975) treated a group of encopretic children aged three to twelve years, using positive reinforcement together with suppositories, and pointed out that a suppository may serve as a discriminative stimulus for correct toileting. Other studies have employed a variety of medical and behavioural treatments for encopresis in normal children (Crowley and Armstrong, 1977; Neale, 1963; Tomlinson, 1970; Wright and Bunch, 1977). Studies of mentally handicapped children (and some of those of normal children) often find that some kind of punishment procedure is necessary for inappropriate toileting behaviour. Giles and Wolf (1966) taught five severely mentally handicapped boys to be continent of both faeces and urine by a combination of shaping, positive and negative reinforcement, suppositories and aversive consequences. Their method, however, involves procedures which are unacceptable to those working with people with severe handicaps in this country — for example, depriving the child of meals until appropriate toileting occurred (although each child was fed at least one large meal a day) and tying one boy to the toilet seat for 36 hours over a three-day period. This same child was placed in a restraining jacket and blindfolded following inappropriate responses. Barrett (1969) describes how parents taught their five-and-a-half-year-old retarded non-verbal boy to use the toilet for bowel movements by a combination of praise and edible reinforcement when he did open his bowels in the toilet, together with contingent isolation and restraint when he defaecated in any other place. The restraint and isolation involved placing the boy in a restraining chair and leaving him alone in his room for 30–45 minutes. The period of restraint and isolation, also used with a normal twelve-year-old by Edelman (1971), would now certainly be considered too long, and Hobbs and Forehand (1977) suggest that four minutes is an optimal period for a time-out procedure. In Edelman's case, punishment alone resulted in a decrease but not a cessation of soiling, which only occurred when the girl was negatively reinforced by being allowed to avoid washing up in the evening if she had not soiled.

Doleys (1984) recommends extremely careful assessment of the encopretic behaviour, including an interview, review of medical records, observation of the degree of constipation and detailed behavioural records. He, like McCartney and Holden (1981), emphasise that the behaviours assessed should include not only appropriate toileting but also records of whether there has been appropriate approach behaviour (it has been noted that many people with mental handicap know how to toilet themselves when they are taken to the toilet, but fail to initiate such behaviour themselves); dressing and undressing skills; ability to wipe clean afterwards; and flushing the toilet. McCartney and Holden recommend the use of backward and forward chaining to teach the necessary skills for toileting. Doley recommends the use of standard behavioural techniques: for example, praise and 'stars' for appropriate defaecation and clean pants, and the use of mild punishments (e.g. washing the pants) for inappropriate behaviour. He suggests caution with the aversive consequences because of the dangers of creating difficult parent–child relationships.

Doleys and Arnold (1975) successfully treated an eight-year-old retarded encopretic boy by using a procedure based on Azrin and Foxx's intensive toilet-training methods. This procedure, called 'full cleanliness training', requires the child to clean himself and his clothing following inappropriate toileting behaviour. The boy's parents checked his pants every fifteen to twenty minutes, reinforcing him for dry and clean pants. They also took him to the toilet each hour for about ten minutes, reinforcing him for any attempt to defaecate. On the way to the toilet they asked him if he wanted to open his bowels in order to draw his attention to the discriminative stimuli that precede a bowel movement. Star charts were also used. Any soiling resulted in:

(1) his parents' displeasure;
(2) the boy washing the soiled clothes for at least 15 minutes;
(3) the boy cleaning himself.

A mild laxative was also used during training. Soiling was eliminated by the sixteenth week, although there was some relapse after this when the parents became careless about the full cleanliness training.

To summarise, if simple 'habit training' proves ineffective, there are three methods for dealing with encopresis: positive reinforcement used alone; positive reinforcement used with a suppository or laxative (if these are to be used, the advice of a doctor should be sought); and positive reinforcement used with punishment for inappropriate toileting responses. Habit-training and positive reinforcement were both tried with Daisy, a five-year-old moderately mentally handicapped girl seen regularly by a paediatrician for this. It was felt, however, that a behavioural treatment might be effective. During the first visit to the home, Daisy's mother described how she had recently taught her to overcome her fear of sitting on the toilet by giving her sweets. Daisy had never been known to defaecate into the toilet. For the first month of treatment, Daisy's mother sat her on the toilet each day after breakfast, as soon as she returned from school and before bed. Again, at no time did Daisy defaecate into the toilet. A star chart and reward system were discussed. Daisy's mother was asked to record every day for two weeks where Daisy had her bowel movement (i.e. in her pants, on the floor, in the toilet). A chart was left for this purpose. Still Daisy did not open her bowels into the toilet although she urinated in the toilet quite happily. By this time Daisy had finished school for the summer holiday. It was explained to her that if she used the toilet for a bowel movement she would get a star on her chart. Each star could be exchanged for a packet of sweets and, if she had any stars at all by the time of the psychologist's next visit, she could go to the shops with her and choose an ice cream or something else that she liked. During the first week Daisy used the toilet twice and, by week 8, was only defaecating into the toilet. Figure 10.1 illustrates Daisy's progress. A side-effect of treatment is that Daisy is now dry at night, although this problem had not been tackled directly.

Figure 10.1: Daisy's toileting programme

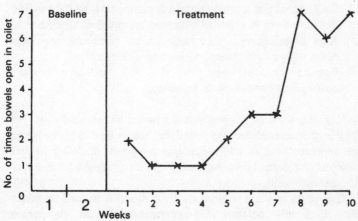

OTHER INAPPROPRIATE TOILETING BEHAVIOURS

Not all toileting problems result from primary enuresis or encopresis. Many people with mental handicaps, even though they are able to use the toilet correctly, engage in various inappropriate toileting behaviours because they like the consequences. Danny, for example, frequently smeared faeces in the classroom. A functional analysis of his smearing showed that it was being maintained by the attention he received each time he smeared, being taken from the classroom by an assistant, bathed, talked to, dressed in clean clothes and, often, given a cup of tea. For this and similar problems, the main treatment method is to remove the positive reinforcement maintaining the behaviour, while ensuring that plenty of positive reinforcement is available for other more acceptable behaviours (Balson, 1973). In Danny's case it was important to see that, as far as possible, he did not receive warm baths, cups of tea and conversation with adults consequent upon his smearing although he was receiving a great deal of adult attention at other times. In this and similar cases it is easier said than done to pay no attention to the smearing. Relatives and staff will, naturally, become angry and want to scold, which may be extremely reinforcing for certain people (see Chapter 3). Furthermore, if the person is not changed immediately, it is difficult to carry on working in the midst of such an unpleasant smell. With Danny, the programme was as follows.

(1) Dress him in a catsuit every day to reduce opportunities to smear.
(2) When he soils his pants, pay no attention for fifteen minutes. Staff agreed that it would be worth putting up with the smell in the short term in order to eliminate the problem altogether.
(3) After fifteen minutes take Danny to the bathroom, wipe him down with a cold flannel without speaking to him.
(4) Bath and change Danny just before he goes home, i.e. not contingently on soiling or smearing.

Soiling and smearing stopped within a matter of two weeks. A very similar programme was used with John, who soiled in his bedroom and appeared to enjoy all the fuss that this produced. When he was removed and cleaned up calmly and the room cleaned in his absence, the smearing stopped.

Overcorrection and restitution may sometimes be used to reduce these kinds of problems. If overcorrection is used, the person cleans up any mess he has made plus cleaning the surrounding area or cleaning the same thing over and over again. This may mean, for example, that he washes his pyjamas and the sheets, scrubs the floor and remakes the bed. Positive practice in this case would include showing the appropriate place for faeces, placing faeces in the lavatory bowl, seating him on the lavatory and similar procedures. A catsuit or pyjama trousers buttoned to pyjamas tops may help to reduce opportunities to smear but, with a person capable of toileting himself, has the disadvantage of making him unable to use the toilet unless he has some means of communicating his need to a caregiver. The advantages and disadvantages of any procedures have to be weighed carefully for each individual.

Other punishment procedures which may be considered include time-out for positive reinforcement and restraint, together with positive reinforcement for not soiling. Again, time-out and restraint must be used for no longer than a few minutes, the person should be under continuous observation, and records should be kept. Furthermore, time-out and restraint should be used contingent on the problem behaviour occurring, and so if the smearing or soiling is discovered some time after the person has actually done it, these methods should not be used.

For certain problems and with some clients 'changing the environment' may provide a solution. Maria, for example, a seven-year-old partly toilet-trained girl, defaecated on the floor in her bedroom approximately twice a week. She did not smear the faeces but covered them with her bedclothes, causing almost as much mess as if she had smeared. Her mother felt that she was frightened to go to the lavatory during the night even though the hall light was left on and a night light was left in Maria's bedroom. Maria's mother tried leaving a potty in the bedroom, but Maria usually knocked this over either by accident or by design. Eventually a heavy wooden commode chair was made by a local carpenter and an eight-week follow-up showed that Maria had defaecated on the floor only once.

Sometimes the problem may be not that the person will not use the toilet but that he uses it too often. This may, of course, be due to an infection or some other physical cause and these should be thoroughly investigated first. There are people, however, who urinate very frequently for no apparent physical reason. Lucy, for example, caused great concern to her teachers by constantly dashing to the toilet and often staying there for ten or fifteen minutes until an adult went to find her. A week's baseline was taken during which

Lucy went to the toilet on average 30 times a day. Lucy's teachers had tried several methods to reduce her visits to the toilet — locking the classroom door, slapping her leg and energetic persuasion — but these had created a number of new problems and had had little effect on the frequency of Lucy's trips to the toilet. No physiological explanation had been found for her frequent micturition and it was felt that the attention she received from staff for going to the toilet was maintaining the behaviour. An extinction programme was considered but rejected as being impracticable. After discussion with the teachers involved it was decided:

Figure 10.2: Treatment

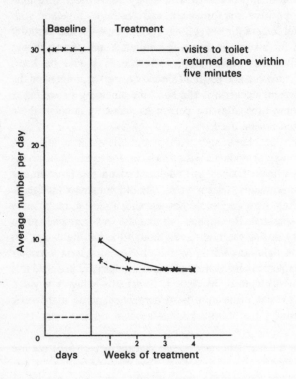

(1) to allow Lucy to go to the toilet no more than once every fifteen minutes. This interval would be increased gradually;

(2) to reward Lucy by attention and approval at frequent intervals so that she would be rewarded for staying in the classroom rather than for going to the toilet;

(3) that when she did go to the toilet, if she had not returned within five minutes, the teacher would collect her, saying once only, 'Time to get off, Lucy', and physically prompting her if necessary. There would be no further verbal communication or eye-to-eye contact on the way back to the classroom.

Figure 10.2 shows that Lucy's visits to the toilet dropped from 30 to seven a day and she returned alone within five minutes on the vast majority of occasions.

CONCLUSIONS

Continence is an important skill for people who are mentally handicapped to acquire because it increases their independence, decreases the workload for caretakers and appears to be a major factor in determining admission into long-term care. Behaviour modification methods can be successfully used to teach toileting even to people with profound handicaps, and technical devices of one sort of another, such as alarm systems and special clothing, may help to speed up or ensure success. The aim here has been to describe a number of methods that may be useful, but no single method can be expected to succeed with every handicapped person; careful observation and analysis must always come first in teaching toilet training as well as other kinds of behaviour.

11

Language and Communication Training

Patricia Howlin

Population studies of people with mental handicap have found a high incidence of language problems. Even in individuals with mild handicaps (IQ 50–69), over 50 per cent are likely to show severe language deficits. In those with moderate handicaps (IQ 35–49) the extent of the language handicap is almost always greater than their overall non-verbal deficit. This gap between verbal and non-verbal skills widens as IQ levels fall. In those with profound handicaps (IQ below 20), spoken language is almost always absent, and comprehension, too, is severely affected (Gould, 1977).

The need to improve communication skills in this group is self-evident. Over the past two decades operant-based procedures have been widely used in an attempt to ameliorate the linguistic deficits commonly associated with mental retardation. Although some of the early studies in this field involved handicapped adults, subsequent research has tended to focus on the acquisition of language skills in children. The effectiveness of language training tends to be limited with older non-verbal subjects, and hence most of the evaluative studies have involved children. For this reason the present chapter concentrates predominantly on the results of training programmes with children rather than adults.

HISTORICAL BACKGROUND

One of the earliest studies to demonstrate the effectiveness of reinforcement techniques in the remediation of language skills was that by Isaacs *et al.* (1960). Using cigarettes and chewing gum as reinforcers, first for lip movements and later for any vocal behaviour, they were able to reinstate speech in two schizophrenic

184

patients who had been mute for over a decade. Later, Sherman (1963, 1965) used similar methods to re-establish speech in institutionalised psychotics. It was about this time, too, that work on the development of speech in non-verbal children began to appear (Hewett, 1965; Hingtgen and Trost, 1964; Lovaas *et al.*, 1966a; Salzinger *et al.*, 1965; Wolf *et al.*, 1964).

Many of these earling training programmes were designed to increase *rates* of vocalisations, rather than the complexity of utterances. Reinforcement (usually with bites of food) would be given for random vocalisation made by the patient, thereby increasing the frequency of such sounds. Subsequent reinforcements would then be given for closer approximations to the sounds required by the therapist.

Lovaas *et al.* (1966a), however, found that although children could learn a few words in this manner, such procedures, despite prolonged training, generally resulted in only very restricted vocabulary growth. The *direct* training of imitative responses, rather than merely reinforcing chance vocalisations, resulted in much greater progress. The success of this approach was subsequently demonstrated in a host of different studies involving children with a wide range of handicaps and varying degrees of language deficit (see Howlin, 1987, for review.) The range of language skills trained has also expanded considerably. Early studies tended to focus on the use of reinforcers to increase appropriate vocalisations or imitative speech, or on the extinction of inappropriate utterances (Cook and Adams, 1966; Hewett, 1965; Nordquist and Wahler, 1973; Sapon, 1966). Treatment programmes have since become much broader in scope and now involve the teaching of relatively complex syntactic, semantic and pragmatic rules (Goetz *et al.*, 1983; Guess *et al.*, 1974; Koegel *et al.*, 1982).

DEVELOPING RECEPTIVE AND EXPRESSIVE LANGUAGE

Typically, language modification programmes have tended to follow the procedures first developed by Lovaas (1966) and Sloane *et al.* (1968). These involve the use of modelling and prompting techniques to increase the frequency of utterances and the use of fading to bring verbalisations under the child's own control. Obviously, however, the stage at which treatment begins and the ultimate goals of training will vary according to the child's basic linguistic competence. The results from a number of research studies make it clear that the success of language intervention programmes is highly dependent on the child's innate language abilty. No matter how intensive the training, attempts to increase verbal imitation in children who are severely handicapped in all aspects of communication are unlikely to be of much practical benefit. Lovaas (1977), for example, reports that it took over 90 000 trials to teach one child just two simple sounds. Instead, for children who lack spontaneous vocalisations, show minimal understanding of speech and have little or no internalised language — as evidenced by imaginative or functional play — it is far better to focus on the development of simple comprehension skills.

INCREASING COMPREHENSION SKILLS

The basic behavioural techniques of prompting and reinforcement are often effective in increasing receptive language skills. Prompts or physical guidance should be combined with clear verbal instructions so that the child learns to associate spoken commands with particular actions. Reinforcement, using praise and possibly some tangible reward, is used to increase co-operation and the rate of correct responses. As the association between the verbal command and the child's action is established, physical prompts or gestures may be withdrawn until the child is able to respond to the spoken instructions alone.

Simple, easily executed movements, such as 'Sit' or 'Stand', should be introduced to begin with. These have the advantage of being readily demonstrable by the therapist, and it is also easy to use physical prompts to ensure that the child carries out the action immediately the command is given. At the same time reinforcement should be given for co-operative responses. Gradually, physical prompts can be faded, and once gross motor actions of this kind are under verbal control a greater range of commands can be introduced. For example, actions such as 'Clap' or 'Wave' might be taught as part of a game sequence. 'Push' or 'Throw' might be taught in relation to playing co-operatively with cars or balls. If, by this stage, interaction with the therapist can be made enjoyable enough in its own right, the need for additional reinforcers, other than praise and verbal encouragement, should be minimal.

Once single word commands can be reliably followed, more complex instructions that are of greater help in daily living can be introduced. These might include instructions such as 'Pick it up',

'Fetch your coat', or 'Go to the toilet'. Again, each stage of the training procedure follows a similar pattern, with physical guidance being used initially to ensure that commands are followed immediately and without error. Verbal and tangible reinforcers are also likely to be needed. Eventually, as appropriate responses become well established, prompts and non-verbal reinforcement can be slowly reduced until the child is able to follow the verbal command alone.

Progress in the early stages of training tends to be slow and arduous, with the first few commands often taking many weeks to acquire. If parents are expected to play a major role in therapy, they may need considerable support at this time if they are not to become discouraged. However, when the child does begin to respond to simple instructions, it is often noticeable that the relationship between him and his parents begins to improve dramatically. When, for the first time, parents are able to control their child's actions by the use of speech and the child himself is able to make some sense of his verbal environment, this frequently results in a marked increase in social interaction and a corresponding decrease in disruptive and non-cooperative behaviours.

EXPRESSIVE LANGUAGE TRAINING

For children who are able to repond to simple commands and already make some spontaneous sounds, training may focus more directly on the development of expressive skills. Typically, the way in which this is done to begin with is to reward the child simply for attending to the therapist when instructed. Training direct eye contact is not necessary and may well interfere with the success of the language programme, but it is essential that the child attends to the therapist and to the materials used in therapy. Physical prompts may be needed to establish such behaviour, but once this is achieved specific training in sound imitation can begin.

To start with, this usually concentrates on sounds that are already frequently emitted by the child and, therefore, relatively easy to bring under control. For example, in the case of a child who constantly repeats the sound /Ba-Ba-Ba/ the therapist might echo this sound after him, and then reinforce the child when he makes his /Ba/ sound again shortly afterwards.

Using sounds that already appear frequently in the child's repertoire increases the likelihood of his 'copying' the therapist's vocalisation and being reinforced for this, and thus also increases the likelihood of his making such sounds more frequently thereafter. It is more difficult to teach children vocalisations that are not already in their repertoire, and work by Koegel *et al.* (1982) has shown that the acquisition of *novel* sounds is a relatively slow process. Nevertheless, verbal and kinaesthetic prompts may be of some help in extending the range of vocalisations made by the child (Nelson and Evans, 1968). Sounds such as /B/ or /oo/ are much easier to demonstrate visually and to shape physically (for example, by gently pushing the child's lips together or pulling them forward) than guttural sounds such as /K/ or /G/.

At first *any* sound which the child makes following the therapist's stimulus-sound should be reinforced immediately, even if this bears little resemblance to the therapist's vocalisations. When the frequency of verbalisations has been increased in this way, subsequent reinforcements should only be given for increasingly closer approximations to the therapist's sound. Physical prompts should be gradually faded until the child is able to repeat the sound without help. New sounds can then be introduced. Initially it is wisest to work on sounds that differ clearly from each other so that the child does not become confused. Later, however, finer and finer discriminations can be introduced. It is often found that the first few sounds can take many hours of training to achieve but subsequent imitations tend to emerge more rapidly.

At this stage of training it is more important to establish the functional value of the child's verbal repertoire than to insist on perfect renditions of the therapist's prompts. A *range* of word approximations that can be used readily by the child to control his environment (such as 'ow' for 'out', 'dinn' for 'dinner', 'toy' for 'toilet' or 'mm' for 'mummy') is worth far more in practical terms than a single, perfectly enunciated word.

Later, when the child is able to imitate a variety of different sounds, he can be taught to 'chain' these together to form simple words or word approximations. Again these should be related to important people or objects in his environment. For example, if he is able to make the sound /Ba/, he might be taught to imitate /Ba-Ba/ as an approximation to 'Baby', when shown a picture of a baby or a doll. /Ma-Ma/ for 'Mummy', or /Da-Da/ for 'Daddy' might also be taught in the same manner. Similarly, if the child is able to make the sounds /K/ and /Ah/, these can be chained together to form the word 'car'. At first each of the paired sounds may need to be prompted separately by the therapist, and the child rewarded for imitating these one at a time. Then, very gradually, the time interval between the presentation of the two sounds should be reduced until reinforcements are obtained only for production of the two sounds together. Later three- and four-sound chains can be introduced. Once chains of two and three sounds have been mastered, imitation of the names of many simple objects can begin.

When the child is able to imitate simple word approximations, the next stage is to encourage the spontaneous use of these in the absence of direct prompts. It is important to begin by introducing objects that are familiar to the child, and whose names he can already easily imitate. Then the child might be prompted with a question such as 'What's this?' and subsequently with the answer, for example: 'Ball'. Gradually these prompts can be faded, and a typical sequence might be: (1) Ball; (2) Ba . . .; (3) B——, leaving the child to supply the missing sounds. Later, merely mouthing the initial letter of the word should be sufficient until eventually the child is able to answer the question in the absence of prompts. When the child appears to be reliably naming specific objects in this way, it is always advisable to test his ability to generalise the word labels to objects other than those originally used for teaching. Unless care is taken over this it is possible for children to associate their newly learned words with specific objects only. The word 'Cup' may be used only when the child sees a particular red and white mug; 'Car' may refer to a single vehicle, not to cars in general. Acquisition of generalised word labels should be tested, and trained, by using a variety of objects from the same class of words. The therapist should confirm that the child is able to produce the correct label when presented with objects that differ from the original in a number of ways. An extensive collection of toy objects can prove very valuable for generalisation training, as can sets of pictures, especially those collected from mail-order catalogues.

Adjectives can be rather more of a problem to teach since even young normal children have difficulty in distinguishing correctly between pairs of adjectives such as big and small, or fat and thin, despite the fact that such words may appear frequently in their spontaneous language. Even colour names can give rise to considerable difficulties. If particular adjectives are already spontaneously used by the child, it is useful to try to increase the frequency of these. Otherwise it is probably safest to leave them until later in the training programme.

It may be much more valuable to teach the use of proper names, such as 'Mummy' or 'Daddy' or the child's own name. These are

obviously necessary for identifying familiar people in the environment or calling attention to the child's own needs. Later, too, they
play an important role in simple phrase constructions. As well as
naming objects or actions or people that are visible at the time, it is
necessary for the child to learn to request items that are not
immediately available. This will often prove more difficult to teach
than simple naming, but is an extremely important stage in the
development of spontaneous speech.

One way of doing this is to make use of an object that is
particularly favoured by the child — perhaps a special toy or even
an object to which he is obsessionally attached. This may be held just
out of the child's reach while he is asked 'What do you want?' and
prompted with the correct answer. Prompts should then gradually be
reduced until the question is answered without help. Later the child
can be taught to select and ask for the item he wants from a range
of different objects, until eventually he is able to express his needs
spontaneously and without necessarily being questioned first.

Teaching phrase speech

Once a fairly extensive single-word vocabulary has been established, two-word chains, such as noun-verb, or adjective-noun
constructions, can be taught. This may be done in a manner similar
to that described for the building up of sound chains, using words
that are already in the child's repertoire. For example, if he can use
individual nouns and verbs, he can be taught to combine these to
form simple phrases such as 'Mummy eating' or 'Baby crying'.

Studies of early phrase speech development in English-speaking
children have indicated that certain semantic structures tend to be
acquired before others (De Villiers and De Villiers, 1978). Although
language acquisition in handicapped children does not necessarily
follow exactly the same stages, it would seem wisest to begin training with structures that are known to be relatively easy for young
normal children to learn. The most common relationships expressed
in early two-word utterances are those of:

Locatives	(Play bed, Pillow here)
Possession	(Mummy's shoe)
Action	(Kick door; Daddy go)
Quality	(Pretty boat; Big chair)

When the child has progressed beyond the two-word stage, longer phrases may be taught successfully by using a backward chaining technique as described in previous chapters. To begin with the child is required to provide the final word to the trainer's prompt. For instance, the therapist, following the question 'What is it?', might prompt with the cue 'It is a red . . .' and the child would then be reinforced for supplying the word 'ball'. The prompt is then reduced so that the penultimate word, too, must be supplied. This process continues until the child is able to answer using a complete, if simple, sentence. When teaching phrase speech in this way it may also be useful to train a set of 'pivotal' phrases to which a variety of different endings can be attached. This helps the child to learn to use more easily basic structures such as 'I want a . . .' or 'It is a . . .' or 'I have a . . .'.

It occasionally happens that children who *can* use simple sentence structures may be unwilling to use more than one or two word utterances if they are able to make themselves understood in this way. This is particularly true of autistic children who are likely to use the very briefest form of utterance they can get away with. For example one 12-year-old boy persisted in using the phrase 'Morris Mummy' whenever he wanted to go out. The phrase had originated when the family lived in an isolated country house and an old Morris car was their only means of transport. Several years and a number of cars later, the same abbreviated and stereotyped utterance was still used. Only when his parents and teachers consistently ceased to respond to this phrase did he bother to use his perfectly adequate language skills to formulate grammatically correct requests such as 'Please can we go to the shops?'

It is important, with more linguistically capable individuals, that stereotyped or 'telegraphic' utterances of this kind should not be reinforced. Children should only be supplied with what they want if they use an appropriate form of request. Higher levels of phrase speech are only likely to be used if the child learns that one- or two-word utterances are *not* sufficient to get what he demands and that he must use simple but complete sentence structures.

As soon as the child has reached the level of two- or three-word utterances, different constructions can be taught. For example, pronoun-verb or pronoun-noun combinations such as 'I have', 'You are', 'Your cup', can be taught. Dolls or puppets can prove very useful in teaching verbs and pronouns. For example, male and female dolls can be shown carrying out various actions and the child is prompted to answer questions such as 'What is he doing?',

'Where are they going?', etc. The therapist's or the child's own actions can be used to teach the various forms of 'I' and 'You' and again these can be turned into play activities. For example, if the child is sitting on a swing or throwing a ball back and forth, he can be prompted to respond to questions such as 'What are you doing?' or 'What am I doing?' The game is then only allowed to continue if the child answers appropriately. To avoid confusion over pronouns it is usually advisable to teach one pronoun at a time to begin with, and only when this is well established to progress to new ones. As with normal children, the pronouns 'He', 'She' and 'It' are usually easier to acquire than 'I' and 'You'. Children frequently show great enjoyment in taking part in such activities, and, if carefully planned, teaching sessions may be very pleasurable for pupil and therapist alike.

INCREASING CONVERSATIONAL AND HIGHER-LEVEL LANGUAGE SKILLS

Other useful structures to teach, in order to introduce maximum flexibility and range into the child's use of language, are prepositions, different verb tenses, singular and plural endings and other simple inflections. Teaching responses to questions that typically occur in social interactions, such as 'What is your name?', 'How are you?', 'Where do you live?', also help the child to take part in very simple conversations, as well as being important if he should get lost. Later, training in more complex verbal skills — such as asking questions, carrying messages, reporting on past events and so on — can be undertaken, again using the techniques of prompting, reinforcement and the gradual fading of prompts.

Generally, the guiding principle of any language training programme is always to proceed in a step-by-step fashion, teaching the child to master one particular sound or word or concept before progressing to another. These existing elements in the repertoire can then be combined to form increasingly complex utterances. Using old, familiar forms in this way to build up new structures ensures that teaching progresses steadily and smoothly towards achieving the goal of communicative language.

The methods described above are, of course, meant only as general guidelines for a language programme and will, of necessity, be modified according to the needs and skills of each particular child. Training for a child who already uses a few spontaneous words will obviously begin at a higher level than for a child who has no communicative sounds. Some children may be so globally mentally handicapped that most of the emphasis will need to be placed on the teaching of receptive skills. Basic instructions such as 'Sit down', 'Look at me', or 'Do this', which are necessary parts of the training programme, may need to be learned before teaching can progress further. Alternatively, for children who possess good use and understanding of simple, concrete speech, the goal of the programme may be to increase their command of more abstract, imaginative language skills.

DECREASING INAPPROPRIATE SPEECH

In cases where echolalic or stereotyped utterances are a problem, the first aim is to reduce these forms of speech. This can be achieved most effectively by consistently ignoring *all* echolalic or stereotyped verbalisations, while at the same time prompting the child to use correct forms of speech. As long as the child receives no response to his echolalic remarks and is attended to only when he uses appropriate constructions, egocentric utterances can generally be brought rapidly under control. Such methods do not, as some parents fear, result in the child becoming discouraged and refusing to talk at all. Instead, socially appropriate speech tends to increase rapidly, and inappropriate echolalia shows a steady decline. However, it should also be noted that echolalia may, for some children, play an important role in early language acquisition. Before attemps are made to eradicate such behaviour entirely, the possible functional value of this type of speech should be carefully assessed (Schuler and Prizant, 1985).

Some children, as already mentioned, may be quite capable of using well-formed sentences or phrases, but prefer to communicate non-verbally, or by means of telegraphic utterances such as 'Want out' or 'Go toilet'. Again prompts for the correct response should be provided at every possible opportunity, and all inadequate or non-verbal forms of communication — whether these be simply placing an adult's hand on the desired object or screaming loudly until someone responds — should be consistently ignored.

It can often be very difficult for parents, nurses or teachers to deal in a consistent manner with such behaviours because many children become extremely adept in communicating in this way. Constantly correcting the child when it is perfectly clear to parents or teachers

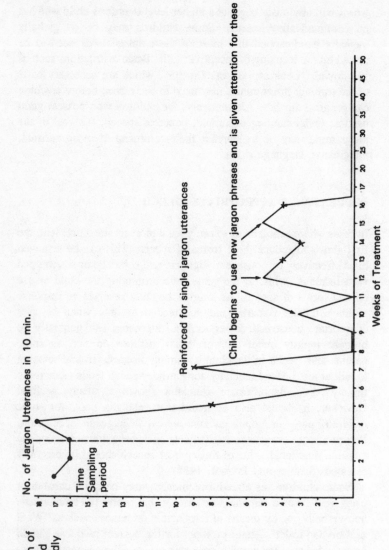

Figure 11.1 Extinction of jargon utterances used by seven-year old mildly retarded boy (IQ 74)

No. of Jargon Utterances in 10 min.

Time Sampling period

Reinforced for single jargon utterances

Child begins to use new jargon phrases and is given attention for these

Weeks of Treatment

what he means is not always easy, but those who are familiar with the child need to be aware that strangers will not necessarily understand him in the way they do. For the child's sake, therefore, it is necessary to insist on the use of correct grammatical utterances. Even the occasional response to an echolalic or stereotyped utterance — perhaps laughing at a particularly funny jargon phrase, or giving the child something he has asked for in an echolalic way — is likely to result in a rapid increase in his use of such phrases and make them very resistant to extinction. Figure 11.1 shows the rapid upsurge in jargon utterances during an extinction programme following any attention for these. The child's utterances were of an extremely provocative kind which his mother had great difficulty in ignoring. Finally, however, she did succeed in consistently ignoring them, and jargon utterances have since remained at a very low level (Howlin, 1980).

MODIFYING THE PROGRAMME ACCORDING TO INDIVIDUAL NEEDS

In order to ensure that the programmes implemented are appropriate to the child's level of development, both verbally and in non-verbal areas, language skills need to be carefully assessed. Formal language tests such as the Reynell Developmental Language Scales (Reynell, 1981) are useful in obtaining standard measures of the child's use and understanding of language. Non-verbal abilities can be reliably assessed by the use of scales such as the Merrill Palmer. If the child is functioning at too low a level to score reliably on language tests, these should be supplemented by observations, made in the child's every-day environment, of what he does say: whether this is spontaneous or echolalic; whether he uses meaningful sounds or single words or phrases; and of how much he can understand in the absence of gestural or other cues. Baseline measures of how much the child is speaking or understanding prior to treatment need to be taken in order to assess the effectiveness of subsequent treatment.

During training, regular measures of the numbers of new sounds or words or constructions acquired are needed to ensure that progress continues. If treatment fails to be effective for any reason, this should be readily discernible from records, and treatment procedures should be modified accordingly. Recording sheets should be simple enough for those in charge of the child to fill in

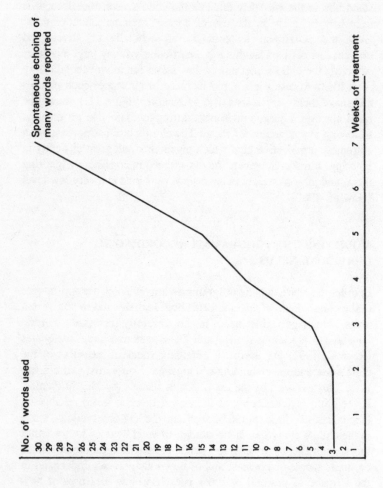

Figure 11.2: Short-term training project with retarded six-year-old boy (IQ ~ 50). Only three words were used prior to training

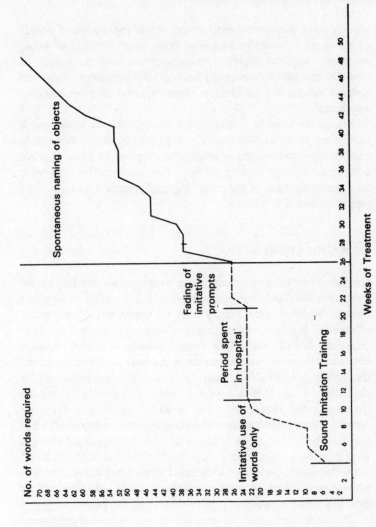

Figure 11.3: Development of verbal imitation and naming vocabulary in 7-year-old non-verbal autistic boy (no imitation or use of words prior to treatment)

No. of words required

70
68
66
64
62
60
58
56
54
52
50
48
46
44
42
40
38
36
34
32
30
28
26
24
22
20
18
16
14
12
10
8
6
4
2

Spontaneous naming of objects

Fading of imitative prompts

Period spent in hospital

Imitative use of words only

Sound Imitation Training

2   4   6   8   10   12   14   16   18   20   22   24   26   28   30   32   34   36   38   40   42   44   46   48   50

Weeks of Treatment

quickly and easily. In the early stages of training, counts of sounds or words used should be adequate. When large numbers of words are being acquired daily, frequency counts may no longer be feasible. Instead records might be kept of the number of days or sessions needed for the child to reach criterion on more complex structures.

Parents or other therapists can frequently obtain considerable reinforcement themselves from keeping such records, as they enable them to see how the child is progressing. Figures 11.2 and 11.3 are both based on data kept by parents. They illustrate the somewhat slow progress made in the early stages of treatment and the more rapid changes that followed.

CHOOSING REINFORCERS

Careful individual assessment is also needed when deciding on the most effective reinforcers for each child. Early studies of language training tended to rely heavily on food reinforcers. These were, admittedly, highly effective for many subjects and could be easily dispensed. It was assumed that if food rewards were always paired with social rewards, such as praise, in the early stages of treatment, then praise alone would eventually assume reinforcing properties for the child. Lovaas (1967), however, found that merely pairing the 'primary' reinforcer, food, with a social reinforcer, the word 'good', was not effective in establishing praise as a secondary reinforcer. When, after many hundreds of such pairings, food rewards were eventually discontinued, 'the child behaved as if he had never heard the word', and failed to respond at all. Only if the child was actively made to attend to the social stimulus before he received the food did praise eventually acquire reinforcing properties.

There are other problems involved in using food as a reinforcer, particularly in a language training programme. Sweets or biscuits, even in small pieces, may interfere with vocalisations, especially when building up chains of words or sounds. In addition, many adults and children with mental handicaps have eating difficulties anyway, and feeding outside regular mealtimes may exacerbate these. Some children actually reject food rewards, whereas others may react very negatively to attempts to reduce these.

In the very early stages of training, particularly with subjects with severe mental handicaps who show very limited interest in their environment, food may well be the only effective reinforcer. If food is required, this should be given in very tiny portions to ensure that training sessions are not unduly interrupted. Care should also be taken to fade schedules of reinforcement steadily, so that the child quickly learns to produce several correct sounds before receiving a reward.

Although food reinforcements may be necessary for some individuals, the possibility of using other effective rewards should be investigated as part of any language training programme.

Language is essentially a social skill, and teaching the child to respond to social rewards is clearly the best means of ensuring that attempts to use language are frequently and consistently reinforced by all those in his environment. There is then no need for therapists and others to go armed with stocks of 'Smarties' or the like which are dispensed each time a word is uttered.

Praise alone can be very effective even with people with severe mental handicaps, although if it is not sufficient other social rewards, such as tickling, hugging or kissing, can also be employed. If social reinforcement is clearly ineffective, alternative methods will need to be tried, although these should always be accompanied by praise and attention. Toys, tokens and visual and auditory stimulation have all been used successfully in language training programmes. If the child shows no positive enjoyment of any particular activity or objects, then rewards based on the Premack principle (see Chapter 3) may be utilised. In this case any activity to which the child reverts when left alone can be used to reinforce attempts to speak. These may include obsessional or ritualistic activities, or simply allowing the child to sit alone doing nothing. Although many therapists, especially parents, may doubt the advisability of using such activities as rewards, they can be very effective in the early stages of treatment. Later, as the child's language and social skills develop, the need for obsessional or ritualised activities tends to decline and more appropriate rewards can be substituted. Non-social rewards should be steadily faded and replaced by social cues during training programmes. If the child learns to use his newly acquired language skills effectively, this alone should become a powerful reinforcer for him.

Satiation can be a problem in lengthy training programmes, and it is always advisable to identify a variety of different reinforcers in order effectively to maintain the child's co-operation. In general, the most effective solution to the problem of reinforcement is to ensure that the training procedures and the skills derived from them are enjoyable and motivating for the child. The materials and activities used in training should themselves be interesting and rewarding enough to constitute effective reinforcers. If developmental processes are to be enhanced through training, it is essential that they do not remain under the direct control of external reinforcers; rather the child should come to want to use the skills because they are useful or pleasurable for him. In this way dependence on extrinsic reinforcers can be minimised, and indeed the use of unnecessary 'rewards' may actually interfere with learning and make it less likely that the behaviour will be maintained (Lepper, 1981).

THE GENERALISATION OF LANGUAGE SKILLS

Problems of generalisation are common, even in normal children, if skills not previously in the child's repertoire have to be taught by operant techniques (Patterson *et al.*, 1973). Difficulties in generalisation tend to be much greater in individuals with learning handicaps, and it is important to ensure that newly learned skills do transfer from trained to untrained settings.

The need to avoid word labels becoming associated with specific objects only rather than with *classes* of objects has already been noted. In addition, care may be needed to ensure that the skills learned with one therapist or in one setting transfer to other people and to other situations. It is essential, if the results of training programmes are to be maintained, that parents, other family members, the child's teachers and all other relevant individuals are involved in therapy. Otherwise the benefits of treatment may remain very restricted. Figures 11.2 and 11.3 for example, show how little of what has been learned at home generalises to the school situation unless training is carried out in both settings. Similarly, behaviours that are apparently well established in a clinic setting are unlikely to transfer to the home unless parents are actively involved in therapy (Koegel *et al.*, 1982).

If newly learned language skills are to generalise successfully, emphasis also needs to be placed on making the child's environment as conducive to language usage as possible. Items in training must be of particular relevance or interest to the child so that attempts at naming are consistently reinforced by his actually obtaining the object. In addition, minor modifications to the child's environment may be necessary to ensure that the use of speech is actively encouraged. Many handicapped individuals become extremely adept at achieving their needs without using any appropriate language.

Parents and teachers need to be firm in *not* responding to non-verbal modes of interaction (such as screaming or grabbing for objects). They may also need to ensure that food or other items are deliberately made inaccessible so that instead of simply taking what he wants the child is obliged to communicate his needs verbally.

Language generalisation may also be enhanced by a careful consideration of the factors that are most likely to motivate the child to communicate. Carr and Durand (1985), for instance, carried out a detailed functional analysis of the reasons for disruptive and self-injurious behaviours in children with mental handicaps. They found that many such behaviours, far from being 'maladaptive', frequently performed an important communicative role for the children. They might be the child's only way of escaping from a situation or of indicating that the task was too difficult for him. If the children were taught alternative ways of making their needs known — by simple signs or verbalisations — not only did rates of disruptive behaviour decrease but the use of communicative skills was far more likely to be maintained and to generalise.

If a child is born with a profound language deficit and does not learn to speak for many years, the inherent difficulties involved in using language may well outweigh any extrinsic reinforcers. Even if a child *can* speak when pressurised or placed in a highly structured teaching environment, he is unlikely to do so in settings where the 'press' to speak is reduced or if his needs can be achieved with less effort. If language skills are to be used effectively, it is essential to make certain that they are of immediate, practical value to the child. The language skills taught must allow the child to attain goals that would be difficult to acquire by other means. In other words, it is important that language provides the child with much more immediate and effective control over his environment. That is, the language taught must have what Goetz *et al.* (1983) have termed 'functional competence'.

The apparent failure of many language programmes may be a function of the lack of any practical value to the child of the skills taught, and not a problem of generalisation as is often assumed. If the speech acquired is not functionally useful, then the 'pay-off' for *not* using speech will almost certainly outweigh any extrinsic encouragement to do so. If language training is unsuccessful, this may well be due to failure to motivate the child to use the skills taught rather than to inherent difficulties of generalisation.

IMPLEMENTING FINDINGS FROM PSYCHOLINGUISTIC RESEARCH

There is still considerable controversy as to whether language acquisition in handicapped children follows the same developmental patterns as in normal children (Howlin, 1984; Johnston and Schery, 1972; Raffin *et al.*, 1978). Nevertheless, the weight of evidence seems to suggest that the linguistic rules acquired easily by normal children are also the easiest for language-delayed children to acquire. When language is trained by artificial means, it is important that attention be given to the child's general cognitive level, and that training programmes be based as far as possible on normal developmental sequences.

Although the relationship between cognitive and linguistic development varies somewhat from child to child (Cromer, 1981), there is a close association between the two. Normal children are not expected to acquire particular levels of language competence until they have reached an appropriate stage of cognitive development. Unfortunately, in work with mentally handicapped children the influence of cognitive development on language acquisition has frequently been overlooked. In many cases the linguistic structures taught have been selected in an apparently arbitrary manner, with little attention being paid to the child's level of cognitive ability. It is apparent, although the pattern is not invariant, that certain aspects of language tend to be acquired at an earlier stage than others and it would seem advisable to incorporate such information into training programmes.

When developing a basic expressive vocabulary the sounds or sound combinations taught should be those that appear early in the speech of normal children. Vowel sounds are usually the first to emerge, followed by the labial consonants (/m/, /p/, /b/). Most other sounds appear between the ages of 18 months and 3 years, although some, such as /th/ (as in three) or /ch/ (as in church) may not be mastered for several years. The first sound combinations to appear are usually of the consonant–vowel, or consonant–vowel–consonant type, such as 'Ta' or 'Dad'.

When words begin to emerge, nouns almost always appear first, and these typically relate directly to the child's main interests: food, toys, clothes, animals, self and parents (Nelson, 1973). Verbs are usually acquired next, and later pronouns and prepositions (McCarthy, 1954). The earliest morpheme rules to be used correctly are the regular /ing/ ending of the present progressive (running, jumping, etc.); the /s/ ending on plurals and possessives ('cups', 'Mummy's', etc.) and simple verb tenses. Irregular morpheme endings are generally acquired some time later, and until this stage is reached there tends to be confusion between regular and irregular forms (e.g. 'wented', 'camed', 'sheeps', etc.). When pronouns emerge, 'it' tends to be used before the personal pronouns 'he', 'she', 'I' or 'you'. Correct use of the latter involves quite complex semantic processing, and errors and confusions may persist up to the age of at least 4 or 5 years.

Concepts of location develop much earlier than concepts of time, and this is reflected in the order in which normal children acquire objectives and questions. 'In' and 'on' occur long before temporal prepositions such as 'before' or 'after'. 'What' and 'where' question forms are used and understood before 'why' or 'when' (Ervin–Tripp, 1973).

As already mentioned, normal children up to 5 years of age or older also have many difficulties with relational or dimensional terms such as big/small, more/less, different/same, even I/you, or with contrasting pairs of verbs such as come/go, bring/take. Experimental work has shown that young children frequently tend to confuse these terms and use them interchangeably. As with other structures that are known to present problems for young normal children, the teaching of more complicated rules is best avoided until a relatively high level of linguistic competence is reached.

In teaching transformational rules the easiest structures to begin with are those that are normally acquired early, such as the use of imperative and question forms (see Clark and Clark, 1977; De Villiers and De Villiers, 1978). When words began to be paired together, training should focus on those semantic relationships that appear in the early phrase speech of normal children. These include possessives (as in 'Mummy's hat'), locatives ('on the chair'), noun plus action ('Daddy sleeps'), action plus object ('hit ball'), and demonstrative and attributive phrases ('that book', 'red car', etc.).

A number of additional guidelines seem to be useful in facilitating language acquisition. Among these 'rules', which are apparently common to many cultures (Slobin, 1973), are the finding that semantically and syntactically consistent structures are acquired earlier than irregular ones. Phrases involving a simple noun–verb–object order are acquired before those involving more elaborate ordering. Full forms of a structure (such as 'I am', 'You are') tend to be used before contracted forms ('I'm', 'You're', etc.).

Finally, short but syntactically correct sentence models seem to be more effective for teaching than abbreviated sentence forms. It has been suggested in the past (Miller and Yoder, 1974) that during language training programmes therapists should 'reduce their syntax to telegraphic speech whenever possible while talking to the child'. This, they postulated, would make it simpler for the child to 'induce latent structures' from the utterances he heard, thereby facilitating his processing of language. However, as Yule and Berger (1975) point out, limiting language models in this way may well inhibit the development of more complex syntactical forms. Certainly normal children seem to respond to full forms of a sentence better than to telegraphic utterances.

Obviously these sequences are not invariant for all children. Moreover, when teaching the handicapped it is important to be aware that they are not a homogeneous group (Cromer, 1981). Different individuals will possess very different language capabilities, and the therapist must take careful account of these. Rigid adherence to any predetermined language programme should always be avoided. Although teaching 'packages' can provide helpful guidelines, they can never be used as a replacement for individually structured therapy that takes account of each child's own strengths and weaknesses.

THE EFFECTIVENESS OF LANGUAGE TRAINING PROGRAMMES

Although behavioural techniques have been extensively used in the treatment of language disorders, experimental evidence supporting the efficacy of these methods is surprisingly limited. The majority of reports in the literature are still uncontrolled single-case studies and, as with any other developmental skill, some improvements in communication are likely to occur over time even without treatment. In the absence of adequate controls, there is always the danger that changes attributed to intervention may be due instead to the child's own growth in maturation rather than to external influences. Moreover it is also apparent that the effects of therapy vary considerably across children, and that certain aspects of language respond more readily to treatment than others.

First, although some programmes have apparently been highly successful after relatively brief periods of intervention, others have achieved little success despite prolonged teaching.

Secondly, therapy seems to be more effective in encouraging the child's use of inherent language skills than in increasing levels of language competence. Changes that do occur following treatment tend to be limited to increases in vocabulary or decreases in inappropriate utterances. Improvements in the complexity of language are much less likely to be reported (Clements *et al.*, 1982; Howlin, 1981).

Finally, the individual characteristics of the children involved in therapy are also likely to affect the success of the programme. Age, IQ, severity of the language handicap and diagnosis are all factors that may influence outcome. On the whole, the younger the child when intervention begins, the greater are the chances of success. There are reports of older children and even adolescents acquiring useful speech but this is rare. Generally, unless some language is acquired before the age of 6 or 7 years the effects of verbal training programmes are likely to be limited.

IQ level also tends to be related to outcome. The greater the overall level of mental handicap the less likely is language to be acquired. Again there are exceptions, but individuals with an IQ in the profoundly handicapped range rarely acquire anything other than very rudimentary communication skills.

The severity of language handicap, too, is important in predicting outcome. Treatment effects tend to be least among individuals who are not only lacking in spoken language but who also show severe limitations in comprehension skills and deficits in non-verbal areas, such as play and social responsiveness. Conversely, children who already possess some simple communication abilities before treatment begins (even if their speech is predominantly echolalic and stereotyped) may be less affected by therapy than is often claimed. Controlled investigations of language training, such as that by Howlin *et al.* (1987) suggest that progress in such children tends to be relatively favourable even in the absence of intervention. Behavioural programmes may result in short-term gains, but in the longer term there are often few differences between treated children and their matching controls. The particular group of children who seem to benefit most from therapy are those on the threshold of developing speech and who have some spontaneous words or word approximations that can be usefully shaped into more complex language skills.

The importance of diagnostic factors should also be borne in mind. As noted above, individuals with language delay are not a homogeneous group, and differences in the handicapping condition may well affect the response to treatment. Autistic children, for example, who have particularly severe communication deficits, tend to respond only slowly to therapy. Non-autistic mentally handicapped children, who do not show marked abnormalities in their social relationships, are more likely to benefit from intervention.

WHAT TO DO WHEN LANGUAGE PROGRAMMES FAIL

As indicated in the above discussion, although behavioural programmes may be beneficial for children with language deficits the results are not always as impressive as originally claimed. The extent of improvement brought about by operant techniques may be limited by the child's inherent linguistic capabilities (Howlin *et al.*, 1987). On the whole, therapy is most successful in increasing the child's use of existing language skills, or in eliminating inappropriate speech. It can do little to overcome fundamental deficits in communication. Children who suffer severe limitations in both their understanding and production of language have little chance of acquiring useful speech. Awareness of the poor outcome of verbal training programmes with such children has led to greater emphasis on alternative or augmentative communication systems.

These have taken several different forms. Manual signing systems, developed mainly from work with the deaf or with individuals suffering from executive (rather than central) language impairments, were among the earliest alternative approaches used (Goodman *et al.*, 1978). However, the success of these tended to depend on the trainee's possessing the social motivation to communicate, relatively intact semantic and syntactic competence (even if their performance were impaired), and normal motor development. In the case of severely mentally handicapped people, none of these requirements may be satisfied, and less complex systems have had to be developed.

One of the simplest of these, commonly used in the UK, is the Makaton vocabulary (Walker, 1980). This is a mainly iconic system (i.e. the signs are meaningfully related to objects rather than having arbitrary associations) but it allows only limited expression of syntactic relationships. More abstract, but at the same time more flexible, systems include British Sign Language (BSL), and the Paget Gorman system (Paget *et al.*, 1972).

Signing systems have been used successfully in many studies, including those involving severely handicapped individuals with additional impairments of sight or hearing (Rittenhouse, 1983).

However, as has been the case with verbal training programmes, most of the reports in the literature have been single-case studies, with minimal experimental controls and anecdotal reporting of results. Such training clearly works well in certain cases, with some children acquiring many hundreds of signs and sign combinations, and even developing spoken language (Deich and Hodges, 1982; Schaeffer, 1980). For others, however, there may be very little benefit (Lancioni, 1983; Murphy *et al.*, 1977).

In such cases it may be necessary to devise even simpler forms of communication. Alternatives to signing include the use of symbols (Carrier, 1976; Porter and Schroeder, 1980; Premack and Premack, 1974), pictures (Lancioni, 1983; Murphy *et al.*, 1977), Bliss symbols (Bliss, 1965) and communication boards (see Bailey and Jenkinson, 1982). These systems have been used successfully with multiply handicapped individuals and have a number of advantages when working with those with severe mental handicaps. Because they depend on recognition rather than recall, they make fewer demands on memory or cognitive skills, and, since they are permanently available to the child, they make it easier to form word combinations; they require less motor proficiency and are more easily understood by untrained observers. However, there are also a number of disadvantages. First, they are a very slow means of communication and they make it difficult to convey syntactic or semantic relations with ease. This may not matter so much when working with very severely handicapped individuals, but it is a serious drawback if the child becomes proficient at the system. Secondly, although the vocabulary is individually tailored to the child's needs, the limited lexicon provided may not be adequate to meet the needs of improved communication skills. Thirdly, they restrict flexibility and spontaneity, and in addition, as vocabulary grows, they may be extremely cumbersome to carry around. Computerised systems may help to overcome problems of restricted vocabulary but they limit the range of situations in which the child can communicate, and, unless carefully designed, may reduce the need for direct interpersonal communication.

Like signing systems, symbolic and pictorial systems have produced many successful results (Carrier, 1976; Porter and Schroeder, 1980). However, the outcome is not universally favourable (Remington and Light, 1983), and even the most successful reports suggest that the spontaneous use of these systems is limited. Mostly they are used in response to adult prompts; spontaneous use tends to be in the form of requests rather than providing information or initiating contact, and generalisation to unfamiliar adults or situations is often poor (Kiernan, 1983).

Although they may have their limitations, it seems that non-verbal communication systems can offer considerable hope for those with severe mental handicaps who have not acquired language by other means. Nevertheless, many questions remain to be answered about the most effective ways of utilising them.

When should they be introduced, for example? Usually non-verbal programmes are not implemented until after verbal pro-grammes have failed. It would seem to be much more beneficial, both for the child and his parents, to avoid this early failure and to introduce non-verbal programmes before verbal ones. This would seem to be particularly advisable when working with older or more severely handicapped individuals, who, statistically at least, are unlikely to learn to speak. Moreover, since the successful teaching of alternative systems can actually lead to the subsequent develop-ment of speech, and certainly does nothing to discourage it, there would seem to be few disadvantages in adopting this approach.

The next question concerns the relative efficacy of the different systems. Although some authors have found that symbols or pictures may be easier to acquire than signs, particularly by individuals with severe mental handicaps (Lancioni, 1983; Murphy et al., 1977), there have been few systematic investigations in this area. There are some suggestions that autistic children may use symbols more readily than signs (De Villiers and Naughton, 1974; McLean and McLean, 1974), but this could be due to the fact that symbols require less in the way of active social interaction. The study of Kiernan and Jones (1981) indicates that the relative ease of acquis-ition seems to depend on the individual characteristics of the children involved in treatment, and MacDonald (1984) found that differences in linguistic intent were also important. Thus, signs may be preferred for the rapid requesting of objects, and symbols are more effective for spontaneous comments.

Within systems, too, there are many as yet unresolved questions. In signing, for instance, is it more effective to teach iconic gestures rather than arbitrary ones? Luftig (1983) reported that concrete signs were acquired more easily than abstract ones, but this finding has not been replicated in all other studies (Kohl, 1981; Wilson, 1983). It should be remembered that judgements about levels of iconicity are largely subjective, and what is abstract for one individual is not necessarily so for another. Kiernan (1983) suggests that the motoric ease with which signs can be executed is more important than iconicity, although, of course, many of the most concrete signs are also the simplest to perform.

A similar problem arises with regard to symbolic/pictorial systems. There has been little attention paid to the comparative merits of abstract symbols (such as those designed by Premack and Premack, 1974) versus pictorial representations, and a number of studies suggest that discriminability of items may be a more important factor in learning than the level of abstraction. However, there would seem to be little practical value in teaching the severely handicapped to use very abstract systems, not least because of the difficulties in generalising these or the problems of interpretation by an untrained audience.

Finally, there is the crucial problem of how alternative systems should be taught. Should non-verbal training be paired with speech at the same time, as many therapists recommend (Barrera *et al.*, 1980; Brady and Smouse, 1978) or should the two systems be kept separate? Again individual child differences should be considered. Autistic children often perform poorly on tasks that involve multi-modal stimuli, and simultaneous communication training may be less useful for this group, or indeed for any child with marked impairments in the understanding of language. On the other hand, for children who can respond equally well to sign and speech, the use of speech and signs or symbols together may well facilitate learning (Kiernan, 1983).

In summary, although alternative communication systems play an important role in language training, they are clearly not universally successful. Much greater attention to the characteristics of children who do respond to different forms of training is urgently required if optimal teaching strategies are to be rapidly and effectively employed. However, no matter how potentially effective the chosen system, probably the most crucial requirement for success is its functional value for the individual child.

CONCLUSIONS

It is evident that behavioural techniques are effective for many although by no means all children with mental handicap. However, reviews of research in this area reveal many unanswered questions and conflicting evidence. Answers to these questions are likely to be forthcoming only if greater attention is given to the basic details of research programmes.

First, more systematic assessments of the children involved are required in order to determine which children respond best to which methods of training. Only in this way will it ultimately prove possible to maximise the chances of treatment effectiveness and to ensure that time is not wasted in inappropriate forms of training.

Secondly, if intervention is to be successful and the results of treatment are to be maintained, the communication skills taught, whether verbal or non-verbal, must be of functional value to the child. Treatment techniques are only likely to endure if they result in the child gaining greater and more immediate control over the environment.

Thirdly, if good generalisation is to be achieved, treatment must involve all the relevant adults in the child's environment and in particular should include parents as therapists.

Fourthly, it is necessary to be aware that although traditional behavioural techniques, such as reinforcement or prompting, are important aspects of treatment they may not be the only factors crucial for success. Psycholinguistic and developmental factors are also likely to play a central role in determining the effectiveness of treatment. Environmental features, too, need to be considered. Thus, the child's environment may have to be subtly altered to ensure that it provides the maximum opportunities for communication. An environment that is too complex, or alternatively one that requires little or no communication from the child, is unlikely to result in improved language development.

Finally greater attention needs to be paid to the longer term effects of therapy. This is an issue that is rarely given adequate consideration but in view of the enormous amount of time and hard work that language programmes entail, assessments of treatment effectiveness over time, and on other aspects of the child's functioning, are needed if the value of therapy is to be properly evaluated.

12

Teaching Parents, Teachers and Nurses

Maria Callias

One of the most important developments in behavioural treatments over the past 20 years has been the move out of special treatment settings into the every-day world. This trend has been especially significant for children and adults with mental handicaps because behavioural approaches have played a fundamental role in the shift from custodial care to fostering independence and alleviating problem behaviour. The recognition that parents, teachers, nurses and others who have ongoing relationships with people with mental handicaps can make an important contribution to their training and treatment has resulted in an ever-growing literature on the issues of training parents and other professionals in behavioural skills (Milne, 1986; O'Dell, 1985), including, more recently, the place of behavioural training in meeting the needs of handicapped persons and their families (Cunningham, 1985) and the nature of the relationships between parents and professionals (Cunningham and Davis, 1985a; Mittler and Mittler, 1983).

The main factors that sparked the widespread move towards training parents (Dangel and Polster, 1984; O'Dell, 1974; Yule, 1975) and other direct care workers (Milne, 1986) are especially salient to meeting the needs of mentally handicapped children and adults. These are: first, the finding that treatment successes achieved in special settings do not necessarily generalise to the every-day environment nor are they maintained when treatment ceases; secondly, inadequate resources in terms of both trained professionals and money to meet the needs of the community through the then conventional dyadic model of treatment where the professional therapist worked directly with the client; and thirdly, the hope that widespread training will serve a preventative function by enabling parents and others to cope with potential future problems before they

211

become established. In addition, early studies were demonstrating the feasibility of teaching behavioural management skills to parents and caregivers who did not have a background in learning theory or psychology; and parents themselves were pressing for more practical guidance with the task of rearing their chronically handicapped children.

Today the need for practical skills-oriented help for parents raising their handicapped children is recognised to be an essential part of comprehensive and co-ordinated services to families with handicapped members (DHSS, 1976; Rutter, 1985; Wing, 1985). If they are to be able to advise on practical management, members of district handicap teams, such as health visitors and social workers who should visit families regularly, need to have some training and experience in behavioural approaches and in how to teach them. At the very least, they need to recognise when to refer families on to other team members for such help. It should be a thing of the past for parents to be given unhelpful general advice like 'treat him like a normal baby' or the kind of idiosyncratic suggestion one parent received on how to get help: 'Take her to the park where someone is sure to see that she is handicapped and help you'.

The need to train nurses and teachers working in the field of mental handicap has been recognised (Milne, 1986). Training varies from short workshops to intensive courses such as the 9-month-long ENB Course 705 (English National Board of Clinical Nursing Studies, 1982) which aims to train senior nurses to play an important role in training colleagues in hospital and community services and to work with parents in addition to using behavioural skills themselves.

The different groups of professionals and parents have to some extent different training needs, because of their diverse roles and settings, but they also have many training needs in common. The aim of this chapter is to offer practical solutions to problems relating to training non-psychologists in the use of behavioural principles with children and adults with mental handicaps. Suggestions are based on the research literature and, where this is lacking, on our clinical experience. The main emphasis is on teaching parents because not only are their needs pre-eminent but much of what is said applies also to training other groups. The literature and additional issues of particular concern to teaching nurses and teachers are discussed later in the chapter.

PARENT TRAINING

The term 'parent training' has come to mean any intervention parents in order to influence their children, and implies that parents need special teaching in order to be effective. Although parent training has been influenced by several theoretical approaches (Henry, 1981), behaviourally oriented training has predominated and has provided the main impetus for systematic and evaluated work. There are several comprehensive critical reviews of behavioural training of parents with handicapped children (Altman and Mira, 1983; Clements, 1985; Cunningham, 1985; Doernberg, 1972; Gath, 1979; Helm and Kosloff, 1986) and those with handicapped infants and pre-schoolers (Cunningham and Davis, 1985b; Marfo and Kysela, 1985) and many general reviews which include work with parents of handicapped children (Berkowitz and Graziano, 1972; Dangel and Polster, 1984; Graziano and Mooney, 1984; Johnson and Katz, 1973; O'Dell, 1974, 1985; Tavormina, 1974; Yule, 1975) but scarcely any work with families of handicapped adolescents and adults although their needs are being recognised (Fairbrother, 1983; Jeffree and Cheseldine, 1983). The issues raised centre mainly around questions of training. For example, can parents be taught to use behaviour modification procedures to change their children's behaviour? What are the most effective ways of training parents? Do training methods relate to success with their children? What exactly, and how much, do parents need to be taught? When are parents successful, and in which circumstances do they fail? What are the reasons for failure? More recently, there has been a shift towards taking a wider perspective in understanding families with a handicapped member, their needs, and their styles of coping (Byrne and Cunningham, 1985; Callias, 1987; Carr, 1985; Crnic et al., 1983; Wilkin, 1979), which raises questions about the place of parent training in meeting the broader needs of families (Cunningham and Davis, 1985a,b) and in service provision generally (Wing, 1985). Though behavioural parent training is not a panacea, and we lack research to help us match intervention strategies systematically to the needs of particular families, some form of parent training continues to be at the heart of most practical help to parents concerned to foster their children's optimal development and to cope with behaviour problems. To date, research on parent training has been patchy, focusing intensively on some issues while neglecting others, and most studies have serious methodological flaws, so we still have a long way to go before our interventions can be said to rest on a sound empirical foundation. However, the problems will not wait, and in making our decisions about how and what to teach it is important to remember that many of our views may be modified by future research.

As O'Dell (1974) states, effective parent training requires three steps: parents must acquire modification skills and changes in their own behaviour; these changes must be implemented with the child; and changes must generalise and persist. Only the second step, implementing change in the child's behaviour, has received sufficient attention, resulting in a relative neglect of systematic information on changes taking place in the parents. There has been an implicit assumption throughout the literature that parents need to learn new skills, essentially those of behaviour modification, in order to help their children. Thus the emphasis has centred around first, showing that parents can effectively change their children's behaviour, and secondly, dimensions of parent training.

Children's problems

Whether parents should be involved in the treatment of their children is no longer questioned. A wealth of studies shows quite clearly that parents can use behavioural methods effectively with their children (reviews cited above). Parents of mentally handicapped children have successfully taught their children a wide variety of skills, including self-help (Lance and Koch, 1973; Longin et al., 1975), dressing (Norrish, 1974), play (Mash and Terdal, 1973), several developmental skills (Bidder et al., 1975; Freeman and Thompson, 1973), attention span (Chamberlain, 1985), parent–child relationship skills (Affleck et al., 1982), and even language and speech (McConkey and O'Connor, 1982; Schumaker and Sherman, 1978; Seitz and Hoekenga, 1974) which seem harder to foster developmentally (Howlin, 1981). Problems treated by parents include both problems common to many children, such as tantrums and noncompliance, and those unlikely to occur among non-handicapped children, such as self-injurious behaviour, self-stimulation, stereotypes (Altman and Mira, 1983; Firth, 1983) and excessive attachment to objects (Marchant et al., 1974). More commonly, parents have been taught both how to encourage a wide range of new skills and how to deal with unwanted problems (Callias and Carr, 1975; Cunningham and Jeffree, 1971; Doernberg, 1972; Galloway and Galloway, 1970; O'Dell et al., 1977a; Rose, 1974; Tavormina, 1975).

Role of parents

Although parents have only been involved in behavioural treatments since the mid-1960s, there has been a shift over time in the manner and extent of their involvement (O'Dell, 1974) and in the nature of their relationship with the therapist within the triadic model (Tharp and Wetzel, 1969) where the therapist imparts skills to the parent who then works with the child. In early studies parents were instructed to carry out certain parts of the treatment (Berkowitz and Graziano, 1972, p. 304); later they co-operated with the psychologist in devising and carrying out treatment programmes (Callias and Carr, 1975; Hemsley *et al.*, 1978; Howlin *et al.*, 1973b); later still, especially where training took place in groups, they were taught the principles of behaviour modification, which they put into practice with minimal direct supervision (Callias and Jenkins, 1973; Callias *et al.*, 1976; Hornby and Singh, 1984b). The latter approach seems promising for parents with chronically handicapped children who are likely to need a strategy for coping with problems, or at least a succession of teaching tasks, in the future. It is not known to what extent parents have succeeded in practice in generalising their new skills or have been able to use them independently.

Individual and group training

Most training in clinical practice is done in individual consultation with one set of parents (or the mother only), in the clinic or in the home (Callias and Carr, 1975). The case for working at home has been well argued (Hemsley *et al.*, 1978; Howlin *et al.*, 1973b; Patterson *et al.*, 1973), two major advantages being that the therapist sees the situation 'for real' and that problems of generalisation are minimised. The main drawbacks are that it is time-consuming for the therapist to travel to the home and, occasionally, that some homes are so busy that parent and therapist are too readily distracted from their main purpose. In this case clinic-based teaching may be preferable. The clinic setting also enables special monitoring devices, like the 'bug in the ear' (Hanf, 1968) or videotape recordings, to be used for immediate feedback and instruction to the learner.

A recent development is that of training parents in groups, usually short-term groups (Baker, 1986; Callias, 1985; Firth, 1982; Hornby and Singh, 1984a,b) but occasionally long-term with members joining an ongoing group (Harris, 1978). Parent group projects have varied in a number of ways including setting, duration, frequency of meetings, group composition, content covered and teaching methods used (Callias, 1985; Carr, 1985; Hornby and Singh, 1984a). Group training has sometimes been combined with an individual approach, for example work with families of aggressive antisocial children (Patterson, 1974; Patterson *et al.*, 1973; Patterson and Reid, 1973), and with pre-school handicapped children (Freeman and Thompson, 1973). Occasionally, supplementary individual work has followed group training for the few families who have not benefited sufficiently from the group (Brightman *et al.*, 1980). In most groups for parents of handicapped children, the children have been seen for assessment only or not at all, and parents have met as a group in a clinic or other setting, sometimes with supplementary home visits to see how they worked with their child. Some projects have chosen to concentrate on a particular content area, such as play (Mash and Terdal, 1973), developmental skills (Bidder *et al.*, 1975), or language (McConkey and O'Connor, 1982), or have focused on a particular age group of children (Attwood, 1978, 1979; Firth, 1982), but most have included a heterogeneous group of children and so have dealt with a wider range of problems and skills (e.g. Attwood, 1978; Tavormina, 1975). Training in behavioural skills has been the main purpose of several projects, but has been only one aspect of other more general courses (Attwood, 1977). The few comparisons between individual and group training show both to be equally effective in teaching skills when other aspects of training are identical (Brightman *et al.*, 1982) though evidence is poor and contradictory on such issues as efficient use of time, cost, client preference and other benefits of either individual or group interventions (Callias, 1985; Cunningham, 1985). Service patterns, resources and therapist preference may well play a large part in determining whether individual or group treatment is offered, but more attention could be directed to matching modality to the needs of families.

Early intervention and Portage Project

Parents of handicapped infants and pre-school children have been encouraged to help their offspring to achieve optimal development in early intervention programmes (Cunningham and Sloper, 1985). Specially trained workers visit the home regularly to offer broad-based counselling which incorporates advice on how to respond sensitively to the infant and on how to structure situations for teaching skills within a developmental framework. The focus is on content, and parents are usually taught behavioural techniques informally and incidentally.

Behavioural approaches have also been incorporated in projects aiming to set up widely available services for advising parents on how to teach their own children. The Portage project (Shearer and Loftin, 1984; Shearer and Shearer, 1972) has provided an attractive and widely used model (Barna *et al.*, 1980; Bidder *et al.*, 1983; Daly *et al.*, 1985; Revill and Blunden, 1979) because of its clear materials and well formulated system of service delivery. Home visitors, professionals of any discipline with experience of handicap and some non-professionals, are trained in the use of Portage guides, principles of behaviour change and how to work with parents. With the back-up of regular meetings with a specialist organiser or team, each home visitor makes weekly visits to each of several families to advise parents on the use of the materials for assessing and teaching skills to their child. At each visit, progress is reviewed, and new goals are set, attempting to ensure that they are ones that the child is likely to achieve within a week or two. Over time, the home visitor tries to fade out so that the parent gains confidence in working more independently with the child.

Content

In most behavioural training the focus is on teaching parents *how* to teach or cope with problems rather than on *what* to teach, though these two threads are often closely intertwined with the emphasis on the curriculum aspects in projects focusing on fostering development.

Parents have been taught either to apply specific techniques to particular circumscribed problems or a more comprehensive range of concepts and techniques (Clements, 1985; Cunningham, 1985). There is very little guidance from the literature on how to decide what to teach. Parents we have worked with clinically and in special workshops have been equally concerned to develop their children's skills and to deal with problem behaviour. Hence, teaching should include strategies for observing carefully, defining the problems or components of a new skill in behavioural terms, and conducting a functional analysis of problems as well as a knowledge of operant principles and techniques for teaching new skills. Parents may also need to know how to facilitate generalisation and maintain changes

217

in their child (Kazdin, 1975; O'Dell *et al.*, 1977a). The curriculum for group training should include all these aspects, although in working with individual families the psychologist can be more flexible and selective.

Teaching methods

Parents have been taught behavioural skills by formal didactic methods (lectures, talks, discussions, films, programmed texts) and/ or direct practical training (modelling, role-play, supervised practice with their child). Systematic studies on teaching methods (Baker, 1986; Milne, 1986; O'Dell, 1985) have shown that all forms of training are more effective than none (e.g. Heifetz, 1977) but that practical training methods are the most effective in enabling parents to acquire the skills (e.g. Glogower and Sloop, 1976; Koegel *et al.*, 1978; Nay, 1975; O'Dell *et al.*, 1977b). Knowledge of general principles facilitates the generalisation of these skills to other problems (Glogower and Sloop, 1976). These findings have obvious implications for both individual and group teaching.

Books and manuals for parents have a useful place in training but are unlikely to substitute entirely for direct contact training, particularly of complex and diffuse problems (Bernal and North, 1978; Callias, 1985; McMahon and Forehand, 1980). Though manuals with minimal therapist contact have been as effective as other direct contact methods for training parents to teach skills, they are less successful for dealing with problem behaviours, and parents lack confidence in their skills (Christensen *et al.*, 1980; Heifetz, 1977; Nay, 1975). Several clear, practical books have been written specially for parents of mentally handicapped children (e.g. Baker *et al.*, 1976; Baldwin *et al.*, 1973; Carr, 1980; Cunningham and Sloper, 1978; Perkins *et al.*, 1976). Such manuals help to introduce concepts and to refresh memories after training.

Context of training

All parent training aims to meet the needs of families but varies in the way it meshes with other services (Dangel and Polster, 1984); sometimes it is service-based (Callias and Carr, 1975; Firth, 1982; Harris, 1978; Holland and Hattersley, 1980; Schopler *et al.*, 1982), but more often it is research-based aiming to meet service needs (Baker, 1986; Hemsley *et al.*, 1978), to investigate technical aspects of training (O'Dell, 1985), or to develop programmes for widespread use (Shearer and Loftin, 1984). Findings from research are combined with clinical experience to suggest strategies for individual and group parent training in clinical practice.

Work with individual families

It is perhaps worth emphasising that the main reason for teaching parents behavioural skills is to enable them to deal with any difficulties they may have in helping their child learn or in managing problem behaviours. To ensure that this is indeed their main or only need, a careful history and assessment of the present circumstances of the child and family should be undertaken. There may be additional problems and stresses (e.g. maternal depression, housing difficulties) in some families that have to be dealt with too (Callias and Carr, 1975; Rutter, 1985; Wilkin, 1979; Wing, 1985). Though some demographic and general characteristics of parents and families, such as lower socio-economic status, less education, single status and marital difficulties, have been associated with poorer outcome and drop-out in some parent training studies, this is by no means always the case (Callias, 1985; Clements, 1985; Cunningham, 1985; O'Dell, 1985; Oltmanns *et al.*, 1977; Feldman *et al.*, 1983), and many families who fail to benefit sufficiently from 'standard package' training do well with training geared to their particular needs (Brightman *et al.*, 1980). There is not sufficient evidence to contraindicate the use of behavioural approaches in such families, unless other problems loom so large that they need attention first or that it is simply not feasible for the child to remain in the family. Undoubtedly some families find it easier to use these approaches than others do, and certain parental and family characteristics may alert the therapist to potential difficulties and to the need to work carefully and realistically. There is at present no satisfactory way of anticipating which families will not be able to benefit from training, so those who seek help should not be denied it on *a priori* grounds.

Individual parent training has the advantage of allowing the therapist to tailor the degree of his involvement, and the amount and nature of training, to the specific requirements of families. Work with individual families is particularly suited to helping those with complex needs, families who have very circumscribed and specific problems, or where special skills teaching or home-based work is needed.

There are several essential steps in carrying out a behavioural intervention. The therapist may carry these out jointly with parents,

219

or advise them on how to do so relatively independently. These steps are:

(1) identification and behavioural description of the problems;
(2) deciding what to tackle first;
(3) carrying out a functional analysis of the problem, including the identification of potential reinforcers;
(4) ensuring that the parent has, or acquires, the relevant skills to carry out the intervention;
(5) implementation of the treatment/training strategy;
(6) monitoring progress;
(7) reviewing the programme if it is proving ineffective; and
(8) ensuring generalisation and maintenance of new behaviours or treatment changes.

The first four steps comprise the behavioural assessment of the problem. The information can be gained through a careful behavioural interview. A home visit to observe the situation at first hand is invaluable. It also provides the opportunity of ensuring that intervention will be realistic. While it is usually desirable to work in the home setting, constraints of time and distance may preclude this. In such cases, care must be taken to ensure that parents can implement the treatment suggestions at home. All too often, for reasons of convenience or parental choice, only one parent, usually the mother, is seen. This works reasonably well provided parents agree on what to do, or one of them has the main responsibility for rearing the child. It is preferable to see both parents at least on some occasions. It is essential to do so if there are major disagreements about crucial aspects of a treatment plan, in order to work for some measure of consistency.

Teaching parents the necessary skills for enabling their child to learn new behaviours is usually relatively straightforward. It is usually possible to visit the home at a convenient time, to teach feeding, dressing, or language. It is often useful to teach parents to use charts such as are included in the Portage materials (Bluma *et al.*, 1976) to provide an assessment of the child's current degree of competence and to act as a framework for selecting suitable training goals. Parents are then taught the necessary training techniques for teaching the skill to their child. The parent can be observed, improvements can be suggested by modelling and/or directly teaching the parent *in situ*. Principles can be discussed and demonstrated. The amount of direct tuition that parents need will vary from minimal to several sessions.

Dealing with problem behaviour is more difficult. Children do not always misbehave at convenient times, so it may not be possible for the therapist to observe the problems directly. Parents need to be taught, through discussion, how to make careful observations and carry out a functional analysis of the problem. This stage is very important, if the therapist and parent are to avoid common pitfalls such as assuming, for example, that all tantrums are 'attention-seeking'. Children can have tantrums for a variety of reasons: they may be fearful of particular situations; unable to understand or carry out demands made on them; tired and irritable — or they may even be trying to gain some adult attention. The intervention will be very different in each case.

Principles for reducing problem behaviours, such as extinction and time-out from positive reinforcement, sound so simple. They are, but their implementation may not be. It is important to discuss fully with parents exactly what they are doing when, for example, they are 'ignoring' Tommy's swearing or tantrum. 'I don't stop him, but tell him not to do it' is not 'ignoring' it in the sense of using extinction. Even when parents do understand and could implement an extinction or time-out from positive reinforcement procedure, they may not be able to in certain circumstances. It is highly unlikely that a parent will be able to ignore Adam when he throws things about in the living room. Removing him from the situation may be problematic, but a feasible intervention may well be possible with a little planning in order to ensure that the important treatment features of time-out from reinforcement are adhered to and that the punishment is not unnecessarily harsh (Hobbs and Forehand, 1977).

Where there is a choice, it is worth trying to plan treatments so that reinforcement or the techniques selected are those that parents find most acceptable. They are likely to find it easier to implement such a plan, and to be enthusiastic about it, and therapeutic changes in the child's behaviour are more likely to persist (Kazdin, 1975). In dealing with problem behaviours, trainee therapists and parents often forget the importance of making sure the children are receiving parental praise, attention and other reinforcement for acceptable behaviour. In circumstances where it is dubious that this is happening in the normal course of events, parents could be encouraged to work on improving particular skills, or on developing play or language with their child, so that an opportunity for some positive interaction is created. Another common fallacy is to assume that the child knows how to behave in a more acceptable way in a given situation, and that the task is simply one of decreasing the unacceptable behaviour. It is important to check on this. Take the complaint that Tom hits and pinches other children. Careful observation and questioning will reveal whether he can also play with them or whether his peer interaction is restricted to hitting and pinching. If the latter is true, it will be necessary to teach him how to interact more appropriately at some level, however simple, as well as, or instead of, aiming to stop the hitting and pinching.

When the parents are implementing projects appropriately, the trainer's role is to review progress, identify any snags or problems and help parents overcome them. It is often necessary to encourage parents to persist when change seems excruciatingly slow, or to change tack when necessary. The generalisation and maintenance phases are often problematic and require more attention than they receive (Forehand and Atkeson, 1977). Trainers should alert parents to the fact that, all too often, their child will not spontaneously demonstrate his new behaviour in a wide variety of appropriate settings and that extending their treatment strategy to these new settings will usually facilitate generalisation. If the same problems occur both at home and school, a consistent treatment approach in both settings should be attempted. Similarly, parents will need to be aware of the reasons why new behaviour patterns may not persist of their own accord, so that they can ensure their maintenance. They need to be taught to fade special training procedures (such as prompts) gradually and how to move from continuous to intermittent schedules of reinforcement in order to strengthen and maintain their child's new behaviour. In addition, the child is likely to persist with using new skills only if these are functional or are maintained by naturally occurring cues and reinforcers. This may be facilitated by teaching skills in their naturally occurring context, for example dressing on rising in the morning.

Ideally, the therapist should continue seeing the family for 'as long as seems necessary': this varies considerably from family to family. If no improvements occur and problems become intolerable, residential observation and intensive treatment may be needed. More commonly, improvement takes place, and contact can cease. With some families of chronically handicapped children, further contact is often required later and parents should be encouraged to renew contact if they need to. A few may prefer regular infrequent appointments (even six-monthly or annually), simply to review their child's progress and needs. Although this may not, strictly speaking, be training, it enables parents to continue fostering their child's development.

Group training for parents

Though the main reason for the recent move to group courses for parents has been the lack of resources for meeting the needs of families on an individual basis (Callias, 1985), working in groups makes it easier to ensure systematic coverage of behavioural principles and techniques; parents welcome the opportunity of sharing with each other their experiences — both of problems and of potential solutions (Tavormina *et al.*, 1976); feelings of isolation, felt by many families, seem to be reduced; hearing about other successful projects often stimulates parents to try to change problems they previously considered immutable; the encouragement and support that parents offer to one another is sometimes more acceptable and sustaining than that offered by a professional because it is perceived as coming from someone who 'knows what it's like' to be in their position.

Possible limitations of group courses includes: the amount of organisation involved in planning and running a workshop; insufficient time for discussing all projects fully at each meeting; the difficulty in offering more intensive training or discussion to those families who need more than can be provided in this context; the unavailability of further contact that many families feel they need at the end of time-limited courses; problems can arise if parents are receiving conflicting advice from other therapists. Many of these difficulties can be avoided or resolved by careful planning and consultation; others are related to the problems of patchy services. Despite these problems, time-limited parent groups do help to fill the enormous gap in the services and are all too often the only source of practical advice to some parents.

The following guidelines for running an effective behaviourally oriented parent group are based on our own experiences of group training and reports in the literature (cited above).

1. Recruitment

The need for a group may arise in a number of different ways, either as an extension of existing services or to meet a newly recognised need. Increasingly, as parents become aware of this form of practical help, professionals will be approached with requests to organise training groups. Such services may be advertised to increase recruitment (Cunningham and Jeffree, 1975), but not all parents, even of those who are thought likely to benefit, will want to join a group (Saunders *et al.*, 1975). Where possible, it seems preferable that the groups should be locally based and part of the community services, for this facilitates travelling for parents and tutors, contacts with local services and follow-up meetings. However, where families are widely scattered or local services are limited, a group without all these advantages may be better than nothing.

2. Selection of parents

Some selection may be necessary if the numbers of parents applying for a course exceeds the number of places available. Our own solution to this was a first-come, first-served policy, and an offer of places on a subsequent course to those not accepted for the first. If more homogeneous groups are preferred, selection can be made on the basis of child characteristics (see Section 4 below) or demographic characteristics of parents, such as marital status (Feldman *et al.*, 1983) or educational background. Although some studies have found it difficult to work in groups with parents of low socio-economic or educational status, or with those parents experiencing personal or marital problems, this is not always the case (Baker, 1986; Callias, 1985; Milne, 1986), making it difficult to forecast accurately which parents will or will not benefit from group teaching. Running the groups in a way that makes minority members feel comfortable (for example, suggesting that single parents attending a mixed group bring a friend — see Baker, 1986), using teaching methods that work well with parents of diverse backgrounds, and being flexible in meeting the needs of participating families (Reese and Serna, 1986) should maximise benefits for most families. Those families who do not benefit sufficiently from group training can be offered supplementary individual training (Brightman *et al.*, 1980). Families with very serious and complex personal and interpersonal problems may do better with individual intervention tailored to their special needs. At present, such decisions are essentially based on clinical judgement.

There are no hard and fast rules about the size of the group; probably four or five families are the minimum, but groups have been run for much larger numbers (Cunningham and Jeffree, 1971), dividing into smaller tutor groups of five to eight families for discussion of projects.

3. Pre-group contact

It is helpful to circulate parents with a short letter outlining the aims of the project, and of the commitment that this would entail in terms

224

of time and work, and to ask them to fill in a brief questionnaire giving demographic data about themselves and basic information about their child's skills and handicaps.

If at all feasible, the families should be visited at home, to clarify the nature of the group, to discuss their particular problems, to meet the child and to carry out any assessments that may be used for evaluation of the group's effectiveness. Acquaintance with the child proves valuable later in the course, when the parents are discussing their projects.

4. Group composition and child characteristics

It may be easier to run groups for parents whose children share common characteristics (Attwood, 1978; Bidder *et al.*, 1975; Mash and Terdal, 1973) although it is perfectly feasible to work with more heterogeneous groups (Cunningham and Jeffree, 1975). If numbers permit, it is probably preferable to choose groups that are homogeneous for age of the child and/or for their degree of handicap. These seem to be the more important factors on which to base the groups, rather than the type of problem or the teaching task chosen by the parent (unless the content is to be restricted in focus, for example to play or language development only) or medical conditions: teaching a child to feed himself requires the parents to apply a similar strategy regardless of the cause of the child's mental handicap. When the grouping is done on the basis of the child's age (for example, under-fives, 5–12, adolescents and young adults) the parents find each other's concerns directly relevant to their own, whereas when the age groups are mixed, parents of the older children may find it boring and unprofitable to listen to discussions on topics like feeding or potty training which they have left far behind them. Degree of handicap is also important. It may be difficult for parents of profoundly handicapped children to maintain realistic goals without becoming too discouraged by their children's comparatively slow progress, especially if they see able children of other group members advancing more rapidly. If all the children in the group are at roughly the same level, this discouraging effect can be minimised.

Parents of children with most kinds of disorders are potentially suitable for inclusion in a behavioural group, the only exception being perhaps those of children with degenerative disorders of known course and limited life expectancy. The main needs of these families are not met by this type of approach.

However the groups are constituted, some parents may drop out of training. Little is known of the reasons for drop-out, but in the case of groups run for parents of mentally handicapped children (Cunningham and Jeffree, 1971; Callias and Jenkins, 1973; Callias *et al.*, 1976; Firth, 1982) the rate seems to be lower than the 36 per cent reported for other parent groups (Rinn *et al.*, 1975).

5. Group tutors

Tutors should have experience of working with handicapped children and their parents using behavioural approaches. In practice, this usually means clinical and educational psychologists, sometimes in conjunction with colleagues from other disciplines (social workers, health visitors, nurses, teachers, etc.). The parent group itself offers a training opportunity in that less experienced workers can collaborate with the more experienced in running the group.

6. Length of the course

Early in the planning stages of a course, a decision has to be taken as to how long it will last. Most have been time-limited, usually meeting about ten times, weekly at first for seven or eight meetings and then less frequently. Intervals between later meetings may be increased to two, three, four or six weeks. This allows for concentrated teaching and supervision of projects early on, and then for increasing independence, with an opportunity for discussing progress. If desired (and in our case it was), follow-up meetings can be arranged.

Evening meetings are preferable from the point of view of the parents, allowing fathers as well as mothers to attend. Two hours seems a reasonable duration for the meetings, though we often found it difficult to end on time.

7. Format of the meetings

Preceding each formal meeting with about 10–15 minutes for coffee and informal chat helps to break the ice and enables participants to get to know each other. The first meeting may then begin with introductions and a brief outline about the aims, format and content of the course. Then this and subsequent meetings are usually divided into two parts: part I contains the didactic teaching aspect of the course; in part II the participants divide, if necessary, into smaller groups of five to eight sets of parents for discussion of the parents' individual projects.

In planning part I of the meetings, decisions will have to be taken about three related teaching problems. First, how far should the

226

teaching emphasise theoretical principles on the one hand, or practical techniques on the other? Secondly, should the focus be on formal teaching or on direct training methods? Thirdly, what should be included in the teaching programme?

From studies on the relative merits of teaching principles or skills, and of different teaching methods (Baker, 1986; Milne, 1986; O'Dell, 1985), a combination of systematic didactic teaching with some supervised practice would seem most suited to parents of handicapped children who face the long-term task of helping their child as they grow up and their needs change. Some form of practical training is essential for parents to acquire behavioural skills, and a knowledge of principles and of strategies for applying them should help parents cope with some new problems independently. Manuals and handouts can provide an introduction to concepts and serve to refresh memories at a later date.

Part I of the meeting usually focuses on the systematic teaching of a particular topic (see below), introducing it in a lecture/discussion with videotape examples. Some role-play practice could be included, either regularly at each meeting or for the whole first part of some of the meetings.

In part II of each meeting the large group divides, if necessary, into smaller groups for discussion of individual projects. Two trainers to a group work well but, at a pinch, one very experienced person can manage.

In the first meeting, parents are asked to describe their child to the group and then they select the areas they wish to work on and, for homework, begin careful observations on these areas. Thereafter, the main focus each week is on helping parents to carry out their projects. Each family selects and works on at least one specific project with their child, and each has a turn to report on progress each week (hopefully, showing off some data too!). They are helped to overcome any difficulties by discussion, role-play, modelling, re-analysis of the situation or any other teaching approach that works. Time should be rationed so that all families have a turn, and different parents take a turn to start each week.

There will, of course, be times when the discussion broadens; parents may have other worries on their mind that they wish to discuss. Non-directive counselling, specific advice or suggestions on how to use other services are all appropriate. Such counselling is quite compatible with a behavioural approach (Tavormina, 1974, 1975).

8. *Programme*

If parents are to be able to deal with a wide range of problems and skills in the future, the teaching content of the first part of the meetings will need to include, first, teaching of several basic behavioural principles and techniques and, secondly, application of these to particular skills and problems. Thus a 10-session course may have the following curriculum.

Week 1: Observation and inference, defining tasks, simple data recording methods.

Week 2: Operant principles — reinforcement.

Week 3: Techniques for teaching new skills: (a) shaping, prompts, fades, chaining.

Week 4: Techniques for teaching new skills: (b) imitation, generalisation and discrimination; (c) generalisation and maintenance.

Week 5: Techniques for decreasing behaviour: extinction, DRO, time-out from positive reinforcement, other mild punishment. Issues in the use of punishment.

Wherever possible these teaching principles should be applied to examples that are relevant to the participants.

In weeks 6–9, content areas that are of particular interest and relevance to the group can be selected for detailed discussion. It is useful to do so both from a developmental perspective, and from the point of view of how parents can apply the above principles and techniques to them. Important areas to consider are: language, play and occupation, self-help skills (including toilet training), adolescence and the future, social behaviour with adults and peers or in certain situations (e.g. shops, parks). If whole sessions are to be allocated to role-play practice, this could be done after week 3 and/or week 5 in the above programme, resulting in six or seven sessions being spent on this part of the curriculum.

Week 10 and other follow-up meetings can be spent on progress reports from the parents and in showing videotapes of the children. During one of these meetings, it is helpful to elicit feedback from the parents and suggestions for improving future courses.

9. *Home visits*

If it can be arranged, it is helpful to make a home visit after the fourth of fifth meeting to see what parents are actually doing with their children, and to sort out difficulties.

10. Assessment and evaluation

There are no well worked out, fully satisfactory simple ways of evaluating group projects. Nevertheless, some attempts should be made at evaluation, at one or all of a number of levels, and using a variety of methods (Milne, 1986). Assessment before and after training is the minimum requirement for studying change; follow-up measures and some group comparisons are desirable in research studies. Examples of ways of assessing changes in the child and in the parents include: parent project data, formal assessments of the child, parent rating scales of the child's behaviour, direct or video-taped observation of parent–child interaction in special or naturalistic settings, and parent attitude scales. Consumer feedback from partici-pants is helpful; it has often been obtained by means of questionnaires and sometimes by interview. Evaluation of the quality of the course and training is a neglected area (Clements, 1985; Milne, 1986).

Problems and issues

Difficulties can arise at home, in spite of genuine concern on the part of adults to help children. If we accept that behavioural learning approaches hold the most promise for helping retarded children develop, it is important to consider what obstacles hinder their use, and what can be done about them.

Several parent trainers have bravely exposed their treatment failures to scrutiny, believing that an examination of cases and conditions in which difficulty or failure occur can illuminate key elements in particular settings which may well go unnoticed in successful inter-ventions (Callias & Carr, 1975; Ferber *et al.*, 1974; Saunders *et al.*, 1975; Sajwaj, 1973; Tharp & Wetzel, 1969, Yule, 1975). These papers offer clinical suggestions for coping with some recurring thorny issues. Problems fall into three main areas: attitudinal, practical and those relating to the constraints of the social context.

Attitudes

Parental attitudes and values that lead to a rejection of or difficulty in implementing behavioural principles have been called resistances (Tharp and Wetzel, 1969). Resistances include a rejection of deter-minism, regarding positive reinforcement as 'bribery', and the expectation that children should behave appropriately for intrinsic reasons. We have found it helpful to avoid getting embroiled in philosophical arguments, and to discuss treatment in practical terms:

229

the child is not behaving as the parents would like him to; we are offering ways they can try out to help him learn new ways of behaving.

The concept and use of positive reinforcement sometimes needs careful discussion. One common objection to the use of reinforcement stems from the notion that extrinsic reinforcement will dampen the child's intrinsic interest in activities (Greene and Lepper, 1974; Lepper *et al.*, 1973). It is perhaps worth emphasising that, in behavioural approaches, extrinsic reinforcement is used precisely because children *lack* the intrinsic motivation to persist in learning skills that will be of intrinsic value to them later. When children enjoy activities for their own sake, extrinsic reinforcement becomes superfluous. A goal of behaviour approaches is that new behaviours should be maintained by intrinsic and naturally occurring reinforcers (Kazdin, 1975, 1977). Some parents may be reluctant to use reinforcers because they mistakenly think reinforcers are always edibles or sweets; others may only be willing to use events that they feel ought to be reinforcing whether this is so or not. Reinforcers should be chosen which are acceptable to the parents and, preferably, from among the things they naturally use. This is not always possible. The therapist's task is then to discuss qualms and objections and to suggest that the parents experiment to see whether or not certain events are better reinforcers than others. Most parents will find the evidence more convincing than any amount of theoretical argument. Reluctance to use positive reinforcement with one particular child often arises from the view that it is 'not fair' to single out one child for special favours. The objection to singling out a child for punishment is less often heard. Discussion of the issue in terms of teaching the child rather than giving 'just desserts', combined with empirical test, usually helps to alter these perceptions.

Other attitudinal problems can emerge in the process of implementing a behavioural approach. Parents may have difficulty in understanding the child's problems and their role in it. Behavioural approaches can raise feelings of anxiety and guilt because the explicit statement that parents can be effective in modifying the child's behaviour can convey the hidden message that they are to blame for causing the current state of affairs in the first place (Yule, 1975). Clinical impression suggests that anxiety about causation is not confined to parents of non-handicapped difficult children but is found, perhaps surprisingly, in some parents of handicapped children too. It is well worth discussing this issue openly at an early stage, making these points: the child definitely has an intrinsic developmental disorder (of known or unknown causation); it may not be possible to know why problems developed as they did but, in helping the child, it is more fruitful to focus on the present situation and to look towards altering things for the future than to dwell on the past; circumstances currently maintaining the difficulties, usually modifiable, need to be differentiated from the original causes which are often unknown and unchangeable; a child's temperamental characteristics and pattern of handicaps may well contribute to difficulties in bringing him up and, consequently, parents need to learn some special ways of coping with and rearing the child. Parents of handicapped children frequently feel they have lost a lot of time for helping their child develop. It is often important to give time to their concerns that 'if only' they could have had advice sooner — and to help them come to a realistic view of what can be achieved. Setting a series of short-term goals rather than one enormous target is frequently helpful.

Parental feelings of inadequacy can be aroused or strengthened by ill-chosen teaching techniques or by other excessive demands during training. For example, the use of modelling on its own may have the effect of decreasing parents' confidence if they see someone else cope so much better with their child. It may be better to train a hesitant, demoralised parent using other techniques such as shaping and direct feedback, which may be slower, but have the advantage of boosting confidence. Parents' broader attitudes toward childbearing, handicap, and the way they construe their role in rearing their handicapped child will have some bearing on their expectations of professional involvement (Cunningham and Davis, 1985a) and how readily they accept particular kinds of interventions including behavioural ones. Such attitudes may be personal ones or common to a particular social or cultural group, and may or may not be alterable by counselling and discussion of the needs of the child. The links between attitudes and behavioural interventions could benefit from empirical investigation.

Practical problems

Several practical problems can arise in behavioural intervention by parents. Simply gathering data can create problems. In spite of the difficulties, some objective record is usually helpful as a device for monitoring progress, as well as for assessing and evaluating projects. Not enough attention has been given to the issues of how to train parents to collect data. Measures such as providing or helping parents to prepare data sheets and using simple but valid indices of change could ensure that data collection does not become an intolerable burden that is neglected (Callias and Carr, 1975). The possible adverse effects of data collection on the parents' perception of their problems need to be borne in mind. Though data collection is viewed as beneficial by therapists, this is not necessarily the case for parents of children with mental handicaps (Yule, 1975). Baseline recordings may be worse than expected, or rate of progress may be discouragingly slow. On the other hand, simply counting or recording specific targets may be therapeutic, either because the parents notice that the problem is less frequent or milder than they thought, or because their own behaviour changes while they are monitoring that of their child. (Behavioural change in the therapeutically desired direction has often been found when individuals are asked to keep records of their own behaviour; see Nelson *et al.*, 1975). The trainer should be on the alert for the effects of data collection, and prepared to discuss these when necessary.

It may be necessary to maintain parents' interest and enthusiasm at the initial stage, when the fruits of their efforts are not yet evident. This is helpful if the parents work on a skill or problem that they perceive as important, whether or not the trainer agrees. If the parents select a very complex or difficult task (for example, self-injury), it may be worth suggesting that they work simultaneously on a simpler project which is likely to be more encouraging, such as imitation or a self-help skill. In addition, clear and repeated discussion about expected rates of change in the child's behaviour may be needed. Obviously, if the current intervention seems to be ineffective, re-evaluation and alteration are called for. Such decisions are at present a matter of clinical judgement rather than founded on clear criteria.

A further important practical issue that has been neglected is that of deciding how to intervene when faced with numerous child problems. There seem to be enormous individual differences in how much parents are able or willing to undertake (Callias and Carr, 1975; Saunders *et al.*, 1975), and deciding on the order of interventions remains an issue (Altman and Mira, 1983). With parents who are willing, there is little to go on, other than to follow our own advice of working in graded steps rather than tackling everything at once. Even if the child presents with numerous problems, it may be preferable for parents to begin by tackling only one or two tasks. One of these should be teaching a new skill, even if the parents originally sought advice over problem behaviours. This provides the opportunity for positive interaction between parent and child, which has often been overshadowed by the problem. Teaching alternative behaviour may be a vital part of dealing with problems, particularly when the child lacks acceptable ways of behaving in that situation. It may also be important to suggest that parents set aside a short period of time regularly every day to work in, rather than attempt to change all their behaviour all day long. Parents can teach some new skills, such as dressing or play, successfully in daily 10 to 15-minute sessions, while the parents of a child who screams virtually all day may at first find it easier to carry out a treatment programme properly for shorter periods (e.g. during meals or a play session) than all day long. Although overall progress may be slower initially, this approach allows parents to learn new patterns of interacting with their children without finding it too exhausting or too disruptive to the family, thus making it less likely that they will opt out. As parents gain skills and see desired changes, generalisation can be introduced, and other tasks can be tackled. On the other hand, it may be necessary from a treatment point of view to deal with problems as and when they arise in the course of the day, because they are relatively infrequent (such as two or three temper tantrums per day) or are totally disruptive anyway (such as throwing furniture). Where teaching skills is concerned, many parents are willing to restructure daily situations such as mealtimes, or bathtime, as learning situations, rather than simply to continue with the chore of feeding or washing the child themselves. Clearly, flexibility is needed in working out practical details to suit the needs of each family.

The issues of generalisation and maintenance of both parents' skills and changes in the child remain in need of study (Altman and Mira, 1983; Helm and Kosloff, 1986). After training, parents tend to use their skills incidentally as part of daily routine rather than in formal projects (Baker, 1986). This seems highly appropriate if the aim of training parents is to enable them, as parents, to foster their child's optimal development and well-being rather than become therapists and teachers, sometimes feeling overburdened by the demands professionals make on them (Sloper *et al.*, 1983; Turnbull and Turnbull, 1982).

Social context

The unexpected obstacles that can arise if due attention is not paid to the home circumstances are clearly highlighted by Sajwaj (1973). Parents were successfully taught to use behavioural principles to modify unwanted behaviour within a clinic setting, but the procedures adopted failed to be effective at home. Observations at home revealed that circumstances were different because of competing demands on the mother. Consequently, there was less attention and reinforcement for appropriate behaviour. A functional analysis done at home at the particular times of difficulty led to the implementation of different procedures, which were successful. Home circumstances need to be known, either by basing treatment there or by eliciting relevant information.

Although the issue of the effects of having a handicapped child on family life and on the siblings is receiving some attention (Carr, 1985; Lobato, 1983; Simeonsson and McHale, 1981; Wilkin, 1979), the effect of behavioural training on siblings and family life has been relatively neglected. Parents sometimes wonder whether giving extra attention or reinforcement to one child will adversely affect the others. In practice, we have not found this to be a problem. It may be that the other children are not surprised that the handicapped child is treated differently. Older children, of course, can understand the problems and frequently participate in the training (Lobato, 1983). Parental concerns should be heeded, and, if real problems arise, suggestions may be offered — for instance, a parallel (even if not strictly necessary) token programme and back-up reinforcers for a younger sib (Carr, 1980), or something to be given to both children for doing the same task, like reading or laying the table.

Early findings that families who have additional concurrent problems such as parental ill-health or martial discord seem to have the most difficulty in carrying out behavioural interventions for problem behaviours (e.g. Callias and Carr, 1975; O'Dell, 1974; Patterson *et al.*, 1973) have led to more attention being directed towards understanding the family and wider social context, assessing difficulties in these areas and taking them into consideration in behavioural parent training (Burgess and Richardson, 1984; Crnic *et al.*, 1983; Embry, 1984; Milne, 1986; Wahler, 1980; Wahler and Dumas, 1984). From the behavioural tradition, this is being done within a broad-based behavioural–cognitive or problem-solving framework with the focus directly on the family interactions and other problems (Blechman, 1984; Patterson, 1982) or through helping mothers understand and control the stresses affecting their interactions with the child (Wahler and Dumas 1984).

At present there is little to show which is the best way of helping families with these multiple problems. In clinical practice, it is quite feasible to offer counselling and behavioural advice on child management concurrently either by the same or different workers, though we have no experience as to which approach is the more effective. Obviously, exposing families to conflicting advice is unhelpful, at best, and may be harmful. Whether the task of implementing treatment should be shared or not depends on the skills and experience of the therapist(s), and the way the clinic or service is organised. In our focused parent groups, we often found ourselves discussing related problems that concerned the parents, and this did not appear to interfere with the main behavioural aims of the group. Mothers in groups in which the treatment was designed to combine behavioural and counselling approaches did better on all kinds of objective measures (Tavormina, 1975), and felt that they both understood and could teach their child better (Tavormina *et al.*, 1976) than did those parents receiving reflective counselling only. It may be that a combination of methods could be most helpful for parents with multiple problems.

Further research is needed to clarify such issues as the role of behavioural training directed at the child in such families; and the timing of various interventions — whether problems are best dealt with simultaneously or in sequence, and in which order. It is perhaps also important to remember that, for whatever family and attitudinal reasons, some families find they cannot or do not see it as their role to work with their children using behavioural approaches (Saunders *et al.*, 1975; Wing, 1975) or feel generally overburdened by expectations of them, particularly if services are not co-ordinated (Turnbull and Turnbull, 1982). However, feedback from parents on behavioural help is usually very positive (Baker, 1986; Callias *et al.*, 1976; Holmes *et al.*, 1982). We need to know much more about the impact of parent training on wider aspects of family life (Helm and Kosloff, 1986); the little evidence available suggests that parent training can have broader beneficial effects than centre-based work with the child (Koegel *et al.*, 1984).

While it is important that we try to find ways of applying behavioural modification principles which parents can accept and make use of, at present there is no way of predicting whether parents who initially express antipathy or experience difficulties will continue to do so. It may be that alternative approaches need to be tried if the parents want help; counselling focused on the parent and child can effectively reduce reported child problems (Tavormina, 1975), though intervention with parents that focuses on non-child-related issues, such as parent advocacy, does not result in changes in the child (Baker and Brightman, 1984).

Behavioural approaches make an important contribution to services for parents of handicapped children, but are not a panacea for all the needs of parents (Wing, 1985). Families also differ widely in their needs, skills and resources (Mittler and Mittler, 1983) and more attention needs to be paid to their individual differences in offering services.

TEACHERS

There is ample evidence that behavioural interventions can be applied successfully by teachers, within a classroom setting, to teach a wide variety of skills to mentally handicapped children, and to cope with their behaviour problems (Barton, 1975; Kazdin, 1977; Kazdin and Craighead, 1973; Ward, 1975). In addition to other problems that parents have dealt with, teachers have been especially interested in language training and work-related skills. Behavioural methods have been used in hospital schools (Barton, 1975) as well as day schools in the community (Saunders *et al.*, 1975; Smith, 1977).

1. Training

Teacher training in behavioural approaches closely parallels parent training in its historical development, moving from teachers carrying out specific behavioural programmes under instruction to courses designed to enable them to carry out behavioural interventions independently (Merrett and Wheldall, 1984; Milne, 1986; Yule *et al.*, 1983). While most intervention in clinical practice is done individually over specific problems, teachers of both handicapped and non-handicapped children have been taught behaviour modification systematically in group courses similar to those held for parents but with principles being applied to school-related behaviour or learning problems (Koegel *et al.*, 1977; Smith, 1977; Yule *et al.*, 1983) and in individually supervised training (Farrell, 1986).

In Britain, the EDY (Education for the Developmentally Young) project has provided widespread in-service behavioural training for teachers and their assistants working in schools for severely and profoundly mentally handicapped children (see Farrell, 1985, and, for a succinct overview, Farrell, 1986). This individually based training programme, based on Kiernan and Riddick's (1973) work on nurse training, was developed at the Hester Adrian Research Centre by Foxen and McBrien (1981) together with instructor's materials (McBrien and Foxen, 1981) and then disseminated via a pyramidal organisational structure. Educational psychologists, special advisory teachers and some headteachers and deputy headteachers were trained in workshops to go on to train teachers and assistants in schools using the curriculum and training methods provided for teaching principles and practice. Small-scale evaluation studies show this training to be effective in improving the skills of teachers and that their skills are maintained over time (McBrien and Edmonds, 1985). However, assistants do not do as well as teachers (Farrell and Sugden, 1984), and well trained teachers fail to improve the skills of profoundly handicapped children (Hogg *et al.*, 1981) — a reminder that even skilled teaching does not automatically help all children to learn.

Studies on training show that teachers, like parents, require practical as well as theoretical training in order to use behavioural principles and techniques effectively (Koegel *et al.*, 1977; McKeowen *et al.*, 1975; Milne, 1986; Smith, 1977). Books and manuals written for teachers of handicapped children tend to focus on skills teaching, and pay attention to task analysis as well as operant principles (e.g. Kiernan, 1981; Koegel *et al.*, 1982).

2. Issues

Many of the problems encountered in training teachers are similar to those found in parent training. In addition, the school setting introduces its own problems (Saunders *et al.*, 1975) — some attitudinal, some practical — and legal and ethical issues relating to acceptable ways of treating children in school are also important (Gast and Nelson, 1977).

Though the need for 'structuring' learning tasks in teaching children is recognised (Gulliford, 1985), teachers still sometimes object to the use of behavioural approaches on philosophical grounds if they hold the view that all children learn best by relatively undirected discovery methods. They may also object to the use of certain procedures (such as time-out from positive reinforcement) or to singling out a particular child for special individual attention. Sometimes such objections can be overcome by avoiding confrontation, discussing the problems in pragmatic terms and emphasising the importance of trying out empirically the treatment intervention to see what happens. For example, the issue of giving special or extra attention to particular children in dealing with problem behaviour can be dealt with by indicating that what is needed is often a change in the *nature* of attention, or its timing, rather than giving more to one child or depriving other children. Most teachers organise their resources (Porterfield and Blunden, 1978; Thomas, 1985) so that they can devote some time to individual teaching, and it is this time that can be set aside for 'special' teaching. It is occasionally necessary to invest extra resources to implement programmes in certain settings, like the playground or certain lessons. Where they see it as necessary, staff are often willing to organise themselves to that they can devote more resources or time to a particular child for a short period of time so that, in the long run, the child can be more independent and less demanding. Once again, it is important to try to devise treatment strategies that the teachers find acceptable, and sufficient time should be spent, at an early stage, on discussion and demonstration in order to ensure this.

When the child presents with similar problems both at home and school, contact and collaboration between teachers and parents becomes important (Saunders *et al.*, 1975). Joint meetings can be useful in setting up a consistent approach, and contact can be maintained via a daily diary and informal meetings between parent and teacher. It may occasionally prove difficult to arrive at a mutually acceptable plan, or the same treatment strategy may not work in different settings. The trainer needs to be on the alert for these potential problems, and to be prepared to use a variety of approaches in trying to overcome them.

Although teachers have been successfully trained in behavioural skills and have been able to help children with behaviour and learning difficulties, this training has been restricted to a limited range of principles and of skills as they apply to the problems of individual children, and thus falls short of giving teachers problem-solving strategies for assessing and dealing with the diversity of individual and group problems they encounter in school. Berger (1982) draws attention to this issue. He suggests ways of helping teachers to conceptualise what goes on in classrooms and ways of extending their problem-solving skills so that they can select interventions from a range of options rather than from only one paradigm.

NURSES

1. Training

Behavioural interventions carried out in hospital or institutional settings with children and adults with mental handicaps have been directed at both reducing maladaptive behaviour (Bates and Wehman, 1977) and increasing self-care, participation in work and activities, and language development of individuals, or of groups in token economy programmes (Kazdin, 1977; Thompson and Grabowski, 1972). Training of nurses, attendants and other staff has ranged from informal instruction to formal courses in the same way as for parents and teachers (Milne, 1986). Studies on teaching methods show that with nurses, too, enactive, practice methods are more effective than purely didactic approaches for imparting skills and knowledge (Gardner, 1973; Milne, 1982; Panyan and Patterson, 1974).

Nurses have been trained to various levels of sophistication, ranging from 'applicator' (using simple procedures under direct supervision) to 'nurse therapist' (an autonomous consultant — Milne, 1985) though often the level of competence and independence that trainers hope their students will achieve is not explicitly stated, especially with short courses and other in-service training. The widespread need to train rapidly direct-care and new staff entering the field of mental handicap has been dealt with in various ways. Teaching materials covering a range of theoretical and practical aspects have been developed for training on an individual basis (Kiernan and Riddick, 1973), a recent development being packages combining materials with guidelines for supervisors of training (Felce *et al.*, 1984). Short intensive group courses for new staff which use theoretical teaching and role play are held at regular intervals at units such as Hilda Lewis House (Callias and Carr, 1975). Similar short courses have been run by itinerent trainers at different hospitals with the purpose of introducing ideas (Williams and Jackson, 1975). Though they meet a demand, such short courses or workshops provide only initial basic training, and staff need to apply and consolidate their knowledge under supervision, if behavioural approaches are to be implemented responsibly (Stein, 1975). Moreover, such courses usually focus on basic principles for teaching skills and managing behaviour problems, giving scant attention to decision-making about goals. Additional training in the use of systematic but broad-based assessment procedures provides a useful adjunct for planning goals (Hegarty, 1981). A more ambitious staff training scheme is the intensive 9-month-long course in behaviour modification sponsored by the English National Board of Clinical Nursing Studies (1982) for qualified nurses. This course aims to impart a sound knowledge of behaviour modification and of how to teach it, so that nurses become qualified to run units along these lines and to teach other hospital staff and parents (Murphy and McArdle, 1978).

While there is ample evidence that nurses working with mentally handicapped people can be taught to use behavioural strategies successfully (e.g. Kazdin, 1977; Thompson and Grabowski, 1972), the extent of generalisation and the long-term effects of training have received little attention (Kazdin, 1977). In a rare follow-up study of extensive in-service training in a hospital, Keith and Lange (1974) found that only 57 per cent of patient behaviours were maintained 3 to 26 months after training. None of the reasons traditionally given for poor maintenance of change (time elapsed since training, degree of mental handicap in clients, staffing) related to relapse rates. There was some evidence to suggest a more complex interaction effect between degree of handicap and staff : resident ratio, such that more programmes were maintained in wards of mildly handicapped residents where there were relatively low staff : residents ratios of 1:8 to 1:11, compared with high ratios of 1:5. Fewest programmes were maintained on highly staffed wards of moderate and severely handicapped residents. The longer term effects of training in behavioural methods on staff's skills remain poorly documented and evaluated (Milne, 1985, 1986).

2. Issues in hospital settings

Introducing behavioural interventions into hospital and other residential settings presents many of the problems already discussed in relation to parents and teachers, and raises additional ones.

Initially, the introduction of behavioural approaches may meet with numerous resistances and objections if it clashes with the existing treatment ethos of the hospital or institution. The common stereotype of people with mental handicaps as incapable of learning and thus in need only of total care and protection, is incompatible with the behavioural emphasis on teaching and encouraging residents to become as independent as possible. Again, behavioural approaches may be rejected for different philosophical reasons, perhaps being seen as overcontrolling. Little attention has been paid to attitudinal or personality variables in staff training projects, yet there is evidence that some of the brightest students resist or opt out of behavioural programmes (Gardner, unpublished; Watson et al., 1971). The importance of adequate discussion, demonstration of efficacy and consultation in setting up the programme is illustrated in two description studies where behavioural programmes were introduced into hospitals for autistic children (Davids and Berenson, 1977; Morrison et al., 1968).

On wards or units where training programmes are introduced successfully, problems of maintaining staff behaviour are common. Such problems of staff motivations may be overcome by providing staff with feedback on their performance and extra incentives (Bricker et al., 1972), or by amusing reminders in the form of a telling cartoon conspicuously pinned on a noticeboard (Fielding et al., 1971), or by more elaborate feedback and management systems (Coles and Blunden, 1982).

There are other difficulties too. The structure and organisation of the institution in which staff work impose limits on their efficiency. Major practical problems can arise from the way the staff shifts are arranged, the physical surroundings, timetabling of activities and staff shortages (Kiernan and Wright, 1973). If the goals of the institutions are to be those of educating residents and reducing their maladaptive behaviours, organisational and administrative change are needed at all levels to facilitate effective programming (Kushlick, 1975; Toogood, 1977). Kushlick (1975) recommends a 'Mager' (Mager and Pipe, 1970) analysis of the service. That is, general aims or 'fuzzies' need to be translated into specific behavioural terms with clear specifications about what criteria should be used to evaluate outcome and the consequences — in other words, an extensive analysis of the structure of the institutions and of the roles and functions of staff at all levels. In such an analysis, staff training has an important place — when staff lack the skills necessary for training the residents. The issues of how changes can best be introduced to institutions is important; Georgiades and Phillimore (1975) provide some useful guidelines for the novice.

Most behavioural interventions on wards have focused on the manipulation of consequences to change client behaviour. Appropriate as this is in most cases, there are times when more attention should be paid to the environmental setting conditions. Differences in behaviour are associated with a wide range of qualitative differences in the physical environment and in the way units are run (King et al., 1971). Moreover, the same residents have been shown to behave more adaptively when they are in a richly equipped recreation room than in a sparsely equipped day-room (Tognoli et al., 1978). Levels of aggression have been reduced considerably simply by enlarging the living space, and then still further by introducing non-contingent reinforcement, though not simply by the provision of more toys (Boe, 1977). Such studies serve an important function in reminding us that behaviour is not independent of the environmental and social context in which both residents and staff live and work. The ethos and physical and social organisation of a hospital or unit are perhaps more important than size alone, in providing a humane and purposeful living situation (Raynes, 1977). Behavioural interventions have a role in such environments, enabling residents to learn skills and to control their unacceptable behaviour so that their lives become richer. They are not a substitute for fundamentally humane living conditions.

Ethical and legal issues concerning the use of behavioural interventions in hospital settings are receiving increasing attention, and have been carefully considered elsewhere (Kazdin, 1975, 1977; Hall, 1978). Where mentally handicapped people in institutions are concerned, questions need to be asked. Who will benefit from intervention? Is it the handicapped person himself or his caregivers only? With clients who cannot give informed consent, and who may not have relatives around to do so, the questions of who decides on goals and how training should proceed are important ones, especially in relation to any plan to use aversive techniques or deprivation of normal rights. Such decisions, the choice of particular techniques and their implementation, need to be carefully considered and monitored. Responsibility for programmes should be made clear, and staff who implement programmes should be adequately trained and supervised. The extent of training needed to ensure competent use of behavioural approaches is unclear, but short courses or experience only in carrying out programmes under supervision, though useful, are unlikely to be sufficient to ensure that staff can implement programmes independently. One of the major strengths of behavioural strategies, the fact that they are simple to understand, is often a disadvantage too. Their implementation may seem easy, but in many cases a complicated behavioural analysis is needed, together with highly skilled intervention.

The issues over ethics, responsibilities and roles of different disciplines are often very sensitive ones in every-day life, but unless they are discussed and acceptable solutions are found, services will continue to be fragmented, and the potentially powerful and valuable contribution of behaviour modification may be abused in many ways (MacNamara, 1977), or dismissed as irrelevant.

CONCLUDING COMMENTS

Parent and staff training continues to expand rapidly to fill the vacuum created by need (O'Dell, 1974), and most of this training continues to be behavioural in content. Though methodological and conceptual problems abound, much has been achieved. Parents, teachers, nurses and others are able to use behavioural approaches to help children and adults with mental handicaps. Some methods of teaching behavioural skills are generally more effective than others, though all are more effective than no training.

Three main themes can be traced in the current literature: a preoccupation with appropriate teaching methods and organisational systems for delivering them; an increasing concern with the characteristics of the adult teachers who are trained; and a growing interest in the contexts in which these adults interact with people with mental handicaps. These issues are being addressed largely from the perspective of how to make behavioural training more effective, efficient and long-lasting. Present research suffers from numerous methodological flaws (Bernstein, 1982; Milne, 1986). Only fragments of the complex processes of influence and inter-action between all members of the triad involved (trainer/consult-ant–caregiver–handicapped person) are addressed by any one study; outcomes are measured at the level of changes either in the handicapped person or in the teacher, but rarely in both — often with rather blunt measuring instruments. The training itself is often poorly described, and its quality and the skill of the trainer/consult-ant are seldom considered. The content of training usually comprises a restricted range of behaviour change methods, the implicit assump-tion being that these are the essential and probably the only relevant strategies and techniques. Developments in cognitive–behavioural and problem-solving strategies have barely impinged on this field. Moreover, especially in 'packaged' courses, little attention is directed towards assessing which skills the caregiver already has in his or her 'natural' repertoire and which are lacking and thus need to be taught. This is a curious state of affairs for trainers who begin their teaching by extolling the virtues of careful definition and assessment of the problem!

Two other implicit assumptions need to be questioned. The first is that the need of parents, nurses and teachers is always or mainly for training in these skills. Yet it may be that many of them have relevant skills, but other factors, such as attitudes to handicapped persons, constraints of the context or personal difficulties, interfere with their efforts to help. Alternatively, ineffective coping techniques may occur together with some of these other problems. Secondly the issue of the maintenance and generalisation of training effects is generally tackled from the point of view of its being a technical matter that the right kind of training will overcome. To some extent this is true, and more attention could be directed to training in such a way as to alter the natural style of caregivers' interactions with these clients rather than focusing almost exclusively on teaching them to carry out formal projects and expect spontaneous generalisation of skills. In addition, it needs to be recognised that other factors such as the characteristics of the client, competing demands on caregivers, life events and other environmental circumstances may greatly influence what happens between the end of training and subsequent follow-up.

The dominant perspective, 'Have tool, will use with problem(s)', seems to lie at the root of many of the limitations of behavioural training. The discernible move to the stance, 'What are the problem(s), which tool(s) shall I use', enables us to apply our broad-based strategies of assessment and problem solving to select interventions that are relevant to the needs of both particular caregivers and people with handicaps. Behavioural training is often what is needed to enable caregivers to cope, but the place of such training in parent counselling and community and other services for people with mental handicaps requires further consideration.

Fruitful developments are likely to emerge not from slavish allegiance to particular theoretical models or from following fashion fads, but from careful problem-oriented research directed towards helping parents, other caregivers and teachers to cope with their task of enabling those people in their care with mental handicaps to develop optimally and to lead lives that are as fulfilling as possible.

13

Evaluation of Treatment Programmes

William Yule

Most of the readers of this book will rarely find themselves involved in large-scale research projects of the sort which compare the efficacy of different treatments. If they find themselves in such a position, then they will know that the classical groups-comparison experimental techniques for demonstrating treatment effects are well described in most introductory books on research design (Maxwell, 1958). Equally, the discerning reader will know that such group studies have particular weaknesses which militate against their use when one wishes to know about the effects of treatment on one individual patient. The results of group studies are often reported only in terms of averages, and such summary statistics describe the whole group, not the individuals within it.

What the clinician wants to know is how many individuals improved by how much, how many were unaffected by treatment and how many were made worse. Even these data are but a guide to deciding whether to apply a particular treatment to a particular patient. Such results cannot guarantee that any treatment will definitely benefit that patient.

At some point, the therapist will want to answer the question, 'Is my treatment helping this patient?' No amount of previously published studies can answer what is very much an empirical question. The way to answer it is to monitor the effects of treatment and, by using an appropriate methodology, to evaluate whether there is a demonstrable relationship between treatment and outcome. The appropriate methodology for such monitoring is the subject of this chapter: single-case research designs.

DEVELOPMENT OF SINGLE-CASE METHODOLOGY

Every patient presents the therapist with unique problems. The job of the therapist is to investigate and understand whatever psychological processes may be at fault and, based on such an analysis of the problem, to develop ways of helping the patient. Somehow, the therapist has to reconcile his knowledge based on studies of large groups of patients with his understanding of the individual patient. This synthesis involves a great deal of clinical skills, but it can be made more powerful by applying experimental methods to the study of the single case.

Experimental studies of single cases have a long history in British clinical psychology, largely as a result of the influence of M.B. Shapiro (Shapiro, 1957, 1966, 1970; Davidson and Costello, 1969). The emphasis of the early studies was more on gaining useful *descriptions* of the patient's psychological functioning than directly on treatment possibilities. None the less, the logic of the investigations is shared with all experimental studies of single cases, namely: define the problem in objective, behavioural terms, then bring those behaviours under experimental control. In other words, the experimenter/therapist searches for independent variables which can be applied so that the particular problem behaviour can be altered in a meaningful, lawful manner.

Once a behaviour is brought under experimental control, therapeutic possibilities are obvious. However, it was the largely American group of behaviour modifiers, coming to treatment problems from a different background of single-organism studies in the animal laboratory, who shifted the emphasis more directly on to the therapeutic possibilities of single-case experimental studies. The parallel in logic between the two approaches has been pointed out by Yates (1970) and by Leitenberg (1973).

SINGLE-CASE STUDIES IN BEHAVIOUR MODIFICATION

Single-case experimental methodology is atheoretical. That is, the methodology is independent of the theoretical framework within which a particular therapeutic technique is formulated. Whether 'treatment' consists of bed rest, catharsis, primal scream, Kleinian interpretation or contingency management, the basic question remains the same. Is there a demonstrable, causal relationship between intervention and outcome? Despite this universality of application, at present most applications of single-case methodology come from investigators working within a behaviour modification framework, and so most of the examples that follow are drawn from this field.

As has been argued in earlier chapters, behaviour modifiers seek to demonstrate a *functional relationship* between treatment and subsequent change in behaviour. Evans (1971) argues that, 'Given our present state of knowledge the functional analysis provides the key link between aetiology and treatment . . . the functional analysis involves identifying the sufficient and necessary conditions for a particular response to occur and persist, so that knowing these conditions allows one to predict behaviour, and manipulation of these conditions allows one to control it.' Kiernan (1973) discusses these issues with special reference to people with mental handicaps. The argument that such investigators are putting forward is that an understanding of what makes the individual tick will automatically provide the therapist with a potential way of intervening therapeutically.

In one of the earliest elaborations of single-case methodology as applied to behavioural treatment, Baer *et al.* (1968) restate the problem as follows: 'An experimenter has achieved an analysis of a behaviour when he can exercise control over it. By common laboratory standards, that has meant an ability of the experimenter to turn the behaviour on and off, or up and down at will'. In a real-life, applied setting, the therapist cannot usually go on repeating this control. The patient, rightly, would not accept it. To demonstrate to his own satisfaction and that of his scientific peers, the therapist must judge how much control is sufficient. This element of judgement enters into all evaluation.

In essence, the problem of demonstrating a causal relationship between treatment and effect can be reduced to the following propositions:

(1) Is there a 'real' change in the patient's behaviour following the application of treatment?
(2) If so, can alternative explanations for the demonstrated improvement be ruled out?

As Birnbrauer *et al.* (1974) point out, the first question can only be answered if data are gathered reliably and repeatedly (see Chapter 2). To answer the second question, some form of experimental manipulation is usually necessary.

SINGLE-CASE EXPERIMENTAL DESIGNS

1. The A–B design

The simplest 'quasi-experimental' design is not really experimental at all. It involves measuring the target behaviour over a baseline period (condition A), followed by continued monitoring during condition B, or treatment. Let us say that a nine-year-old boy with a mild degree of mental handicap is referred because of severe distractibility in class, and that after a careful consideration of relevant data it is found that he is 'off-task' on 80 per cent of occasions over a 10-day baseline period. When the teacher alters her interaction with the boy so that settling to work is immediately rewarded, his off-task behaviour drops to an average of 20 per cent three weeks after treatment is started. Clearly a change has occurred, but was treatment responsible for the improvement?

The problem in this simple case is that there are too many competing explanations which could plausibly account for the change. If treatment lasts over a lengthy period, how does one allow for the effects of 'maturation'? Chance events outside the teacher's control may be important. For instance, in checking attendance records it might transpire that the boy normally sits next to a very interfering playmate, who was present during baseline but absent during 'treatment'. Campbell and Stanley (1963) discuss these and many other factors which behavioural scientists working with children ignore at their peril.

Many external events can influence the course of a problem. 'Spontaneous remission' (Eysenck, 1963) can occur, unwilling as we are to admit that patients can improve independently of treatment. It is all too easy in using the simple A–B design to commit the fallacy of *post hoc, ergo propter hoc*.

Fleming (1984) reports the case of Peter, a 36-year-old man with Down's syndrome who had been hospitalised for 20 years and was very dependent. For the four years prior to referral Peter had developed the irritating habit of throwing items of clothing from a ward window. These mainly belonged to other patients who had left them lying around. Peter did not throw out his own clothes, but kept them in his locker.

For ten days, staff recorded the number of items found on the roof outside the windows (another example of using a 'permanent product' as an index of behaviour — see Chapter 2. Peter's throwing was inferred rather than observed). The intervention built upon

Peter's ability to spot clothes left lying around and his ability to put his own clothes away correctly. Staff asked Peter to collect clothes and place them in a clothing cupboard on the ward. He was hugged and praised for doing this. Peter was given six to ten trials of the activity per day, the trials being dropped as the behaviour was established.

As can be seen in Figure 13.1, 7.6 items were collected from the roof per day on average during baseline. This dropped rapidly during the first week of treatment but reached an all-time high during the second week. Circumstantial evidence suggested that clothing from another ward had been thrown on to the roof that week! Thereafter, the number of items quickly dropped to zero and remained there at a six-week follow-up. The author is well aware of the limitations of this design, but rightly argues that it illustrates the value of a constructional approach (Goldiamond, 1974) to dealing with such disruptive behaviour as Peter's.

Figure 13.1: ×——× Items of clothing ejected from ward windows. ●——● Practice trials of appropriate behaviour carried out by staff with client

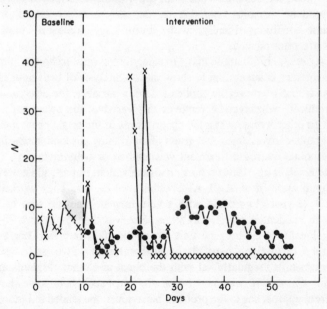

Source: Fleming (1984), p. 353. Reprinted with the permission of the author and editor. Copyright © 1984, British Association for Behavioural Psychotherapy.

Recently, there has been a renewal of interest in the A–B design, with the application of time-series analysis to such data. These developments have been discussed more fully elsewhere (Kazdin, 1984; Yule and Hemsley, 1977). For present purposes, it is sufficient to note that, although such data analysis techniques allow one to conclude that there has been a significant *shift* in the previous pattern at the point at which treatment was introduced, all the same problems of separating treatment effects from chance effects remains.

2. The reversal design (or A–B–A–B design)

Baer *et al.*'s (1968) formulation leads almost directly to one of the commonly used single-case experimental designs: the reversal design. During an initial period, the patient is carefully observed and a basal or *baseline* level of the problem behaviour is obtained. Then, during the second phase, treatment is applied while the target behaviour continues to be monitored. During the third phase of the experiment, the treatment conditions are withdrawn: effectively, the independent variables operating on the patient are 'reversed' to baseline conditions. Finally, in the fourth stage, treatment conditions are reintroduced.

Baer *et al.* (1968) argue that, 'In using the reversal technique, the experimenter is attempting to show that an analysis of behaviour is at hand: that whenever he applies a certain variable, the behaviour is produced; whenever he removes this variable, the behaviour is lost'. In other words, when the observations of the target behaviour are graphed over time, the graph should show discontinuities at those points when the treatment was applied or withdrawn.

De Kock *et al.* (1984) report on a case which, in part, illustrates the application of an A–B–A–B withdrawal design. They worked with a 32-year-old woman with severe mental handicap who had lived in residential care for 27 years. She was then living in a 25-place locally based hospital unit where the staff described her as severely disruptive, particularly at mealtimes. Two staff, on opposite shifts, regularly sat with the client and other residents at mealtimes, and it was noted that the two staff had somewhat different approaches to the problem behaviour: one tended to ignore her more than the other.

The therapists observed the behaviour of both staff and clients at succesive mealtimes, intending to implement a multiple-baseline-

Figure 13.2: Proportion of intervals during which the subject was engaged in appropriate mealtime behaviour

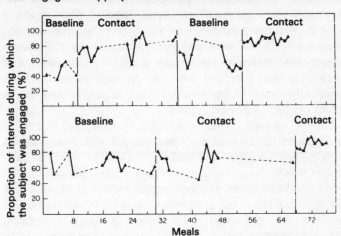

Source: de Kock *et al.* (1984), p. 171. Reprinted with the permission of the authors and editor. Copyright © 1984, British Association for Behavioural Psychotherapy.

across-settings design (see below), but found that one staff member failed to alter her behaviour to criterion level so that a reversal and reinstatement was undertaken with the first staff member. Basically staff were instructed to use differential reinforcement of incompatible behaviour — that is, they were given attention for engaging in appropriate mealtime behaviour such as eating, conversing and handling meal-related materials.

The results can be seen in Figure 13.2. The top half of the graph relates to the staff member who increased her appropriate attention from around 25 per cent of the times the client was appropriately engaged at mealtimes to over 70 per cent of the time, the criterion level fixed upon. As can be seen, the client responded by behaving appropriately around 78 per cent of each mealtime. This dropped to 61 per cent when the staff member tried to go back to ignoring appropriate behaviour, and was reinstated at 86 per cent of the time when 'treatment' was reinstated.

The lower graph refers to the second staff member who eventually managed to praise appropriate behaviour to criterion level at the 68th meal. The client responded by providing more stable, high levels of appropriate mealtime behaviour.

Considering only the reversal data with the first staff member, it can be seen that the client's appropriate mealtime behaviour rose appreciably when treatment was started, dropped when treatment was withdrawn and re-established at a high level when treatment was reintroduced. This is fairly convincing evidence that the changes resulted from treatment. The authors comment on the problem of withdrawing treatment, and note that the staff member did not immediately return to her baseline level of activity and this is reflected in the client's behaviour.

A second example comes from a study by Zlutnick *et al.* (1975), who reported the case of a 17-year-old girl with severe mental handicaps who presented with major motor epilepsy. She had daily seizures despite large doses of anti-epileptic medication. Careful behavioural observations revealed a characteristic 'chain' of events leading up to seizure, and so treatment consisted of interrupting this chain at a very early stage. As can be seen in Figure 13.3, during a five-week baseline period, seizures occurred on an average of 16 per day. This fell to near zero during the first treatment period. When treatment conditions were reversed, the number of seizures quickly rose, only to be controlled again when treatment was reinstated. A nine-month follow-up showed that the girl's seizures remained at a near-zero level.

In both these studies, the data provide convincing demonstrations of a functional relationship between the application of an active treatment (the independent variable) and the patient's clinical condition (the dependent variable). It can be seen that, under certain circumstances, this is an elegant yet simple design to employ in evaluating the effectiveness of treatment in an individual case.

As with traditional group experimental studies, there is an intimate relationship between the problem under investigation and the research design which is most appropriate to demonstrate experimental control. Thus, as the reversal design has been used more frequently, so its limitations have been documented (Barlow and Hersen, 1984; Gelfand and Hartmann, 1984; Leitenberg, 1973; Yule *et al.*, 1974). It is unreasonable to ask a parent or nurse or teacher to withdraw an apparently effective treatment which appears to have resulted in the client ceasing some unpleasant activity such as spitting, smearing faeces or hitting. Desirable as reversal may be on scientific grounds, such a request will appear bizarre to the caretakers.

More importantly, there are some behaviours which, once established, will not reverse. For example, when a non-talking child

Figure 13.3: The number of minor motor seizures per day for a seventeen-year-old girl with major motor epilepsy

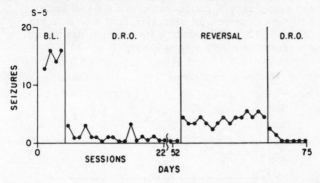

Source: Zlutnick *et al.* (1975), p. 10. Reprinted with the permission of the author and editor. Copyright © 1975; the Society for the Experimental Analysis of Behavior, Inc.

is trained to use some language meaningfully, that skill will probably become self-reinforcing, and similarly with the acquisition of other skilled behaviour such as reading, writing, swimming or riding a bicycle. It is probable that the reversal design is not appropriate for demonstrating experimental control over the acquisition of new skills. Its value is probably greatest where the frequency of occurrence of an already existing skill is being manipulated.

In passing it is as well to note that, if a behaviour change is so quickly reversible, cynics may question the value of the initial intervention. Such cynicism is, in part, misplaced. It is increasingly being recognised that changing behaviour is but the initial step in treatment. Maintenance of change over the longer term presents a different set of technical challenges. To be able to demonstrate that even the initial change has been effected rationally must be seen as a major advance in evaluating therapeutic intervention.

3. Multiple-baseline designs

An alternative set of designs was introduced by Baer *et al.* (1968) which they termed the 'multiple-baseline' technique. As originally conceived, the therapist identifies a number of different responses which are troubling the patient. Each of these responses is monitored simultaneously. Then, while continuing to monitor all the selected

Figure 13.4: Results of the five subjects from the first group home who were trained by skilled trainers. The data are presented as per cent of correct responses per trial across various training situations for each skill. Follow-up data are presented at 6, 12, or 18 weeks; data points in this phase represent assessment following retraining

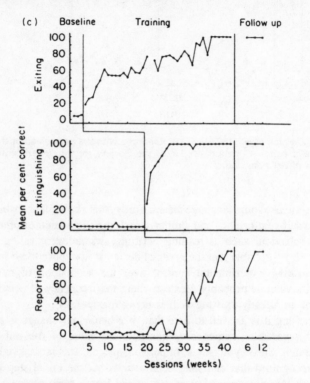

Source: Katz and Singh (1986) p. 64. Reprinted with permission of the authors and editor.

behaviours, treatment is applied to one behaviour only. After an appropriate length of time, treatment is next applied to a second behaviour, leaving the others still untouched, and so on in sequence. By this means, 'The experimenter is attempting to show that he has a reliable experimental variable, in that each behaviour changes maximally only when the experimental variable is applied to it' (Baer *et al.*, 1968). This is an ingenious way of demonstrating a one-to-one relationship between intervention and outcome, utilising the well-known observation that troubles rarely present singly in real-life cases.

254

When appropriate, this design is relatively easy to apply. Katz and Singh (1986) report on the important issue of training adult residents appropriate fire-safety behaviours. As more residents lead more independent lives in community settings, the ability to deal appropriately with emergencies assumes new importance, although a good case can be made for undertaking this form of training in hospital settings as well. The authors chose to teach three sets of behaviours: (a) for getting out of (exiting) a burning building, (b) reporting a fire to the proper authorities, and (c) extinguishing a fire by the 'stop, drop and roll' procedure. They worked with nine residents aged 30–50 years in two group homes. Illustrative data from one resident are shown in Figure 13.4.

During baseline, each resident was asked to show what they would do if a fire broke out, if their own or another's clothing caught fire, and if they had to report a fire. Interventions started for the first behaviour, in this case getting out of the burning building, after three baseline probes. The other behaviours were not targeted. As can be seen, this particular adult resident quickly learned how to get out of a burning building. During this time, there were no changes in the other behaviours. Then, when extinguishing burning clothing was targeted, these skills were quickly acquired but no change occurred in the ability to make correct reports. The latter improved only when specifically taught. All three skills remained high at 12-week follow-up. The behaviour improved only when taught, providing strong evidence for the causal effects of the intervention.

For the multiple-baseline (across responses) design to be applicable, the therapist must be able to select behaviours which are (relatively) functionally unrelated. It is no use if the successful treatment of the first problem is associated with the disappearance of the second or subsequent problems, since this would fail to demonstrate the predicted experimental control (Birnbrauer et al., 1974; Gelfand and Hartmann, 1984; Leitenberg, 1973). It would be all too easy to claim that the predicted effects did not occur, and therefore the behaviours must really have belonged to the same reponse class. Such special pleading should not become the behaviour modifier's 'reaction formation' or let-out clause.

A second variation of the multiple-baseline design takes cognisance of the fact that very often people's behaviour is situation specific. Children can be angels at school, yet devils at home. Johnny might urinate in the hall but never in the kitchen. It is now well recognised that treatment changes do not automatically generalise from one setting to another (Baer et al., 1968; Patterson

255

Figure 13.5: Rate of toy play and stereotypies for each subject during baseline and reinforcement of toy play conditions. The last few sessions in each condition are plotted

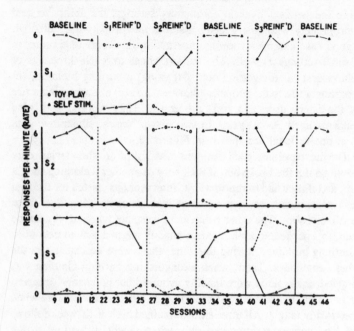

Source: Flavell (1973), p. 22. Reprinted with the permission of the author and editor.

et al., 1967). This observation is capitalised on in the multiple-baseline (across stimulus settings) design.

The de Kock *et al.* (1984) study attempted to capitalise on the fact that their client was supervised by two different staff members at different mealtimes. They observed the client's mealtime behaviour with each and began intervention with the first staff member after the ninth meal. Then, after the 30th meal, the intention was that the second staff member initiate differential reinforcement of acceptable mealtime behaviour. Unfortunately, she did not do this to an acceptable criterion level until the 68th meal. Nevertheless, for present illustrative purposes, the data in Figure 13.4 show how a multiple-baseline-across-setting design can be set up. The particular study also illustrates the value of recording therapist as well as client behaviour. The logic of the design is to show that the client's behaviour alters only when the treatment is implemented, and not before.

A third variation on the multiple-baseline design is, strictly speaking, not a single-case subject design at all, in that it is the multiple-baseline across subjects. In other words, this is a design to apply across a small group of subjects. Nevertheless, this design already shows signs of being widely used, and may well prove to be the most useful in most real-life settings.

In this case, one selects two or more patients with closely similar problems. The target behaviours are monitored for baseline levels. Then, treatment is introduced to one subject at a time, maintaining all the others in baseline conditions. In other words, this is a sort of multiple-replication of A–B designs across subjects. The point is that if treatment effects are repeatedly associated across subjects with the start of intervention, then chance factors are less likely to provide plausible alternative explanations.

Two examples will suffice. Flavell (1973) uses a multiple-baseline-across-subjects design with reversals to demonstrate that stereotypies could be reduced by training children with mental handicaps to play appropriately with toys. As can be seen in Figure 13.5, as each child was reinforced in turn for playing with toys, so their amount of play increased and the amount of stereotypies decreased. Thus, the third subject showed no noticeable increase in play until this was specifically targeted during sessions 40 to 43. Such regularities in data are too strong to be merely coincidence, and so one is forced to conclude both that play did respond to positive reinforcement and that stereotyped behaviour was reduced as play was increased.

Barton *et al.* (1975) describes a number of studies carried out in a hospital school for children with severe mental handicap. In one study, four children in the special care unit were given systematic toilet training. Following a short baseline, all four were put on the same programme whereby they were potted every half-hour and reinforced for passing urine. As can be seen in Figure 13.6, 'accidents' were reduced from 5 to 10 per subject per day to only about one per day after only three weeks of intensive treatment. This improvement was maintained in three children at 12 months' follow-up.

In this last example treatment was started simultaneously in all four subjects. This does little to weaken the logic of the demonstration. In fact, subjects can even be treated sequentially — a much more convenient state of affairs for the busy clinician. Clements and Hand (1985) have argued that if such treatment series are undertaken,

Figure 13.6: Toilet programme — accidents per week

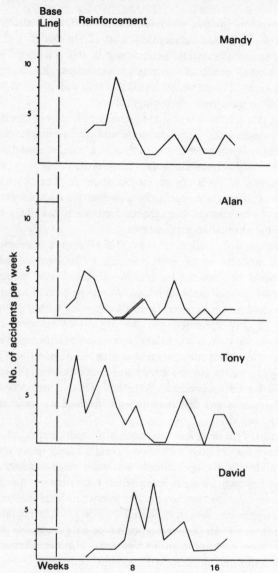

Source: Re-drawn from Barton (1975), p. 31. Reprinted with the permission of the authors and editor.

the point at which one moves from baseline to treatment conditions should be determined at random to allow appropriate statistical treatment of the data and to avoid potential bias in selecting the beginning of intervention. Whether this complex approach will have wide applicability remains to be seen. It must be emphasised that, in this small-group design, the focus of interest is on the treatment rather than on the analysis of the individual patient's difficulties. Even so, this is a valuable means of evaluating treatment.

CONCLUSIONS

Whereas the logic of single-case studies is elegantly simple, it can be seen that there is quite an art in selecting the appropriate research design. Moreover, as is discussed in detail elsewhere (Barlow and Hersen, 1984; Yule and Hemsley, 1977), the problems of measurement and the arguments about the statistical treatment of data are both complex and sophisticated.

The selection of the appropriate single-case design involves considering at least four related problems. First, the appropriate index of change has to be selected. Increasingly, multiple-outcome measures are being employed. Secondly, in accordance with the arguments given above, the appropriateness of applying a reversal design has to be examined. Thirdly, the length of the baseline must be determined. Fourthly, even where changes occur, the clinician has always to ask whether the change is *clinically* (as opposed to statistically) significant. Provided all of these problems are discussed, the therapist is well on the way to evaluating the therapeutic effectiveness of the intervention.

It is recognised that the application of sound single-case experimental methodology is still in its infancy, but it is already obvious in the publications of the last decade that such sophisticated analytical techniques have helped to create a therapeutic breakthrough in the field of mental handicap. It is confidently predicted that single-case reversal designs will be improved upon and become more sophisticated as applied research progresses.

14

Organising a Residential Service

Judith Jenkins with David Felce, Jim Mansell, Ursula de Kock
and Sandy Toogood

Over the last 15 years, interest in using behavioural theory and
applied behaviour analysis for helping people with severe and
profound intellectual handicaps has become extensive. It is now
commonplace to talk about training or teaching programmes,
behavioural management procedures for 'problem' behaviour, goal
setting, reinforcing emerging skills, room management, and so on.
There are training courses and workshops for teachers, nurses,
residential care staff, parents, and day-care instructors. Additionally
there is a wide range of books, assessments and training packages
to assist people who wish to use behavioural approaches.

That is the theory, and the gap between that and real life can seem
a wide one. It can be extraordinarily hard to ensure that reinforcement is given consistently, immediately and contingently for a new
behaviour. In the middle of a tiring, busy shift it is undeniably
difficult for people to remember *not* to respond to an irritating,
persistent problem behaviour from which they have been asked to
withhold attention, with the aim of extinguishing it. And how easy
it can be to omit spending five or ten minutes with an individual to
work on a teaching programme which was so carefully drawn up!
Work pressures seem unremitting, progress can seem so slow as to
be invisible on a day-to-day basis, and staff morale can be very
fragile at times.

How then to lessen the gap between theory and practice, to
support and maintain staff morale and activity so that they can work
with behavioural procedures in an organised and coherent yet practical and personal way? And how to do all this within the constraints
of arranging the complicated necessary activities involved in daily
living? The approach to be described in this chapter was developed
in Andover, Hampshire (part of the Winchester Health District) by

a group of service workers and researchers, with the aim of providing a residential service for the most severely and profoundly mentally handicapped adults in the catchment area. Although the details relate to the development of a new service, providing a home for up to eight people in an ordinary house, many aspects of the approach can be (and indeed have been) used in other group care settings, including schools, adult training centres, large hostels and hospital accommodation (e.g. Barrowclough and Fleming, 1986; Clements, 1979; Crisp and Sturmey, 1984; de Kock *et al.*, 1984; Felce *et al.*, 1984; Marston and Gupta, 1977; Porterfield and Blunden, 1978).

THE OPERATIONAL POLICY

The starting point for the structure of the service is the operational policy, which was worked out in detail even before the house was purchased and fitted. This policy, which has since been adopted in essence for all the small residential homes run by Winchester Health District's mental handicap service, aims to state clear objectives on what the service is trying to do for its clients, and some of the processes or procedures staff must use in pursuing the objectives. Among the key objectives is the following statement:

> The overall aim is to provide for each person living in the home the same range of opportunities as exist for anyone else; this means that, in a high quality service, people living in the home will
>
> (i) acquire new skills that enhance their ability to cope with the normal social environment
> (ii) engage in a wide range of ordinary activities to practise and consolidate skills they have acquired
> (iii) lose disruptive or inappropriate behaviours that limit or deny access to ordinary activities.

It also means that the service must be tailored to each person's individual preferences, stengths and needs, that the service provides the *least restrictive environment* in which the objectives can be met, and that the service promotes responses from staff and other people that are *appropriate to the person's age* and *respect the person's dignity*.

261

The focus here is on stating unequivocally that the service has a clear obligation to promote adaptive behaviour and to form wide-ranging experiences and opportunities for learning by its clients. Other statements in the policy focus on practical aspects which will help support the major objectives, for example:

Housekeeping

The day-to-day running of the home will be organised to include use of local shops and amenities as an important part of the planned programme of activities.

Food, supplies and . . . materials will be purchased from local shops by staff with people living in the home.

Each person living in the home will have their own effects, toiletries and clothing. Personal clothing will be laundered at home. Given adequate continence or use of incontinence materials, bed linen will be laundered at home or at a local launderette.

The garden will be maintained by residents and staff, with advice from District staff, as part of the normal range of daily activities.

There is recognition here that domestic and catering activities are *not* 'hotel' services to be provided for the people living in the home, but part and parcel of daily living which yield valuable activities and experiences, both in the house and in the local community. In support of this there are statements which place clear obligations on the staff to involve the people living in the home in all domestic activities, regardless of their degree of handicap, while recognising that some people may need substantial help in sharing in the activities.

Organisation of the day

Staff will provide each person living in the home with access to at least one activity at any time of the waking day. Activities will be carefully planned and sequenced to avoid time spent by clients passively waiting.

   (i) materials are arranged so that the client can get to them and use them

  (ii) help and encouragement is readily available from a member of staff, as appropriate to the person's development level

 (iii) the activity is appropriate to the chronological age of the people participating

(iv) a range of activities is available for each person (including those who are most severely handicapped or disruptive) each week, including activities outside the home which bring people living in the house into contact with other citizens and integrate them into the local community

(v) priority is given to organising housework activities so that people living in the home can join in, rather than providing 'occupational' activities with pre-school toys.

In addition, the focus of the service as being a learning environment as well as a home is reinforced in the policy by including statements such as the following:

Individual programme plans

Every person living in the home will have a written individual programme plan which will set long-term and/or medium-term goals for

(i) teaching the person new skills

(ii) arranging the person's participation in particular activities (including family contact)

(iii) weakening and replacing disruptive behaviours

(iv) remedying or ameliorating health problems (including problems of disfigurement or stigmatising appearance).

Each individual programme plan will be reviewed at least once every nine months, and goals will be amended, added or deleted on the basis of the client's current strengths and needs.

The operational policy cannot on its own ensure that a residential service works in accordance with its guidelines or that it works well. However, a detailed policy can be a genuine support to staff because the expectations of the service managers are explicit. It is thus possible to develop the details of daily activities, learning and behavioural management procedures knowing that they are clearly working within policy guidelines. The procedures described below have been developed by the staff in the residential service in Andover to assist them to implement the policy, to monitor the progress and activities of the people living in the home, and to have a consistent framework or structure for staff activity which can be maintained across different shifts, and over the weeks and months.

STRUCTURE OF THE SYSTEM

A visitor to the home would see a well appointed, well furnished, ordinary (though fairly substantial) house. Depending on the time of day, the visitor would see staff helping the people living in the home to undertake housework, shopping, cooking, laundry, gardening, personal care, and leisure pursuits in or out of the house. At some times of day, some (if not all) the people living in the home would be out at day-care activities, extended or further education, or, possibly, supported work. The visitor would at times see staff encounter a range of inappropriate and sometimes very difficult behaviours, including throwing or damaging objects, tantrumming, stripping of clothes, breaking windows, aggression, self-inflicted injury, extreme withdrawal, stereotyped behaviour, and single or double incontinence. What the casual visitor would not see is the thought and discussion that goes on daily and weekly to keep the routines and rhythms of the day running smoothly, to plan and implement the teaching and experiential aspects of the service, and to monitor and modify the inappropriate behaviours that may severely limit someone's access to community resources or affect the person's participation in other more valued activities. Behind the 'ordinary life' of the people in the home lies a strong system of planning the day, creating learning opportunities and recording results together with a behavioural framework taught to staff both 'on the job', at weekly staff meetings, and at in-service training sessions.

THE HOME AS A LEARNING ENVIRONMENT

Following from the key objectives in the operational policy it is clear that a major set of tasks for staff concerns teaching the people living in the house to join in with the myriad of daily living tasks involved in running a home, and to learn the skills where presently these are lacking. For the people who learn most quickly, this may mean them becoming independent in activities such as cleaning, taking a bath, making whole meals or parts of them, and so on. For people with more profound handicaps it may mean polishing part of a table with hands-on help from staff, carrying empty milk bottles from the kitchen to the front doorstep, or holding a flannel while the staff member guides her wrist to wash her face. Throughout all activities there is an awareness by staff of the need to create chances to learn, and these can be formalised at several levels. First, there is the

Figure 14.1: Individual Programme Planning. Needs List

Client's name: ..*Miss Sally Pritchard*.............. Key worker: *Miss S. Renton*...
Form completed ...*July 1982*..................... (month, year)
IPP meeting to be held on ..*13 July 1982*..... (date) ...*10.00 am*......... (time)
at ..*Adult Training Centre*........................... (place)

PROGRAMME PLANNING TEAM

The keyworker should establish which people on the following list have
been in contact with the client since the last IPP meeting. Each of these
people should be asked what they would like to put on the Needs List as
priority areas for work, and invited to the meeting.

Client   ✓
Family/advocate   *No contact with family*
Residential care person-in-charge   ✓
ATC Manager/employer   ✓
Special Care Unit Manager
Head teacher/class teacher
Psychologist   ✓
Community Nurse
Social Worker
General Practitioner
Psychiatrist/other medical specialist   ✓   *Unable to attend meeting*
Speech therapist
Physiotherapist
Occupational therapist
Other

---

1. PREDICTED REQUIREMENTS AND NEED FOR MAJOR SERVICES

Long-term accommodation
Short-term care
Day care/training   *Attend ATC*
Education
Work
Finance   *Very short of clothes*

---

2. TEACHING OR LEARNING PRIORITIES:
Skills to acquire in the next 9 months

Self care   *Undress and dress correctly. Comb hair. Hold appropriate foods with
       both hands*
Domestic   *Wash small items of clothing*
Daily living
Community living }
Communication   *Speech not clear*

265

Figure 14.1: *contd.*

Personality and
social adjustment   *Accosts shop assistants, calls them nurses*
Behaviour problems
Close personal
relations
Use of leisure   *Riding*
Physical development

Needed in the next nine months concerning the areas of:

3. Health/Hygiene   *Chiropody. Medication review. Teeth. Problem with right arm.*
4. Physical appearance and co-ordination   *Gait is awkward.*
5. Social relationships/companionship   *Needs friend apart from others living in house and staff.*
6. Opportunities for increased or different occupation:
   Household   *Do more activities on own initiative.*
   Day care/work
   Leisure   *Increase range of indoor leisure activities.*
7. Opportunities for participation in Community events.   *Swimming*

Individual Programme Plan (Jenkins *et al.*, 1987). Each person living in the house has an Individual Programme Plan (IPP) meeting every nine months. This meeting, to which everyone currently involved with the person is invited to contribute, aims to provide a co-ordinated, forward-looking set of goals that people will be working on over the next nine months. A Needs List is constructed in advance of the meeting, and in effect forms the agenda for the meeting. The Needs List (Figure 14.1) has a set of headings to be considered when thinking of a person's needs, including 'major' change such as a move in residence or day-time activity, a list of skill areas to help people consider the learning priorities, and other types of need including health, appearance, companionship, range of activities and so on. At the IPP meeting the Needs List, which may be extremely lengthy, is discussed and fined down into a Personal Priorities List (Figure 14.2) where each objective is stated clearly. Thus the various people at an IPP meeting end up with a joint document which they have agreed to use as an Individual Programme Plan. This plan is not only helpful in getting different disciplines to agree what they will work on, but is also written in performance terms and is thus easily monitorable at any time. It is in a sense the backbone of the goal-setting system in the home.

The second level of providing a learning environment is called

266

Figure 14.2: Individual Programme Plan. Co-ordinated forward goal planning, including teaching needs, range of experiences, service needs

Client: Miss Sally Pritchard

Date: 13 July 1982

People present at IPP meeting: Mr Johnson (Person-in-charge), Dr Peters (Psychologist), Mr Taylor (ATC Manager), Miss Renton (key worker, Care Staff)

Areas	Discussion	Objective	Person responsible	Outcome nine months later
Place of training	Place in special care unit is agreed to be appropriate.	Sally to attend Special Care Unit following appointment of staff by end of August.	Mr Taylor	
Finance	Need for clothes: Sally is being given a disproportionate share of budget as it is. Has max. NCIP.	Review spending arrangements for tights.	Mr Johnson	
	Possible alternative for tights is to teach her to pull tights on without damaging them so much.	Sally will put on and take off tights without causing holes.	Mr Johnson	
Self-care	Can undress but takes off clothes all together as opposed to sequentially	Sally will take off pullover before blouse, skirt before tights, tights separately from pants	Mr Johnson	
	Can comb hair but does not look in a mirror	Sally will look in mirror image for 30 seconds while combing hair or adjusting clothing	Mr Johnson	
	Eating sandwiches — currently separates layers and eats filling separately. Possible problem of lack of teeth	Sally will eat sandwiches complete	Mr Johnson	

Figure 14.2: *contd.*

Areas	Discussion	Objective	Person responsible	Outcome nine months later
Domestic	Washing small items of clothing	Sally will wash tights, pants, daily	Mr Johnson	
Communication	Sally's vocabulary has improved enormously but clarity is poor	Refer to speech therapist for advice	Mr Johnson	
Community living	Sally calls shop assistants in overalls 'nurses', and tends to hold on to them	Devise a standard procedure for correction and liaise with Special Care Unit when Sally starts to attend	Mr Johnson, Dr Peters	
Health/hygiene	False teeth needed	Consultation with dentists at Health Centre to be arranged	Mr Johnson	
	Medication is currently under review. Sally was on large amounts of tranquillisers and anti-convulsants when moved in, probably more than necessary	Ask Dr Black to complete the medication review	Mr Johnson	
	Awkward gait, poor posture. Limited use of right arm possibly because of fractured collar bone that healed in a misshapen form	Refer to physiotherapist for advice	Mr Johnson	
	Need for chiropody. ATC has regular chiropody sessions, and could include Sally in these even before	Book Sally into next chiropody sessions at ATC, and notify Mr Johnson when this will be	Mr Taylor	

Social relationships	she begins to attend ATC Special Care Unit		
	Given absence of next-of-kin there is a need for an adult friend other than among staff. Someone locally is showing interest in Sally	Encourage contact from local person	Mr Johnson
	Also need to encourage relationships with other people living in the house	To offer Sally range of recreational activities involving other members of the house	Mr Johnson
Opportunities for increased household activities	Sally is learning to do many household activities, but needs prompting. Would like her to do various tasks more on own initiative	Sally will hoover carpet without continuous prompting	Mr Johnson
		Sally will put milk jug in fridge without spilling	Mr Johnson
		Sally will put clean clothes into drawers	Mr Johnson
Opportunities for increased leisure activities	Need to expand range of experience Sally has had for leisure activities	Try macramé, French knitting, rug making music, swimming, and gauge Sally's reaction	Mr Johnson

unstructured opportunities. It is created by the very fact that the setting is an ordinary house, with an ordinary variety of furnishings and domestic equipment, and with the domestic tasks all being done by the people living there with help from staff. This provides a richness of opportunities to learn skills and regularly control the materials available in the house, which are far more complex than often appreciated. For example, someone who had for 20 years lived in a locked ward in a large mental handicap hospital learned not only when it is appropriate to switch on and off the light in a room, but also at what level of daylight it is appropriate to draw the curtains. Both these behaviours were unavailable to her in her previous environment where lights were centrally controlled and curtains were drawn by staff. Similarly, someone who for years had heard 'piped' music, organised by the ward charge nurse from his office, was able to buy his own cassette recorder and learned to operate it at his own discretion with his choice of music. The wide range of domestic chores involved in running a household provides a rich 'curriculum' to which the people living in the house are exposed daily. Even without formal goal-setting or teaching, daily practice has been found to improve people's skills (Felce and de Kock, 1983). The crucial element is that they should *have* the practice, that staff involve people living in the house in every single activity with just enough help to further their present skill level. This approach is very similar to the incidental teaching approach described by Hart and Risley (1975) in the context of a different client group.

As with the Individual Programme Plan, it is possible to monitor the provision of unstructured opportunities by staff. A simple household activity chart (Figure 14.3) is kept for each person living in the house of which domestic activities he or she has shared in each day (at whatever level is possible given the person's current skills). This chart is summarised weekly, and changes in level of involvement by the person can be looked for over the weeks. This sort of record obviously only samples people's participation and cannot reflect all the detail. However, it also forms a visible reminder to staff that they should involve the people living in the house in all activities, since they are required to complete the chart on each shift. Direct observation will yield richer information on skill levels, degree of participation, and how often staff do jobs on their own (they should not!). But direct observation is a luxury in terms of observer time, and the household activities chart is a practical substitute for most occasions. A similar type of chart is used to log community participation by noting each occasion, and for what

270

Figure 14.3: Client activity record. Unstructured opportunities that occur by being in a house and organising domestic life

Client: _Sally Pritchard_   week ending _13/9/82_

	Activity	Sun	Mon	Tues	Wed	Thurs	Fri	Sat	SUMMARY
PREPARE/ COOK FOOD	Breakfast		✔		✔		✔		
	Lunch	✔		✔					7
	Tea					✔			
	Drink/Snack							✔	

		Sun	Mon	Tues	Wed	Thurs	Fri	Sat	SUMMARY
LAY TABLE	Breakfast								
	Lunch			✔	✔	✔			4
	Tea							✔	

		Sun	Mon	Tues	Wed	Thurs	Fri	Sat	SUMMARY
CLEAR TABLE	Breakfast			✔		✔			
	Lunch		✔						
	Tea							✔	
CLEAN DINING ROOM	Breakfast						✔		
	Lunch	✔			✔				10
	Tea		✔						
CLEAN KITCHEN	Breakfast						✔		
	Lunch								
	Tea								
	Other				✔				

		Sun	Mon	Tues	Wed	Thurs	Fri	Sat	SUMMARY
WASHES UP	Breakfast	✔						✔	
	Lunch			✔					5
	Tea								
	Other		✔			✔			

		Sun	Mon	Tues	Wed	Thurs	Fri	Sat	SUMMARY
LOADS DISHWASHER	Breakfast				✔				
	Lunch					✔			
	Tea						✔	✔	
	Other								7
CLEARS DISHWASHER/ PUTS CROCK- ERY AWAY	Breakfast			✔					
	Lunch		✔			✔			
	Tea								
	Other								

Figure 14.3: *contd.*

	Activity	Sun	Mon	Tues	Wed	Thurs	Fri	Sat	SUMMARY
DAILY	Lounge	✓							
CLEAN	Bathroom		✓	✓					
(e.g. dust,	Hall			✓			✓		16
tidy,	Stairs/landing								
polish	Bedroom		✓					✓	
hoover)	Make bed	✓	✓	✓	✓	✓	✓	✓	

	Lounge		✓						
THOROUGH	Dining room								
WEEKLY	Kitchen				✓				3
CLEAN	Bedroom					✓			
	Office								

	Machine					✓			
WASH	Hand	✓	✓	✓	✓	✓	✓	✓	9
CLOTHES	Clean Utility room				✓				

	Hang out	✓	✓	✓	✓	✓	✓	✓	
DRY	Fetch in								7
CLOTHES	Use tumbler								

	Fold/iron								
IRON	Put in/take out of		✓				✓		2
CLOTHES	airing cupboard								

	Shopping		✓		✓	✓			
	Put shopping away		✓		✓	✓			
OTHER	Gardening	✓							9
	House maintenance								
	Leisure outings			✓		✓			

Figure 14.4: Opportunity Plan. Fortnightly goal-setting meeting, often providing substeps for an IPP goal. ✓ indicates goal attained; Ⓧ goal not attained

Goals set	Mon	Tues	Wed	Thurs	Fri	Sat	Sun	Mon	Tues	Wed	Thurs	Fri	Sat	Sun
Look into mirror when combing hair before going out	✓✓	Ⓧ	✓✓Ⓧ	✓✓	✓✓	✓✓Ⓧ	✓	✓✓	✓✓	✓✓	✓Ⓧ			
Fasten buttons into corresponding holes	✓✓Ⓧ	Ⓧ ✓	✓Ⓧ	Ⓧ✓✓	✓✓	✓	✓	✓	✓✓	✓✓				
Wash tights daily with help to squeeze out	Ⓧ	✓Ⓧ	✓	✓Ⓧ	✓Ⓧ	✓	✓	✓	Ⓧ	✓	✓			
Sweep dining room floor using broom	✓	Ⓧ	Ⓧ		✓	✓	Ⓧ	✓	✓	✓	✓			
Collect hoover from hall cupboard and ask for help to plug in	Ⓧ	Ⓧ	Ⓧ	Ⓧ	✓	✓	Ⓧ	✓	✓	✓	Ⓧ			
Carry milk jug from worktop to fridge and place in fridge without spilling	✓	Ⓧ	Ⓧ		✓	Ⓧ	✓	✓	Ⓧ	✓	✓			
Clean false teeth with help and place in container every night		✓	✓	✓	✓	✓	✓	✓	✓	✓	✓			

GOALS ATTAINED FROM LAST PERIOD

Collects waste bin from office and empties it, sweeps with broom with staff guiding weak hand, carries milk jug to fridge without spilling.

OTHER AREAS	STAFF SELECTING GOALS
Purchase denture container, brush, denture cleaner.	T.R., J.H., R.D.

purpose, someone goes out of the house or has contact with people living outside the house.

The third level of providing a learning environment is a simple goal-setting system called *Opportunity Planning* (Toogood, Jenkins, Felce and de Kock, unpublished). As the name suggests, a more systematic approach is added to the natural opportunities offered by the domestic environment by focusing on certain skills for someone to learn. These skills might be chosen because they are stated as high priority on an Individual Programme Plan, or staff might have noticed that someone is almost independent in a certain skill and decide to work more systematically to ensure independence. The Opportunity Plan is worked out at a small in-house meeting (usually held at shift changeover time) for every person on a fortnightly basis. The results of the meeting are recorded on a chart (Figure 14.4), and staff are expected to provide at least one opportunity daily for the person to practise the stated skill. However, teaching techniques are left to the staff's initiative in this system.

At the fourth level of learning environment provided by the small house comes the highly developed *precision teaching* system (Mansell *et al.*, 1983). Here, a skill to be taught (usually stated as a goal in the Individual Programme Plan) is broken down into small, weekly teaching steps, with a detailed teaching programme written for each step (Figure 14.5) including a space for staff to record the results of each teaching session.

This detailed approach is more demanding of time than Opportunity Planning, both when writing the programmes and when systematically carrying them out. Therefore staff usually work through unstructured, natural opportuities and Opportunity Plans, and only if these are unsuccessful in enabling the person to master the skills do they move on to the precision teaching approach.

Reducing problem behaviours can be seen as a parallel theme to teaching new skills. Problem behaviours will be recognised as important issues in an Individual Programme Plan. Often the provision of natural opportunities to participate in constructive, valued behaviour will lead to major improvements without more formal methods being tried. When these fail, staff work hard to develop alternative incompatible behaviours by carefully structuring the person's time and activities. Where necessary they employ carefully defined and recorded behavioural procedures for reducing the problem behaviour to back up the development of alternative behaviour.

Figure 14.5: Bereweeke Activity Chart. Precision teaching: highly structured teaching programme usually relating to an IPP goal

Name: Sally Pritchard			**Week ending:** 23.12.1982				
Long-term goal: Pick up and eat quarter square sandwich unaided.							
Teaching target: Use pincer grip to hold quarter square sandwich (jam filling) with physical guidance to position fingers above and below sandwich.							
Criterion: 3 out of 4 trials, 2 consecutive sessions.							
Place of sessions: Dining room			**Times of sessions:** 8–10 p.m.				
Materials and preparation: 2 small plates, 4 quarter-square sandwiches filled with jam. Plate of sandwiches placed on table.							
Instructions (what to say and what help to give): Say to Sally "Let's go into the dining room, to eat your sandwiches". Once there, ask her to sit at end of table, you stand to her right hand side, slightly behind. Place your right hand over the back of Sally's hand so that her forefinger and thumb form an open pincer shape, the other 3 fingers fold into her palm. Say "Sally, pick up the sandwich" and release your guidance. Repeat for each quarter square.							
Correct response: Sally picks up and holds sandwich without guidance after fingers have been positioned.							
Reinforcement for correct response: You say "well done Sally"; Sally eats the sandwich.							
Correction procedure: If Sally lifts the top layer of the sandwich up say "Stop, Sally". Place your hand over hers and guide her to pick up sandwich and take it to her mouth.							
What to record: ✔ when successful ⊘ if correction needed							

Number of sandwiches							
Days	Wed	Thurs	Fri	Sat	Sun	Mon	Tues
Staff	T.B.	J.H.	A.P.	A.P.	J.H.	R.A.	B.D.

PLANNING THE STAFF DAY

Being aware of the four levels of work described above, together with viewing people living in the house as individuals each with personal strengths, needs, emotions and interests, creates heavy demands on staff time and organisation. To help them, staff are shown how to plan each shift to take account of major tasks to be done (e.g. the big weekly shop, a thorough lounge clean, a trip to the dentist or hairdresser) and at the same time to work out who will be responsible for which of the people living in the house for that shift (Felce and de Kock, unpublished). This does not mean that a staff member works with the same one or two people throughout the shift, but that the staff on duty decide as a group how to organise the jobs and people's different needs most constructively. Whereas personal care activities are always done individually and in private, domestic and leisure activities may involve a staff member working with three or four people at a time (not necessarily all in the same room). This calls for staff to develop skills in planning and preparing the jobs to be done, interacting with the people living in the house to keep them involved at whatever their current skill level may be, and providing help as necessary and reinforcing participation rather than passivity or inappropriate behaviour. All this, together with extremely high standards demanded for the personal care and appearance of the people living in the house, and for the cleanliness of the house, places very high demands on the care staff. They therefore need teaching, support and advice on a regular basis.

STAFF SUPPORT STRUCTURE

The most crucial source of support and advice is the *weekly meeting* of 2½ hours, attended by all staff in the house and sometimes also by outside professionals such as the psychologist or speech therapist. At this meeting each person living in the house is discussed in a systematic way, new goals will be described, feedback and monitoring of the last week is presented (using the records collected) and details of programmes and procedures for the next week are agreed. As this is the only time in the week when all staff meet, it is a crucial forum for expressing views, recognising successes or discussing anxieties about the programmes. Following the discussion, staff are expected to abide by the decisions made, at least until the next meeting, to ensure consistency in carrying out the programmes and activities.

A further source of support and advice to staff in the behavioural aspect of working in the house is *direct observation and feedback*. The observation may be of a behaviour being presented by a person living in the house, or it may be of modes of staff interaction, or both. Discussion of a problem in the weekly meetings is always used to generate the first line of approach, but sometimes a period of systematic observation by a senior staff member or the psychologist will yield hypotheses hitherto unthought of. Observation and feedback is also helpful to check the accuracy with which staff follow procedures, as sometimes even experienced staff can allow procedures to slide. Observation is often of most value when helping a staff member to find ways of arranging tasks so several people can participate in them. An independent observer, without other responsibilities at the time, can see the effect of what a staff member does much more easily than can the staff themselves.

The staff meeting is a major forum too for outside profesionals to offer advice on teaching procedures and behavioural management procedures. The presence of all the care staff together with the records collected over the previous week yields a large quantity of valuable information about the progress of a teaching programme or a behaviour problem. As well as concerning individuals, discussion at the meeting may well indicate any organisational difficulties. For example, from direct observation and then discussion, it became apparent that meals were organised and served somewhat differently depending on which staff were working at the time. Staff clearly recognised that this (which happened by accident) was creating confusion for the people living in the house, and as a result were able to agree at a staff meeting details of how to arrange mealtimes. Similarly, incipient behaviour problems are raised and staff are able to say, in a non-threatening atmosphere, how each of them deals with a problem as it occurs. Collective discussion, and a focus on likely antecedents and consequences of the behaviour of concern, lead to a practical, detailed way of responding to the behaviour which is agreed by all staff. A 'behavioural' cause is not always assumed when a problem occurs; physical illness, premenstrual tension, family stresses are among other reasons which have been recognised as having given rise to some major behaviour problems. However, a behavioural focus to the staff meeting helps in two ways: (i) it encourages staff to describe and record behaviours in clear ways, and (ii) it has been found helpful to have a consistent way for staff to respond when a problem behaviour occurs. Whether or not the behaviour has originated from faulty learning, staff work hard to prevent further reinforcement of it.

In-service training also provides a source of staff support. The care staff employed in the service are all local people, often inexperienced in working with people who have major learning difficulties or in residential settings. Immediate, on-the-job instruction is supported by written details of all current teaching and behaviour management procedures and by handbooks of guidance (e.g. Jenkins *et al.*, 1987; Mansell *et al.*, 1983; Felce and de Kock unpublished; Toogood, Jenkins, Felce and de Kock, unpublished). In addition regular programmes of in-service training are arranged which include workshops on goal-setting procedures, how to describe behaviour in objective performance terms, concepts of reinforcement, shaping, prompting, working with groups of people rather than individuals by using room management principles, dealing with problem behaviour in a behavioural framework, and so on. Care staff may also attend District-based in-service training courses on other aspects of the work, but the behavioural component is arranged locally and tailored to the particular needs of the staff working within the house. This training provides a framework for the practical aspects of behavioural theory encountered day by day. Most importantly, the theory and procedures taught in the in-service training are backed up by daily involvement in teaching programmes, goal-setting, recording practices and procedures for problem behaviour which are developed at staff meetings. Thus, in a workshop, staff will hear, talk about and practise procedures which they then continue to see in their daily work. The psychologist teaching the workshops is also the psychologist working on a clinical basis in the house. So, again, continuity of approach should be maximal.

THE ADVANTAGES OF THE APPROACH

The residential care model described above is complex, with many interwoven threads. To work within it requires staff commitment in no uncertain terms. They must be thorough in their attention to detail and honest in their perception of what they do and how they respond, and must have great perseverance and determination. These qualities may seem hard to come by, but there are certain aspects of the approach which may positively support them.

First, the approach presents a consistently *positive view* of the people for whom the service is created. While acknowledging the sometimes enormous difficulties which someone may experience, and the extreme learning delay they may have, the model described above focuses always on helping the person develop in skills and in breadth of experiences. As a result, the vicious circle of initial handicap creating low expectations, leading to reduced opportunities and experiences and so to poor performance, can be reversed. People are treated in a valued way, are offered culturally valued experiences and activities, are taught (in small steps and easy stages) more and wider skills, and have often confounded expectations.

For example, one woman now takes herself to and from the Adult Training Centre daily, using public transport, after some years of being collected in a minibus. Another woman, after 30 years of living in a hospital (for much of the time on a locked ward), has held a daily cleaning job in a local pub for 2½ years. As well as a mental handicap, she has a profound hearing loss and is blind in one eye and partially sighted in the other, so this is no mean feat. Another young woman, who for years had worn one-piece, purpose-designed jumpsuits as a strategy to prevent her from stripping off her clothes, has learned over about one-and-a-half years to wear attractive clothes appropriate for her age and to keep them on. Someone else who for years was described as unable to walk up and down stairs has learned to do so, which opens up many new opportunities both indoors and in the local community.

A second strength of the approach is that the domestic environment itself yields hundreds of *relevant activities* without staff having to think up leisure occupations for hours on end. While housework is certainly not the sum total of activities, it forms a substantial part of them — just as it would in any individual's own home.

Learning domestic skills can lead ultimately to people being able to use them at their own discretion, and therefore to increase control over their own lives. Full independence may never happen for most of the people living in the house, but each new self-determined activity is a matter for celebration. For example, staff were astonished and delighted the first time one person got out bread, butter and Marmite and proceeded to make herself a sandwich without referring to anyone or asking anyone for permission.

Third, the approach, while complex in detail, has a *coherence* in its focus on learning and behavioural orientation which should help staff to put principles into practice. Large IPP goals can be traced, over the months, through Opportunity Plans, community activity records, behavioural records of problems and so on. The same

279

principle of reinforcement is at work in so many different ways that staff do learn to generalise its use.

A fourth strength of the approach is the *quantity and range of data* collected. Staff are asked to keep many records (Opportunity Plans, precision teaching records, household activity records, community contact records, records of observation of behaviour). But every one of these records is directly relevant to the staff's day-to-day work; the information is fed back regularly to the weekly staff meeting, out of which come the practical decisions. This means that the people filling in the records and the people using them are virtually one and the same group (together with the immediate senior staff and a few outside professionals). So the records are conscientiously kept and thorough, giving staff good information on which to base their decisions. In addition, the records can be summarised, across time for any individual person, to across everyone living in the house at a defined time, in order to provide some highly relevant information on the successes and the difficulties in the house as they occur. Although at present the records are used at in-house meetings and Individual Programme Plan meetings only, it is likely that in the future they may be used as part of a wider system to monitor and support the quality of the service. Hence managers could have summaries of records created by care staff, which would provide a systematic picture of the effectiveness of service delivery.

CONCLUSION

In considering this approach to running, advising and supporting a residential service, it should not be thought an easy option. The people receiving the service are the same people who have in the past been admitted to 'difficult' or 'disturbed' wards in institutions, and include people with the most profound and often multiple handicaps. Teaching them to overcome difficulties and change behaviours that have been established for years is a long and effortful business. Reversing the vicious circle indeed happens but not overnight.

Most of the aspects of the approach described here can be (and indeed have been) employed in larger environments, including day-care settings, hostels and hospital wards. For example, the Individual Programme Planning sytem is used for the severely and profoundly handicapped people living in the geographical area covered by the service, not just for people living in a small house with all the other features of the system described here. Opportunity Plans or similar approaches have been used easily and successfully in many residential and day settings in Hampshire, whether or not the staff have been trained in the use of detailed teaching. Opportunity Plans help sensitise the staff in focusing on quite a small number of goals to work on at a time, which can be spread throughout the day and tailored to natural occasions. Similarly the precision teaching system has been implemented in full or in part in larger residential units, hospital wards and special care day units (e.g. Felce *et al.*, 1984). Although in many ways precision teaching is the hardest part of the 'learning environment package' to practise successfully, it seems to provide a clear structure within which staff can operate, and so is a useful practical support in the job.

The difficulties of *maintaining* Individual Programme Plan systems, room management procedures, behavioural management procedures and so on in large institutions have been well documented elsewhere (Ivancic *et al.*, 1981; Kyle and Roche, 1983; Partridge *et al.*, 1985; Quilitch, 1975; Woods and Cullen, 1983). What is responsible for maintaining all the procedures in the small residential service described here is not totally clear. It seems likely that the way in which parts of the system dovetail and interrelate may be a relevant factor, as also may be the very positive and highly valued perception staff have of the people living in the house. Two other features may also have a bearing on the matter. One is that the operational policy makes clear that the care staff and immediate senior staff have control of all domestic arrangements. So not only is the responsibility clear for who is to arrange shopping, cleaning and so on, but it is also explicitly stated that all the people living in the house should be directly involved in all these activities. This measure of local control is rather different from most institutions where different categories of staff will be responsible for many domestic tasks, and where residents may actually be denied the opportunity of being involved.

The second feature of the service which may help to maintain the range of procedures described relates to the eligibility rules for coming into the service. A catchment area is defined for each house which is based on prevalence figures and people known to live (or have close relations) in the area. The service is available to people of 'health service dependency' (Wessex Regional Health Authority's definition) within that area. Although all the people are defined as severely or profoundly handicapped, there nevertheless exists a wide range of skills and problems within the definition. Therefore, not everyone would be expected to have a severe behaviour disorder (though many do), and not everyone would have multiple handicaps. The catchment area as the primary eligibility criterion *avoids* the deliberate concentration of the most difficult people together (unlike many hospital 'back' wards or 'special care' settings). The relatively mixed grouping could be an additional relevant factor in assisting staff to continue using the range of procedures in so far as not everyone is being difficult all the time. Finally, progress can always be seen, however small any one step may be.

15

Ethical Concerns in the Use of Behaviour Modification

William Yule and Janet Carr

Changing people is the aim of many interventions. Parents, teachers, doctors, nurses and other therapists all aim to influence other people's lives, albeit with the best of intentions and for the benefit of the clients. Whatever the form of intervention used, the person doing the intervening should always ask whether the intervention is justified. Who asked for the intervention? Do they have the right to ask for such help? Does the client agree? How will the intervention help the client? What are the dangers or disadvantages? Will the benefits outweigh the disadvantages?

These, and many other, questions should be considered before intervention is started. We may think that they should be considered whatever form of help is offered, and yet the ethical issues behind these questions seem to have been more openly debated regarding the use of behaviour modification than about the use of medical treatments and other forms of education and psychotherapies. Partly this may be because the very label, 'behaviour modification', announces itself as concerned with altering behaviour thus arousing anxieties. We see four other possible reasons for the interest and concern.

First, many techniques of behaviour modification are noticeably successful. The teacher sees fairly quickly that appropriate use of positive reinforcement increases social co-operation. The nurse is soon made aware that her use of the toileting programme has helped the patient gain continence. As long as treatments were not clearly effective, they seemed less powerfully controlling. When therapeutic outcomes, specified beforehand, are regularly being achieved, these seem to pose a threat to the patient's own self-determination.

Secondly, behaviour modification ensures that the goals to be aimed at are made explicit and measurable. Therapists see what is being achieved and this indicates that they influence or control clients' behaviour. Somehow, more ephemeral objectives such as 'increasing self-awareness', which make it almost impossible to see whether or not the goal has been achieved, are less associated with notions of control. Many people associate 'control' with uncomfortable ideas about totalitarianism, and it jars uncomfortably against ideas of free will.

Thirdly, the objective procedures and deliberately delivered consequences used in behaviour modification are seen as manipulative and inhuman. We all like to think that we exercise our free will and make rational choices in our lives. We become uncomfortable when we see how some apparently simple techniques can determine other people's behaviour, and wonder about the determinants of our own behaviour. To apply laws of behaviour derived from the laboratory study of pigeons and rats is somehow demeaning.

Fourthly, more than most other forms of intervention, behaviour modification techniques can be carried out in the normal, every-day environment by non-professionals. Not only does this involve a loss of the mystique which attaches to some other procedures; it raises very real issues about the responsibilities of professionals for providing services and ensuring their quality. The dangers of placing powerful therapeutic techniques in the hands of those not used to carrying responsibility for others are real, and will be returned to later.

Thus, the power, success and explicitness of behaviour techniques in the hands of professionals and non-professionals have forced a healthy examination of the ethical dilemmas that underlie all interventions. Many of these dilemmas are magnified when considering interventions with people with mental handicaps. In the remainder of this chapter, we will consider some of the general ethical principles guiding treatment and some particular areas of concern with clients with mental handicaps before suggesting some ways in which the interests of clients and therapists can be safeguarded.

SOME GENERAL PRINCIPLES

Most professional organisations have codes of conduct or guidelines for good practice to which their members subscribe. Those of the British Association for Behavioural Psychotherapy and the American Association for the Advancement of Behavior Therapy deal most explicitly with the actions of behaviour therapists. However, these quasi-legal codes have as much to do with intra-profession activity as with the ethical issues concerning the practice of behaviour modification. Rather than take readers through such specific codes, we will address ourselves to some more general issues. We will take it for granted that therapists will respect the confidentiality of their clients and will not seek to exploit them, although it has been pointed out that in part the careers of professionals are built out of their work with their clients (Foskett, 1986).

Informed consent

Before embarking on any investigation or treatment, the therapist should have the patient's informed consent. In every-day practice with clients of normal ability, this is usually a very cursory matter. Clients go of their own volition to consult professionals. For example, a patient has been feeling off colour and the general practitioner feels a blood test would clarify the nature of the complaint. The GP says 'I would like to take a sample of blood. Roll up your sleeve, please'. By rolling up her sleeve, the patient is normally deemed to have given her informed consent to the procedure, even though the GP did not spell out in detail the risks involved in the invasive procedure of inserting the needle in a vein to get a sample of blood. However, for more elaborate medical procedures involving anaesthesia and surgery, written consent is usually sought after further explanation.

How does this relate to behaviour modification for people with mental handicaps? In the first instance, it is unusual for the client to initiate the request for help. Requests come from parents, guardians, caregivers and other professionals. To whom is the therapist accountable: the client or the parent, the adult client or the day-centre manager? Who decides what is in the best interest of the client?

Secondly, most children of normal intelligence are deemed incapable in law of giving fully informed consent, although the law is being interpreted more liberally in the UK in recent years. There is now a sort of sliding scale of competence with children regarded as gaining more competence (and hence control over their own lives) as they grow older. But where does this place the rights of children and adults with severe mental handicaps? Those who cannot appreciate cause–effect relationships or have difficulty in dealing with time relationships cannot be regarded as being able to give informed consent. That is not to say that there is not still a duty on the therapist to explain as far as possible to the client how they see the problem and what the proposed intervention will be. Wherever possible, the client's expressed wishes must be considered. If these cannot be elicited, then consent should be sought from the parent or legal guardian, although in the case of adults aged 18 and over this has no legal standing. Either way, there clearly needs to be agreement from legal guardians in such cases.

What about informal patients and clients in community settings who have no legal guardians? Who acts as their advocates and protectors? In settings where there are multidisciplinary teams providing services, discussions within those teams may, to a large extent, function to safeguard the interests of clients who cannot give fully informed consent. Other safeguards, as suggested below, may also be desirable.

Least intrusive intervention

All interventions are intrusive, and most have both desirable and undesirable aspects — the latter usually being referred to as 'side-effects' when drugs form the intervention (although these are as much effects as are the desired ones). A long-standing principle is that one should use the form of intervention which is least intrusive to the client before proceeding to one that is more intrusive, other things being equal.

Thus, using this principle it is easy to see that giving advice which can be implemented at home is to be preferred to regular attendance at an out-patient clinic which, in turn, is to be preferred to admission to a unit. This hierarchy is based on the degree of interference with the client's daily life. In most cases, the particular hierarchy also reflects the financial costs to the community. Problems of choice arise when these two considerations do not coincide.

We slipped in the well known legal phrase, 'other things being equal'. What other factors need to be considered? Consider the treatment of epilepsy. Some types of epilepsy respond to behavioural treatment. Patients can be taught to avoid situations that trigger fits or to practise relaxation or diversionary tactics when they get warning of a possible fit. Most types of epilepsy can be partially controlled by various drugs, although most drugs have unwanted 'side effects' such as effects on alertness or learning ability. A few serious forms of epilepsy require surgical intervention. The decision as to which treatment to offer then depends in part on the nature and seriousness of the epilepsy and the question of the reversibility of the procedure. Thus, surgical intervention is irreversible and would normally only be considered after adequate trials of other procedures. Drug therapy is, in our view, more intrusive than behavioural intervention and so in suitable cases the latter should be tried first.

Notice that in this example, as in most we face in real life, there are no clear-cut, absolute answers. Judgements are based on the evidence known about the condition at a particular time, and they are influenced by the views of fellow professionals and society at large. For example, it might have been expected that the widespread use of the irreversible surgical procedure of lobotomy which was current in the 1940s would not have been tolerated after the advent of the powerful tranquillisers in the 1950s, and indeed the use of the procedure did drop dramatically. Nowadays, with better behaviour techniques for dealing with self-injurious and difficult behaviour (see Chapter 8, and below), one has seriously to ask about the ethics of using powerful tranquillisers as 'chemical strait-jackets'.

Effectiveness and efficiency of treatment

One factor to be brought into the decision-making process is how effective a treatment is, and the amount of time and resources that an intervention will require. One fact about most behavioural interventions is that they can be time consuming and therefore expensive in therapist's (and client's) time. Take the treatment of hyperactivity in children. There is considerable controversy over whether medication or behaviour modification is the treatment of choice (Yule, 1986). Drugs can act quickly but can suppress growth, interfere with learning and have temporary effects; behaviour modification takes much longer to analyse the problem and to teach new ways of behaving, but, once learned, the skills remain. Thus, a treatment decision may depend on how crucial it is to influence the behaviour quickly.

Indeed, this determines a number of decisions. Where a patient may harm himself or others, there is a duty to protect the patient and others. That may involve interfering with the patient's normal freedom of movement until the problem is resolved. It may involve the use of a more intrusive intervention for a brief period until a less intrusive one is identified, implemented and has a chance of working. For example, aversive conditioning procedures (see Chapter 8) can suppress undesirable behaviours quickly. Positive training of alternative behaviours takes longer. Therefore, in instances where self-injury is threatening to destroy tissue (or even life) there may be a case for using aversive conditioning as an emergency measure. However, in the light of the evidence on the long-term effects of aversive conditioning only, it would be unethical to continue such a programme without serious efforts to train up incompatible, positive behaviours.

Another aspect of efficiency concerns the use of resources. It is all too easy to focus on the needs of the individual client whose problems are already known to the therapist. Someone needs to be concerned with the needs of the community as a whole and therefore with how best therapists' time should be allocated. As is seen in Chapter 12, behavioural skills can be taught to a wide variety of caregivers and, in principle, this model of service delivery has a great deal to commend it. An ethical problem arises when the caregiver has mastered some, but not all, the skills and needs to refer back to an experienced therapist for advice. If such advice is not readily available, is it ethical to offer brief training in the first place?

Rights of the client

Unless a client has had his or her civil rights legally restricted under the Mental Health Act or other legislation, the therapist has a duty to respect these rights. These rights are variously enshrined in international declarations, clarified by legal rulings in bodies such as the European Courts of Justice or by national legislatures.

The United Nations Declarations of General and Special Rights of the Mentally Handicapped (1971) states that 'The mentally retarded person has, to the maximum degree of feasibility, the same rights as other human beings'. This has been elaborated by both the Jay Committee (1979) and the National Development Group for the Mentally Handicapped (1980). Both sets of guidelines embrace a normalisation philosophy.

The Jay Committee identified three broad sets of principles underlying a coherent philosophy and model of care:

(a) Mentally handicapped people have a right to enjoy normal patterns of life within the community.

(b) Mentally handicapped people have a right to be treated as individuals.

(c) Mentally handicapped people will require additional help from the communities in which they live and from professional services if they are to develop to their maximum potential as individuals (para. 89).

These broad principles were then spelled out so that being 'treated as individuals' was seen to include:

(a) The right of an individual to live, learn and work in the least restrictive environment appropriate to that particular person.

(b) The right to make or be involved in decisions that affect oneself.

(c) Acceptance that individual needs differ not only between different handicapped individuals, but within the same individual over time.

(d) The right of parents to be involved in decisions about their children (para. 92).

Thus, it is clear that an increasing number of authorities endorse the right of individuals to be involved in making decisions about their treatment. This has major implications for the providers of all services.

It is sometimes difficult for therapists to see how their every day activities relate to these somewhat abstract ideals. Let us take a recent example of how different rulings affect interventions.

There has long been a fierce debate about the use of corporal punishment in homes and schools. Surveys show that most parents use mild slaps at some stage in disciplining their children. Child-care advisors have usually ignored the literature on the efficacy of punishment and argued, on *a priori* grounds, that it should not be used. Until recently, schools in Britain used corporal punishment, usually for serious misdemeanours. A recent ruling of the European Court has made such practices effectively illegal. Meanwhile, in Sweden, parliament has outlawed the use of corporal punishment in the home. Clearly, all therapists must be aware both of the prevailing attitudes of society towards the use of punishment and of the law of the land.

In Britain, at present, residential treatment facilities are in some considerable difficulties over the treatment of children who are formally in the care of local authority social services departments. The Secretary of State for Social Services has ruled that in order to prevent abuse, children in care cannot be held in secure accommodation without application to a court. Strictly interpreted, this means that if a child in care is in a residential treatment facility where rooms are locked or where time-out from reinforcement involving seclusion is being used, application should be made to a court. Other children in the same facility who are not 'in care' are not covered by the legislation, leading to difficulties for the staff in having different regimes for different children.

Returning to the needs of people with mental handicap, the current moves to deinstitutionalise patients and meet their needs within the community raises uncomfortable questions about the rights of individuals and the quality of consent being given by adults now leaving hospitals. Behavioural methods are sometimes used to help people live in community settings by providing skills of daily living. What happens when a hospital resident, having sampled the alternative, expresses a now-informed choice to remain in a large hospital? Indeed, what happens when a careful evaluation of needs results in the conclusion that the needs are best met in other than a community setting? There are worrying ethical concepts regarding normalisation as there are regarding behaviour modification and other treatments (P. Mittler, personal communication, 1986).

THREE MAIN AREAS OF ETHICAL CONCERN

Three areas are constantly raised when we run courses on behaviour modification for people with mental handicaps: reinforcement, the setting of goals, and the use of aversive techniques. Let us examine each in turn.

Reinforcement

A common reaction of parents and teachers to the suggestion that they use tangible reinforcement to help a child learn a new behaviour is to dub it 'immoral'. They do not want to use 'bribery'. After all, why should they reward a child for doing something that he or she should be doing anyway?

These are really 'moralistic' rather than ethical arguments. Bribes are used to induce someone to commit an immoral act — to do something against their better judgement — or to induce somebody to do something that will benefit the briber rather than

290

themselves. This should never pertain in the course of treatment. In any case, if it did, it would not be the use of reinforcement that was unethical, but the goal that was selected.

The goal of all behavioural treatment is to enrich the lives and extend the personal choices of clients. Many people with mental handicaps, both children and adults, have very restricted lives. For many of them, few pleasures are available and their long histories of failure may lead to both a difficulty in anticipating pleasure and an expectation of failure in any new task.

This is recognised in both the theory and practice of using positive reinforcement to motivate people (see Chapters 3 and 4). The aim of most treatment programmes is to enhance the use of existing skills and to build up new ones. In order to maintain therapeutic gains, behaviours should eventually be reinforced by naturally occurring or social reinforcement. Before the goal is reached, extrinsic reinforcement will often have to be used to facilitate the motivation which others get intrinsically.

Two separate ethical concerns are raised by this. First, there is a worry that the unnecessary use of extrinsic reinforcement will interfere with intrinsic pleasure in doing something for its own sake. In theory this could happen, and critics often cite Lepper et al.'s (1973) work in support of their arguments. However, Ogilvie and Prior (1982) in a critical review suggest that the existence of the overjustification effect has not been convincingly demonstrated in practical behavioural work in which, far from showing pleasure in a task for its own sake, clients are typically brought by means of extrinsic reinforcers to experience tasks which they later often discover to be enjoyable.

Secondly, there is a worry that the use of extrinsic reinforcers may interfere with the civil rights of the clients. Two examples will illustrate some of the dilemmas. An all too familiar problem with chronically handicapped and institutionalised people is to get them to leave their chairs to participate in any activity. In one token economy (Atthowe and Krasner, 1968) sitting in chairs was made a reinforcer rather than a right, using the Premack principle. After a few months, the patients were participating in many more activities and, almost paradoxically, sitting in the chairs far less often.

In discussing the ethical issues raised by this intervention, Atthowe (1976) asks what the therapist is to do when the patient may agree on the long-term goals (rehabilitation and discharge) but not with the early steps in the programme.

Should you carry out a treatment plan with which the patient does not agree even if you are convinced he will benefit? . . . By making sitting in special chairs a 'contingent right' that had to be earned, the therapist was denying the patient the right to choose a custodial form of existence. Yet creating the special contingencies eventually led to more self-determination and increased the patient's options for living. Still, we must be on guard to minimize the possibility of interfering with the right of hospitalized patients; some form of a peer or advocate review should be part of any treatment plan' (Atthowe, 1976, p. 251).

Many forms of contingency contract use the ploy of changing a freely available activity into a special treat, access to which is denied if criterion performance is not reached. There seems to be no ethical problem provided the client fully understands the contract. Where the client is mentally handicapped or a minor or both, safeguards need to be met (see earlier section on informed consent).

It is no accident that the issue arises clearly in token economies. The second example gave rise to a lively exchange a decade ago between Jack Tizard and Geoff Thorpe (Kiernan and Woodford, 1975b). Thorpe had introduced a discussion on the feasibility of establishing token economies in hospitals for the mentally handicapped with a quotation from Agras (1972):

Instituting such an economy implies total environmental control. If privileges are to be used as reinforcers, then they must be obtainable as a token exchange. This means that the hospital or school administration must agree with the aims of the project and take the necessary administrative measures to allow for such control . . . The mere giving of tokens is not a token economy. Properly done, the token economy is a complex motivating environment.

To Tizard, this was '. . . very chilling. As a statement of objectives it might sound all right for the Gulag Archipelago or Dachau, but as a way of thinking about patients and people it is unacceptable' (Kiernan and Woodford, 1975b, p. 258). He doubted whether such programmes really worked, and feared that they became ends in themselves. He felt there were other ways of improving the quality of patients' lives. Other participants in the debate agreed that most early token economies seemed unnecessarily controlling.

A British Working Party later looked predominantly at issues surrounding the use of token economies in National Health Service hospitals (Zangwill, 1980), although it had originally been brought into being because of abuses of patients by staff following a Langian approach to the treatment of schizophrenia (Yule, 1982). The working party was concerned that a balance should be struck between meeting a patient's basic needs and using ordinary activities to motivate poorly motivated patients. They, like Atthowe and others before them, came to the view that patients' rights can best be safeguarded by having such programmes regularly reviewed by local ethical committees and not by decrying their use altogether. In the decade since the report was published, such ethical committees are not very visible.

Goal-setting

Goals of treatment '. . . should be adopted . . . to foster the development of the client [not for] the convenience of staff, parents or guardians' (Roos, 1979). Critics of some of the earliest published studies of work in mainstream classrooms were concerned that techniques were misused to make children sit still and be good — that is, to make life easier for the teacher — when encouraging them to be active and to question things might be more appropriate. Who is to decide which goal is correct? When may the therapist be inadvertently bolstering up another adult's distorted view of a client's difficulties?

Given that most clients with mental handicaps cannot give truly informed consent, then it is incumbent on the therapist to involve parents, guardians and other team members in setting treatment objectives. Some goals are non-controversial: people should be helped to communicate more effectively; wetting and soiling should be reduced; self-help skills should be increased. But when it comes to reducing aggressive interactions or non-compliance, a different feel enters into the discussion.

If we are to respect the individuality of a person with a mental handicap, shouldn't we allow him to express his likes and dislikes? Given that he cannot do so conventionally with spoken language, shouldn't we tolerate his hitting other residents? Apart from begging the question about the functional meaning of the hitting, this form of argument ignores two other important elements. First, other people also have rights: parents, siblings, other clients and staff have the right not to be assaulted. In any case, if a client is regularly aggressive, he will soon lose out socially and educationally. Secondly, on normalisation principles, clients should not be encouraged in behaviours that will stigmatise them in the community.

Different analyses may have to be performed on short-term and long-term goals. It is all too easy for short-term expedients to prevent the attainment of long-term goals. If short-term deprivation will increase motivation and lead to the attainment of more normal living, is it justified? There are never any easy answers.

As the power of behavioural technology is appreciated, and as the needs of individuals with mental handicaps are better understood, so the two can be married. Consensus across caregivers, relatives and professionals about the goals of services for those with mental handicaps can be reached in broad terms. What each therapist needs to do is to ensure that he or she is in touch with current, local views, both on the goals themselves and on how best to reach them. This implies the need to have regular discussions with peers and others.

There is now a strong self-advocacy movement among people with physical disabilities who insist on the right to consultation concerning their Individual Service Programmes. Crawley (1982) demonstrated that self-advocacy can also be encouraged among people with mental handicaps, again underlining the need to involve clients in goal setting and other aspects of their own care and treatment.

Aversive procedures

The use of aversive procedures, especially electric shock but also seclusion, in behaviour modification programmes is still most controversial. At the outset, one has to acknowledge that like all intervention techniques they are open to abuse. The techniques are more fully defined and discussed in Chapter 8. Here, we will address some of the ethical issues in their use. Ross (1981) summarises these succinctly: 'The presentation of painful stimuli can be justified as a treatment procedure when the alternative is permanent injury or death, as in cases of chronic vomiting or severe self-injurious behavior, and when more benign treatment methods have failed or would be too slow' (p. 313). In other words, the principle of least intrusive intervention demands that while normally other methods should have been tried first and failed, the question of efficacy and the time available may mean that aversive techniques have to be applied to save further damage or death.

Again Ross (1981) elaborates:

> No one should apply punishment as a treatment procedure without full awareness, exploration and discussion of its ethical implications and never before less drastic measures have been considered . . . no one should undertake to punish self-injurious behavior who is not prepared to invest much time and effort in establishing and maintaining adaptive response patterns that can take the place of the suppressed behavior and serve the child as a means of obtaining social reinforcers . . . In the absence of such efforts, procedures employing punishment, especially those that involve the infliction of pain, are totally unacceptable. The elimination of self-directed behavior should not be an end in itself but always a means towards the end of increasing a child's reper-toire of adaptive responses (pp. 323–4).

All that Ross says about children applies to adults with severe handicaps.

In part, this means that punishment techniques are rarely, if ever, justified unless strenuous efforts are in hand to implement a positive, carefully monitored training programme. In part, it is also an argument for better assessment and functional analysis of problem behaviours. As is seen in Chapters 2 and 8, more careful and elaborate functional analyses of self-injurious behaviours are beginning to identify in some cases less punitive ways of intervening.

As always, the least traumatic possible intervention should be used when a punitive technique is considered necessary. Water mist can serve as a punisher instead of electric shock in some cases; brief restraint can be less intrusive than isolation in a bare room. One has constantly to be on guard for poorly trained staff using isolation in a punitive way in the mistaken belief that they are implementing a programme of time-out from positive reinforcement. The scrupulous collection of records of such incidents should permit managers to monitor such activities and prevent abuses. After all, if a time-out from positive reinforcement programme has been properly set up, there should be a noticeable change in behaviour within a very short period of time.

Where some unacceptable behaviours are maintained on a thin schedule of social reinforcement, some people have objected to the use of extinction on the grounds that institutionalised patients already live in an impoverished environment. That is, of course, a criticism of the institution, not of behaviour modification. Even so, where such fears are voiced, it is possible in many instances to use differential reinforcement of other behaviours (DRO) instead, or as well, in order to ensure a plenitude of positive factors in the person's environment.

The whole issue of using aversive procedures with clients who cannot give informed consent highlights the need to have such programmes overseen by an accessible local ethical committee. It also highlights the need for staff training of those people using the techniques (see Chapter 12), and the need for supervision, advice and support for junior workers, and for regular planned reviews of programmes, as well as for their monitoring by local ethical committees.

Training others

In running training programmes and in editing this book, we are aware of another set of ethical problems inherent in behaviour modification. In the rush to 'give psychology away' to others, it is all too easy to pass over isolated techniques without ensuring a thorough understanding of the principles on which the techniques are based. Anyone can learn to dispense reinforcement contingently. The difficult skills lie in the functional analysis of the presenting problem and the task analysis needed to shape up new behaviours.

As Ross (1981) puts it:

It is grossly irresponsible, if not unethical, to attempt to influence a child's behavior for ostensibly therapeutic purposes without first studying the particulars of the specific situation. This point is especially pertinent in the case of behavior therapy where many aspects involve well-defined, easily learned procedures that lend themselves to 'treatment packages' that can be heedlessly applied even by people with little training or experience or can be dispensed as standard prescriptions for intervention solely on the basis of parents' or teachers' complaints (p. 22).

We know of one case in Britain where nurses in a mental subnormality hospital were prosecuted for assaulting a patient. Whenever he performed an unacceptable act he was thrown to the ground and sat upon. Their defence was that they were merely following timeout procedures that had been taught them at a short training course.

296

The video recordings used in the training course were subpoenaed and the court agreed with the organisers of the short course that the nurses' actions bore scant resemblance to the procedures taught. The nurses were found guilty of assault.

At one level this sad story reflects poor management and supervision within the hospital. At another, one has to note what responsibility organisers of short courses have for ensuring that what they teach is not abused. The answer can only be: very little, although organisers of locally based courses are taking their responsibilities more seriously (see Chapter 16). Our job as teachers must be to disseminate knowledge and skills. We must caution people of the need to obtain continuous supervision. But we need not censor knowledge which can be put to good use.

CONCLUSIONS AND SUGGESTIONS

Behaviour modification does carry dangers and can be abused, but this is no reason for abandoning it. Over the past twenty years it has demonstrated that it has good potential for teaching and enriching the lives of people with mental handicaps: indeed, it is often the only way of introducing them to new and valuable experiences.

In our view, behaviour modification poses no unique ethical problems. It merely poses them more explicitly. We have tried to illustrate some of the real ethical dilemmas facing therapists, and to indicate some solutions. In brief, better training of professionals is one key to safeguarding the interests of dependent clients. Fuller, more open discussion of the ethical problems involved in treating patients who cannot give informed consent is a good place to start.

At various points, we have noted that all judgements are relative, seeking to balance the advantages and disadvantages of a particular course of intervention at a particular point in time. No one therapist should be expected to do this alone. Reference to other colleagues helps share the burden and safeguard the rights of clients. More formally, we see advantages in having treatment programmes of all kinds regularly reviewed by a local ethical committee which has representatives of parents and guardians, and lay members as well as professional members. In our experience, these can be very helpful and usually reassuring. After all, everyone is trying to act in the best interests of the client. It is just that the best interests in the short and long term are not always clear to any one individual.

16

The Organisation of Short Courses

Janet Carr

Behaviour modification is seen more and more as a valuable approach to teaching the mentally handicapped, and demand for courses on the topic is considerable. One of the aims of this book is to provide some practical help to those who wish to run such a course. Nobody, however, will want to rush into setting up a course without first determining certain basic requirements such as:

how long a course it should be — a day? a week?

for whom it should be intended — teachers? nurses? parents? psychologists? a combination of workers?

what the course should aim to achieve — increase theoretical knowledge? practical skills? both of these?

and how the organisers expect to draw conclusions on whether or not the aims have been accomplished — what methods of evaluation will be used?

LENGTH OF COURSE

Most courses run in this country have been brief and concentrated, lasting from a few days to a week (Milne, 1984; Williams and Jackson, 1975); some, especially those for parents, have been spread out over a number of weeks (Bidder *et al.*, 1975; Cunningham and Jeffree, 1971, 1975; Firth, 1982; Heifetz, 1977).

Other courses have been much longer and more thorough, and have incuded written and practical examinations leading to the award of a certificate or diploma (Jackson, 1976; Murphy and McArdle, 1978; Speight, 1976). The basic content of these courses is similar (and is contained in the preceding chapters of this book).

The essential difference between them lies in the amount of detail, practical experience and revision that can be included. Clearly the length of the course will constraint its objectives and the expectations of its participants. Different types of course, of differing lengths, will suit some people better than others. Course organisers may be in a position to offer one kind of course and not others. All these factors must be taken into account when a course is being planned. However, as a general rule, all short courses, up to and including those lasting six months, may be expected to be felt by the participants to be too short. It may be advisable for short courses to be explicitly described as offering no more than an introduction to behaviour modification (Williams and Jackson, 1975); for participants to be told that they cannot expect to gain a full working knowledge of the theory and skills involved; and for organisers to be prepared for a demand for follow-up meetings.

COURSE STUDENTS

Many courses have been designed to cater for one type of student: for nurses or for psychologists, for teachers or for parents. In general, this approach seems an appropriate one, in that the course organisers know that the students share a common background of knowledge and experience. It may not, however, be essential to restrict membership of a course to one discipline. The courses run at the Institute of Psychiatry were designed for psychologists, but applicants from other disciplines — social workers, teachers, doctors, nurses — were also accepted; and the courses run at Hilda Lewis House deliberately include staff of all disciplines and also parents. The apparent success of these courses may be attributed to the fact that all students, of whatever discipline, are assumed to have virtually no knowledge of behaviour modification. With a very few exceptions this assumption seems, from the participants' performance on the courses, and especially where practical skills are concerned, to be justified; the basic principles and skills taught are relevant to all the students. Where different groups are known to differ markedly in their knowledge and experience of behaviour modification, it may be advisable to offer different types of courses.

AIMS OF THE COURSE

Whether a course is to be aimed at increasing theoretical knowledge (for instance, with academic students), or at giving the participants skills which they can use to help and teach the mentally handicapped, must be decided at the outset. In our experience, the demand is almost entirely for the latter type of course. Some further suggestions for running this kind of course are given in the section on 'The Teaching Component' on p. 304.

EVALUATION OF SHORT COURSES

Behaviour modification is becoming widely recognised as a useful approach, and the need for courses for psychologists, other professionals and non-professionals is acknowledged (Working Party on Behaviour Modification, 1978). Demand increases and courses proliferate. Some are carefully evaluated (Murphy and McArdle, 1978), but of the others, and especially of the mushrooming short courses, the question must be asked: what good do they do? Do the students who attend them learn anything? Or anything useful? Does attendance at a short course enable a student to do anything more or better than he was able to do before it? If a short course is less than ideal, is it better than nothing at all? There are suggestions that it may not be (Woods and Cullen, 1983). It seems important that those who run these courses should try to provide answers to at least some of these questions, and that some attempt should be made to study the effectiveness of the course. Although a variety of evaluative approaches is possible, the four to be discussed are: by questionnaire; by written tests; by assessment of practical skills; and by assessment of client change.

1. Questionnaires

This is the simplest level of evaluation and has been widely used (Cunningham and Jeffree, 1971, 1975; Milne, 1984; Smith, 1977; Tavormina, 1975). Participants are typically asked to record on a standard form their opinion of various aspects of the course, both didactic and organisational, and of the effect the course has had or is likely to have on their practising skills (see Appendix 3 in the first edition of this book). Typically the response to these questionnaires is predominantly positive, as may also be other subjective reactions (Houston *et al.*, 1979). Gratifying as this response is to the course organisers, it should be viewed with some caution, especially where the course has been the only teaching experience to which the participants have had access. The organisers (the present authors among them) must reflect, particularly where courses for parents are concerned, that teaching of almost any kind might be welcome, and that the appreciation shown by the questionnaire respondents may not necessarily be due to the particular type of course undertaken. Nevertheless, questionnaires may be useful. Responses are not invariably favourable, and if the questionnaire is designed so as to elicit criticism as well as praise, it may provide helpful suggestions for future courses.

2. Written tests

Some form of written test of knowledge of behaviour modification has been used in a number of studies (Doleys *et al.*, 1976; Gardner *et al.*, 1970; Gardner and Giampa, 1971; Milne, 1984). A brief test was developed by one of us (JC) and used in the assessment of the Hilda Lewis House short courses; later this was expanded in collaboration with other authors of this book, and this version of the test (the Behaviour Modification Information Test) was used in the evaluation of courses run at the Institute of Psychiatry, and of a course for teachers (Smith, 1977) and for nurses (Murphy and McArdle, 1978). The test is simple to administer and to score. It tests memory for technical terms and awareness of theoretical principles. The full test and scoring standards are given in Appendix 2 in the first edition of this book. Results from the two Institute of Psychiatry courses showed that mean scores on the Behaviour Modification Information Test (BMIT) increased in each case by nearly 13 points (out of a maximum possible score of 51). Rank order correlations of BMIT scores before and after the courses were highly significant, showing that gains on the test were spread fairly evenly over those who at the outset knew a good deal about behaviour modification and those who knew very little. Rank order scores on the BMIT were also significantly associated with video ratings (see p. 302), both before and after the course; thus, results from the BMIT can give some indication of students' probable performance on a practical test.

More recently a multiple-choice version of the BMIT has been developed, which has the advantages of being easier to score and somewhat less alarming perhaps for relatively unsophisticated trainees. It has now been used to assess acquisition of knowledge in participants on training courses for adult day-centre and hostel staff, nursery nurses, social workers, etc. Out of a maximum possible score of 46 the mean pre-course score for all 95 participants was 20 (range 8–38) and the mean post-course score was 28.3 (range 13–43) giving a mean gain of 8.3.

3. Assessment of practical skills

If practical skills are taught, it is important to assess how effectively they have been taught. Increasingly the emphasis is on practical skills: of 17 published studies of training courses reviewed by Milne (1985), two-thirds were evaluated in this way. In some courses students have been assessed in their real-life interactions with clients (Bricker *et al.*, 1972; Doleys *et al.*, 1976; McBrien and Edmonds, 1985), while other students have been assessed also through video vignettes (Milne, 1984) or role-playing situations (Gardner *et al.*, 1970; Murphy and McArdle, 1978; Smith 1977). The student's performance is scored for the presence of appropriate responses (reinforcement given for positive behaviour, prompting and fading used correctly, etc.) and for the absence of inappropriate responses (e.g. attention paid to undesirable behaviour).

A potential source of error in many studies is that students are rated by interested parties (course organisers), who are fully aware of where the students have got to in the course and whether the ratings being made are at the beginning or the end of the course. Although it is extremely difficult to avoid this situation when ratings are made *in vivo*, it seems probable that it would influence the outcome of the evaluation in a direction favourable to the expectations of the course organisers. In order to avoid this, where the assessments of the courses run at the Institute of Psychiatry were concerned, the role-play sessions were videotaped and were rated blind by independent raters. Although laborious and time-consuming, this method ensures that the benefits to be derived from a course are impartially evaluated.

Results from the two Institute of Psychiatry courses show that on the videotaped test of practical skills scored by blind raters, participants' scores increased in each case by about 8 points. When the ratings were done by course tutors, who were aware of which were 'before' and which 'after' tapes, the mean difference was 10.6 points. Participants who undertook the practical tests felt strongly that much of the improvement in their performance could be attributed not to what they learned on the course, but to familiarity with the test situation: on the second occasion they knew the layout of the video studio, the kind of behaviour the stooge could be expected to show, what they, themselves, would have to do and so on. All this they had had a week to think about, and it was this, they suggested, that made the major difference to their performance. Consequently, on two further courses (Murphy and McArdle, 1978), student nurses took the videotaped test at the outset and again a week later, before they embarked on an intensive course in behaviour modification, and again a week later following this course. Results showed that about half of the overall increase in scores occurred between the first and second tests — e.g. before any formal training took place.

This group of student nurses spent the intervening week between tests 1 and 2 working in Hilda Lewis House, and therefore had the opportunity to observe behaviour modification being carried out and, if they wished, to ask questions (how far they did so is unknown). It is not clear at present whether the same increase in pre-training scores would take place if the students were not in this kind of environment. Nevertheless, it seems that some of the improvement shown by students may be due not to learning but to familiarity with the test situation.

As a refinement of the method discussed above, teachers were videotaped pre- and post-test and at follow-up in interactions with a real child (i.e. not in role-play) and the videotapes were rated blind by independent raters (McBrien and Edmonds, 1985). The results showed a significant improvement from pre- to post-test, the improvement being maintained at follow-up. The authors point out that this study does not include any assessment of a possible 'pre-course training effect' as described above, but the use of real, rather than role-played, subjects and situations which were then rated blind from videotapes is particularly interesting.

4. Client change

In the final analysis the main justification for courses in behaviour modification must be the benefit to the clientele served by the course participants. To demonstrate this effect requires pre- and post-course measures of the abilities and behaviours of the client group served by the participants or of experimental and control groups. Either is a daunting undertaking, especially where the course participants come from widely scattered settings, and only a few studies have attempted this type of evaluation. Of the 17 studies of nurse training reviewed by Milne (1985), only five evaluated course effectiveness in terms of the effects shown by the patients. One of these, a study in which the main measure of teaching effectiveness consisted of measures of client progress, Carsrud *et al.* (1980) showed that people with mental handicaps who were cared for by staff trained in behaviour modification methods made, highly significantly, better progress than did those cared for by staff with no such training. Milne (1985) compared long-stay patients treated by groups of nurses some of whom had completed a course in behaviour modification and some who were waiting to go on the course. Patients treated by the former group of nurses showed 'large improvement' compared with the 'small change' in those under the care of the latter, patient change being assessed on objective measures such as cessation of incontinence. No details are given, but the difference between the two groups is said to be significant at the 0.05 level (Mann Whitney U-test).

In other studies participants demonstrated following their training courses that they were able successfully to teach their clients (Watson and Uzzell, 1980; Carr and Hayward, 1986), but with no pre-course or control data the evidence for an effect of the training is less impressive.

THE TEACHING COMPONENT

Once the structural aspects of the course have been determined, the course organisers will need to decide how the course will be taught, and in particular the weight to be given to didactic and to practical teaching.

Behaviour modification comprises not only a body of knowledge but also a number of techniques and skills. Since these latter must be applied in practical situations it seems obvious that they should be taught, at least partly, by practical methods: students should have a chance to learn not only the theory but also the practice of the techniques. The underlying principle has been amply acknowledged; psychologists have often pointed out to other professionals that there is a difference between saying and doing, between 'telling what' and 'showing how' to do something. Advice on teaching new skills is readily available, and exhortations such as, 'Active learning is better than passive recognition', abound in the literature. And yet many of the early texts and descriptions of the training of both professional and lay people in behaviour modification techniques appear to have ignored practical skills training. It was, it seemed, enough to *tell* psychologists what to do rather than to show them and to give them practice. It is clear enough where this type of training can lead: all those involved in professional teaching will recognise the student who can pass written examinations while still being a one-person disaster in inter-personal work with patients. How to ensure that students acquire practical skills as well as the theory of behaviour modification has not been an easy problem to solve, and a variety of methods have been tried in the teaching of parents, nurses, teachers and others.

At an elementary level of training, parents were 'instructed' in the treatment procedure (Williams, 1959) and then closely supervised in its application (Mackay, 1971). In another study parents were required to interact with a child while being watched by an experienced therapist, who then corrected their performance; this was supplemented by occasions when the therapist worked with the child while the parent watched and discussed with another therapist what was going on (Terdal and Buell, 1969). Video feedback of the student's own performance has been found a useful teaching technique (Bernal, 1969; Bricker *et al.*, 1972; Doleys *et al.*, 1976; Kiernan and Riddick, 1973). Behavioural rehearsal and role-play have been widely used, to teach teaching-parents and pre-delinquent boys (Phillips *et al.*, 1971), ward attendants (Carsrud *et al.*, 1980), with trainees alternating the roles of therapist and child (Gardner, 1972; Watson *et al.*, 1971), and parents (Patterson *et al.*, 1973; Hirsch and Walder, 1969, cited by Berkowitz and Graziano, 1972). Milne (1982) compared an 'active' course comprising role-playing, modelling, etc. with a more 'passive' chalk-and-talk type approach and found that the 'active' group gained higher scores on a knowledge test and on a videotaped simulated performance test, although the two groups did not differ on a test of attitudes. Role-playing has also been used to evaluate the effects of training. Kirigin *et al.* (1975) using pre- and post-training tests in five role-playing situations showed that parents who had undergone a five-day workshop made significantly greater gains than those who had had access only to written materials. Gardner (1973) also used role-playing techniques to assess the skills acquired in training by ward

305

attendants. He pointed to the advantages of using a trainee to act as the retarded child: that learning can be speeded up and complexities of training dealt with in one session which would normally take far longer to cover; that the staff under assessment are not subjected to the differences in behaviour of different residents but experience near-uniform behaviours; and that problem behaviours such as hyperactivity can be programmed at will in order to assess the competence of staff in dealing with such a problem.

The role-play method seemed to us to offer much of value to students learning behaviour modification techniques. Although it is widely used, there is no detailed account in the literature of how to go about it. For those who may want to use role-playing in their teaching, what follows is a description of the method as we used it.

WORKSHOPS

In our five-day course, each day was divided into a morning and an afternoon session. Each session began with a one-hour lecture with videotaped illustrations on one of the topics covered by Chapters 2–8 and 11–13 in the present book. From time to time it has been suggested that the lectures are unnecessary, and we have considered dispensing with them. Although we do not have experimental evidence either way, we have felt that it would be difficult for students to embark on practical training without having some prior knowledge of what they were supposed to do. The lectures also ensure that all students have in common at least a minimum fund of theoretical knowledge to draw on. Hence, on balance, we think the lectures useful and have continued to use them in our teaching. Each lecture was followed by a 1½-hour workshop focusing on the lecture material. The students were divided into workshop groups, eight or nine to a group, and each workshop was run by two tutors, one of whom acted as trainer and the other as 'stooge' — the mentally handicapped person. The trainer explained the problems and learning difficulties, apropos of the particular workshop, of the mentally handicapped person, and gave a short demonstration of the appropriate techniques to be used, already discussed in the preceding lecture (e.g. prompting, modelling, etc.). The students then took it in turns to act as therapist to the mentally handicapped person, attempting to put into practice the principles and techniques which had been described and demonstrated. The tutor asked for comments from the other students on the therapist's methods, and gave suggestions of her own. The stooge, although usually maintaining the part of a person who was mentally handicapped and, often, mute, would occasionally remark on the therapist's handling as seen from the receiving end.

For the students, attempting to use the techniques in a practical situation, as opposed to hearing them described or even watching them on videotape, offered an entirely different learning experience. All sorts of problems in the use of the techniques, both major and minor, emerged which had not been apparent until then. For example, in the workshop on reinforcement, students often found it difficult at first to deliver edible reinforcers quickly enough, or to have them readily to hand and yet not available for the stooge to grab. Many students had difficulty in giving clear directions, whether verbally or by gesture or physical prompting. Fading prompts was found to be a much more delicate and complicated task than it sounds. Even after they had been told that attention was a reinforcer, students would find their attention unwittingly glued to the stooge's inappropriate behaviour. With practice, discussion, demonstration and more practice it was possible to overcome many of these difficulties and for the students to feel they had a clearer idea of how to undertake this kind of work.

More recently an alternative format in which didactic material and practical role-play are interdigitated has been developed for course members who may not be accustomed to sitting through hour-long lectures. Each topic (e.g. reinforcement) is introduced, one sub-area (e.g. immediate delivery of reinforcement) is described, followed by demonstration and participation in role-play by the course members (Carr and Hayward, 1986).

Role of the stooge

The two tutors in any one group alternated roles as trainer and stooge and usually found a session as stooge a rest-cure compared with one as trainer. Nevertheless, the stooge also has an exacting part to play. It is essential that she should be familiar with a wide range of people with mental handicaps and with their various behaviours and responses. She must be constantly alert to the behaviours of the trainer-therapists and to how these would affect her own behaviour as a person with a mental handicap. A very real difficulty is knowing how far her own reactions as a normally intelligent person can be a guide to how the person she is impersonating would react in a similar situation. For example, rough or feeble handling may be experienced similarly, but boredom with a task perhaps differently. Some stooges found it helpful to take as a model a particular person whom they knew well, and to behave as they felt he would in similar circumstances. However, it was important that this should not be carried too far, and that the stooge should always be aware of the needs of the teaching situation. On one course a stooge became so engrossed in her role as a profoundly handicapped passive child that she failed to react to the inappropriate behaviours of the trainer-therapists such as leaving reinforcers within reach. Another pitfall the stooge must avoid is playing for laughs. This applies particularly in workshops on decelerating undesirable behaviours, or in others where tantrums are scheduled. It is all too easy for the stooge to be carried away by the disinhibiting effects of diminished responsibility, especially as the audience usually enjoys the sight of a professional person stamping and screaming and throwing chairs. The stooge has to remember to use behaviours to enable the students to learn how to cope with them, not to feed her own ego.

On another course, another problem concerning the stooge became apparent. It is accepted that the stooge must be fully acquainted with people with mental handicaps; what now became obvious was that the stooge must also be very well acquainted with behaviour modification. This emerged during a course for parents, run by one tutor on her own, and based at a school. In order that the teachers at the school should have a part in the course they were asked to act as stooges in the workshops, and accepted with enthusiasm. However, in spite of careful briefing on the lines of the previous paragraph, they were not really successful as stooges because they did not know enough about behaviour modification to respond to appropriate techniques when these were used. For example, in a session on extinction a parent-therapist correctly withheld attention, but the teacher-stooge continued with the inappropriate behaviour far beyond what would have been reasonable, to the point where the tutor wondered whether to intervene. At long last, however, the stooge responded appropriately. This might be what would happen in a real-life situation with a real mentally handicapped child, but one of the advantages of working with a stooge is that action and learning are packed into a shorter time than is possible in real-life; by the time the stooge finally capitulated there was no time to go on to other aspects of the workshop. So, ideally, stooges should be at a fairly high level of sophistication. Where this is not possible, some intensive training of the stooges, not just written instructions and verbal discussion, might be helpful.

Being a stooge is a highly instructive process. One experiences for the first time the frustration of being inarticulate, the irritation of inappropriate handling, the ineffectiveness of unvarying reinforcers be they edible or social, and the compelling effectiveness of a varied schedule of reinforcement. This being so, the question arises as to whether each student should have the opportunity of doing a stint as stooge. Much depends on the time available. Students need to have had considerable experience of workshops — say half a dozen sessions — before they can be asked to change from trainee therapist to stooge; and they need a considerable time as stooge, at least one whole workshop each, to allow them to gain the maximum benefit from experiencing several different therapists. Other factors to be taken into account are the greater difficulty of programming students to carry out the role of stooge in a way that will give the most benefit to the other participants, and the resulting uncertainty of the participants as to whether the behaviours shown are really those that they are expected to be able to cope with. On the whole, we have not usually thought it feasible, on our short courses, to allow students to act as stooges, but have recommended they try to arrange for sessions as such when they return to their own places of work. On a longer course, experience as a stooge might be possible and valuable for the students.

Students have sometimes asked whether it would be possible for workshops to centre around a real child or adult rather than a stooge. Apart from the ethical problems involved, we feel that this is not desirable because of the impossibility of programming the real person's behaviour. A stooge can be asked to be profoundly or mildly handicapped, to learn slowly or quickly or, if necessary, to skip essential stages of learning, to stop a tantrum or to throw another straight away. What we lose in realism we more than make up for in flexibility. The course is a teaching device aimed at covering a broad spectrum of possible behaviours in a short time. We hope that the students will be able to use and try out their skills more realistically on real clients when they return to their places of work.

Workshop problems

For the tutors there are many problems in running a workshop.

There is the question of how much the tutor should demonstrate the 'right' way to carry out the techniques. Since time on our course was limited, it seemed preferable that the students should use as much of it as possible in working with the stooge and gaining practical experience, but some students felt that they had had too little chance of seeing the techniques appropriately modelled. More time spent in modelling the techniques in person, or in repeated video demonstrations, might pay dividends.

Another problem concerned how long any one student should be allowed to go on working with the stooge. If the student's method of working was faulty, should the tutor interrupt the session and point out what was wrong, or allow the student to continue in order that his error might become apparent from the stooge's failure to make progress and the student be compelled to try different tactics? Ideally, the latter might have been the best way for the students to learn, but in practice, with all the constraints of time, it was not always possible. Instead, when a student-therapist persisted with a faulty technique, the tutor would usually stop him, and ask the other students whether they had any comments on how the session was going. Where necessary the tutor would steer these comments round to cover the point he wished to make to the student. Following the discussion the student would try again, hopefully using a new approach, although sometimes students found it difficult to alter their habitual ways of behaving and might need to be stopped and corrected several times. Some students found it very difficult to show more than lukewarm enthusiasm in giving social reinforcement; others repeatedly failed to give reinforcement when it was appropriate or allowed long delays before delivery. When this happened they would be stopped again for more discussion and demonstration.

It is, however, very important not only to point out the student's mistakes and failures. Participating in a workshop is an alarming business, and some students found it extremely unpleasant to have to leave their seats and perform as trainee-therapists. If it is left to them, some participants will refuse to act as therapists, leaving this to a small number of braver volunteers.

In our workshops it was made clear to the participants that everyone was expected to take his turn as therapist and nobody would be allowed to act only as audience. The result of this was that, first, however nervous a student was of acting as therapist, he or she knew that all the other students were in the same position; secondly, perhaps partly because of this, the students were generally supportive of each other, and their criticism of any one therapist's performance was tempered by an awareness that 'it's my turn next'; and lastly, because they were not allowed to avoid the alarming situation, the students may have found it less unpleasant than they had feared.

Nevertheless, almost all students, of whatever discipline, are nervous of having to come forward and take the part of therapist. It therefore behoves the tutors to make this as easy as possible for the students; to set each in turn a limited task which should be well within her capacity to accomplish given the teaching that has gone before; above all, to be generous with praise and sparing with criticism, concentrating on the reinforcement of the student's appropriate behaviours rather than on the punishment of her inappropriate ones. If they are to derive maximum benefit from the course, students should not only learn to use the techniques efficiently, but should also be encouraged to gain confidence in their own increasing skills.

Ideally, each student would have had the chance to work with the stooge on every aspect of every workshop, but in practice this was for us not possible. Indeed, in a 1½-hour workshop each student usually had only one or at most two sessions as trainer, although this could be stepped up in sessions that required more than one trainer at a time, as for instance when we worked on imitation, when a prompter as well as a trainer could be used. How long to go on working on a particular aspect of a workshop was another problem: it was tempting to continue with one aspect — for instance, prompting spoon feeding — until it had been thoroughly mastered, but this could only be done at the expense of other parts of the workshop. In fact we often found ourselves unable to complete the schedule for the workshops, in spite of much careful planning and timing. Nevertheless, we felt it necessary to allow ourselves some flexibility, so that if a particularly difficult problem arose it could receive special attention.

Preparation of workshops

In order to ensure that as far as possible all students completing the course had had similar training experience, the workshops on any one particular topic followed an identical format in each of the workshop groups. Before the course opened, the content of the workshops was thoroughly discussed between the tutors after which the trainers' and stooges' guides were drawn up (see Appendix 1 in the first edition of this book) and copies made for each group, mounted on cardboard for ease of handling. The two sets of guides were designed to be complementary; the trainer's guide gives the sequence of tasks to be worked through in the workshop, together with important points to be brought out and discussed; the stooge's guide also gives the sequence of tasks plus instructions as to how he is to behave: how 'bright' he is (this may vary from one task or session to another), when to throw a tantrum, when to show boredom with tasks or reinforcers and so on. Of course, the occasion for many of these behaviours depends partly on the trainee-therapist's method of working: we have sometimes been unable as stooges to display undesirable behaviours because the skilful handling of the trainee-therapist precluded them — in which case this too was explained and discussed.

LONGER-TERM EFFECTS OF SHORT COURSES

In the early days of behaviour modification training it seemed to be assumed that any training was bound to have beneficial effects. Older, sadder and wiser, we now realise, not least because of the weight of evidence from the literature (Quilitch, 1975; Woods and Cullen, 1983) that any initial effect of a short course in promoting behavioural interactions with clients is likely to wear off rapidly. In view of this an attempt was made to increase the usefulness of behavioural methods to course participants by involving them in practical projects and by providing them with follow-up supervision. A series of 3-day courses was planned in the early 1980s, and these had built into them the requirement that after the course each participant would undertake at least one practical project, using the behavioural methods taught. Thus at the outset each participant was asked to select at least one client and one problem that he or she would work on following the course. The bulk of the last afternoon of the course was set aside for discussion of these projects, how they would be set up and how they would be expected to proceed, and a mutually convenient date was fixed for a follow-up meeting. These follow-up meetings were, in the main, well received and well attended; an impressive amount of work and many gratifying outcomes were reported. Of 113 participants at 13 short courses, 68 (60 per cent) carried out at least one project following the end of the course, and of these 28 (25 per cent of the whole group) carried out two or more. These figures compare with the 26 per cent of course participants who have been reported elsewhere as having carried out post-course projects (Milne, 1984).

Some participants moved out of the area, changed jobs or dropped out, but many were enthusiastic about continuing to meet. One group has now held its sixth meeting and two their seventh, where new clients, new projects and new problems were brought forward. Providing opportunities for further meetings and supervision may then do something to enhance the use made of short courses in behavioural work, even if this still falls far short of what is in theory possible, and much work in this area remains to be done.

CONCLUSIONS

Short courses in behaviour modification are popular, and those that are organised are well attended. Their organisation takes considerable planning, time and effort and may be difficult for those already fully committed in demanding jobs, but running such a course can also be rewarding to the tutors as they see the response of the students, their enthusiasm and their increasing expertise. Students often discuss the relation of their new knowledge to their own background and experience and the problems and situations that they have encountered, and this, in raising new areas of application of the techniques, can be informative too for the tutors. Follow-up meetings, with students encouraged to report back — preferably with recorded data — on projects undertaken following the course, provide an opportunity for revision for the students and feedback for the tutors.

In spite of the problems attendant upon the running of practical workshops, we ourselves are convinced of their usefulness. Students too are enthusiastic about them, commenting that the workshops bring out and clarify questions that had not occurred to them before to ask; and that the students themselves feel a new confidence in embarking on using behaviour modification in real-life projects. In the ideal situation students would receive further teaching and supervision in these real-life projects. Where this is not possible, a short course may provide at least a starting point to learning for those wishing to use behaviour modification to help people with mental handicaps.

313

References

Abelew, P.H. (1972) Intermittent schules of reinforcement applied to the conditioning treatment of enuresis. *Dissert. Abst. Int.*, **33**, 2799B–800B

Abramson, E.E. & Wunderlich, R. (1972) Dental hygiene training for retardates: an application of behavioural techniques. *Ment. Retard.*, **10** (3), 6–8

Ackerman, A.M. & Shapiro, E.S. (1984) Self-monitoring and work productivity with mentally retarded adults. *J. Appl. Behav. Anal.*, **17**, 403–7

Affleck, G., McGrade, B.T., McQueeney, M. & Allen, D. (1982) Relationship-focused early intervention in developmental disabilities. *Excep. Child.*, **49**, 259–61

Agras, W. (1972) *Behavior modification: principles and clinical applications*. Boston: Little and Brown

Albin, J.B. (1977) Some variables influencing the maintenance of acquired self feeding behavior in profoundly retarded children. *Ment. Retard.*, **15** (5), 49–52

Alevizos, K.J. & Alevizos, P.N. (1975) Effects of verbalizing contingencies in time-out procedures. *J. Behav. Ther. Exper. Psychiat.*, **6**, 253–5

Allen, K.D. & Fuqua, R.W. (1985) Eliminating selective stimulus control: a comparison of two teaching procedures for teaching mentally retarded children to respond to compound stimuli. *J. Exp. Child Psychol.*, **39**, 55–71

Altman, K. & Mira, M. (1983) Training parents of developmentally disabled children. In: J.L. Matson & F. Andrasik (Eds), *Treatment issues and innovations in mental retardation*. New York and London: Plenum Press, pp. 303–71

Anderson, N. & Rincover, A. (1982) The generality of overselectivity in developmentally disabled children. *J. Exp. Child Psychol.*, **34**, 217–30

Aronwitz, R. & Conroy, C.W. (1969) Effectiveness of the automatic toothbrush for handicapped persons. *Am. J. Phys. Med.*, **48** (4), 193–205 (from abstract in *Mental Retardation Abstracts*, 1971, **8**, No. 576)

Ashkenazi, Z. (1975) The treatment of encopresis using a discriminative stimulus and positive reinforcement. *J. Behav. Ther. Exper. Psychiat.*, **6**, 155–7

Atthowe, J.M. (1976) Treating the hospitalized person. In: W.E. Craighead, A.E. Kazdin and M.J. Mahoney (Eds) *Behaviour modification: principles, issues and applications*. Boston: Houghton Mifflin

Atthowe, J.M. & Krasner, L. (1968) A preliminary report on the application of contingent reinforcement procedures (token economy) on a 'chronic' psychiatric ward. *J. Abn. Psychol.*, **73**, 37–43

Attwood, T. (1977) The Priory parents' workshop. *Child: Care, Health Devel.*, **3**, 81–91

Attwood, T. (1978) The Croydon workshop for parents of pre-school mentally handicapped children. *Child: Care, Health Devel.*, **4**, 79–97

Attwood, T. (1979) The Croydon workshop for the parents of severely handicapped school-age children. *Child: Care, Health Devel.*, **5**, 177–88

Ayllon, T. & Azrin, N.H. (1968) *The token economy: a motivational system for therapy and rehabilitation.* New York: Appleton-Century-Crofts

Azrin, N.H. & Armstrong, P.M. (1973) The 'mini-meal' — a rapid method for teaching eating skills to the profoundly retarded. *Ment. Retard.*, **11** (1), 9–13

Azrin, N.H. & Besalel, V.A. (1979) *A parents' guide to bedwetting control: a step-by-step method.* New York: Simon & Schuster

Azrin, N.H. & Foxx, R.M. (1971) A rapid method of toilet training the institutionalized retarded. *J. Appl. Behav. Anal.*, **4**, 89–99

Azrin, N.H., Gottlieb, L., Hughart, L., Wesolowski, M.D. & Rahn, T. (1975) Eliminating self-injurious behavior by educative procedures. *Behav. Res. Ther.*, **13**, 101–11

Azrin, N.H. & Holz, W.C. (1966) Punishment. In: W.K. Honig (ed.) *Operant behavior: areas of research and application.* New York: Appleton-Century-Crofts

Azrin, N.H., Schaeffer, R.M. & Wesolowski, M.D. (1976) A rapid method of teaching profoundly retarded persons to dress by a reinforcement-guidance method. *Ment. Retard.*, **14** (6), 29–33

Azrin, N.H., Sneed, T.J. & Foxx, R.M. (1973) Dry-bed: a rapid method of eliminating bed-wetting (enuresis) of the retarded. *Behav. Res. Ther.*, **11**, 427–34

Azrin, N.H., Sneed, T.J. & Foxx, R.M. (1974) Dry-bed training: rapid elimination of childhood enuresis. *Behav. Res. Ther.*, **12**, 147–56

Azrin, N.H. & Thienes, P.M. (1978) Rapid elimination of enuresis by intensive learning without a conditioning apparatus. *Behav. Ther.*, **9**, 342–54

Azrin, N.H., Thienes-Hontos, P. & Besalel-Azrin, V. (1979) Elimination of enuresis without a conditioning alarm: an extension by office instruction of the child and parents. *Behav. Ther.*, **10**, 14–19

Bachman, J.E. & Fuqua, R.W. (1983) Management of inappropriate behaviours of trainable mentally impaired students using antecedent exercise. *J. Appl. Behav. Anal.*, **16**, 477–84

Baer, D.M., Peterson, R.F. & Sherman, J.A. (1967) The development of imitation by reinforcing behavioral similarity to a model. *J. Exp. Anal. Behav.*, **10**, 405–16

Baer, D.M. & Stokes, T.F. (1977) Discriminating a generalisation technology: recommendations for research in mental retardation. In: P. Mittler (Ed.), *Research to practice in mental retardation. Education and training*, Vol. II. I.A.S.S.M.D.

Baer, D.M., Wolf, M.M. & Risley, T.R. (1968) Some current dimensions of applied behavior analysis. *J. Appl. Behav. Anal.*, **1**, 91–7

Baer, R.A., Williams, J.A., Osnes, P.G. & Stokes, T.F. (1984) Delayed reinforcement as an indiscriminable contingency in verbal/non-verbal correspondence training. *J. Appl. Behav. Anal.*, **17**, 429–40

Bailey, P.A. & Jenkinson, J. (1982) The application of Bliss symbols. In: M. Peter & R. Barnes (Eds), *Signs, symbols and schools*. Stratford:

National Council for Special Education

Baker, B.L. (1986) Parents as teachers: a programme of applied research. In: D. Milne (Ed.), *Training behaviour therapists*. London, Croom Helm, pp. 92–117

Baker, B.L. & Brightman, R.P. (1984) Training parents of retarded children: program specific outcomes. *J. Behav. Ther. Exper. Psychiat.*, **15**, 255–60

Baker, B.L., Brightman, A.J., Heifetz, L.J. & Murphy, D.M. (1976) *Steps to independence: a skills training series for children with special needs*. Champaign, Ill.: Research Press

Baker, R., Hall, J.N. & Hutchinson, K. (1974) A token economy project with chronic schizophrenic patients. *Brit. J. Psychiat.*, **124**, 367–84

Baldwin, V.L., Fredericks, H.D.B. & Brodsky, G. (1973) *Isn't it time he outgrew this? or, A training program for parents of retarded children*. Springfield, Ill.: Charles C. Thomas

Balsam, P.D. & Bondy, A.S. (1983) The negative side effects of reward. *J. Appl. Behav. Anal.*, **16**, 283–96

Balsam, P.D. & Bondy, A.S. (1985) Reward induced response covariation: side effects revisited. *J. Appl. Behav. Anal.*, **18**, 79–80

Balson, P.N. (1973) Case study: encopresis: a case with symptom substitution. *Behav. Ther.*, **4**, 134–6

Bandura, A. (1969) *Principles of behaviour modification*. New York: Holt, Rinehart & Winston

Barlow, D.H. & Hersen, M. (1984) *Single case experimental designs: strategies for studying behaviour change*, second edition. New York: Pergamon Press

Barna, S., Bidder, R.T., Gray, O.P., Clements, J. & Gardner, S. (1980) The progress of developmentally delayed pre-school children in home-training scheme. *Child: Care, Health Devel.*, **6**, 157–64

Barrera, R., Lobato-Barrera, D. & Sulzer-Azaroff, B. (1980) A simultaneous treatment comparison of expressive language training programmes with a mute autistic child. *J. Autism Devel. Dis.*, **10**, 21–6

Barrett, B.H. (1969) Behavior modification in the home: parents adapt laboratory developed tactics to bowel-train a 5½-year-old. *Psychother. Theory Res. Prac.*, **6**, 172–6

Barrowclough, C. & Fleming, I. (1986). Training direct care staff in goal planning with elderly people. *Behav. Psychother.*, **14**, 192–210

Barton, E.S. (1975) Behaviour modification in the hospital school for the severely subnormal. In: C.C. Kiernan & F.P. Woodford (Eds) *Behaviour modification with the severely retarded*. Amsterdam: Elsevier North Holland, Associated Scientific Publishers

Barton, E.S., Guess, D., Garcia, E. & Baer, D.M. (1970) Improvement of retardates' meal-time behaviors by time-out procedures using multiple baseline techniques, *J. Appl. Behav. Anal.*, **3**, 77–84

Barton, E.S., Robertshaw, M.S., Barrett, H. & Winn, B. (1975) The introduction and development of behaviour modification in an ESN(S) school. *Behav. Mod.*, **8**, 20–38

Bates, P. & Wehman, P. (1977) Behavior management with the severely retarded: an empirical analysis of the research. *Ment. Retard.*, **15** (6), 9–12

Bath, K.E. & Smith, S.A. (1974) An effective token economy program for mentally retarded adults. *Mental Retard.*, **12**, 41–4

Batson, P.N. (1973) Case study: encopresis a case with symptom substitution. *Behav. Ther.*, **4**, 134–6

Baumeister, A.A. (1967) Learning abilities of the mentally retarded. In: Baumeister, A.A. (Ed.), *Mental retardation: appraisal, education and rehabilitation.* London: University of London Press

Baumeister, A.A. (1978) Origins and control of stereotyped movements. In: C.E. Meyer, (Ed.) *Quality of life in severely and profoundly mentally retarded people: research foundations for improvement.* Washington, DC: American Association on Mentally Deficient

Baumeister, A.A. & Maclean, W.E. (1984) Deceleration of self-injurious and stereotypic responding by exercise. *Appl. Res. Ment. Ret.*, **5**, 385–93

Bayley, M. (1973) *Mental handicap and community care: a study of mentally handicapped people in Sheffield.* London: Routledge & Kegan Paul

Bell, J. & Richmond, G. (1984) Improving profoundly mentally retarded adults performance on a position discrimination. *Am. J. Ment. Defic.*, **89**, 180–6

Berger, M. (1982) Applied behaviour analysis in education: a critical assessment and some implications for training teachers. *Educ. Psychoe.*, **2**, 289–300

Berkowitz, B.P. & Graziano, A.M. (1972) Training parents as behaviour therapists: a review. *Behav. Res. Ther.*, **10**, 297–317

Berkowitz, S., Sherry, P.J. & Davis, B. (1971) Teaching self-feeding skills to profound retardates using reinforcement and fading procedures. *Behav. Ther.*, **2**, 62–7

Bernal, M.E. (1969) Behavioral feedback in the modification of brat behaviors. *J. Nerv. Ment. Dis.*, **148**, 375–85

Bernal, M.E. and North, J.A. (1978) A survey of parent training manuals. *J. Appl. Behav. Anal.*, **11**, 533–44

Bernstein, G. (1982) Training behaviour change agents: a conceptual review. *Behav. Ther.*, **13**, 1–23

Bertsch, G., Fox, C.J. & Kwiecinski, J. (1984) Teaching developmentally disabled persons how to react to fires. *Appl. Res. Ment. Retard.*, **5** (4), 483–97

Besalel, V.A., Azrin, N.H., Thienes-Hontos, P. & McMorrow, M. (1980) Evaluation of a parent's manual for training enuretic children. *Behav. Res. Ther.*, **18**, 358–60

Bidder, R.T., Bryant, G. & Gray, O.P. (1975) Benefits to Down's Syndrome children through training their mothers. *Arch. Dis. Childhood*, **50**, 383–6

Bidder, R.T., Hewitt, K.E. & Gray, O.P. (1983) Evaluation of teaching methods in a home-based training scheme for developmentally delayed pre-school children. *Child: Care, Health Devel.*, **9**, 1–12

Birnbrauer, J.S., Peterson, C.R. & Solnick, J.V. (1974) Design and interpretation of studies of single subjects. *Am. J. Ment. Defic.*, **79**, 191–203

Birnbrauer, J.S., Wolf, M.M., Kidder, J.D. & Tague, C.E. (1965) Classroom behavior of retarded pupils with token reinforcement. *J. Exp. Child Psychol.*, **2**, 219–35

Blackman, D. (1974) *Operant conditioning: an experimental analysis of behaviour.* London: Methuen

317

Blechman, E.A. (1984) Competent parents, competent children: behavioural objectives of parent training. In: R.F. Dangel & R.A. Polster (Eds), *Parent training: foundations of research and practice.* New York/London: Guilford Press, pp. 34–63

Bliss, C.K. (1965) *Semantography (Blissymbolics)* (2nd edn.) Australia: Semantography Publications

Bluma, S., Shearer, M., Frohman, A. & Hilliard, J. (1976) *Portage guide to early education: manual* (revised edition). Portage, Wis.: The Portage Project

Boe, R.B. (1977) Economical procedures for the reduction of aggression in a residential setting. *Ment. Retard.,* 15 (5), 25–8

Bollard, J. & Nettlebeck, T. (1981) A comparison of dry-bed training and standard urine-alarm conditioning treatment of childhood bedwetting. *Behav. Res. Ther.,* 19, 215–26

Bollard, J., Nettlebeck, T. & Roxbee, L. (1982) Dry bed training for childhood bedwetting: a comparison of group with individually administered parent instruction. *Behav. Res. Ther.,* 20, 209–17

Bouter, H.P. & Smeets, P.M. (1979) Teaching tooth-brushing behaviour in severely retarded adults: systematic reduction of feedback and duration training. *Int. J. Rehab. Res.,* 2 (1), 61–9

Brady, D. & Smouse, A. (1978) A simultaneous comparison of three methods for language training with an autistic child: An experimental single case analysis. *J. Autism Child Schiz.,* 8, 271–9

Bricker, D.D. (1972) Imitative sign training as a facilitator of word–object association with low-functioning children. *Am. J. Ment. Defic.,* 76, 509–16

Bricker, W.A. & Bricker, D.D. (1970) A program of language training for the severely language handicapped child. *Excep. Child.,* 37, 101–11

Bricker, W.A., Morgan, D.G. & Grabowski, J.G. (1972) Development and maintenance of a behaviour modification repertoire of cottage attendants through T.V. feedback. *Am. J. Ment. Defic.,* 77, 128–36

Brierton, G., Garms, R. & Metzger, R. (1969) Practical problems encountered in an aide administered token reward cottage program. *Ment. Retard.,* 7, 40–3

Brightman, R.P., Ambrose, S.A. & Baker, B.L. (1980) Parent training; a school-based model for enhancing teaching performance. *Child Behav. Ther.,* 2, 35–47

Brightman, R.P., Baker, B.L., Clark, D.B. & Ambrose, S.A. (1982) Effectiveness of alternative parent training formats. *J. Behav. Ther. Exper. Psychiat.,* 13, 113–17

Brown, B.J. & Doolan, M. (1983) Behavioural treatment of faecal soiling: a case study. *Behav. Psychother.,* 11, 18–24

Bry, P.M. (1969) The role of reinforcement in imitation by retardates. Unpublished doctoral dissertation, University of Missouri. Quoted by Gardner, W.I. (1971)

Bundschuh, E.L., Curtis Williams, W., Hollingworth, J.D., Gooch, S. & Shirer, C. (1972) Teaching the retarded to swim. *Ment. Retard.,* 10 (3), 14–17

Burchard, J.D. & Barrera, F. (1972) Analysis of time-out and response cost in a programmed environment. *J. Appl. Behav. Anal.,* 5, 271–82

Burgess, R.L. & Richardson, R.A. (1984) Coercive interpersonal contingencies as a determinant of child maltreatment. In: R.F. Dangel & R.A. Polster (Eds), *Parent training: foundations of research and practice.* New York/London: Guilford Press, pp. 239–59

Byrne, E.A. & Cunningham, C.C. (1985) The effects of mentally handicapped children on families — a conceptual review. *J. Child Psychol. Psychiat.*, **26**, 847–64

Byrne, D. & Stevens, C. (1980) Mentally handicapped children's responses to vibrotactile and other stimuli as evidence for the existence of a sensory hierarchy. *Appex, J. Brit. Inst. Ment. Handicap,* **8**, 96–8

Calhoun, K.S. & Matherne, P. (1975) The effects of varying schedules of time-out on the aggressive behaviors of a retarded girl. *J. Behav. Ther. Exper. Psychiat.*, **6**, 139

Callias, M. (1985) Group treatments. In: M. Rutter & L. Hersov (Eds), *Child and adolescent psychiatry: modern approaches,* Second edition. London: Blackwell Scientific Publications, pp. 871–87

Callias, M. (1987) Working with parents of handicapped children. In: J. Tsiantis & S. Manolopoulos (Eds), *Modern issues in child psychiatry.* Athens: Kastaniotis. (In Greek.)

Callias, M. & Carr, J. (1975) Behaviour modification programmes in a community setting. In: C.C. Kiernan & F.P. Woodford (Eds), *Behaviour modification with the severely retarded.* Amsterdam: Elsevier-North Holland, Associated Scientific Publishers

Callias, M., Carr, J., Murphy, G., Tsoi, M. & Yule, W. (1976) Parent group training. Unpublished

Callias, M. & Jenkins, J.A. (1973) Group training in behaviour modification: a pilot project with parents of severely retarded children. Unpublished

Campbell, D.T. & Stanley, J.C. (1963) Experimental and quasi-experimental designs for research and teaching. In: N.L. Gage (Ed.), *Handbook of research on teaching.* Chicago: Rand McNally

Campbell, H.J. (1972) Getting through to the handicapped child. *World Medicine,* 28 June, 17–20

Campbell, M.F. (1970) Neuromascular uropathy. In: M.F. Campbell & H. Harrison (Eds), *Urology 2.* Philadelphia, PA: Saunders

Carr, E.G. (1977) The motivation of self-injurious behaviour: a review of some hypotheses. *Psychol. Bull.*, **84**, 800–16

Carr, E.G. (1979) Teaching autistic children to use sign language: some research issues. *J. Autism Devel. Dis.*, **9**, 345–59

Carr, E.G. & Durand, V.M. (1985) Reducing behaviour problems through functional communication training. *J. Appl. Behav. Anal.*, **18**, 111–26

Carr, E.G., Newsom, C.D. & Binkoff, J.A. (1980) Escape as a factor in the aggressive behaviour of two retarded children. *J. Appl. Behav. Anal.*, **13**, 101–7

Carr, J. (1975) *Young children with Down's syndrome.* London: Butterworth

Carr, J. (1980) *Helping your handicapped child: a step-by-step guide to everyday problems.* Harmondsworth: Penguin Books

Carr, J. (1985) The effect on the family of a severely mentally handicapped child. In: A.M. Clarke, A.D.B. Clarke & J.M. Berg (Eds), *Mental* deficiency: the changing outlook. London: Methuen, pp. 512–48

Carr, J. (1987) Bedwetting: a new approach to treatment in a mentally handicapped boy. *Child: Care, Health Devel.*, **13** (4)

Carr, J. & Hayward, E. (1986) Help for problem pre-schoolers. *Nursery World*, 16 January, 11–15

Carrier, J.K. Jr (1976) Application of a nonspeech language system with the severely language handicapped. In: L.L. Lloyd (Ed.), *Communication assessment and intervention strategies*. Baltimore, MD, University Park Press

Carsrud, A.L., Carsrud, K.B. and Dodd, B.G. (1980) Randomly monitored staff utilization of behavior modification techniques: long-term effects on clients. *J. Consult. Clin. Psychol.*, **48** (6), 704–10

Chamberlain, P. (1985) Increasing the attention span of five mentally handicapped children using their parents as agents of change. *Behav. Psychother.*, **13**, 142–53

Christensen, A., Johnson, S.M., Phillips, S. & Glasgow, R.E. (1980) Cost effectiveness in behavioral family therapy. *Behav. Ther.*, **11**, 208–26

Christensen, D.E. (1975) Effects of combining methylphenidate and a classroom token system in modifying hyperactive behavior. *Am. J. Ment. Defic.*, **80**, 266–76

Clark, H. & Clark, E.V. (1977) *Psychology and language: an introduction to linguistics*. New York: Harcourt-Brace

Clark, H.B., Rowbury, T., Baer, A.M. & Baer, D.M. (1973) Time-out as a punishing stimulus in continuous and intermittent schedules. *J. Appl. Behav. Anal.*, **6**, 443–55

Clarke, A.D.B. & Cookson, M. (1962) Perceptual motor transfer in imbeciles: a second series of experiments. *Brit. J. Psychol.*, **53**, 321–30

Clement, P.W. (1973) Training children to be their own behaviour therapists. *J. School Health*, **43**, 615–20

Clements, C.B. & McKee, J.M. (1968) Programmed instruction for institutionalized offenders: contingency management and performance contracts. *Psychol. Rep.*, **22**, 957–64

Clements, J. (1979) Goal planning in residential care for the severely mentally handicapped. *Behav. Psychother.*, **7**, 1–6

Clements, J. (1985) Update: training parents of mentally handicapped children. *Association for Child Psychology and Psychiatry Newsletter*, **7** (4), 2–9

Clements, J., Evans, C., Jones, C., Osborne, K. & Upton, G. (1982) Evaluation of a home-based language training programme with severely mentally handicapped children. *Behav. Res. Ther.*, **20**, 243–69

Clements, J. & Hand, D.J. (1985) Permutation statistics in single case design. *Behav. Psychother.*, **13**, 288–99

Clements, J., Wing, L. & Dunn, G. (1986) Sleeping problems in handicapped children: a preliminary study. *J. Child Psychol. Psychiat.*, **27**, 399–407

Cohen, I.L. (1984) Establishment of independent responding to a fire alarm in a blind, profoundly retarded adult. *J. Behav. Ther. Exp. Psychiat.*, **15** (4), 365–7

Cole, C.L., Gardner, W.I. & Karan, O.C. (1985) Self-management training of mentally retarded adults presenting severe conduct difficulties. *Appl. Res. Ment. Retard.*, **6**, 337–47

Coles, E. & Blunden, R. (1982) Maintaining new procedures using feedback to staff, a hierarchical reporting system, and a multidisciplinary management group. *J. Org. Behav. Management*, **3**, 19–33

Colvin, G.T. & Horner, R.H. (1983) Experimental analysis of generalisation: an evaluation of a general case programme for teaching motor skills to severely handicapped learners. In: J. Hogg & P.J. Mittler (Eds), *Advances in mental handicap research*, Vol. 2, New York: John Wiley

Cone, J.D., Anderson, J.A., Harris, F.C., Goff, D.K. & Fox, S.R. (1978) Developing and maintaining social interaction in profoundly retarded young males. *J. Abn. Child Psychol.*, **6**, 351–60

Cook, C. & Adams, H.E. (1966) Modification of verbal behaviour in speech deficient children. *Behav. Res. Ther.*, **4**, 265–71

Coon, M.E., Vogelsberg, R.T. & Williams, W. (1981) Effects of classroom public transportation instruction on generalisation to the natural environment. *J. Assoc. Severely Handicapped*, **6**, 46–53

Couch, J.V. & Clement, T.H. (1981) Free time as a reinforcer for on-task behaviour in a special education classroom. *Psychol. Rep.*, **48**, 369–70

Craighead, W.E., Kazdin, A.E. & Mahoney, M.J. (Eds) (1976) *Behaviour modification: principles, issues and applications*. Boston, Mass: Houghton Mifflin

Crawley, B. (1982) The feasibility of trainee-committees as a means of self-advocacy in Adult Training Centres in England and Wales. Unpublished PhD Thesis, University of Manchester

Crisp, A.G. & Sturmey, P. (1984) Organising staff to promote purposeful activity in a setting for mentally handicapped adults: an evaluation of alternative strategies — small groups and room management. *Behav. Psychother.*, **12**, 281–99

Crnic, K.A., Friedrich, W.N. & Greenberg, M.T. (1983) Adaptation of families with mentally retarded children: a model of stress, coping and family ecology. *Am. J. Ment. Defic.*, **88**, 285–305

Crnic, K.A. and Pym, H.A. (1979) Training mentally retarded adults in independent living skills. *Ment. Retard*, **17** (1), 13–16

Cromer, R. (1981) Reconceptualizing language acquisition and cognitive development. In: R. Schiefelbusch & D. Bricker (Eds), *Early language acquisition and intervention*, Baltimore, MD: University Park Press, pp. 51–138

Cronin, K.A. & Cuvo, A.J. (1979) Teaching mending skills to mentally retarded adolescents. *J. Appl. Behav. Anal.*, **12** (3), 401–6

Crosson, J.E. (1969) A technique for programming sheltered workshop environments for training severely retarded workers. *Am. J. Ment. Defic.*, **73**, 814–18

Crowley, C.P. & Armstrong, P.M. (1977) Positive practice, overcorrection and behaviour rehearsal in the treatment of three cases of encopresis. *J. Behav. Ther. Exp. Psychiat.*, **8**, 411–16

Cullen, C. & Partridge, K. (1981) The constructional approach: a way of using different data. *Apex: J. Brit. Inst. Ment. Handicap*, **8**, 135–6

Cunningham, C. (1985) Training and education approaches for parents of children with special needs. *Brit. J. Med. Psychol.*, **58**, 285–305

Cunningham, C. & Davis, H. (1985a) *Working with parents: frameworks for collaboration*. Milton Keynes & Philadelphia: Open University Press

Cunningham, C.C. & Davis, H. (1985b) Early intervention. In: M. Craft, J. Bicknell & S. Hollins (Eds), *Mental handicap: a multidisciplinary approach*. London: Bailliere Tindall, pp. 162–76

Cunningham, C.C. & Jeffree, D.M. (1971) *Working with parents: developing a workshop course for parents of young mentally handicapped children*. NSMHC, N.W. Region

Cunningham, C.C. & Jeffree, D.M. (1975) The organisation and structure of workshops for parents of mentally handicapped children. *Bull. Br. Psychol. Soc.,* **28**, 405–11

Cunningham, C.C. & Sloper, P. (1978) *Helping your handicapped baby*. Human Horizon Series, London: Souvenir Press

Cunningham, C.C. & Sloper, P. (1985) Early intervention for the child. In: M. Craft, J. Bicknell & S. Hollins (Eds), *Mental handicap: a multidisciplinary approach*. London: Balliere Tindall, pp. 209–28

Cuvo, A.J., Leaf, R.B. & Borakove, L.S. (1978) Teaching janitorial skills to the mentally retarded: acquisition, generalization, and maintenance. *J. Appl. Behav. Anal.,* **11**, 345–55

Daly, B., Addington, J. Kerfoot. S. & Sigston, A. (Eds) (1985) *Portage: the importance of parents*. Windsor, Berks: NFER-Nelson

Dangel, R.F. & Polster, R.A. (Eds) (1984) *Parent training: foundations of research and practice.* New York/London: Guilford Press

Davids, A. & Berenson, J.K. (1977) Integration of a behavior modification program into a traditionally oriented residential treatment center for children. *J. Autism Child Schiz.,* **1**, 269–85

Davidson, P.O. & Costello, C.G. (Eds) (1969) *N = 1: Experimental studies of single cases*. New York: Van Nostrand

Deich, R.F. & Hodges, P.M. (1982) Teaching nonvocal communication to nonverbal retarded children. *Behav. Mod.,* **6**, 200–28

Deitz, S.M. (1977) An analysis of programming. DRL schedules in educational settings. *Behav. Res. Ther.,* **15**, 103–11

Deitz, S.M. & Repp, A.C. (1973) Decreasing classroom misbehavior through the use of DRL schedules of reinforcement. *J. Appl. Behav. Anal.,* **6**, 457–63

Deitz, S.M. & Repp, A.C. (1974) Differentially reinforcing low rates of misbehavior with normal elementary school children. *J. Appl. Behav. Anal.,* **7**, 622

de Kock, U., Mansell, J., Felce, D. & Jenkins, J. (1984). Establishing appropriate alternative behaviour of a severely disruptive mentally handicapped woman. *Behav. Psychother.,* **12**, 163–74

Department of Health and Social Security (1976) *Fit for the future*. London: HMSO

Department of Health and Social Security (1980) *Mental Handicap: progress, problems and priorities. A review of mental handicap services in England and Wales since the 1971 White Paper, Better Services for the Mentally Handicapped*. London: HMSO

Department of Health and Social Security (1983) *Mental Handicap hospitals and units in England: results from the Mental Health Enquiry. Statistical Bulletin*. London: HMSO

De Villiers, J.G. & Naughton, J.M. (1974) Teaching a symbol language to autistic children. *J. Consult. Clin. Psychol.*, **42** 111–17

De Villiers, P. & De Villiers, J.G. (1978) *Language acquisition.* Cambridge, Mass.: Harvard University Press

Dische, S., Yule, W., Corbett, J.A.C. & Hand, D. (1983) Childhood nocturnal enuresis: factors associated with outcome of treatment with an enuresis alarm. *Devel. Med. Child Neurol.* **25**, 67–80

Dixon, J. & Smith, P.S. (1976) The use of a pants alarm in daytime toilet training. *Brit. J. Ment. Subn.*, **42**, 20–5

Doernberg, N.L. (1972) Parents as teachers of their own retarded children. In: J. Wortis (Ed.) *Mental retardation: an annual review*, Vol. 4, New York: Grune & Stratton

Doleys, D.M. (1977) Behavioral treatments for nocturnal enuresis in children: a review of recent literature. *Psychol. Bull.*, **84** (1), 30–54

Doleys, D.M. (1984) Enuresis and encopresis. In: T.H. Ollendick & M. Hersen (Eds), *Handbook of child psychopathology.* New York and London: Plenum Press

Doleys, D.M. & Arnold S. (1975) Treatment of childhood encopresis: full cleanliness training. *Ment. Retard.*, **13**, 14–16

Doleys, D.M., Doster, J. & Cartelli, L.M. (1976) Parent training techniques: effects of lecture-role playing followed by feedback and self recording. *J. Behav. Ther. Exp. Psychiat.*, **7**, 359–62

Doleys, D.M., Stacy, D. & Knowles, S. (1981) Modification of grooming behaviour in adult retardates. *Behav. Mod.*, **5**, 119–28

Doleys, D.M. & Wells, K.L. (1975) Changes in functional bladder capacity and bedwetting during and after retention control training: a case study. *Behav. Ther.*, **6**, 685–8

Donnellan, A.M. & Mirenda, P.L. (1983) A model for analysing instructional components to facilitate generalisation for severely handicapped students. *J. Spec. Educ.*, **17**, 317–22

Doty, D.W., McInnis, T. & Paul, G.L. (1974) Remediation of negative side effects of an on-going response-cost system with chronic mental patients. *J. Appl. Behav. Anal.*, **7**, 191–8

Douglas, J. & Ryan, M. (1987) A pre-school severely disabled boy and his powerful wheelchair: a case study. *Child Care, Health Devel.* (in press)

Douglas, J. & Richman, N. (1984) *My child won't sleep.* Harmondsworth: Penguin Books

Duker, P. (1975) Behavioural control of self-biting in the Lesch–Nyan patient. *J. Ment. Defic. Res.*, **19**, 11–19

Edelman, R.I. (1971) Operant conditioning treatment of encopresis. *J. Behav. Ther. Exp. Psychiat.*, **2**, 71–3

Edelson, S.M., Taubman, M.T. & Lovaas, O.I. (1983) Some social contexts of self-destructive behaviour. *J. Abn. Child Psychol.* **11**, 299–312

Embry, L.H. (1984) What to do? Matching client characteristics and intervention techniques through a prescriptive taxonomic key. In: R.F. Dangel & R.A. Polster (Eds), *Parent training: foundations of research and practice.* New York/London: Guilford Press, pp. 443–73

English National Board of Clinical Nursing Studies (1982) *Training syllabus for nurses caring for people with mental handicap.* London: English and Welsh National Boards for Nursing, Midwifery and Health Visiting

Epstein, L.H. & McCoy, J.F. (1977) Bladder and bowel control in Hirschsprung's disease. *J. Behav. Ther. Exper. Psychiat.*, **8**, 97–9

Epstein, R. (1985) The positive side effects of reinforcement: a commentary on Balsam and Bondy (1983). *J. Appl. Behav. Anal.* **18**, 73–8

Ervin-Tripp, S. (1973) *Language acquisition and communicative choice.* Stanford, CA: Stanford University Press

Evans, I.M. (1971) Theoretical and experimental aspects of the behaviour modification approach to autistic children. In: M. Rutter (Ed.) *Infantile autism: concepts, characteristics and treatment.* London: Churchill Livingstone

Eyman, R.K. & Call, T. (1977) Maladaptive behaviour and community placement of mentally retarded persons. *Am. J. Ment. Defic.*, **82**, 137–44

Eysenck, H.J. (1963) Psychoanalysis — myth or science? In: S. Rachman (Ed.), *Critical essays on psychoanalysis.* Oxford and New York: Pergamon

Fabry, B.D. Mayhew, G.L. & Hanson, A. (1984) Incidental teaching of mentally retarded students within a token system. *Am. J. Ment. Defic.*, **8**, 29–36

Fairbrother, P. (1983) Needs of parents of adults. In: P. Mittler & H. McConachie (Eds), *Parent, professional and mentally handicapped people: approaches to partnership.* London: Croom Helm, Cambridge, MA: Brookline Books

Farrell, P.T. (Ed.) (1985) *EDY: Its impact on staff training in mental handicap.* Manchester: Manchester University Press

Farrell, P. (1986) Teachers as therapists: an account of the EDY project. In: D. Milne (Ed.), *Training behaviour therapists.* London: Croom Helm, Cambridge, MA: Brookline Books

Farrell, P. & Sugden, M. (1984) An evaluation of an EDY course in behavioural techniques for classroom assistants in a school for children with severe learning difficulties. *Educ. Psychol.*, **4**, 185–98

Faw, G.D., Reid, D.H., Schepis, M.M., Fitzgerald, J.R. & Welty, P.A. (1981) Involving institutional staff in the development and maintenance of sign language with profoundly retarded persons. *J. Appl. Behav. Anal.*, **14** (4), 411–23

Felce, D. & de Kock, U. (1983) *Small homes for severely and profoundly mentally handicapped people.* University of Southampton: Annual report to DHSS

Felce, D. & de Kock, U. (unpublished). *Planning client activity, a handbook*

Felce, D., de Kock, U., Mansell, J. & Jenkins, J. (1984). Providing systematic individual skill-teaching for severely disabled and profoundly mentally handicapped adults in residential care. *Behav. Res. Ther.*, **22**, 299–309

Feldman, W.S., Manella, K.J. & Varni, J.W. (1983) A behavioural parent training programme for single mothers of physically handicapped children. *Child: Care, Health Devel.*, **9**, 157–68

Ferber, H., Keeley, S.M. & Shemberg, K.M. (1974) Training parents in behaviour modification: outcome and problems encountered in a programme after Patterson's work. *Behav. Ther.*, **5**, 415–19

Fernandez, J. (1978) Token economies and other token programmes in the United States. *Behav. Psychother.*, **6**, 56–69

Ferster, C.B. & Skinner, B.F. (1957) *Schedules of reinforcement*. New York: Appleton-Century-Crofts

Fewtrell, W.D. (1973) A way of toilet training retarded children. *Apex*, **1**, 26–7

Fielding, D. (1980) The response of day and night wetting children who wet only at night to retention control training and the enuresis alarm. *Behav. Res. Ther.*, **18**, 305–17

Fielding, D., Berg, I. & Bell, S. (1978) An observational study of postures and limb movements of children who wet by day and at night. *Devel. Med. and Child Neurol.*, **20**, 453–61

Fielding, L., Errickson, E. & Bettin, B. (1971) Modification of staff behavior: a note. *Behav. Ther.*, **2**, 550–3

Fincham, F.D. & Spettell, C. (1984) The acceptability of dry bed training and urine alarm training as treatments of nocturnal enuresis. *Behav. Ther.*, **15**, 388–94

Finley, W.W., Besserman, R.L., Bennett, L.F., Clapp, R.K. & Finley, R.M. (1973) The effects of intermittent and 'placebo' reinforcement on the effectiveness of the conditioning treatment of enuresis nocturna. *Behav. Res. Ther.*, **11**, 289–97

Finley, W.W., Rainwater, A.J. & Johnson, G. (1982) The effect of varying alarm schedules on acquisition and relapse parameters in the conditioning of enuresis. *Behav. Res. Ther.*, **20**, 69–80

Finley, W.W. & Wakeford, O.S. (1984) Reinforcement ratios and relapse parameters following conditioning for nocturnal enuresis: a reply to Sacks and DeLeon. *Behav. Res. Ther.*, **22** (5), 591

Firth, H. (1982) The effectiveness of parent workshops in a mental handicap service. *Child: Care, Health Develp.*, **8**, 77–91

Firth, H. (1983) Difficult behaviour at home: a domiciliary service for handicapped children. *Ment. Handicap*, **11**, 61–4

Flavell, J.E. (1973) Reduction of stereotypies by reinforcement of toy play. *Ment. Retard.*, **11** (4) 21–3

Fleming, E. (1982) Enuretic bedwetting alarm and toilet training. Correspondence. *Brit. Med. J.*, **285**, 512

Fleming, I. (1984) The constructional approach to 'problem behaviour' in an institutionalized setting. *Behav. Psychother.*, **12**, 349–55

Forehand, R. & Atkeson, B.M. (1977) Generality of treatment effects with parent therapists: a review of assessment and implementation procedures. *Behav. Ther.*, **8**, 575–93

Foskett, J. (1986) Personal communication

Foxen, T. & McBrien, J.A. (1981) *Trainee workbook*. Manchester: Manchester University Press

Foxx, R.M. (1976) The use of overcorrection to eliminate the public disrobing (stripping) of retarded women. *Behav. Res. Ther.*, **14**, 53–61

Foxx, R.M. & Azrin, N.H. (1972) Restitution: a method of eliminating aggressive disruptive behaviour of retarded and brain damaged patients. *Behav. Res. Ther.*, **10**, 15–27

Foxx, R.M. & Azrin, N.H. (1973) *Toilet training the retarded*. Champaign, Ill.: Research Press

Foxx, R.M., McMorrow, M.J., Bittle, R.G. & Bechtel, D.R. (1986) The successful treatment of a dually diagnosed deaf man's aggression with a programme that included contingent electric shock. *Behav. Ther.*, **17**, 170–86

Frankel, F. (1976) Unravelling the effects of programme inconsistency: a reply to Gilbert. *Ment. Retard.*, **13**, Oct., 8–9

Fraser, D. (1978) Critical variables in token economy systems: a review of the literature and a description of current research. *Behav. Psychother.*, **6**, 46–55

Freeman, S.W. & Thompson, C.L. (1973) Parent-child training for the MR. *Ment. Retard.*, **11** (4), 8–10

Gable, R.A., Hendrickson, J.M. & Strain, P.S. (1978) Assessment, modification and generalisation of social interaction among severely retarded, multi-handicapped children. *Educ. Train. Ment. Retard.*, **13**, 279–86

Gadberry, S., Borroni, A. & Brown, W. (1981) Effects of camera cuts and music on selective attention and verbal and motor imitation by mentally retarded adults. *Amer. J. Ment. Defic.*, **86** (3), 309–16

Galloway, C. & Galloway, K.C. (1970) Parent groups with a focus on precision behavior management. *IMRID Papers & Reports*, Vol. 7, No. 1, Nashville, Tennessee

Galvin, J.P. & Moyer, L.S. (1975) Facilitating extinction of infant crying by changing reinforcement schedules. *J. Behav. Ther. Exper. Psychiat.*, **6**, 357–8

Garcia, E., Baer, D.M. & Firestone, I. (1971) The development of generalized imitation within topographically determined boundaries. *J. Appl. Behav. Anal.*, **4**, 101–12

Gardner, J.M. (1972) Selecting non-professionals for behavior modification programs. *Am. J. Ment. Defic.*, **76**, 680–5

Gardner, J.M. (1973) Training the trainers: a review of research on teaching behavior modification. In: R.D. Rubin, J.P. Brady & J.D. Henderson (Eds), *Advances in behavior therapy*, Vol. 4, London: Academic Press

Gardner, J.M. (Unpublished) Results of training in behavior modification on experienced and inexperienced institution attendants. Cited in Gardner, J.M. (1973)

Gardner, J.M., Brust, D. & Watson, L.S. (1970) A scale to measure skill in applying behaviour modification techniques to the mentally retarded. *Am. J. Ment. Defic.*, **74**, 633–6

Gardner, J.M. & Giampa, F.L. (1971) The attendant behavior check-list: a preliminary report. *Am. J. Ment. Defic.*, **75**, 617–22

Gardner, W.I. (1971) *Behavior modification in mental retardation*. Chicago: Aldine Atherton

Gardner, W.I. & Cole, C.L. (1984) Aggression and related conduct difficulties in the mentally retarded: a multi-component behavioural model. In S.E. Breuning, J.L. Matson & R.P. Barrett (Eds), *Advances in mental retardation and developmental disabilities*, Vol. 2. Greenwich, CT: Jai Press

Gast, D.L. & Nelson, C.M. (1977) Legal and ethical considerations for the use of time out in special education settings. *J. Spec. Educ.*, **11**, 457–67

Gath, A. (1979) Parents as therapists of mentally retarded children. *J. Child. Psychol. Psychiat.*, **20**, 161–5

Gaylord-Ross, R.J., Haring, T.G., Breen, C. & Pitts-Conway, V. (1984) The training and generalisation of social interaction skills with autistic youth. *J. Appl. Behav. Anal.*, **17**, 229–48

Gelfand, D.M. & Hartmann, D.P. (1984) *Child Behaviour Analysis and Therapy*, 2nd Edition. New York: Pergamon

Georgiades, N.J. & Phillimore, L. (1975) The myth of the hero-innovator and alternative strategies for organizational change. In: C.C. Kiernan & F.P. Woodford (Eds), *Behaviour modification with the severely retarded*. Amsterdam: Elsevier-North Holland, Associated Scientific Publishers

Gewirtz, J.L. & Baer, D.M. (1958) Deprivation and satiation of social reinforcers as drive conditions. *J. Abn. Soc. Psychol.*, **57**, 165–72

Gilbert, G.D. (1975) Extinction procedures: proceed with caution. *Ment. Retard.*, **12**, 28–9

Giles, D.K. & Wolf, M.M. (1966) Toilet training institutionalized, severe retardates: an application of behaviour modification techniques. *Am. J. Ment. Defic.*, **70**, 766–80

Girardeau, F.L. & Spradlin, J.E. (1964) Token rewards in a cottage program. *Ment. Retard.*, **2**, 345–51

Glidden, L.M. & Warner, D.A. (1982) Research on imitation in mentally retarded persons: theory-bound or ecological validity run amuck? *Appl. Res. Ment. Retard.*, **3** (4), 383–95

Glogower, F. & Sloop, E.W. (1976) Two strategies of group training of parents as effective behavior modifiers. *Behav. Ther.*, **7**, 177–84

Goetz, L., Schuler, A. & Sailor, W. (1983) Motivational considerations in teaching language to severely handicapped students. In: M. Hersen, V. Van Hasselt & J. Matson (Eds), *Behavior therapy for the developmentally and physically disabled*. New York: Academic Press

Goldberg, J., Katz, S. & Yekutiel, E. (1973) The effects of token reinforcement on the productivity of moderately retarded clients in a sheltered workshop. *Brit. J. Ment. Subn.*, **19**, 80–4

Goldiamond, I. (1974) Towards a constructional approach to social problems. Ethical and constitutional issues raised by applied behavioral analysis. *Behaviorism*, **2**, 1–84

Goodall, E., Corbett, J., Murphy, G. & Callias, M. (1981) Sensory reinforcement table for severely retarded and multiply handicapped children. *Apex, J. Brit. Inst. Ment. Handicap*, **9** (3), 96–7

Goodman, L., Wilson, P. & Bornstein, H. (1978) Results of a national survey of sign language programs in special education. *Ment. Retard.*, **16**, 104–6

Gould, J. (1977) Language development and non-verbal skills in severely mentally retarded children. *J. Ment. Defic. Res.*, **20**, 129–45

Graziano, A.M. & Mooney, K.C. (1984) *Children and behavior therapy*. New York: Aldine Press

Greene, D. & Lepper, M.R. (1974) Effects of extrinsic rewards on children's subsequent intrinsic interest. *Child Devel.*, **45**, 1141–5

Griffin, J.W., Williams, D.E., Stark, M.T., Altmeyer, B.K. & Mason, M. (1984) Self-injurious behaviour: a state-wide prevalence survey, assessment of severe cases and follow-up of aversive programs. In: J.C. Griffin, *et al.* (Eds), *Advances in the treatment of self-injurious behaviour.* Austin, Texas: Dept. of Health and Human Services, Texas Planning Council for Developmental Disabilities

Griffiths, P., Meldrun, C. & McWilliam, R. (1982) Dry bed training in the treatment of nocturnal enuresis in childhood. A research report. *J. Child Psychol. Psychiat.*, **23**, 485–95

Gripp, R.F. & Magaro, P.A. (1974) The token economy program in the psychiatric hospital: a review and analysis. *Behav. Res. Ther.*, **12**, 205–28

Guess, D., Sailor, W. & Baer, D.M. (1974) To teach language to retarded children. In: R.L. Schiefelbush & L.L. Lloyd (Eds) *Language perspectives — acquisition, retardation and intervention.* London: Macmillan

Gulliford, R. (1985) Education. In: A.M. Clarke, A.D.B. Clarke & J.M. Berg (Eds), Mental deficiency: the changing outlook London: Methuen, pp. 639–85

Gunzburg, A. (1976) An operational philosophy of enrichment applied to the design of a children's family unit. *Brit. J. Ment. Subn.*, **22** (2), 112–7

Gunzburg, H.C. (1965) *Progress assessment charts.* London: National Society for Mentally Handicapped Children

Gunzburg, H.C. (1968) *Social competence and mental handicap.* London: Bailliere Tindall

Hall, J. (1978) Ethics, procedures and contingency management. *Behav. Psychother.*, **6**, 70–5

Hall, R.V. (1971a) *Managing Behavior, Parts I, II and III.* Lawrence, Kansas: H & H Enterprises

Hall, R.V. (1971b) Training teachers in classroom use of contingency management. *Educ. Technol.*, **9**, 33–8

Hallahan, D.P., Kaufmann, J.M., Kneedler, R.D., Snell, M.E. & Richards, H.C. (1977) Being imitated by an adult and the subsequent imitative behaviour of retarded children. *Am. J. Ment. Defic.*, **81**, 556–60

Halle, J.W., Marshall, A.M. & Spradlin, J.E. (1979) Time delay: a technique to increase language use and facilitate generalisation in retarded children. *J. Appl. Behav. Anal.*, **12**, 431–9

Hanf, C. (1968) Modifying problem behaviors in mother–child interaction. Standardized laboratory situations. Paper presented at the meetings of the Association of Behavior Therapies, Olympia, Washington. Cited in Berkowitz & Graziano (1972)

Haring, T.G. (1985) Teaching between class generalisation of toy play behaviour to handicapped children. *J. Appl. Behav. Anal.*, **18**, 127–40

Harris, J. (1978) Working with parents of mentally handicapped children on a longterm basis. *Child: Care, Health Devel.*, **4**, 121–30

Hart, B. & Risley, T.R. (1975) Incidental teaching of language in the preschool. *J. Appl. Behav. Anal.*, **8**, 411–20

Hart, B. & Risley, T.R. (1980) *In vivo* language intervention: unanticipated general effects. *J. Appl. Behav. Anal.*, **13**, 407–32

Hartmann, D.P. (1984) Assessment strategies. In: D.H. Barlow & M. Hersen (Eds), *Single case experimental designs*, Second Edition. New York: Pergamon Press

Hedbring, C. & Newsom, C. (1985) Visual overselectivity: a comparison of two instruction remediation procedures with autistic children. *J. Aut. Devel. Disord.*, **15**, 9–22

Hegarty, J. (1981) *Audio-visual methods for staff training*. Chelmsford, Essex: Graves Medical Audio-visual Library.

Heidorn, S.D. & Jensen, C.C. (1984) Generalization and maintenance of the reduction of self injurious behavior maintained by two types of reinforcement. *Behav. Res. Ther.*, **22** (5), 581–6

Heifetz, L.J. (1977) Behavioural training for parents of mentally retarded children: alternative formats based on instructional manuals. *Am. J. Ment. Defic.*, **82**, 194–203

Heitman, R.J. & Justen, J.E. (1982) Effects of social reinforcement on motor performance of trainable retarded students on speed and persistence tasks. *Percept. Mot. Skills*, **54**, 391–4

Heitman, R.J., Justen, J.E. & Gilley, W. (1980) Effects of mental age, knowledge of results, and social reinforcement on motor performance. *Am. J. Ment. Defic.*, **85**, 200–2

Hekkema, N. & Freedman, P.E. (1978) Effects of imitation training on immediate and delayed imitation by severely retarded children. *Am. J. Ment. Defic.*, **83** (2), 129–34

Helm, D.T. & Kosloff, M.A. (1986) Research on parent training: shortcomings and remedies. *J. Autism Devel. Dis.*, **16**, 1–22

Hemsley, D. (1978) Limitations of operant procedures in the modification of schizophrenic functioning: the possible relevance of studies of cognitive disturbance. *Behav. Anal. Mod.*, **2**, 165–73

Hemsley, R., Howlin, P. Berger, M., Hersov, L., Holbrook, D., Rutter, M. & Yule, W. (1978) Treating autistic children in a family context. In: M. Rutter & E. Schopler (Eds) *Autism: reappraisal of concepts and treatment*. New York: Plenum

Henriksen, K. & Doughty, R. (1967) Decelerating undesired mealtime behavior in a group of profoundly retarded boys. *Am. J. Ment. Defic.*, **72**, 40–4

Henry, S.A. (1981) Current dimensions of parent training. *School Psychol. Rev.*, **10**, 4–14

Herbert, M. & Iwaniec, D. (1981) Behavioural treatment of faecal soiling: a case study. *Behav. Psychother.*, **9**, 55–7

Hersov, L. (1985) Faecal soiling. In: M. Rutter & L. Hersov (Eds), *Child and adolescent psychiatry: modern approaches*. Blackwell Scientific, Oxford

Hewett, F.M. (1965) Teaching speech to an autistic child through operant conditioning. *Am. J. Orthopsychiat.*, **35**, 927–36

Hill, J.W., Wehman, P. & Horst, G. (1982) Toward generalisation of appropriate leisure and social behaviour in severely handicapped youth: pinball machine use. *J. Assoc. Severely Handicapped*, **6**, 38–44

Hingtgen, J.N. & Trost, F.C. (1966) Shaping co-operative responses in early childhood schizophrenics: II. Reinforcement of mutual physical

329

contact and vocal responses. In: R. Ulrich, T. Stachnik & J. Mabry (Eds), *Control of human behavior*. Chicago: Scott Foresman

Hirsch, I. & Walder, L. (1969) Training mothers as reinforcement therapists for their own children. *Proceedings of the 77th Annual Convention of the American Psychological Association*, **4**, 561–2. Cited by O'Dell (1974)

Hobbs, S.A. & Forehand, R. (1975) Effects of differential release from time-out on children's deviant behavior. *J. Behav. Ther. Exper. Psychiat.*, **6**, 256–7

Hobbs, S.A. & Forehand, R. (1977) Important parameters in the use of time-out with children: a re-examination. *J. Behav. Ther. Exper. Psychiat.*, **8**, 365–70

Hogg, J., Foxen, T. & McBrien, J. (1981) Issues in the training and evalua-tion of behaviour modification skills for staff working with profoundly retarded multiply handicapped children. *Behav. Psychother.*, **9**, 345–57

Hogg, J. & Sebba, J. (Eds) (1986) Definition and prevalence of profound mental and multiple handicap. *Profound Retardation and Multiple Impairment*. London: Croom Helm, Rockville, MD: Aspen Publishers

Holland, C.J. (1970) An interview guide for behavioural counselling with parents. *Behav. Ther.*, **1**, 70–9

Holland, J.M. & Hattersley, J. (1980) Parent support groups for the families of mentally handicapped children. *Child: Care, Health, Devel.*, **6**, 165–73

Holmes, N., Hemsley, R., Rickett, J. & Likierman, H. (1982) Parents as cotherapists: their perceptions of a home-based behavioural treatment for autistic children. *J. Autism Devel. Dis.*, **12**, 331–42

Holz, W.C., Azrin, N.H. & Ayllon, T. (1963) A comparison of several procedures for eliminating behavior. *J. Exper. Anal. Behav.*, **6**, 399–406

Hornby, G. & Singh, N.N. (1984a) Group training for parents of mentally retarded children: a review and methodological analysis of behavioural studies. *Child: Health, Care Devel.*, **9**, 199–213

Hornby, G. & Singh, N.N. (1984b) Behavioural group training with parents of mentally retarded children. *J. Ment. Defic. Res.*, **28**, 43–52

Horner, R.D. & Keilitz, I. (1975) Training mentally retarded adolescents to brush their teeth. *J. Appl. Behav. Anal.*, **8**, 301–9

Houston, J.C., Bradbury, R., Jelley, C., Adams, R.J., McGill, P., Samp-son, M., Davies, J.H, de Castro, M., Lees, J., Bush, A., Harper, J. & Ager, A. (1979) The behavioural approach in mental handicap. *Bull. Br. Psychol. Soc.*, **32**, 41

Howlin, P. (1976) How to help the parents and the children. Paper read at National Society for Autistic Children Conference on 'Early childhood autism and other problems affecting language and communication'. Churchill College, Cambridge

Howlin, P. (1980) The home treatment of autistic children. In: L.A. Hersov, M. Berger and R. Nichol (Eds), *Language and language disorders in children*. Oxford: Pergamon

Howlin, P. (1981) The effectiveness of operant language training with autistic children. *J. Autism Devel. Dis.*, **11**, 89–106

Howlin, P. (1984) The acquisition of grammatical morphemes in autistic children: a critique and replication of the findings of Bartolucci, Pierce and Steiner 1980. *J. Autism Devel. Dis.*, **14**, 127–36

Howlin, P. (1987) Behavioural approaches to language training. In: W. Yule & M. Rutter (Eds) *Language development and disorders*. London: Blackwell Scientific Publications/S.I.M.P.

Howlin, P., Cantwell, D., Marchant, R., Berger, M. & Rutter, M. (1973a) Analyzing mother's speech to young autistic children: a methodological study. *J. Abn. Child Psychol.*, **1**, 317–39

Howlin, P., Marchant, R., Rutter, M., Berger, M., Hersov, L. & Yule, W. (1973b) A home-based approach to the treatment of autistic children. *J. Autism Child. Schiz.*, **3**, 308–36

Howlin, P. & Rutter, M. with Berger, M., Hemsley, R., Hersov, L. & Yule, W. (1987) *Treatment of autistic children*. Chichester: Wiley.

Hughson, E.A. & Brown, R.I. (1975) A bus training programme for mentally retarded adults. *Br. J. Ment. Subn.*, **21** (2), 79–83

Hunt, J.G., Fitzhugh, L.C. & Fitzhugh, K.B. (1968) Teaching 'exit-ward' patients appropriate personal appearance by using reinforcement techniques. *Am. J. Ment. Defic.*, **73**, 41–5

Hunt, J.G. & Zimmerman, J. (1969) Stimulating productivity in a simulated sheltered workshop setting. *Am. J. Ment. Defic.*, **74**, 43–9

Isaacs, W., Thomas, J. & Goldiamond, I. (1960) Applications of operant conditioning to reinstate verbal behavior in psychotics. *J. Speech Hear. Dis.*, **25**, 8–12

Ivancic, M.T., Reid, D.H., Iwata, B.A., Faw, G.D. & Page, T.J. (1981) Evaluating a supervision program for developing and maintaining therapeutic staff–resident interaction during institutional care routines. *J. Appl. Behav. Anal.*, **14**, 95–107

Ivy, R. & Dubin, W. (1979) Acquisition and generalisation of instruction following behaviour in profoundly retarded individuals. *Percept. Mot. Skills*, **49**, 163–9

Iwata, B.H. & Bailey, J.S. (1974) Reward versus cost token systems: an analysis of the effects on students and teachers. *J. Appl. Behav. Anal.*, **7**, 567–76

Iwata, D.A., Dorsey, M.F., Slifer, K.J., Bauman, K.E. & Richman, G.S. (1982) Toward a functional analysis of self-injury. *Anal. Intervent. Devel. Dis.*, **2**, 3–20

Jackson, M.W. (1976) A course member's view. *Nursing Mirror*, 30 Sept.

Jay, P. (1979) *Report of the Committee of Enquiry into Mental Handicap Nursing and Care*. London: HMSO

Jeffree, D. & Cheseldine, S. (1983) Working with parents of adolescents: the work of the PATH Project. In: P. Mittler & H. McConachie (Eds), Parent, professionals and mental handicapped people: approaches to partnership. London: Croom Helm, Cambridge, MA: Brookline Books, pp. 465–511

Jenkins, J., Felce, D., Toogood, S., Mansell, J. & de Kock, U. (1987) *Individual programme planning*. Kidderminster: British Institute of Mental Handicap

Johnson, B.F. & Cuvo, A.J. (1981) Teaching mentally retarded adults to cook. *Behav. Modific.*, **5**, 187–202

Johnson, C., Bradley-Johnson, S., McCarthy, R. & Jamie, M. (1984)

Token reinforcement during WISC-R administration: (II) Effects on mildly retarded black students. *Appl. Res. Ment. Retard.*, **5**, 43–53

Johnson, C.A. & Katz, R.C. (1973) Using parents as change agents for their children. *J. Child Psychol. & Psychiat.*, **14**, 181–200

Johnson, M. (1985). Social policy and service development. In: M. Craft, J. Bicknell & S. Hollins (Eds) *Mental handicap*. London: Bailliere Tindall

Johnson, S.B. (1980) Enuresis. In: R.D. Daitzman (Ed.), *Clinical behaviour therapy and behaviour modification*, Vol. 1, New York: Garland STPM Press, pp. 81–142

Johnson, S.M. & Bolstad, O.D. (1973) Methodological issues in naturalistic observation: some problems and solutions for field research. In: L.A. Hamerlynck, L.C. Handy & E.J. Mash (Eds), *Behavior change: methodology, concepts and practice*. Champaign, Ill.: Research Press

Johnston, J.M. (1972) Punishment of human behavior. *Am. Psychol.*, **27**, 1033–54

Johnston, J.R. & Schery, T.K. (1972) The use of grammatical morphemes by children with communication disorders. In: D. Moorehead & A. Moorehead (Eds), *Normal and deficient child language*. Baltimore, MD: University Park Press

Joint Board of Clinical Nursing Studies (1974) *Outline curriculum in behaviour modification in mental handicap for registered nurses*. Course No. 700. London: JBCNS

Jones, C. (1980) The uses of mechanical vibration with the severely mentally handicapped. Part II: Behavioural effects. *Apex, J. Brit. Inst. Ment. Handicap*, **7**, 112–14

Jones, F.H., Simmons, J.Q. & Frankel, F.C. (1974) An extinction procedure for eliminating self-destructive behaviour in a 9 year old autistic girl. *J. Autism Child. Schiz.*, **4**, 241–50

Jones, M.C. (1983) *Behaviour problems in handicapped children: the Beech Tree House approach*. London: Souvenir Press

Jones, R.R. (1973) Behavioral observation and frequency data: problems in scoring, analyses and interpretation. In: L.A. Hamerlynck, L.C. Handy & E.J. Mash (Eds), *Behavior change: methodology, concepts and practice*. Champaign, Ill.: Research Press

Jones, R.R. (1974) Design and analysis problems in program evaluation. In: P.O. Davidson, F.W. Clark & L.A. Hamerlynck (Eds), *Evaluation of behavioral programmes in community, residential and school settings*. Champaign, Ill.: Research Press

Jordan, R. & Saunders, C. (1975) Development of social behaviour. In: C.C. Kiernan & F.P. Woodford (Eds), *Behaviour modification with the severely retarded*. IRMMH Study Group No. 8. Amsterdam, Elsevier North Holland, Associated Scientific Publishers

Kanfer, F.M. & Grimm, L.G. (1977) Behavioral analysis: selecting target behaviors in the interview. *Behav. Mod.*, **1**, 7–28

Kanfer, F.M. & Saslow, G. (1969) Behavioral diagnosis. In: C.M. Franks (Ed.), *Behavior therapy: appraisal and status*. New York: McGraw Hill, Chapter 12

Karen, R.L., Astin-Smith, S. & Creasy, D. (1985) Teaching telephone-answering skills to mentally retarded adults. *Am. J. Ment. Defic.*, **89** (6), 595–609

Karniol, R. & Ross, M. (1977) The effects of performance-relevant and performance-irrelevant rewards on childrens' intrinsic motivation. *Child Devel.*, **48**, 482–7

Katz, R.C. & Singh, N.N. (1986) Comprehensive fire-safety training for adult mentally retarded persons. *J. Ment. Defic. Res.*, **30**, 59–69

Kaufmann, J.M., Hallahan, D.P. & Ianna, S. (1977) Suppression of a retardate's tongue protrusion by contingent imitation: a case study. *Behav. Res. Ther.*, **15**, 196–8

Kaufmann, J.M., Lafleur, N.K., Hallahan, D.P. & Chanes, C.M. (1975) Imitation as a consequence for children's behaviour. Two experimental case studies. *Behav. Ther.*, **6**, 535–42

Kaufman, K.F. & O'Leary, K.D. (1972) Reward, cost and self-evaluation procedures for disruptive adolescents in a psychiatric hospital school. *J. Appl. Behav. Anal.*, **5**, 293–309

Kazdin, A.E. (1975) *Behavior modification in applied settings.* Illinois: Dorsey Press

Kazdin, A.E. (1977) *The token economy: a review and evaluation.* New York & London: Plenum Press

Kazdin, A.E. (1978) *History of behavior modification.* Baltimore, MD: University Park Press

Kazdin, A.E. (1984) Statistical analyses for single case experimental designs. In D.H. Barlow & M. Hersen *Single case experimental designs*, Second Edition. New York: Pergamon Press, Chapter 9

Kazdin, A.E. & Bootzin, R.R. (1972) The token economy: an evaluative review. *J. Appl. Behav. Anal.*, **5**, 343–72

Kazdin, A.E. & Craighead, W.E. (1973) Behavior modification in special education. In: L. Mann & D.A. Sabatino (Eds) *The first review of special education*, Vol. 2, Philadelphia: Buttonwood Farms

Keith, K.D. & Lange, B.M. (1974) Maintenance of behavior changes in an institution-wide training program. *Ment. Retard.*, **12** (2), 34–7

Keller, F.S. (1968) 'Good-bye teacher . . .' *J. Appl. Behav. Anal.*, **1**, 79–89

Kendall, P.C., Nay, W.R. & Jeffers, J. (1975) Time-out duration and contrast effects: a systematic evaluation of a successive treatment design. *Behav. Ther.*, **6**, 609–15

Kennedy, W.A. & Sloop, E.W. (1968) Methedrine as an adjunct to conditioning treatment of nocturnal enuresis in normal and institutionalized retarded subjects. *Psychol. Rep.*, **22**, 997–1000

Kiernan, C.C. (1973) Functional analysis. In: P. Mittler (Ed.), *Assessment for learning in the mentally handicapped.* London: Churchill

Kiernan, C.C. (1974) Behaviour modification. In: A.M. Clarke & A.D.B. Clarke (Ed.), *Mental Deficiency: the changing outlook.* London: Methuen

Kiernan, C.C. (1981) *Analysis of programmes for teaching.* Basingstoke, Hampshire: Globe Education

Kiernan, C.C. (1983) The exploration of sign and symbol effects. In: J.H. Hogg & P.J. Mittler (Eds), *Advances in mental handicap research*, Vol. 2. New York and Chichester: Wiley

Kiernan, C.C. (1986) Communication, language and behaviour problems. In: J.A. Corbett & C. Oliver (Eds), *Understanding behaviour disorders in* people with mental handicap. Collins, London

Kiernan, C.C. & Jones, M.S. (1981) The heuristic programme: a combined use of signs and symbols with severely mentally handicapped children. Unpublished manuscript, Thomas Coram Research Unit, University of London

Kiernan, C.C. & Riddick, B. (1973) A draft programme for training in operant techniques: practical units. Univ. of London Institute of Education. Thomas Coram Research Unit. Research Papers Nos. 1 & 2

Kiernan, C.C. & Saunders, C. (1972) Generalized imitation: experiments with profoundly retarded children. Second European Conference on Behaviour Modification, Wexford, Ireland. Quoted by Kiernan, C.C. (1974)

Kiernan, C.C. & Woodford, F.P. (1975a) Training and reorganisation for behaviour modification in hospital and community settings. Institute for Research into Mental and Multiple Handicap, Action Workshop No. 2. Summarized in *Brit. Ass. Behav. Psychother. Bull.*, **3**, 31–4

Kiernan, C.C. & Woodford, F.P. (1975b) *Behaviour modification with the severely retarded*. Amsterdam: Associated Scientific Publishers

Kiernan, C.C. & Wright, E.C. (1973) The F6 Project — a preliminary report. *Proc. Roy. Soc. Med.*, **66**, 1137–40

King, R.D., Raynes, N.V. & Tizard, J. (1971) *Patterns of residential care.* London: Routledge & Kegan Paul

Kirigin, K.A., Ayala, H.E. Braukmann, C.J., Brown, W.J., Minkin, N., Phillips, E.C., Fixsen, D.L. & Wolf, M. (1975) Training teaching parents: an evaluation of workshop training procedures. In: E. Ramp & B. Semb (Eds) *Behavior analysis: areas of research and application.* Englewood Cliffs, NJ: Prentice Hall

Koegel, R.L., Glahn, T.J. & Nieminen, G.S. (1978) Generalization of parent training results. *J. Appl. Behav. Anal.*, **11**, 95–109

Koegel, R.L. & Rincover, A. (1977) Research on the difference between generalization and maintenance in extra-therapy responding. *J. Appl. Behav. Anal.*, **10** (1), 1–12

Koegel, R.L., Rincover, A. & Egel, A. (1982) *Educating and understanding autistic children.* California: College Hill Press

Koegel, R.L., Russo, D.C. & Rincover, A. (1977) Assessing and training teachers in the generalized use of behavior modification with autistic children. *J. Appl. Behav. Anal.*, **10**, 197–206

Koegel, R.L., Shreibman, L., Britten, K. & Laitinen, R. (1979) The effects of schedule of reinforcement on stimulus overselectivity in autistic children. *J. Autism Devel. Dis.*, **9**, 383–97

Koegel, R.L. Schreibman, L., Johnson, J., O'Neill, R.E. & Dunlap, G. (1984) Collateral effects of parent training of families with autistic children. In: R.F. Dangel & R.A. Polster (Eds), *Parent training: foundations of research and practice.* New York/London: Guilford Press, pp. 358–78

Kohl, F.L. (1981) Effects of motoric requirements on the acquisition of manual sign responses by severely handicapped students. *Am. J. Ment. Defic.*, **85**, 396–403

Konarski, E.A. & Diorio, M.S. (1985) A quantitative review of self-help research with the severely and profoundly mentally retarded. *Appl. Res.*

Ment. Retard., **6** (2), 229–45

Kushlick, A. (1975) Improving the services for the mentally handicapped. In: C.C. Kiernan & F.P. Woodford (Eds) *Behaviour modification with the severely retarded*. Amsterdam: Elsevier North-Holland, Associated Scientific Publishers

Kyle, N. & Roche, V. (1983). Individual Programme Plan and behaviour modification: a system of care for the residential setting. *Ment. Handicap*, **11**, 17–19

Lal, H. & Lindsley, O.R. (1968) Therapy of chronic constipation in a young child by re-arranging social contingencies. *Behav. Res. Ther.*, **6**, 484–5

Lance, W.D. & Koch, A.C. (1973) Parents as teachers: self-help skills for young handicapped children. *Ment. Retard.*, **11** (3), 3–4

Lancioni, G.E. (1982) Normal children as tutors to teach social responses to withdrawn mentally retarded schoolmates: training, maintenance and generalisation. *J. Appl. Behav. Anal.*, **15**, 17–40

Lancioni, G.E. (1983) Using pictorial representation as communication means with low functioning children. *J. Autism Devel. Dis.*, **13**, 87–105

Larsen, L.A. & Bricker, W.A. (1968) *A Manual for parents and teachers of severely and moderately retarded children*. IMRID Papers and Reports, V, No. 22: George Peabody College, Nashville, Tennessee

Leff, R. (1974) Teaching the TMR to dial the telephone. *Ment. Retard.*, **12** (2), 12–13

Leitenberg, H. (1973) The use of single-case methodology in psychotherapy research. *J. Abn. Psychol.*, **82**, 87–101

Lent, J.R., LeBlanc, J. & Spradlin, J.E. (1970) Designing a rehabilitative culture for moderately retarded adolescent girls. In: R. Ulrich, T. Stachnik & J. Mabry (Eds), *Control of human behavior*, Vol. 2. Illinois: Scott Foresman

Lepper, M. (1981) Intrinsic and extrinsic motivation in children with autism. In: W. Collins (Ed.), *Aspects of the development of competence*. Hillsdale, NJ: Laurence Erlbaum, pp. 155–216

Lepper, M.R., Greene, D. & Nisbett, R.E. (1973) Undermining children's intrinsic interest with extrinsic rewards: a test of the 'over-justification' hypothesis. *J. Pers. Soc. Psychol.*, **28**, 129–37

Levine, M.D. (1982) Encopresis: its potentiation, evaluation and alleviation. *Paed. Clin. N. Amer.*, **29**

Lindsley, O.R. (1964) Direct measurement and prosthesis of retarded behavior. *J. Educ.*, **147**, 62–81

Lobato, D. (1983) Siblings of handicapped children: a review. *J. Autism Devel. Dis.*, **13**, 347–64

Longin, N.S., Cone, J.D. & Longin, H.E. (1975) Teaching behavior modifiers: mothers' behavioral and attitudinal changes following general and specific training. *Ment. Retard.*, **13** (5), 42

Lovaas, O.I. (1966) A program for the establishment of speech in psychotic children. In: J.K. Wing (Ed.), *Early childhood autism*. London: Pergamon

Lovaas, O.I. (1967) A behavior therapy approach to the treatment of childhood schizophrenia. In: J.P. Hill (Ed.) *Minnesota symposia on child psychology*, Vol. I. Minneapolis: Univ. Minnesota Press

Lovaas, O.I. (1977) *The autistic child: language development through* behaviour modification. New York: Wiley

Lovaas, O.I., Berberich, J.P., Perloff, B.F. & Schaeffer, B. (1966a) Acquisition of imitative speech in schizophrenic children. *Science*, **151**, 705–7

Lovaas, O.I., Freitag, G., Kinder, M.I., Rubinstein, B.D., Schaeffer, B. & Simmons, J.Q. (1966b) Establishment of social reinforcers in two schizophrenic children on the basis of food. *J. Exp. Child Psychol.*, **4**, 109–25

Lovaas, O.I., Koegel, R.L. & Schreibman, L. (1979) Stimulus overselectivity in autism: a review of research. *Psychol. Bull.*, **86**, 1236–54

Lovett, S. (1985) Microelectronic and computer-based technology. In: Clarke, A.M., Clarke, A.D.B. & Berg, J.M. (Eds), *Mental deficiency: the changing outlook*, 4th Edition. London and New York: Methuen

Lowther, R.M. (1980) Additional settings versus additional trainers as sufficient stimulus exemplars for programming generalisation of a greeting response of severely retarded persons. *Dissert. Abst. Int.*, **40**, 5850 B–5851 B

Lucero, W.J., Frieman, J., Spoering, K. & Fehrenbacher, J. (1976) Comparison of three procedures in reducing self-injurious behavior. *Am. J. Ment. Defic.*, **80**, 548–54

Luftig, R.L. (1983) Translucency of sign and concreteness of gloss in the manual sign learning of moderately/severely mentally retarded students. *Am. J. Ment. Defic.*, **88**, 279–86

Luiselli, J.K. (1984) *In vivo* training of a fire emergency skill with a severely retarded adult. *J. Behav. Ther. Exper. Psychiat.*, **15** (3), 277–80

Luiselli, J.K., Myles, E., Evans, T.P. & Boyce, D.A. (1985) Reinforcement control of severe dysfunctional behaviour of blind, multihandicapped students. *Am. J. Ment. Defic.*, **90**, 328–34

McBrien, J.A. & Edmonds, M. (1985) An evaluation of an E.D.Y. training course in behavioural techniques for staff working with severely mentally handicapped children. *Behav. Psychother.*, **13**, 202–17

McBrien, J.A. & Foxen, T. (1981) *Instructors' handbook*. Manchester: Manchester University Press

McCarthy, D.S. (1954) Language development in children. In: L. Carmichael (Ed.), *Manual of child psychology*, 2nd Edition. New York: Wiley

McCartney, J.R. & Holden, J.C. (1981) Toilet training for the mentally retarded. In J.L. Matson & J.R. McCartney (Eds), *Handbook of behaviour modification with the mentally retarded*. New York and London: Plenum Press

McConahey, O.L. (1972) A token system for retarded women: behavior modification, drug therapy and their combination. In: T. Thompson & J. Grabowski (Eds), *Behavior modification of the mentally retarded*. New York: Oxford University Press

McConahey, O.L., Thompson, T. & Zimmerman, R.A. (1977) A token system for retarded women: behavior modification, drug therapy and their combination. In: T. Thompson & J. Grabowski (Eds), *Behavior modification of the mentally retarded*. New York: Oxford

McConkey, R. & O'Connor, M. (1982) A new approach to parental involvement in language intervention programmes. *Child: Care, Health Devel.*, **8**, 163–76

McCoull, G. (1969–71) Report on the Newcastle-upon-Tyne Regional Aetiological Survey, Mental Retardation, Prudhoe Hospital, Northumberland

McDonagh, E.C., McIlvane, W.J. & Stoddard, L.T. (1984) Teaching coin equivalence via matching to sample. *Appl. Res. Ment. Retard.*, **5** (2), 177–97

MacDonald, A. (1984) Blissymbolics and manual signing — a combined approach. *Communicating Together*, **2** (4), 20–1

McDonald, G., McCabe, P. & Mackle, B. (1976) Self-help skills in the profoundly subnormal. *Brit. J. Ment. Subn.*, **22**, 105–11

MacDonough, T.S. & Forehand, R. (1973) Response contingent time-out: important parameters in behavior modification with children. *J. Behav. Ther. Exper. Psychiat.*, **4**, 231–6

McInnis, T., Himelstein, H.C., Doty, D.W. & Paul, G. (1974) Modification of sampling exposure procedures for increasing facilities ulitization by chronic psychiatric patients. *J. Behav. Ther. Exper. Psychiat.*, **5**, 119–27

Mackay, D. (1971) Behaviour modification of childhood psychiatric disorders using parents as therapists. *London Hospital Gazette, Clinical & Scientific Supplement.* May, III–XIV

McKeowen, D., Jr., Adams, H.E. & Forehand, R. (1975) Generalization to the classroom of principles of behavior modification taught to teachers. *Behav. Res. Ther.*, **13**, 85–92

Mackowiak, M.C., Chvala, V.B., Masilotti, V.M. & Hermann, G.P. (1978) A developmental guide for the education of severely and profoundly handicapped individuals, Part I. *Brit. J. Ment. Subn.*, **24**, 35–45

McLean, L.P. & McLean, J.E. (1974) A language training program for non-verbal autistic children. *J. Speech. Hear. Dis.*, **39**, 186–93

McMahon, R.J. & Forehand, R. (1980) Self-help behavior therapies in parent training. In: B.B. Lahey & A.E. Kazdin (Eds), *Advances in clinical child psychology*, Vol. 3. New York: Plenum, pp. 149–76

MacNamara, R. (1977) The complete behavior modifier: confessions of an over-zealous operant conditioner. *Ment. Retard.*, **15** (1), 34–7

Mace, F.C., Page, T.J., Ivancic, M.T. & O'Brien, S.O. (1986a) Effectiveness of brief time-out with and without contingent delay: a comparative analysis. *J. Appl. Behav. Anal.*, **19**, 79–86

Mace, F.C., Shapiro, E.S., West, B.J., Campbell, C. & Altman, J. (1986b) The role of reinforcement in reactive self-monitoring. *Appl. Res. Ment. Ret.*, **7**, 315–27

Mager, R.F. & Pipe, R. (1970) *Analyzing Performance Problems, or 'You Really Oughta Wanna'.* California: Fearon

Mahoney, K., van Wagenen, R.K. & Meyerson, L. (1971) Toilet training of normal and retarded children. *J. Appl. Behav. Anal.*, **4**, 173–81

Maisto, C.R., Baumeister, A.A. & Maisto, A.A. (1978) An analysis of variables related to self injurious behavior among institutionalised retarded patients. *J. Ment. Defic. Res.*, **22**, 27–36

Mansell, J., Felce, D., Flight, C. & Jenkins, J. (1983) *Bereweeke skill-*

teaching system, Windsor, Berks: NFER–Nelson

Marchant, R., Howlin, P., Yule, W. & Rutter, M. (1974) Graded change in the treatment of the behaviour of autistic children. *J. Child Psychol. Psychiat.,* **15**, 221–7

Marfo, K. & Kysela, G.M. (1985) Early intervention with mentally handicapped children: a critical appraisal of applied research. *J. Pediat. Psychol.,* **10**, 305–34

Marston, N. & Gupta, H. (1977) Interesting the old. *Community Care,* 16 November, 26–8

Martin, G. & Pear, J. (1984) *Behaviour modification — what it is and how to do it,* 2nd Edition. New York, Prentice-Hall

Martin, G.L., Kehoe, B., Bird, E., Jensen, V. & Darbyshire, M. (1971a) Operant conditioning in dressing behavior. *Ment. Retard.,* **9**, 24–31

Martin, L., McDonald, S. & Omichinski, M. (1971b) An operant analysis of response interactions during meals with severely retarded girls. *Am. J. Ment. Defic.,* **76**, 864–8

Mash, E.J. & Terdal, L. (1973) Modification of mother–child interactions: playing with children. *Ment. Retard.,* **11** (5), 44–9

Mash, E.J. & Terdal, L.G. (Eds) (1981) *Behavioral assessment of childhood disorders.* New York: Guilford Press

Matson, J.L. (1981) Use of independence training to teach shopping skills to mildly mentally retarded adults. *Am. J. Ment. Defic.,* **86** (2), 178–83

Maxwell, A.E. (1958) *Experimental design in psychology and the medical sciences.* London: Methuen

May, J.G., McAlister, J., Risley, T., Twardosz, S. & Cox, C.H. (1974) *Florida guidelines for the use of behavioral procedures in state programmes for the retarded.* Tallahassee, Florida: Florida Division of Retardation

Mayhew, G.L., Enyart, P. & Anderson, J. (1978) Social reinforcement and the naturally occurring social responses of severely and profoundly retarded adolescents. *Am. J. Ment. Defic.,* **83** (2), 164–70

Meador, D.M. (1984) Effects of colours on visual discrimination of geometric symbols by severely and profoundly mentally retarded individuals. *Am. J. Ment. Defic.,* **89**, 275–86

Meadow, R. (1977) How to use buzzer alarms to cure bed-wetting. *Brit. Med. J.,* **2**, 1073–5

Measel, C.J. & Alfieri, P.A. (1976) Treatment of self-injurious behaviour by a combination of positive reinforcement for incompatible behaviour and overcorrection. *Am. J. Ment. Defic.,* **81**, 147–53

Merrett, F. & Wheldall, K. (1984) Training teachers to use the behavioural approach to classroom management: a review. *Educ. Psychol.,* **4**, 213–34

Miller, R.S. & Morris, W.N. (1974) The effects of being imitated on children's responses in a marble-dropping task. *Child Devel.,* **45**, 1103–7

Miller, J.F. & Yoder, D.E. (1974) An ontogenic language teaching strategy for retarded children. In: R.L. Schiefelbusch, & L.L. Lloyd (Eds), *Language perspectives — acquisition, retardation and intervention.* London: Macmillan

Milne, D.A. (1982) A comparison of two methods of teaching behaviour modification to mental handicap nurses. *Behav. Psychother.*, **10**, 54–64

Milne, D. (1984) The development and evaluation of a structured learning format introduction to behaviour therapy for psychiatric nurses. *Brit. J. Clin. Psychol.*, **23**, 175–85

Milne, D. (1985) A review of the in-service training of nurses in behaviour therapy. *Behav. Psychother.*, **13**, 120–31

Milne, D. (Ed.) (1986) *Training behaviour therapists.* London: Croom Helm Cambridge, MA: Brookline Books

Minge, M.R. & Ball, T.S. (1967) Teaching of self-help skills to profoundly retarded patients. *Am. J. Ment. Defic.*, **71**, 864–8

Mischel, W. (1968) *Personality and assessment.* New York: Wiley

Mittler, P. (1986) Personal communication

Mittler, P. & Mittler, H. (1983) Partnership with parents: an overview. In: P. Mittler & H. McConachie (Eds), *Parent, professional and mentally handicapped people: approaches to partnership.* London: Croom Helm Cambridge, MA: Brookline Books, pp. 8–43

Monaco, T.M., Peach, W., Blanton, R.S. & Loomis, D. (1968) Pilot study: self-care program for severely retarded girls. *Central Missouri Synthesis on Mental Retardation*, **1** (1), 8–20 (from abstract in *Mental Retardation Abstracts*, 1970, **7**, No. 2788)

Moore, P. & Carr, J. (1976) Behaviour modification programme (to teach dressing to a severely retarded adolescent). *Nursing Times*, 2 September, and *Communication*, **11** (2), 20–7

Morrison, D., Mejia, B. & Miller, M.A. (1968) Staff conflicts in the use of operant techniques with autistic children. *Am. J. Orthopsychiat.*, **38**, 647–52

Morse, W.J. (1966) Intermittent reinforcement. In: W.K. Honig (Ed.), *Operant behaviors: areas of research and application.* New York: Appleton-Century-Crofts

Mosk, M.D. & Bucher, B. (1984) Prompting and stimulus shaping procedures for teaching visual–motor skills to retarded children. *J. Appl. Behav. Anal.*, **17**, 23–34

Muellner, S.R. (1960) Development of urinary control in children. *J. Am. Med. Assoc.*, **172**, 1256–61

Muir, K.A. & Milan, M.A. (1982) Parent reinforcement for child achievement: the use of a lottery to maximise parent training effects. *J. Appl. Behav. Anal.*, **15**, 455–60

Murphy, G.M. (1978) Overcorrection: a critique. *J. Ment. Defic. Res.* **22**, 161–73

Murphy, G. (1982) Sensory feedback in the autistic and mentally handicapped child: a review. *J. Autism Devel. Dis.*, **12**, 265–78

Murphy, G. (1986) Direct observation as an assessment tool in functional analysis and treatment. In J. Hogg & N. Raynes (Eds), *Assessment in mental handicap: a guide to tests, batteries and check lists.* London: Croom Helm Cambridge, MA: Brookline Books

Murphy, G., Callias, M. & Carr, J. (1985) Increasing simple toy play in the profoundly mentally handicaped child. *J. Autism Devel. Dis.*, **15**, 375–88

Murphy, G., Carr, J. & Callias, M. (1986) Increasing simple toy play in the profoundly mentally handicapped child. *J. Autism Devel. Dis.*, **16**, 45–58

Murphy, G. & Goodall, E. (1980) Measurement error in direct observation: a comparison of common recording methods. *Behav. Res. Ther.*, **18**, 147–50

Murphy, G.M. & McArdle, M. (1978) Behaviour modification with the retarded: a six-month training course for nurses. *Nursing Mirror*, 27 April, 31–4

Murphy, G., Steele, K., Gilligan, T., Yeow, J. & Spare, D. (1977) Teaching a picture language to a non-speaking retarded boy. *Behav. Res. Ther.*, **15**, 198–201

Murphy, G. & Wilson, B. (1981) Long term outcome of contingent shock treatment for self-injurious behaviour. In: P. Mittler (Ed.), *Frontiers of knowledge in mental retardation*, Vol. 2. Baltimore, MD: University Park Press

Musick, J.K. & Luckey, R.E. (1970) A token economy for moderately and severely retarded. *Ment. Retard.*, **8**, 35–6

Myers, J.J. & Deibert, A. (1971) Reduction of self-abusive behavior in a blind child by using a feeding response. *J. Behav. Ther. Exper. Psychiat.*, **2**, 141–4

National Development Group for the Mentally Handicapped (1980) *Improving the quality of services for mentally handicapped people: a checklist of standards.* London: DHSS

Nay, W.R. (1975) A systematic comparison of instructional techniques for parents. *Behav. Ther.*, **6**, 14–21

Neale, D.H. (1963) Behavior therapy and encopresis in children. *Behav. Res. Ther.*, **1**, 139–49

Neef, N.A., Iwata, B.A. & Page, T.J. (1978) Public transportation training: *in vivo* versus classroom instruction. *J. Appl. Behav. Anal.*, **11**, 331–44

Nelson, G.L., Cone, J.D. & Hansen, C.R. (1975) Training correct utensil use in retarded children: Modelling *vs.* physical guidance. *Am. J. Ment. Defic.*, **80**, 114–22

Nelson, K. (1973) Structure and strategy in learning to talk. *Monogr. Soc. Res. Child Devel.*, **38**, Serial No. 149

Nelson, R.O. & Evans, I.M. (1968) The combination of learning principles and speech therapy techniques in the treatment of non-communicating children. *J. Child Psychol. Psychiat.*, **9**, 111–24

Nelson, R.O., Lipinski, D.P. & Black, J.L. (1975) The effects of expectancy on the reactivity of self-recording. *Behav. Ther.*, **6**, 337–49

Nirje, B. (1970) The normalization principle — implications and comment. *J. Ment. Subn.*, **16** (2), 62–70

Nolley, D., Butterfield, B., Fleming, A. & Muller, P. (1982) Non-aversive treatment of severe self-injurious behaviour: multiple replications with DRO and DRI. In: J.H. Hollis & C.E. Meyers (Eds), *Life-threatening behaviour*. Washington: A.A.M.D. Monograph

Nordquist, F.M. & Wahler, R.G. (1973) Naturalistic treatment of an autistic child. *J. Appl. Behav. Anal.*, **6**, 79–87

Norrish, M.P. (1974) Training parents to teach their young retarded children self-help skills. M. Phil. dissertation, University of London

Nutter, D. & Reid, D.H. (1978) Teaching retarded women a clothing selection skill using community norms. *J. Appl. Behav. Anal.*, **11**, 475–87

O'Brien, F. & Azrin, N.H. (1972) Developing proper mealtime behaviors

of the institutionalized retarded, *J. Appl. Behav. Anal.*, **5**, 389–99

O'Brien, F., Bugle, C. & Azrin, N.H. (1972) Training and maintaining a retarded child's proper eating. *J. Appl. Behav. Anal.*, **5**, 67–72

O'Dell, S. (1974) Training parents in behaviour modification: a review, *Psychol. Bull.*, **81**, 418–33

O'Dell, S. (1985) Progress in parent training. In: M. Hersen, R.M. Eisler & P.M. Miller (Eds) *Progress in Behaviour Modification*, Vol. 19. London: Academic Press, pp. 97–108

O'Dell, S., Blackwell, L.J., Larcen, S.W. & Hogan, J.L. (1977a) Competency based training for severely behaviorally handicapped children and their families. *J. Autism Child. Schiz.*, **7**, 231–42

O'Dell, S., Flynn, J. & Benlolo, L. (1977b) A comparison of parent training techniques in child behavior modification. *J. Behav. Ther. Exp. Psychiat.*, **8**, 261–8

Ogilvie, L. & Prior, M. (1982) Behaviour modification and the overjustification effect. *Behav. Psychother.*, **10**, 26–39

Oliver, C. (1986) Self-injurious behaviour. *Talking Sense*, **33** (4), 23–4

Oliver, C., Crayton, L. & Murphy, G. (1987) Formal functional analysis of self-injurious behaviour: the development of further analogue conditions. *J. Appl. Behav. Anal.*, in press

Olness, K., McFarland, M.D. & Piper, J. (1980) Biofeedback: a new modality in the management of children with faecal soiling. *Behav. Paed.*, **96**, 505–9

Oltmanns, T.F., Broderick, J.A. & O'Leary, K.D. (1977) Marital adjustment and the efficacy of behavior therapy with children, *J. Consult. Clin. Psychol.*, **45**, 724–9

Orlando, R. & Bijou, S.W. (1960) Single and multiple schedules of reinforcement in developmentally retarded children. *J. Exp. Anal. Behav.*, **3**, 339–48

Ottenbacher, K. & Altman, R. (1984) Effects of vibratory edible and social reinforcement on performance of institutionalised mentally retarded individuals. *Am. J. Ment. Defic.*, **89** (2), 201–4

Owusu-Bempah, J. (1983) Contingent imitation as an on-ward behaviour modification technique. *Brit. J. Ment. Subn.*, **29** (2), 92–5

Pace, G., Ivancic, M., Edwards, G., Iwata, B. & Page, T. (1975) Assessment of stimulus preference and reinforcer value with profoundly retarded individuals. *J. Appl. Behav. Anal.*, **18**, 249–55

Paget, R., Gorman, P. & Paget, G. (1972) *A systematic sign language.* Mimeographed Manual, London

Paloutzian, R.F., Hasazi, J., Streifel, J. & Edgar, C.L. (1971) Promotion of positive social interaction in severely retarded young children. *Am. J. Ment. Defic.*, **75**, 519–24

Panyan, M.C. & Patterson, E.T. (1974) Teaching attendants the applied aspects of behavior modification. *Ment. Retard.*, **12** (5), 30–2

Parker, G. (1984) Training for continence among children with severe disabilities. *Br. J. Ment. Subn.*, **30**, 38–43

Partridge, K., Chisholm, N. & Levy, B. (1985) Generalisation and maintenance of ward programmes: some thoughts on organisational factors. *Ment. Handicap*, **13**, 26–9

Patterson, G.R. (1973) Multiple evaluations of a parent training program.

In: T. Thompson & W.S. Dockens (Eds) *Proceedings of the International Symposium on Behavior Modification*. New York: Appleton-Century-Crofts.

Patterson, G.R. (1974) Interventions for boys with conduct problems: multiple settings, treatments and criteria. *J. Consult. Clin. Psychol.*, **42**, 471–81

Patterson, G.R. (1982) *Coercive family process*. Eugene, Oregon: Castalia Publishing Company

Patterson, G.R., Cobb, J.A. & Ray, R.S. (1973) A social engineering technology for re-training the families of aggressive boys. In: H.E. Adams & I.P. Unikel (Eds), *Issues and trends in behavior therapy*. Springfield, Ill.: Charles C. Thomas

Patterson, G.R. & Gullion, M.E. (1968) *Living with children: new mehods for parents and teachers*. Champaign, Ill.: Research Press

Patterson, G.R., McNeal, S., Hawkins, N. & Phelps, R. (1967) Reprogramming the social environment. *J. Child Psychol. Psychiat.*, **8**, 181–95

Patterson, G.R., Ray, R.S., Shaw, D.A. & Cobb, J.A. (1969) A manual for coding of family interactions. Unpublished manuscript, Oregon Research Institute

Patterson, G.R. & Reid, J.B. (1973) Intervention for families of aggressive boys: a replication study: *Behav. Res. Ther.*, **11**, 382–94

Peek, R.M. & McAllister, L.W. (1974) *Behavior modification guidelines*. State of Minnesota: Dept. of Public Welfare

Perkins, E.A., Taylor, P.D. and Capie, A.C.M. (1976) *Helping the retarded: a systematic behavioural approach*, Institute of Mental Subnormality, Kidderminster

Perske, R. & Marquiss, J. (1973) Learning to live in an apartment: retarded adults from institutions and dedicated citizens. *Ment. Retard.*, **11** (5), 18–19

Petersen, G.A., Austin, G.J. & Lang, R.P. (1979) Use of teacher prompts to increase social behaviour. Generalisation effects with severely and profoundly retarded adolescents. *Am. J. Ment. Defic.*, **84**, 82–6

Phibbs, J. & Wells, M. (1982) The treatment of nocturnal enuresis in institutionalised retarded adults. *J. Behav. Ther. Exper. Psychiat.*, **13**, 245–9

Phillips, E.L., Phillips, E.A., Fixsen, D.L. & Wolf, M.M. (1971) Achievement Place: modification of the behaviors of predelinquent boys within a token economy. *J. Appl. Behav. Anal.*, **4**, 45–59

Porter, P.B. & Schroeder, S.F. (1980) Generalization and maintenance of skills acquired in non-speech language imitation program training. *Appl. Res. Ment. Retard.*, **1**, 71–84

Porterfield, J. & Blunden, R. (1978). Establishing an activity period and individual skill training within a day setting for profoundly mentally handicapped adults. *J. Pract. Appr. Devel. Handicap*, **2**, 10–15

Powell, J., Martindale, B., Kulp, S., Martindale, A. & Bauman, R. (1977) Taking a closer look: time sampling and measurement error. *J. Appl. Behav. Anal.*, **10**, 325–32

Premack, D. (1959) Towards empirical behaviour laws. 1. Positive reinforcement. *Psychol. Rev.*, **66**, 219–33

Premack, D.A. & Premack, A.J. (1974) Teaching visual language to apes and language-deficient persons. In: R.L. Schiefelbusch & L.L. Lloyd (Eds), *Language perspectives — acquisition, retardation and intervention*. London: Macmillan

Quilitch, H.R. (1975) A comparison of three staff management procedures. *J. Appl. Behav. Anal.*, **8**, 59–66

Raffin, M., Davis, J. & Gilman, L. (1978) Comprehension of inflectional morphemes of deaf children exposed to a visual English sign system. *J. Speech Hear. Dis.*, **21**, 387–400

Raynes, N.V. (1977) How big is good? The case for cross-cutting ties. *Ment. Retard.*, **15** (4), 53–4

Redd, W.H. & Birnbauer, J.S. (1969) Adults as discriminative stimuli for different reinforcement contingencies with retarded children. *J. Exp. Child. Psychol.*, **7**, 440–7

Reese, R.M. & Serna, L. (1986) Planning for generalization and maintenance in parent training: parents need I.E.P.s too. *Ment. Retard.*, **24**, 87–92

Reid, J.B. (1970) Reliability assessment of observation data: a possible methodological problem. *Child Devel.*, **41**, 1143–50

Remington, B. & Light, P. (1983) Some problems in the evaluation of research on non-oral communication systems. In: J. Hogg & P.J. Mittler (Eds), *Advances in mental handicap research*, Vol. 2, Chichester: Wiley

Repp, A.C., Deitz, S.M. and Speir, N.C. (1979) Reducing stereotypic responding of retarded persons by the differential reinforcement of their behavior. *Amer. J. Ment. Defic.*, **79**, 279–84

Revill, S. & Blunden, R. (1979) A home training service for pre-school developmentally handicapped children. *Behav. Res. Ther.*, **17**, 207–14

Reynell, J. (1981) *Reynell Developmental Language Scales* (Revised). Windsor, Berks: NFER

Richman, G.S., Reiss, M.L., Bauman, K.E. & Bailey, J.S. (1984) Teaching menstrual care to mentally retarded women: acquisition, generalization and maintenance. *J. Appl. Behav. Anal.*, **17**, 441–51

Richman, J.S. Sonderby, T. & Kahn, J.V. (1980) Prerequisite vs. *in vivo* acquisition of self-feeding skill. *Behav. Res. Ther.*, **18**, 327–32

Richman, N., Stevenson, J. & Graham, P.J. (1982) *Pre-school to school: a behavioural study*. London: Academic Press

Richmond, G. (1983) Shaping bladder and bowel continence in developmentally retarded pre-school children. *J. Autism Devel. Dis.*, **13**, 2, 197–204

Rincover, A. (1978) Variables affecting stimulus fading and discriminative responding in psychotic children. *J. Abn. Psychol.*, **87**, 541–53

Rincover, A., Cook, R., Peoples, A. & Packard, D. (1979) Sensory extinction and sensory reinforcement principles for programming multiple adaptive behaviour change. *J. Appl. Behav. Anal.*, **12**, 221–33

Rinn, R.C., Vernon, J.C. & Wise, M.J. (1975) Training parents of behaviorally-disordered children in groups: a three years' program evaluation. *Behav. Ther.*, **6**, 378–87

Risley, T.R. & Baer, D.M. (1973) Operant behavior modification: the deliberate development of behavior. In: B.M. Caldwell & H.N. Ricciuti (Eds), *Review of Child Development Research*, Vol. 3, Chicago: Univ. Chicago Press

Risley, T.R., Hart, B. & Doke, L. (1971) Operant language development: the outline of a therapeutic technology. In: R.L. Schiefelbusch (Ed.), *Language of the mentally retarded*. Baltimore, MD: University Park Press

Rittenhouse, R.K. (1983) The acquisition of a functional vocabulary in severely disabled children using systematic sign language instruction. *J. Rehab. Deaf*, **17** (3), 1–3

Robertson, S.J., Simon, S.J., Pachman, J.J. & Drabman, R.J. (1979) Self-control and generalisation procedures in a classroom of disruptive retarded children. *Child Behav. Ther.*, **1**, 347–62

Robson, I. (1988) Overcoming nocturnal enuresis: an altenative to the Dry Bed approach. *Behav. Psychother.* (in press)

Romanczyk, R.G. & Goren, E.R. (1975) Severe self-injurious behaviour: the problem of clinical control. *J. Consult. Clin. Psychol.*, **43**, 730–9

Roos, P. (1979) Ethical use of behaviour modification techniques. In: P. Mittler (Ed.), *Research to practice in mental retardation*, IASSMD

Rose, S.D. (1974) Training parents in groups as behavior modifiers of their mentally retarded children. *J. Behav. Ther. Exper. Psychiat.*, **5**, 135–40

Ross, A.O. (1981) *Child behavior therapy: principles, procedures and empirical basis*. New York: Wiley

Ross, R.T. (1972) Behavioral correlates of levels of intelligence *Amer. J. Ment. Defic.*, **76**, 545–49

Rudrud, E.H., Ziarnik, J.P. & Colman, G. (1984) Reduction of tongue protrusion of a 24-year-old woman with Down's syndrome through self-monitoring. *Am. J. Ment. Defic.*, **88**, 647–52

Rutter, M. (1985) The treatment of autistic children. *J. Child Psychol. Psychiat.*, **26**, 193–214

Rutter, M., Tizard, J. & Whitmore, K. (Eds) (1970) *Education, health and behaviour*. London: Longman

Sackett, G.P. (Ed.) (1978) *Observing behavior, Volume 1: Theory and applications in mental retardation*. Baltimore, MD. University Park Press

Sajwaj, T. (1973) Difficulties in the use of behavioral techniques by parents in changing child behavior: guides to success. *J. Nerv. Ment. Dis.*, **156**, 395–403

Sajwaj, T. & Hedges, D. (1973) A note on the effect of saying grace on the behavior of an oppositional retarded boy. *J. Appl. Behav. Anal.*, **6**, 711–12

Sajwaj, T., Libet, J. & Agras, S. (1974) Lemon juice therapy: the control of life-threatening rumination in a six-month old infant. *J. Appl. Behav. Anal.*, **7**, 557–63

Sajwaj, T., Twardosz, S. & Burke, M. (1972) Side-effects of extinction procedures in a remedial pre-school. *J. Appl. Behav. Anal.*, **5**, 163–72

Salend, S.J. & Kovalich, B. (1981) A group response–cost system mediated by free tokens: an alternative to token reinforcement. *Am. J. Ment. Defic.*, **86** (2), 184–7

Salzberg, B. & Napolitan, J. (1974) Holding a retarded boy at a table for 2 minutes to reduce inappropriate object contact. *Am. J. Ment. Defic.*, **78**, 748–51

Salzinger, K., Feldman, R.S., Cowan, J.E. & Salzinger, S. (1965) Operant conditioning of verbal behavior of two young speech deficient boys. In: L.P. Ullman & L. Krasner (Eds), *Case studies in behavior modification*.

New York: Holt, Rinehart & Winston

Sandford, D. & Nettelbeck, T. (1982) Medication and reinforcement within a token programme for disturbed mentally retarded residents. *Appl. Res. Ment. Retard.*, **3**, 21–36

Sapon, S.S. (1966) Shaping productive verbal behavior in a non-speaking child: a case report. *Monogr. Ser. Lang. Linguist.*, **19**, 155–75

Saunders, C.A., Jordan, R.R. & Kiernan, C.C. (1975) Parent–school collaboration. In: C.C. Kiernan & F.P. Woodford (Eds) *Behaviour modification with the severely retarded*. Amsterdam: Elsevier North Holland, Associated Scientific Publishers

Schaeffer, B. (1980) Spontaneous language through signed speech. In: R.L. Schiefelbusch (Ed.), *Nonspeech language and communication*. Baltimore, MD: University Park Press

Schaffer, H.R. & Emerson, P.E. (1964) The development of social attachment in infancy. *Monogr. Soc. Res. Child Devel.*, **29**, Serial No. 94

Schleien, S.J., Wehman, P. & Kiernan, J. (1981) Teaching leisure skills to severely handicapped adults: an age-appropriate darts game. *J. Appl. Behav. Anal.*, **14** (4), 513–19

Schoelkopf, A.M. & Orlando, R. (1965) Delayed *vs.* immediate reinforcement in simultaneous discrimination problems with mentally retarded children. *Psychol. Rec.*, **15**, 15–23

Schopler, E., Mesibov, G. & Baker, A. (1982) Evaluation of treatment for autistic children and their parents. *J. Am. Acad. Child Psychiat.*, **21**, 262–7

Schover, L.R. & Newsom, C.D. (1976) Overselectivity, developmental level and overtraining in autistic and normal children. *J. Abn. Child. Psychol.*, **4**, 289–98

Schreibman, L. (1975) Effects of within-stimulus and extra-stimulus prompting on discrimination learning in autistic children. *J. Appl. Behav. Anal.*, **9**, 81–119

Schreibman, L. & Charlop, M.H. (1981) S+ versus S− fading in prompting procedures with autistic children. *J. Exp. Child Psychol.*, **31**, 508–20

Schreibman, L., Charlop, M.H. & Koegel, R.L. (1982) Teaching autistic children to use extra stimulus prompts. *J. Exp. Child Psychol.*, **33**, 475–91

Schroeder, S.R., Schroeder, C.S., Smith, B. and Dalldorf, J. (1978) Prevalence of self-injurious behavior in a large state facility for the retarded: A three-year follow-up study. *J. Autism. Child. Schiz.*, **8**, 261–9

Schuler, A. & Prizant, B. (1985) Echolalia. In: E. Schopler & G. Mesibov (Eds), *Communication problems and autism*, New York: Plenum

Schumaker, J.B. & Sherman, J.A. (1978) Parent as intervention agent. In: R.L. Schiefelbusch (Ed.), *Language intervention strategies*. Baltimore, MD: University Park Press

Seitz, S. & Hoekenga, R. (1974) Modeling as a training tool for retarded children and their parents. *Ment. Retard.*, **12** (2), 28–31

Sewell, E., McCoy, J.F. & Sewell, W.R. (1973) Modification of an antagonistic social behavior using positive reinforcement for other behavior. *Psychol. Rec.*, **23**, 499–504

Shaffer, D. (1985) Enuresis. In M. Rutter & L. Hersov (Eds), *Child and adolescent psychiatry*, Oxford: Blackwell Scientific

Shaffer, D., Gardner, A. & Hedge, B. (1984) Behaviour and bladder disturbance of enuretic children: a rational classification of a common disorder. *Devel. Med. Child Neurol.*, **26**, 781–92

Shapiro, E.S. (1981) Self control procedures with the mentally retarded. In: M. Hersen, R.M. Eisler & P.M. Miller (Eds), *Progress in behaviour modification*, Vol. 12. New York: Academic Press

Shapiro, M.B. (1957) Experimental method in the psychological description of the individual psychiatric patient. *Int. J. Soc. Psychiat.*, **3**, 89–103

Shapiro, M.B. (1966) The single case in clinical–psychological research. *J. Gen. Psychol.*, **74**, 3–23

Shapiro, M.B. (1970) Intensive assessment of the single-case: an inductive–deductive approach. In: P. Mittler (Ed.), *The psychological assessment of mental and physical handicaps*. London: Methuen

Shattuck, R. (1981) *The forbidden experiment*. London: Quartet Books

Shearer, D.E. & Loftin, C.R. (1984) The Portage Project: teaching parents to teach their preschool children in the home. In: R.F. Dangel & R.A. Polster (Eds), *Parent training: foundations of research and practice*. New York/London: Guilford Press, pp. 93–126

Shearer, M. & Shearer, D. (1972) The Portage Project: a model for early childhood education. *Except. Child.*, **36**, 172–8

Sherman, J.A. (1963) Reinstatement of verbal behavior in a psychotic by reinforcement methods. *J. Speech Hear. Dis.*, **28**, 398–401

Sherman, J.A. (1965) Use of reinforcement and imitation to reinstate verbal behavior in mute psychotics. *J. Abn. Psychol.*, **70**, 155–64

Sidman, M. and Stoddard, D.T. (1967) The effectiveness of fading in programming a simultaneous form discrimination for retarded children. *J. Exper. Anal. Behav.*, **10**, 3–15

Simeonsson, R.J. & McHale, S.M. (1981) Review: research on handicapped children: sibling relationships. *Child: Care, Health Devel.*, **7**, 153–71

Sines, D. & Bicknell, J. (1985) *Caring for mentally handicapped people in the community. Lippincott Nursing Series*. New York: Harper & Row

Singh, N.N. & Winton, A.S.W. (1985) Controlling pica by components of an overcorrection procedure. *Am. J. Ment. Defic.*, **90**, 40–45

Slifer, K.J., Ivancic, M.T., Parrish, J.M., Page, T.J. & Burgio, L.D. (1986) Assessment and treatment of multiple behaviour problems exhibited by a profoundly retarded adolescent. *J. Behav. Ther. Exper. Psychiat.*, **17**, 203–13

Sloane, H.N., Johnson, M.K. & Harris, F.R. (1968) Remedial procedures for teaching verbal behavior to speech deficient or defective young children. In: H.N. Sloane & B.D. MacAuley (Eds), *Operant procedures in remedial speech and language training*. Boston: Houghton Mifflin

Slobin, D.I. (1973) Cognitive pre-requisites for the development of grammar. In: C.A. Ferguson & D.I. Slobin (Eds) *Studies of child language development*. New York: Holt Rinehart & Winston

Sloop, E.W. & Kennedy, W.A. (1973) Institutionalized retarded enuretics treated by a conditioning technique. *Am. J. Ment. Defic.*, **77**, 717–21

Sloper, P., Cunningham, C.C. & Arnjotsdottir, M. (1983) Parental reactions to early intervention with their Down's syndrome infants. *Child: Care, Health Devel.*, **9**, 357–76

Slukin, A. (1975) Encopresis: a behavioural approach described. *Social Work Today*, **5**, 643–6

Smeets, P.M., Bouter, R.F. & Bouter, H.P. (1976) Teaching toothbrushing behaviour in severely retarded adults: a replication study. *Brit. J. Ment. Subn.*, **22** (1), 5–12

Smeets, P.M., Lancioni, G.E. & Hoogeveen, F.R. (1984) Using stimulus shaping and fading to establish stimulus control in normal and retarded children. *J. Ment. Defic. Res.*, **28**, 207–18

Smith, J. (1977) An evaluation of behavioural skills training. Unpublished M. Phil. thesis, University of London Institute of Psychiatry

Smith, L.J. (1981) Training severely and profoundly mentally handicapped nocturnal enuretics. *Behav. Res. Ther.*, **19**, 67–74

Smith, M. & Meyers, A. (1979) Telephone skills training for retarded adults: group and individual demonstration with and without verbal instruction. *Am. J. Ment. Defic.*, **83** (6), 581–7

Smith, P.S. (1979) A comparison of different methods of toilet training the mentally handicapped. *Behav. Res. Ther.*, **17** (1), 33–43

Smith, P.S., Britton, P.T., Johnson, M. & Thomas, D.A. (1975) Problems involved in toilet training profoundly mentally handicapped adults. *Behav. Res. Ther.*, **15**, 301–7

Smith, P.S. & Smith, L.J. (1977) Chronological age and social age as factors in intensive daytime toilet training of institutionalized mentally retarded individuals. *J. Behav. Ther. Exp. Psychiat.*, **8**, 269–73

Solnick, J.V., Rincover, A. & Peterson, C.R. (1977) Some determinants of the reinforcing and punishing effects of time out. *J. Appl. Behav. Anal.*, **10**, 415–24

Song, A.Y. & Gandhi, R. (1974) An analysis of behavior during the acquisition and maintenance phases of self-spoon feeding skills of profound retardates. *Ment. Retard.*, **12** (1), 25–8

Song, A.Y., O'Connell, R.D., Nelson, H.L. & Apfel, S. (1976) Cottage bound self-help skill teaching and intensive school training for the profoundly and severely retarded. *Brit. J. Ment. Subn.*, **22** (2), 99–104

Sorotzkin, B. (1984) Nocturnal enuresis: current perspectives. *Clin. Psychol. Rev.*, **4**, 293–316

Sowers, J., Verdi, M., Bourbeau, P. & Sheehan, M. (1985) Teaching job independence and flexibility to mentally retarded students through the use of a self control package. *J. Appl. Behav. Anal.*, **18**, 81–5

Spain, B., Hart, S.A. & Corbett, J.A. (1985) The use of appliances in the treatment of severe self-injurious behaviour. In: G. Murphy & B. Wilson (Eds), *Self-injurious behaviour*. Kidderminster: B.I.M.H. Publications

Speight, I.M. (1976) Course No. 700: Behaviour modification in mental handicap. *Nursing Mirror*, 30 September

Spradlin, J.E. & Girardeau, F.L. (1966) The behavior of moderately and severely retarded persons. In: N. Ellis (Ed.), *International Review of Research in Mental Retardation*, Vol. 1, New York: Academic Press

Sprague, R. & Toppe, T. (1966) Relationship between activity level and delay of reinforcement in the retarded. *J. Exp. Child. Psychol.*, **3**, 390–7

Stainback, S. & Stainback, W. (1980) *Educating children with severe maladaptive behaviours*. New York: Grune & Stratton

Stainback, W., Stainback, S. & Strathe, M. (1983) Generalisation of positive social behaviour by severely handicapped students: a review and analysis of research. *Educ. Train. Ment. Retard.*, **18**, 293–9

Stein, T.J. (1975) Some ethical considerations of short-term workshops in the principles and methods of behaviour modification. *J. Appl. Behav. Anal.*, **8**, 113–15

Stoffelmayr, B.E., Faulkener, G.R. & Mitchell, W.S. (1973) The rehabilitation of chronic hospitalised patients — a comparative study of operant conditioning methods and social therapy techniques. Final report to the Scottish Home and Health Dept. Quoted by Fraser, D. (1978)

Stokes, T.F. & Baer, D.M. (1977) An implicit technology of generalisation. *J. Appl. Behav. Anal.*, **10**, 349–67

Strichart, S.S. (1974) Effects of competence and nurturance on imitation of non-retarded peers by retarded adolescents. *Am. J. Ment. Defic.*, **78**, 665–73

Strichart, S.S. & Gottlieb, J. (1975) Imitation of retarded children by their non-retarded peers. *Am. J. Ment. Defic.*, **79**, 506–12

Sugaya, K. (1967) Survey of the enuresis problem in an institution for the mentally retarded with emphasis on the clinical psychological aspects. *Jap. J. Child Psychiat.*, **8**, 142–50

Taplin, P.S. & Reid, J.B. (1973) Effects of instructional set and experimenter influence on observer reliability. *Child Devel.*, **44**, 547–54

Tarnowski, K.J. & Drabman, R.S. (1985) The effects of ambulation training on the self-stimulatory behaviour of a multiply handicapped child. *Behav. Ther.*, **16**, 275–85

Tavormina, J.B. (1974) Basic models of parent counselling: a critical review. *Psychol. Bull.*, **81**, 827–35

Tavormina, J.B. (1975) Relative effectiveness of behavioral and reflective group counselling with parents of mentally retarded children. *J. Consult Clin. Psychol.*, **43** (1), 22–31

Tavormina, J.B., Hampson, R.B. & Luscomb, R.L. (1976) Participant evaluations of the effectiveness of their parent counselling groups. *Ment. Retard.*, **14** (6), 8–9

Taylor, P.D. & Turner, R.K. (1975) A clinical trial of continuous, intermittent and overlearning 'bell-and-pad' treatments for nocturnal enuresis. *Behav. Res. Ther.*, **13**, 281–93

Terdal, L. & Buell, J. (1969) Parent education in managing retarded children with behavior deficits and inappropriate behaviors. *Ment. Retard.*, **7** (3), 10–13

Terrace, J.S. (1966) Stimulus control. In: W.K. Honig (Ed.), *Operant behavior: areas of research and application*. New York: Appleton-Century-Crofts

Tharp, R.G. & Wetzel, R.J. (1969) *Behavior modification in the natural environment*. New York: Academic Press

Thomas, M. (1985) An introduction to room management. In: P.T. Farrell (Ed.), *EDY: Its impact on staff training in mental handicap*. Manchester: Manchester University Press

Thompson, T. & Grabowski, J. (Eds) (1972) *Behavior modification of the mentally retarded*. New York: Oxford University Press

Thompson, T.J., Braam, S.J. & Fuqua, R.W. (1982) Training and generalization of laundry skills: a multiple probe evaluation with handicapped persons. *J. Appl. Behav. Anal.*, **15** (1), 177–82

Thorpe, J.G. (1975) Token economy systems. In: C.C. Kiernan & F.P. Woodford (Eds), *Behaviour modification with the severely retarded*. Amsterdam: Associated Scientific Publishers

Tizard, J. (1975) Discussion of Thorpe (1975) Token economy systems. In: C.C. Kiernan & F.P. Woodford (Eds), *Behaviour modification with the severely retarded*. Amsterdam: Elsevier North Holland, Associated Scientific Publishers

Tizard, J. & Grad, J.C. (1961) *The mentally handicapped and their families: a social survey*. London: Oxford University Press

Tognoli, J., Hamad, C. & Carpenter, T. (1978) Staff attitudes toward adult male residents' behavior as a function of two settings in an institution for mentally retarded people. *Ment. Retard.*, **16**, 142–6

Tomlinson, J.R. (1970) The treatment of bowel retention by operant procedures: a case study. J. Behav. Ther. Exper. Psychiat., **1**, 83–5

Toogood, R. (1977) Behaviour modification and mental handicap hospitals. *Apex, J. Brit. Inst. Ment. Handicap*, **5** (2), 26–7

Toogood, S., Jenkins, J., Felce, D. & de Kock, U. *Opportunity plans*. Unpublished

Topper, S.T. (1975) Gesture language for a severely retarded male. *Ment. Retard.*, **13**, 30–1

Torpy, D.M. (1981) Day wetting: a bar to leaving hospital? *Apex, J. Brit. Inst. Ment. Handicap*, **9**, 78–9

Touchette, P.E. & Howard, J.S. (1984) Errorless learning: reinforcement contingencies and stimulus control transfer in delayed prompting. *J. Appl. Behav. Anal.*, **17**, 175–188

Treffry, D., Martin, G.L., Samuels, J. & Watson, C. (1970) Operant conditioning of grooming behavior of severely retarded girls. *Ment. Retard.*, **8** (4), 29–33

Turnbull, A.P. & Turnbull, H.R. (1982) Parent involvement in the education of handicapped children: a critique. *Ment. Retard.*, **20**, 115–22

United Nations (1971) *Declaration of general and special rights of the mentally handicapped*, New York: UNO

van den Pol, R.A., Iwata, B.A., Ivancic, M.T., Page, T.J., Neef, N.A. & Whitley, F.P. (1981) Teaching the handicapped to eat in public places: acquisition, generalization and maintenance of restaurant skills. *J. Appl. Behav. Anal.*, **14** (1), 61–9

Van Houten, R. & Nau, P.A. (1980) A comparison of the effects of fixed and variable ratio schedules of reinforcement on the behavior of deaf children. *J. Appl. Behav. Anal.*, **13**, 13–21

Vukelich, R. & Hake, D.F. (1971) Reduction of dangerously aggressive behaviour in a severely retarded resident through a combination of positive reinforcement procedures. *J. Appl. Behav. Anal.*, **4**, 215–25

Wacker, D., Berg, W., Wiggins, B., Muldoon, M. & Cavanagh, J. (1975) Evaluation of reinforcer preferences for profoundly handicapped students. *J. Appl. Behav. Anal.*, **18**, 173–8

Wahler, R.G. (1980) The insular mother: her problems in parent–child treatment. *J. Appl. Behav. Anal.*, **13**, 207–19

Wahler, R.G. & Cormier, N.H. (1970) The ecological interview: a first step in outpatient behavior therapy. *J. Behav. Ther. Exper. Psychiat.*, **1**, 279–89

Wahler, R.G. & Dumas, J.E. (1984) Changing the observational coding styles of insular and non-insular mothers: a step toward maintaining parent training effects. In: R.F. Dangel & R.A. Polster (Eds), *Parent training: foundations of research and practice*. New York/London: Guilford Press, pp. 379–416

Wahler, R.G. & Leske, G. (1973) Accurate and inaccurate observer summary reports: reinforcement theory interpretation and investigation. *J. Nerv. Ment. Dis.*, **156**, 386–94

Wakefield, M.A., Woodbridge, C., Steward, J. & Croke, W. (1984) A treatment programme for faecal incontinence. *Devel. Med. Child. Neurol.*, **26**, 613–16

Walker, M. (1980) The revised Makaton vocabulary. Unpublished paper, The Makaton Vocabulary Development Project, Camberley, Surrey

Ward, J. (1975) Behaviour modification in special education. In: K. Wedell (Ed.), *Orientations in special education*. London: John Wiley

Waters, J. (1970) Adapt dressing, clothes to child. *Ment. Retard. News*, **19** (3), 7 (from abstract in *Mental Retardation Abstracts*, 1971, **8**, No. 2043)

Watson, L.S. (1973) *Child behavior modification: a manual for teachers, nurses and parents*. New York: Pergamon

Watson, L.S., Gardner, J.M. & Sanders, C. (1971) Shaping and maintaining behavior modification skills in staff members in an MR institution: Columbus State Institute Behavior Modification Programme. *Ment. Retard.*, **9** (3), 39–42

Watson, L.S. & Uzzell, R. (1980) A program for teaching behavior modification skills to institutional staff. *Appl. Res. Ment. Retard.*, **1**, 41–53

Wehman, P. (1974) Maintaining oral hygiene skills in geriatric retarded women. *Ment. Retard.*, **12**, 20

Welch, S.J. & Pear, J.J. (1980) Generalisation of naming responses to objects in the natural environment as a function of training stimulus modality with retarded children. *J. Appl. Behav. Anal.*, **13**, 629–43

Westling, D.L. & Murden, L. (1978) Self-help skills training: a review of operant studies. *J. Spec. Educ.*, **12**, 253–83

White, G.D., Nielson, G. & Johnson, S.M. (1972) Time-out duration and the suppression of deviant behavior in children. *J. Appl. Behav. Anal.*, **5**, 111–20

Whitman, T.L., Scibak, J.W., Butler, K.M., Richter, R. & Johnson, M.R. (1982) Improving classroom behaviour in mentally handicapped children through correspondence training. *J. Appl. Behav. Anal.*, **15**, 545–64

Whitman, T.L., Zakaras, M. & Chardos, J. (1971) Effects of reinforcement and guidance procedures on instruction-following behavior of severely retarded children. *J. Appl. Behav. Anal.*, **4**, 283–90

Whitney, L.R. & Barnard, K.E. (1966) Implications of operant learning theory for nursing care of the retarded child. *Ment. Retard.*, **4**, 26–31

Wickings, S., Jenkins, J., Carr, J. & Corbett, J. (1974) Modification of behaviour using a shaping procedure. *Apex, J. Brit. Inst. Ment. Handicap*, **2**, 6

Wigley, V., Yule, W. & Berger, M. (1982) A primary solution to soiling. *Spec. Educ. Forward Trends*, Vol. 9, No. 4

Wilkin, D. (1979) *Caring for the mentally handicapped child*. Croom Helm: London

Williams, C.D. (1959) The elimination of tantrum behavior by extinction procedures. *J. Abn. Soc. Psychol.*, **59**, 269

Williams, C. & Jackson, M.W. (1975) Nurse training in behaviour modification. In: C.C. Kiernan & F.P. Woodford (Eds), *Behaviour modification with the severely retarded*. Study Group No. 8, IRMMH. Amsterdam: Associated Scientific Publishers

Willoughby, R.H. (1969) The effects of time-out from positive reinforcement on the operant behaviour of pre-school children. *J. Exp. Child Psychol.*, **7**, 299–313

Wilson, A.R.S. (1983) The use of manual communication with deaf–blind mentally handicapped children. In J. Hogg & P.J. Mittler (Eds), *Advances in mental handicap research*, Vol. 2. Chichester: Wiley

Wing, L. (1971) Severely retarded children in a London area: prevalence and provision of services. *Psychol. Med.*, **1** 405–15

Wing, L. (1975) Practical counselling for families with severely retarded children living at home. *REAP*, **1**, 113–27

Wing, L. (1985) Services for severely retarded children and adolescents. In: M. Rutter & L. Hersov (Eds), *Child and adolescent psychiatry: modern approaches*, 2nd Edition. Oxford: Blackwell Scientific Publications, pp. 753–65

Wing, L. (1987) The epidemiology and classification of behaviour disorders in people with mental retardation. In J.A. Corbett and C. Oliver (Eds) *Behaviour disorders and mental retardation — understanding and management* London: Collins (in press)

Winkler, R.C. (1971) The relevance of economic theory and technology of token reinforcement systems. *Behav. Res. Ther.*, **9**, 81–8

Winton, A.S.W., Singh, N.N. & Dawson, M.J. (1984) Effects of facial screening and blindfold on self-injurious behaviour. *Appl. Res. Ment. Retard.*, **5**, 29–42

Wolery, M., Kirk, K. & Gast, D. (1986) Stereotypic behaviours as a reinforcer: effects and side effects. *J. Autism Devel. Dis.*, **15**, 149–61

Wolf, M., Risley, T. & Mees, H. (1964) Applications of operant conditioning procedures to the behavior problems of an autistic child. *Behav. Res. Ther.*, **1**, 305–12

Wolfe, V.F. & Cuvo, A.J. (1978) Effects of within-stimulus and extra-stimulus prompting on letter discrimination by mentally retarded persons. *Am. J. Ment. Defic.*, **83**, 297–303

Woods, P.A. & Cullen, C. (1983). Determinants of staff behaviour in long term care. *Behav. Psychother.*, **11**, 4–17

Woods, T.S. (1983) The selective suppression of a stereotypy in an autistic child: a stimulus control approach. *Behav. Psychother.*, **11**, 235–48

Woods, T.S. (1984) Generality in the verbal tacting of autistic children as a function of 'naturalness' in antecedent control. *J. Behav. Ther. Exper. Psychiat.*, **15**, 27–32

Working Party on Behaviour Modification (1978) *Bull. Brit. Psychol. Soc.*, **31**, 368–9

Wright, D.F. & Bunch, G. (1977) Parental intervention in the treatment of chronic constipation. *J. Behav. Ther. Exper. Psychiat.*, **2**, 93–5

Wunderlich, R.A. (1972) Programmed instruction: teaching coinage to retarded children. *Ment. Retard.*, **10** (5), 21–3

Wyatt *v.* Stickney (1972) 344 Federal Supplement 373 and 387, Middle District, Northern Division, Alabama

Yates, A.J. (1970) *Behavior therapy.* New York: Wiley

Young, G.C. & Morgan, R.T. (1972) Overlearning in the conditioning treatment of enuresis. *Behav. Res. Ther.,* **10**, 147–51

Young, R.M., Bradley-Johnson, S. & Johnson, C.M. (1982) Immediate and delayed reinforcement on WISC-R performance for mentally retarded students. *Appl. Res. Ment. Retard.,* **3**, 13–20

Yule, W. (1975) Teaching psychological principles to non-psychologists: Training parents in child management. *J. Assoc. Educ. Psychol.,* **10** (3), 5–16

Yule, W. (1977) Behavioural approaches to treatment. In: M. Rutter & L. Hersov (Eds), *Child psychiatry: modern approaches.* London: Blackwell Scientific Publications

Yule, W. (1982) Special review of the Zangwill report on behaviour modification. *Behav. Res. Ther.,* **20**, 411–13

Yule, W. (1986) Behavioural treatments. In: E.A. Taylor (Ed.), *The Overactive child.* Clinics in Developmental Medicine No. 97. London: MacKeith Press

Yule, W. & Berger, M. (1975) Communication, language and behavior modification. In: C.C. Kiernan & F.P. Woodford (Eds), *Behaviour modification with the severely retarded.* Amsterdam: Associated Scientific Publishers

Yule, W., Berger, M. & Howlin, P. (1974) Language deficit and behaviour modification. In: N. O'Connor (Ed.), *Language and cognition in the handicapped.* London: Churchill

Yule, W., Berger, M. & Wigley, V. (1983) Behaviour modification and classroom management. In: N. Frude & H. Gault (Eds), *Children's aggression at school.* Chichester and New York: Wiley

Yule, W. & Hemsley, D. (1977) Single-case method in medical psychology. In: S. Rachman (Ed.), *Contributions to Medical Psychology,* Vol. I. Oxford: Pergamon

Zangwill, O.L. (Chairman) (1980) *Behaviour modification: report of a Joint Working Party to formulate ethical guidelines for the conduct of programmes of behaviour modification in the National Health Service: a consultation document with suggested guidelines.* London: HMSO

Zeiler, M.D. & Jervey, S.S. (1968) Development of behavior: self-feeding. *J. Consult. Clin. Psychol.,* **32**, 164–8

Zimmerman, J. & Baydan, N.T. (1963) Punishment of S^Δ responding of humans in conditional matching to sample by time-out. *J. Exper. Anal. Behav.,* **6**, 589–97

Zimmerman, J. & Ferster, C.B. (1963) Intermittent punishment of S^Δ responding in matching to sample. *J. Exper. Anal. Behav.,* **6**, 349–56

Zimmerman, J., Stuckey, T.E., Garlick, B.J. & Miller, M. (1969) Effects of token reinforcement on productivity in multiply handicapped clients in a sheltered workshop. *Rehab. Lit.,* **30**, 34–41

Zlutnick, S., Mayville, W.J. & Moffat, S. (1975) Modification of seizure disorders: the interruption of behavioral chains. *J. Appl. Behav. Anal.,* **8**, 1–12

Index